Check-in

Die ersten zwei Seiten stimmen dich auf das Thema der Unit ein.
In der blauen Kompetenzbox siehst du, was du in dieser Unit lernen wirst.

Die roten Dreiecke zeigen dir, dass du hinten im Diff pool z. B. Hilfen und leichtere oder weiterführende Aufgaben findest.

Stations

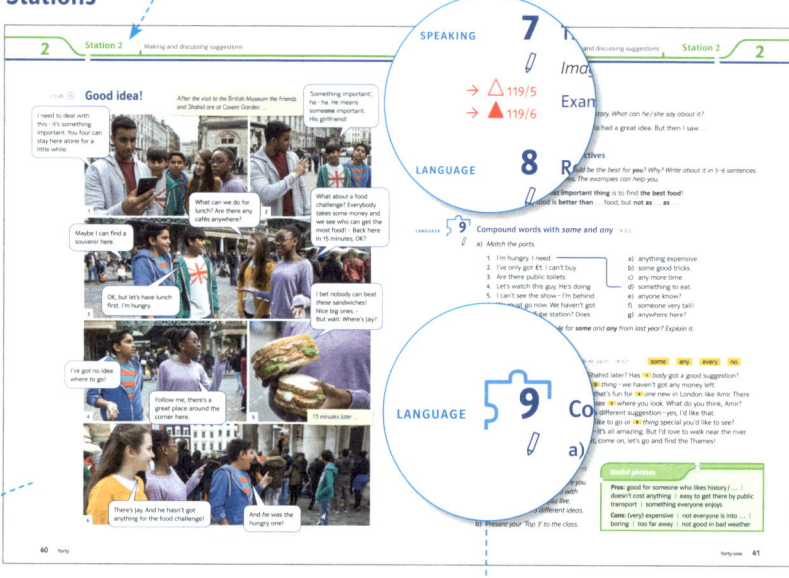

In den 2 bis 3 Stations pro Unit findest du deinen neuen Lernstoff, tolle Texte und passende Aufgaben.

Die Aufgaben mit dem Puzzle-Symbol unterstützen dich besonders dabei, deine Lernziele zu erreichen und helfen dir bei der Vorbereitung der Unit task.

Unit task

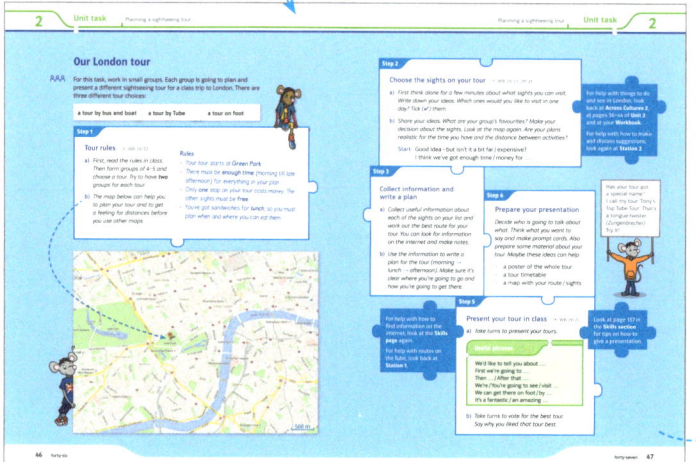

Und hier kommt alles zusammen. Anhand dieser großen Unit-Aufgabe kannst du deine neu erworbenen Fähigkeiten schrittweise überprüfen und festigen und dabei auf kreative Weise zeigen, was du nun kannst.

Check-out

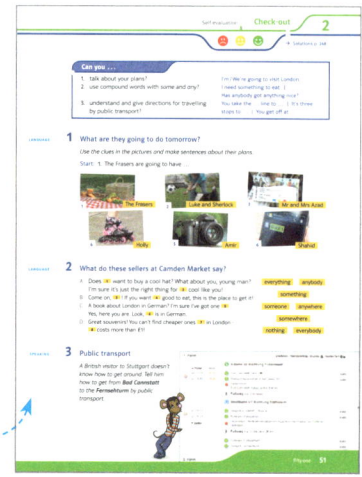

Mit diesen Übungen am Ende der Unit kannst du deinen Lernfortschritt selbst überprüfen. Lösungen stehen dir im Anhang zur Verfügung.

Story

Hier findest du lustige und spannende Texte über die *friends* in Greenwich.

Action UK!

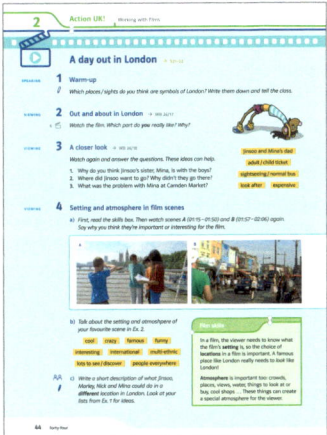

Und hier gibt es tolle Filme aus Greenwich!

Across cultures

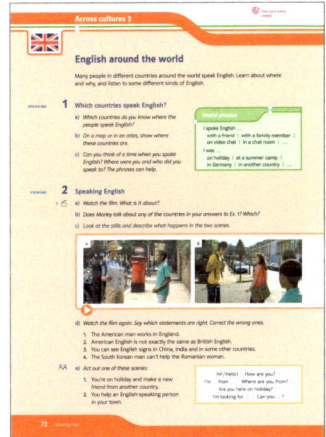

Vergleiche auf diesen Seiten deinen Alltag mit der Alltagskultur und der Geschichte Großbritanniens.

Diff pool

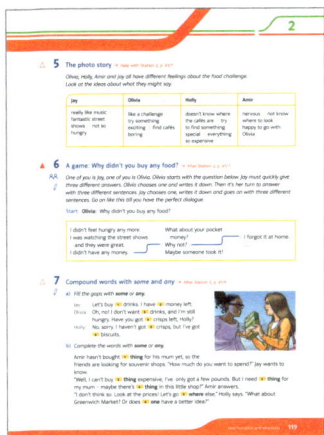

Skills

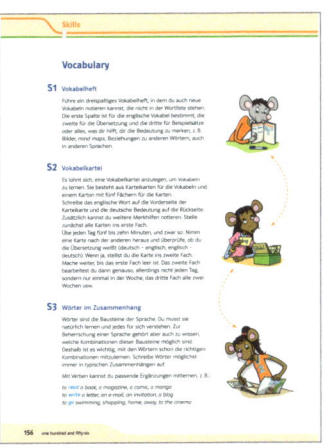

Grammar, Vocabulary

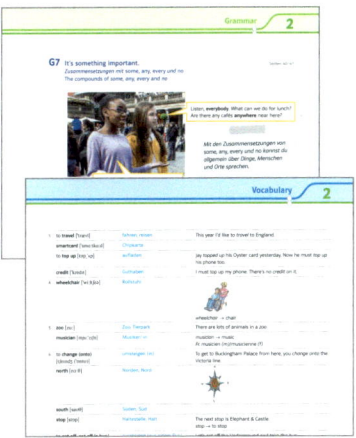

Im hinteren Buchteil stehen dir hilfreiche Anhänge zur Verfügung. *Diff pool*, *Grammar* und *Vocabulary* kennst du schon aus dem letzten Jahr. Neu ab Green Line 2 ist der *Skills*-Anhang. Hier findest du zu den Lernbereichen *Reading*, *Writing*, *Speaking*, *Listening*, *Viewing*, *Mediation* und *Vocabulary* allerlei Lernhilfen und Methodentipps. Die gelben Verweise → S17 bei den Unit-Aufgaben sagen dir, dass es sich lohnt, dort nachzuschlagen!

Symbole

→ △ 132/1	Verweis auf leichtere Aufgaben / Hilfen im Diff pool
→ ▲ 132/2	Verweis auf anspruchsvollere Aufgaben im Diff pool
→ WB 7/4	Verweis auf eine Übung im Workbook
→ G2	Verweis auf die Grammatik im Anhang
→ S2	Verweis auf die Skills im Anhang
🙎🙎	Partnerarbeit
🙎🙎🙎	Gruppenarbeit
🗐	Hier entsteht ein Produkt für dein Portfolio.

✐	Schreiben (geschlossen / einfach)
✏	Schreiben (offen / kreativ)
S1/14 ⊙	Verweis auf die Schüler-CDs im Workbook (Audio)
L1/19 ⊙	Verweis auf die Lehrer-CDs (Audio)
🖺	Verweis auf die Lehrer-DVD (Film)
🌐	Code auf www.klett.de eingeben und Zusatzmaterial nutzen
🔁2	Übungen, die die Unit task besonders vorbereiten
🏴󠁧󠁢	Across cultures

Green Line 2 für Klasse 6 an Gymnasien in Baden-Württemberg

Herausgeber: Harald Weisshaar, Bisingen

Autorinnen und Autoren: Marion Horner, Ipswich; Carolyn Jones, Beckenham; Jon Marks, Ventnor; Alison Wooder, Ventnor sowie Jennifer Baer-Engel, Göppingen; Paul Dennis, Lahnstein; Barbara Greive, Dortmund; Cornelia Kaminski, Fulda
unter Mitwirkung von Monique Kunhar, Schwaikheim; Manuela Moll, Eislingen

Beratung: Paul Dennis, Lahnstein; Cornelia Kaminski, Fulda; Nilgül Karabulut, Aachen; Hartmut Klose, Seevetal; Antje Körber, Merseburg; Jörg Nieswand, Berlin; Jörg Schulze, Dresden

Für besondere Unterstützung danken wir herzlich Ms Susan Bolton von der **Thomas Tallis School**, London.

Zusatzmaterial für Schülerinnen und Schüler zu diesem Band:

Workbook + Audio-CD + Übungssoftware	978-3-12-834128-6
Workbook + Audio-CD	978-3-12-834125-5

sowie eine Reihe von abgestimmten *English Readers*

1. Auflage

1 6 5 4 3 2 | 2021 20 19 18 17

Alle Drucke dieser Auflage sind unverändert und können im Unterricht nebeneinander verwendet werden.
Die letzte Zahl bezeichnet das Jahr des Druckes.

Redaktion: Michael Mattison; Anette Mohamud; Manuela Moll; Lektorat editoria: Cornelia Schaller, Fellbach
Herstellung: Anita Bauch

Gestaltung: Petra Michel, Essen
Umschlaggestaltung: know idea, Freiburg; Koma Amok, Stuttgart
Illustrationen: Peer Kramer, Düsseldorf; jani lunablau, Barcelona *(Maskottchen und Story)*
sowie Christian Dekelver, Weinstadt *(Karten)*
Satz: Satzkiste GmbH, Stuttgart; Mediengestaltung Elke Kurz, Waiblingen
Reproduktion: Schwaben-Repro, Stuttgart
Druck: PASSAVIA Druckservice GmbH & Co. KG, Passau

Printed in Germany
ISBN 978-3-12-834120-0 (fester Einband)
ISBN 978-3-12-834121-7 (flexibler Einband)

Green Line 2

von
Marion Horner
Carolyn Jones
Jon Marks
Alison Wooder
Jennifer Baer-Engel
Paul Dennis
Barbara Greive
Cornelia Kaminski

herausgegeben von
Harald Weisshaar

Ernst Klett Verlag
Stuttgart · Leipzig

Inhalt

● Across cultures 1 🇬🇧

	Lektionsteil/Thema	Kompetenzen	Inhalte/Sprachliche Mittel (R = Revision)
8	**Let's discover TTS!**	**s/voc** Über eine britische Schule sprechen	**L** Einen Vortrag über TTS verstehen	**w/sk** Einen Flyer erstellen	**v** Eine Filmsquenz verstehen	school subjects and activities, timetable

Unit 1: My friends and I

	Lektionsteil/Thema	Kompetenzen	Inhalte/Sprachliche Mittel (R = Revision)
12	**Check-in**	**s/L** Situationen beschreiben	**s** Gefühle beschreiben	**voc/sk** *Mind maps*	🇬🇧 *Yearbooks*	feelings
14	**Station 1** **I love Red Nose Day**	**s** Über die Vergangenheit sprechen	**w** Einen Bericht schreiben	**M/sk** Die Inhalte eines deutschen Flyers auf Englisch wiedergeben / Ein Gespräch aufrechterhalten	🇬🇧 *Charities*	special group activities *simple past: regular and irregular verbs*
17	**Station 2** **How did they know?**	**s** Herausfinden, was passiert ist	**w** Eine Rätselgeschichte schreiben	**L** Eine längere Erzählung verstehen	puzzle stories *simple past: questions and negative statements* ***R:** questions (simple present)*
20	**Station 3** **Everyone can enjoy a challenge**	**s** Dinge beschreiben und vergleichen	🇬🇧 *Wales*	outdoor activities *adjectives (comparative & superlative forms)*
22	**Story** **It was amazing**	**R** Einen Reisebericht verstehen	**s/w** Das Ende einer Geschichte erfinden	**w/sk** Einen Reisebericht planen	**voc/sk** Einen Text sprachlich interessant gestalten	a class trip headings; words and phrases for time and place; feelings; exciting words
25	**Skills** **Dictionaries**	**voc/sk** Mit einem zweisprachigen Wörterbuch arbeiten	elements of a dictionary / a dictionary entry
26	**Unit task** **Our travel report**	🧩 Einen Reisebericht planen und schreiben	events in the past; making a report interesting
28	**Action UK!** **The new boy**	**v** Eine Filmsequenz verstehen: Der Neue	**v/sk** Musik als filmisches Mittel	
29	**Check-out**	Selbstkontrolle: Die Lernziele der Unit überprüfen	

Unit 2: London is amazing!

Inhalt

Unit 4: Stay in touch

Inhalt

Legende

L	Listening	W	Writing	VOC	Vocabulary	🇬🇧	Across cultures
S	Speaking	M	Mediation	SK	Skills	‹ ›	Fakultativ
R	Reading	V	Viewing		Kompetenzaufgabe	R	Revision

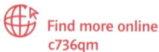

Find more online:
c736qm

Let's discover TTS!

There are quite a few differences between British and German schools – subjects, for example: At Thomas Tallis School, you can also take exams in Dance, Drama, Film studies or Fashion. And there's more than just lessons at British schools. In the afternoons, clubs offer a lot of additional activities like sports, birdwatching, cooking or games like chess. Learn more about TTS and British schools on these pages.

1   A wall painting in the school building

3   Assembly

2   Basketball Club

4   Sign Language Club

5   Dance class

SPEAKING

1 What you can do at TTS

a) *Look at the quotes in the speech bubbles below. What are they about?*
Match them to the photos on the left.

A We start school with our tutor at 8:30. Or sometimes we go to the hall for Assembly.

D We love competitions against other schools – well, we love winning.

B This school is full of art!

E Everyone is special and everyone belongs here. We all try to help students with special needs.

C We practise a lot and we sometimes do shows.

b) *Now talk about what is the same or different at your school.*

c) *Your turn: What pictures can you use to present your school?*

LISTENING

2 This is a fantastic school!

L 1/1

a) *Listen to Olivia. Who is she talking to? Take notes about the different parts of her presentation and say what each part is about.*

→ S18–20

b) *Choose one of the quotes from A–E. Listen again. What reactions are there from the listeners after the part with that quote?*

School subjects:
English
Maths
Science
Technology

LISTENING

3 New friends

L 1/2

a) *Gwen is a new girl at TTS. She's partially sighted. Listen to her conversation with Holly and Olivia. Why does Gwen need their help?*

b) *Listen again. Which subjects do they talk about? How can teachers and other students help Gwen?*

c) *Now that you know a lot about TTS, what do you think: Is it a fantastic school? Say why or why not.*

d) *Your turn: Talk about how your school / your class helps students with special needs.*

VOCABULARY

4 **School subjects: Gwen's timetable**

a) *Look at Gwen's timetable. Compare it with your timetable.*
The useful phrases can help you.

Time	Monday	Tuesday	Wednesday	Thursday	Friday
08:30	Registration				
08:50	Technology	Science	Maths	RE	English
09:50	Technology	Science	Maths	French	French
10:50	Break				
11:10	Maths	Art	Science	English	Humanities
12:10	English	Music	Technology	Geography	Humanities
13:10	Lunch				
14:00	Dance	English	PE	Maths	Dance
15:00	Registration in tutor group / Assembly				
15:10	Home / Clubs				

Useful phrases

Our school day starts at 7:30 / …
We have … lessons in the
afternoon / every day / only on
Mondays / Tuesdays / …

There's a break at …
Lunch is from … till …

Gwen and I have the same subjects, but I
also have lessons in …

In Maths / History / RE / … we learn / talk
about … / we often work on projects.

We have / don't have lots of clubs / activities /
… in the afternoon

b) *Write your own timetable in English.*

c) *Your turn: Look at the pictures. Say which subjects they show. Then talk about which*
subjects you like best and why.

WRITING

5 The TTS Eco Club → WB 2/1–2

a) *Holly's favourite club at TTS is the Eco Club. Look at a flyer for that club. Would you like to join it? Say why or why not.*

b) *Read the skills box. Choose **one** of the clubs on the right. Write and design a flyer for it.*

c) *Exchange your flyers with another pair of students and peer-edit each other's work.*

| Maths Club | Singing Club |
| Tallis TV | Football Club | Science Club |

Writing skills

When you write a flyer make sure that
- it's easy to read
- it has all the important information about your club:
  the **name** of the club
  what you do
  when you meet (day and time)
  where you meet
  why people should join your club
- you welcome people with a special **welcome message** and a **slogan**!

The TTS Eco Club

When?	Tuesdays at 3:15
Where?	Room G23 & The Wildlife Garden
What?	Work on our Wildlife Garden or our Green Classroom projects
Why?	We want to find ways to

Love and protect nature! Think green! Recycle!

Save energy! Stop pollution!

Come and join us –
EVERYONE CAN MAKE A DIFFERENCE!

VIEWING

6 The film star

2 *Drama is one of the most interesting classes at TTS. It's fun! But not always, as Laura finds out.*

Watch the film. Say what Laura wants to win. Explain what her problem is.

VIEWING

7 Good advice?

a) *Watch (01:38–04:00) again. What advice do people give Laura? Take notes.*

b) *Talk about the advice for Laura. Here are some ideas:*

A: Polly is a star, so she knows best!
B: Well Marley isn't an actor but *his* advice is great too: "Believe in yourself".

c) *Look at the still (04:35). What is Laura thinking at this moment in the film? Look at the phrases for help.*

d) *Now watch the rest of the film. Explain why Laura thanks Polly.*

Useful phrases

Don't panic! | Don't be nervous! |
Just relax! | I'm sure you're good at … |
You're always so confident. | Try again. |
Take a deep breath. | Believe in yourself!

Find more online:
7ru95v

Unit 1

My friends and I

Your classmates –
CAUGHT ON CAMERA!

A

Jay, don't you know that embarrassing outfits always end up in the yearbook? LOL! ☺

B

Dave, Olivia and Luke after a round of boxing. Ouch, those red noses! Oh, wait – it's Red Nose Day, of course! (Nice cake, mmm…)

SPEAKING

1 Talk about the yearbook photos

What can you see? Where are the girls and boys? What do you think they're doing or saying?

LISTENING

2 Caught on camera

L 1/3 ◎ **a)** *Listen to the dialogues. Which photo are the characters talking about? (There is no dialogue for one of the photos.)*

→ S18–20 **b)** *Listen again and then answer the questions.*

1. How does Jay feel about the photo of himself and Holly? **2.** Which two characters are on the yearbook team? **3.** Who is doing which pages in the yearbook? **4.** Why does Holly like the photo of the three boys?

In Unit 1 you learn

… how to talk about special activities in the past and how to give information about places. You learn:

- words about feelings
- the simple past
- words and phrases that describe and compare

C

D

The eyes say it all for lovebirds Holly and Jay. (The camera never lies!)

Luke, Dave and Jay are practising for the class trip. Hey guys, we know that you're funny – but now we know that you're silly too!

SPEAKING **3** **Feelings** → WB 3/1–2

 a) *Take turns to act different feelings. Can the others guess your word?*

 b) *Look at the photos again. Say how you think the characters feel and why.*

Example: Photo D: I think Dave feels happy because he's having fun with his friends.

→ △114/1 **c)** *Make a mind map for 'feelings'. Add new words to your personal vocabulary.*

| happy | shy | excited | embarrassed | proud |

Across cultures

Yearbooks are an American tradition, but now they are popular in British schools too. Students on a yearbook team work together to make a fun book for their class, with photos of students and reports about activities during the school year. How do you collect the highlights in the school year?

L1/4 ◎ **I love Red Nose Day**

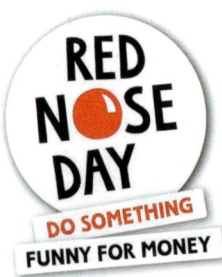

YES, IT'S RED NOSE TIME AGAIN!

Here at TTS we always do our best for COMIC RELIEF. Two years ago we raised lots of money, but this year let's raise even more! Check the TTS website for more information.

COMIC RELIEF is a great charity. It helps people in need in Africa and also the UK. The comedian Lenny Henry started Comic Relief – that's how it got its name – and on the first Red Nose Day in 1988 people wore red noses, did fun activities to raise money and watched a big comedy show on TV. That was many years ago, but today we still do the same things!

I love Red Nose Day. So when I saw the poster on the school noticeboard last month I felt really excited. My friends and I had lots of crazy ideas about how to raise money. In the end we made and sold cakes with funny faces. After school we went into Greenwich and did our own comedy show in the street. Luke's dog Sherlock was a real star, and lots of people gave us money for the TTS collection. It was great fun! I can't wait till next time.

Olivia Fraser

READING **1 Charity work: Olivia and her friends**

→ ▲ 114/2 *Look at what Olivia writes about Red Nose Day. What things sound fun to you?*

Across cultures 🇬🇧

People in the UK often help **charities**. What charities in Germany do you know about?

LANGUAGE **2 Irregular simple past forms** → WB 4/3 → G1

a) *Look again at Olivia's text and find the past forms of these verbs. Make a list.*

be   do    feel   get

give   go   have   make

see   sell   wear

Verb	Past form
be	was / were
do	did
feel	…

 There are no rules for irregular past forms. You must learn them by heart.

→ △ 114/3 b) *Put in the correct past forms. (The list of irregular verbs on page 246 can help you.)*

Two years ago the students **1** (do) fun activities and **2** (get) money for Comic Relief. They **3** (bring) the money to school. Then the school **4** (put) all the money together and **5** (give) it to the charity. Red Nose Day **6** (be) a non-uniform day, so everyone **7** (come) to school in different clothes. But they all **8** (wear) something red. Of course they all **9** (have) red noses too. Some students **10** (take) funny photos for the school website.

→ △ 115/4
→ S14

LANGUAGE **3** Find the rule: Regular simple past forms

a) *Look at the example. Find the rule for regular past forms and write it down.*

Example: Lenny Henry **started** Comic Relief in 1988. Last time we **raised** lots of money. In the evening we **watched** the big TV show.

b) *Be careful how you say **-ed**. There are three different sounds. Listen and say:*

1. [d] Two years ago we organis**ed** a great Red Nose Day. I lov**ed** it. We plann**ed** lots of activities.
2. [t] First we help**ed** to raise money. Then we watch**ed** TV. I lik**ed** Lenny Henry's jokes!
3. [ɪd] I want**ed** to look funny so I paint**ed** my face. I need**ed** a red nose too, of course.

LANGUAGE **4** The friends' comedy show → WB 4/4–5

Look at the picture and write 5–6 sentences about the comedy show. Choose from these verbs and use the simple past.

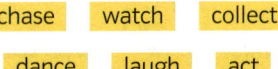

Example: The friends did the comedy show after school.

LANGUAGE  **5** The star of the show → WB 5/6, 6/7

What does Sherlock tell his dog friends the next day? Write the text again in his words, with the verbs in the simple past. Check if the forms are regular or irregular.

Start: I **did** lots of great tricks in the comedy show yesterday.

Sherlock *does* lots of great tricks in the comedy show. First he *jumps* over a big box. Then he *runs* around and *chases* his tail. After that he *dances* on a skateboard, and when Olivia *starts* to play the sax he also *sings*. The people *love* it. They *laugh* and *clap* and *give* lots of money for Comic Relief. Luke and his friends *try* to do their best too but everyone's eyes *are* on Sherlock. He *feels* happy and proud – he *is* the real star of the show!

Look at G1 on page 144. You must be careful with the spelling of some regular forms.

SPEAKING

6 Play a game: Something funny for money

People often pay money when you do funny or hard activities for charity. Take turns to say what you did on Red Nose Day. Roll two dice, for an activity and a comment.

Example: **2** + **5** I went everywhere in pyjamas. I enjoyed the day.

Activities
1 turn off my phone for the day
2 go everywhere in pyjamas
3 swim for 30 minutes
4 eat baby food
5 try not to laugh all day
6 speak in a funny voice

Comments
1 have lots of fun
2 find that hard
3 feel great
4 do my best
5 enjoy the day
6 raise lots of money

> If you like, you can think of new ideas for activities and comments.

WRITING

7 Your turn: A report about a special activity

→ △ 115/6

Write a report about an activity that you did with your friends or family. Write 6–8 sentences.

Example: Last year my friends and I helped to tidy a park. We …

Useful phrases	
When?	Last week / A month ago / In July / …
Who?	My friends and I / My dad / …
What?	We did a project / show … | We organised a … / made … / helped …
Feelings?	It was fun / I felt happy / nervous / proud / …

MEDIATION

8 A flyer in a German classroom

→ S17

Answer a British student's questions.

1. I know 'groß', so I can see this flyer is about something big. But what is it?
2. Who wants to sell cakes? And why?
3. Is the sale here in the school building?
4. 10th October – that's the date of your sale, right?
5. What's this about Africa?

> **Mediation skills**
>
> A **quick answer** helps to keep the conversation going.
>
> Don't worry **if the answer isn't in the text**. Just say there's no information.

GROSSER KUCHENVERKAUF

++ Wichtige Ankündigung! ++

Wir brauchen noch Geld für unsere Klassenfahrt. Deshalb planen wir einen großen Kuchenverkauf. (Erinnert ihr euch? Letztes Jahr haben wir auf diese Weise viel Geld für eine Schule in Afrika gesammelt.) Lasst uns also bald wieder in der Küche fleißig werden und viele leckere Kuchen backen!
Um zu besprechen, wann unser Kuchenverkauf stattfindet und wer was macht, treffen wir uns am 10. Oktober in der ersten Unterrichtsstunde. Merkt euch bitte dieses Datum – und bringt viele Ideen mit!

L 1/7 ⊚ # How did they know?

Luke: Only ten days till our class trip! I can't wait!

Dave: Sit down and help us, Luke! It's our group's job to think of games to play on the coach.

Luke: Hey, what about puzzle stories?

5 Holly: I don't know that game. How do you play it?

Dave: I know it! Great idea, Luke. Someone tells a little story with missing information. Then the others ask questions to try and find the solution. Here's a puzzle story for you …

10 After an anonymous phone call the police went to an address to arrest a dangerous man. They didn't know what the man looked like. They only knew that his name was John and that he was at that address. When they got to the house they found four people at a table in the kitchen:

15 a taxi driver, a mechanic, a farmer and a postman. The police didn't ask any questions and the other people didn't say anything, but right away the police arrested the postman. How did they know that they had the right person? Why were they so sure?

Luke: Did the police really arrest the right person?	Dave: Yes, they did.
20 Luke: Were there any photos of the man?	Dave: No, there weren't.
Holly: Did the postman try to run away?	Dave: No, he didn't.
Luke: Did the other people help the police?	Dave: No, they didn't.
Holly: Was it the man's home?	Dave: I don't know. But that isn't important.
25 Luke: Was the man's name a clue?	Dave: Yes, it was.

→ Solution on p. 19

SPEAKING ## 9 Talk about games

Do you like guessing games? What ideas have you got for games on a coach trip?

LANGUAGE ## 10 Ask and answer questions about the puzzle story → WB 6/8 → G2–3

1. Did the phone call help the police?
2. Was the man's name Peter?
3. Did the police ask any questions?
4. Was the man dangerous?
5. Were the four people in the kitchen?
6. Were the other people postmen too?

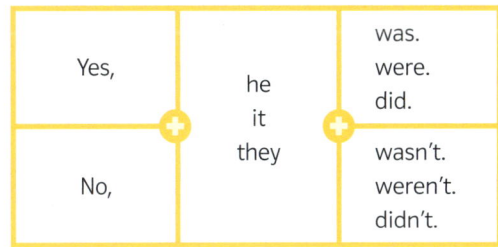

Yes,	he it they	was. were. did.
No,		wasn't. weren't. didn't.

LANGUAGE **11** **Find the rule: Differences between present and past** → G2-3

 *Look at the sentences in the present and the past. What are the differences for **questions** and **negative sentences**? Write down the rule.*

Simple present	Simple past
Do you like the story?	Did you like the story?
What does she say?	What did she say?
I don't know the game.	I didn't know the game.
He doesn't want to play.	He didn't want to play.

LANGUAGE **12** **Guess what we did**

→ △ 116/7
→ ▲ 116/8

Think of a fun activity that you and a friend did on a coach. (It needn't be true.) Your partner guesses what you did.

Example:
Did you tell puzzle stories? – No, we didn't.
Did you count all the red cars? – No, we didn't.
Did you send funny texts? – Yes, we did!

I spy with my little eye …

LANGUAGE **13** **Problems on the coach** → WB 6/9

*Complete the sentences. Use **didn't**.*

Example: I felt hungry but I (not have any food) → … but I didn't have any food.

1. I wasn't happy because my best friend (not sit next to me)
2. I helped a girl with her bag but she (not say thank you)
3. It was very loud on the coach so some people (not hear our puzzle stories)
4. The driver was friendly but he (not speak much English)
5. I needed the toilet but the coach (not stop)
6. The coach was slow so we (not get there till late)

LANGUAGE  **14** **Make fun questions and answers** → WB 7/10–11 → G2

a) *Work in groups of three or four. Think of six fun questions. Start with question words and use the simple past. Write each question on a piece of paper.*

How? Why? What? Where?

Who? laugh? get? see?

be? meet? …?

Examples:

What did you find in your schoolbag?
Why were you in a tree all day?

b) *Swap questions with another group and write funny answers to their questions.*

c) *With the other group, look at all the questions and answers. Choose the three best ideas and read them to the class.*

SPEAKING   15   Revision: Who am I?   → WB 8/12

Think of a famous person. It can be a real person (e.g. singer, sports star) or a character from a film or book. Your partner must guess who you are.

Example:

Are you a real person? – No, I'm not.
Can I see you in a film? – Yes, you can.
Is the film a comedy? – No, it isn't.
Do you do dangerous things? – Yes, I do.
Does Daniel Craig act your role? – Yes, he does.
I know! You're James Bond. – Yes, that's right.

> You can only ask questions with yes/no answers.
> Are you …? Have you got …?
> Do/Does …? Is …? …?

LISTENING   16   Luke's dream

L 1/8 ⊙
→ S18–20

a) *Listen and find five pictures for Luke's dream. (One picture is wrong.)*
Put the five pictures in the correct order.

b) *Listen again and answer the questions.*

1. What was Luke's problem with Sherlock?   **2.** How did Luke feel when the coach went without him?   **3.** Who did Luke ask for help first?   **4.** Why were the police suddenly too busy to help Luke?   **5.** Why didn't Luke stay on the train?   **6.** What did Luke find out about the horse in the past?   **7.** Why didn't Luke find out the end of his dream?

WRITING   17   Your turn: Your puzzle story

Write your own short puzzle story (5–6 sentences).
You can use your own idea or maybe you already know a story like this.
Can your friends guess the solution?

Solution to the puzzle story on page 17: There was only one man in the house – the postman. The other people were all women.

L 1/9 ◎   **Everyone can enjoy a challenge**

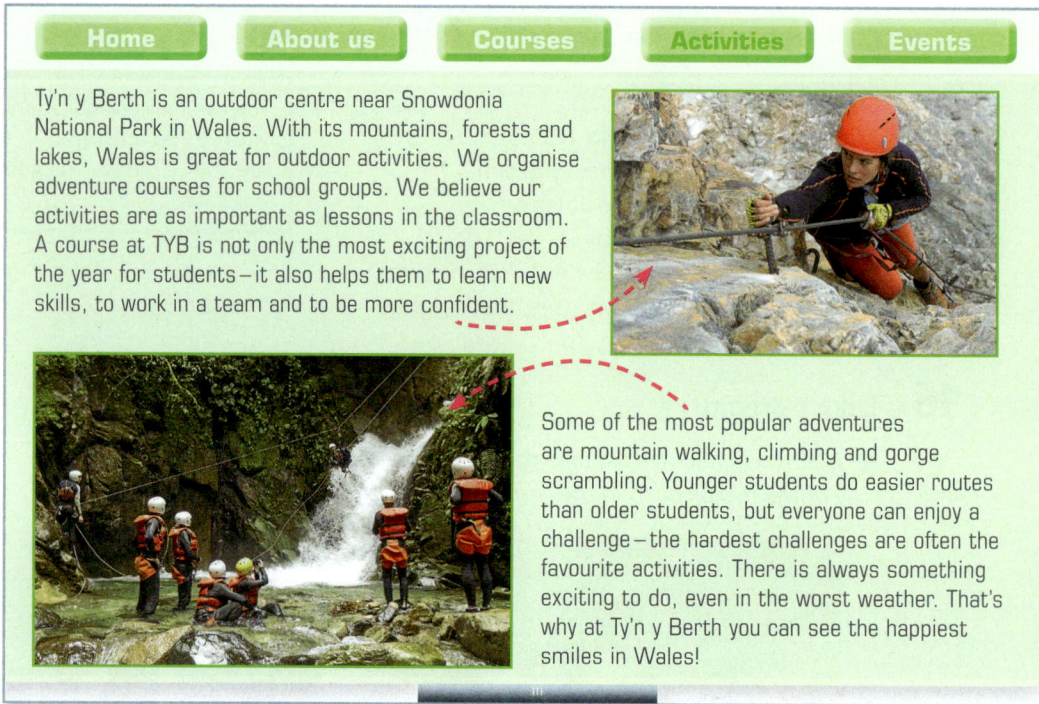

Home   About us   Courses   Activities   Events

Ty'n y Berth is an outdoor centre near Snowdonia National Park in Wales. With its mountains, forests and lakes, Wales is great for outdoor activities. We organise adventure courses for school groups. We believe our activities are as important as lessons in the classroom. A course at TYB is not only the most exciting project of the year for students – it also helps them to learn new skills, to work in a team and to be more confident.

Some of the most popular adventures are mountain walking, climbing and gorge scrambling. Younger students do easier routes than older students, but everyone can enjoy a challenge – the hardest challenges are often the favourite activities. There is always something exciting to do, even in the worst weather. That's why at Ty'n y Berth you can see the happiest smiles in Wales!

SPEAKING   **18**   **Talk about the outdoor centre**

a) *Close your books. Say what you remember about Wales and the outdoor centre.*

b) *Would you like to go there? What looks fun or interesting to you?*

c) *Your turn: Tell the class about a time when you had a challenge.*

Across cultures

Wales is an important part of the UK, but it's also a separate country with its own Celtic culture. Many people there speak two languages, English and Welsh. Ty'n y Berth is a Welsh name. You say it like this: [tiːnˌə ˈbɜːθ]

LANGUAGE   **19**   **Find the rule: Comparative and superlative forms** → G4

 a) *Copy and complete the grid. Look in the text for the missing forms.*

b) *Collect more examples from the text and add them to the grid.*

c) *Write down the rule for comparative and superlative forms of adjectives.*

adjective	comparative	superlative
hard	harder	…
big	…	biggest
easy	…	easiest
popular	more popular	…
confident	…	most confident
bad	worse	…
…	…	…

LANGUAGE **20** **Practise the new forms**

a) *Say the comparative and superlative forms of these adjectives.*

proud   good   interesting   funny

dangerous   quiet   brave   excited

→ △ 116/9   b) *What do you think about these things? Compare your ideas.*

Example: A: I think mountain walking is the **most exciting** outdoor activity.
B: Oh, I think climbing is **more exciting than** mountain walking.

exciting outdoor activity   good place for a holiday   interesting hobby   (any more ideas?)

LANGUAGE **21** **Say it in different words** → WB 8/13, 9/14–15 → G5

→ △ 117/10   *Use a different adjective and a different form.*

Example: 1. Wales is **smaller than** England.

1. Wales isn't as big as England. (small)
2. The weather today isn't as good as yesterday. (bad)
3. Route A is harder than route B. (easy)
4. The courses are cheaper than most people think. (expensive)
5. I'm more confident than I was about new challenges. (nervous)

Be careful with **than** and **as**.
When do you use which word?
younger **than** = **not as** old **as**

VOCABULARY **22** **Find adjectives to describe what you can see** → WB 9/16

→ △ 117/11
→ ▲ 117/12

Take turns to describe. Use comparative or superlative forms or '(not) as … as …'

fast   small   low   big   slow   tall   high

S 1/3–7
L 1/11–15

It was amazing

1 Before you read

→ S5–6, 8 *Look only at the words in* blue *in part A of the text. What do you think the text is about? Collect ideas.*

This text and the exercises help with the Unit task on pages 26–27.

Dave Preston's report for the class yearbook:

A It was a trip to a different planet! We came from a place with busy streets and shops and lots of people, but in this new place
5 there were only mountains and lakes and lots of sheep …
    Everyone on the coach was excited when we started our class trip to the Ty'n y Berth Outdoor Centre that
10 Saturday morning. Even our teacher Mr Swindon was excited . "Who wants to go to Wales?" he shouted. "We all do!" we shouted back.
    It was a long way from Greenwich,
15 but we played games and ate our sandwiches, and when at last we saw the big sign "Croeso i Gymru" we all clapped. Now the roads were quieter. Everything looked green and the villages and farms
20 had strange Welsh names. Soon we were in the mountains.

B At last the coach stopped in front of an old grey building next to fields and trees. Lots of the buildings in Wales are grey.
25   A man with a friendly face met us at the door of the building. "Welcome to Ty'n y Berth, everyone!" he said with a smile. "I'm Will, one of the instructors at the centre. And this is your home for
30 the next few days."
    Years ago it was a village school. But now it's all different inside. The biggest room is for meals and free time activities, and most of the smaller rooms are
35 bedrooms for people on courses at the centre.
    I was in a bedroom with five other boys. Right away there was a problem because Luke and Jay wanted the same bed near the window. "Maybe you can
40 take turns," I said. They thought that was a good solution, and Luke slept in the bed first. For all of us that night it felt a bit strange to be in a new place without our families.
45

C Most of the time at Ty'n y Berth we were too busy to think of home. Every morning and afternoon there were new and exciting activities to try. Then in the evening we usually played games.
50   Everyone loved gorge scrambling. It was funny when Olivia, Holly and I tried to help each other to get across a little river. In the end we just helped each other to fall *into* it. The water in
55 mountain rivers is very cold!
    We all found some activities harder than others. For me, climbing was the greatest challenge. But our instructor Ceri was great. She gave me lots of tips,
60 and then I felt more confident.
    Late one evening there was a surprise. Will gave everyone a torch and we went for a walk in the dark. "Don't talk, just listen," Will said. So we listened and it
65 was amazing because it was so very quiet. In Greenwich there's always noise, even at night. Then we all turned off our torches and that was amazing too. It was much darker than
70 in London so the stars looked much bigger and clearer.

D Too soon it was the last day, but when
75 we went to bed Luke whispered to me,
"I've got a torch so let's go for a night walk
again. Just you, Jay and me." We knew it
was against the rules, but we wanted one
last adventure. We waited till the others
80 were asleep. Then, as quiet as mice, we
tiptoed from the bedroom.

It was very dark outside, but with
Luke's torch we found our way across a
field and through some trees. Then Luke
85 turned off the torch. Well, I thought he
did, and I didn't know why. "Er, Luke –
it's a cloudy night so we can't look at the
stars, you know. I can't even see you," Jay
said. "I know," Luke's voice answered.
90 "The torch needs a new battery."

Oh no! Now we had a problem. The
night was as black as – well, as black as
night. We tried to be cool but we didn't
feel it. Which was the way back to the
95 centre? We had no idea. We started to
walk. We just hoped it was the right way.
Then suddenly – "Hoo-hoo!" What was
that? The strange noise made us nervous.
"Hoo-hoo!" It was nearer now. What was
100 it? We started to run, but in the dark it
was dangerous. Jay fell over something.
"Help! It's moving! It's a monster!" he

shouted. We tried to run away together.
Something awful hit my face and I
shouted too. We were really scared. 105
It was crazy. I don't know how we got
back to the centre again. We were so
happy to see that old grey building. We
tiptoed to the door and – oh no, the door
was locked! What now? We didn't want 110
trouble, but we needed to get back to our
beds. How did we do it? That's a secret.

E Early the next morning the coach came
to take us back to Greenwich. We were
sad to say goodbye to Wales, but we've all 115
got great memories of our amazing class
trip. (And now everyone knows why Luke,
Jay and I were tired and slept all the way
home!)

READING

2 **Questions about the text** → WB 10/17–18

a) *Take turns to ask and answer questions about Dave's report.*

Example: Where did the students go for their class trip? – They went to Wales.

What …?	the students / go for their class trip	Dave / find the hardest challenge
Why …?	everyone / get to Ty'n y Berth	the stars / look so big and clear
Where …?	the girls and boys / eat their meals	the three boys / go for a night walk
How …?	Luke and Jay / want the same bed	Luke's torch / need?
When …?	the students / do on the course	(*your own idea for questions?*)

b) *Something to think about: What do you think these things were?*

1. the "hoo-hoo" noise (line 97)   **2.** the monster (line 102)   **3.** something awful (line 104)

SPEAKING **3** The secret → WB 10/19

a) *In the report Dave doesn't say how he, Luke and Jay got back to their beds. How do you think they did this? What ideas have you got?*

→ S16

→ 117/13

b) *Role play: Work in groups. Think of an ending and write a short scene. Act your scene for the class.*

Maybe they found an open window.

Maybe they …

WRITING **4** How to: Plan a travel report

→ S7 **a)** *In one or two sentences say what each of the five parts of the report (A–E) is about.*

Start: Part A is about how the students got from Greenwich to Wales.

b) *Find two or three key phrases in each part that can make good headings for that part.*

Example: Part A: Our class trip – A long way from Greenwich – Croeso i Gymru

→ S10–13 **c)** *Use your ideas from a) and b) to make Dave's plan for his report. Use a grid to show the five parts and the main ideas in each part.*

Part	Main ideas
A	class trip – from Greenwich to Wales – long way
B	

Writing skills

Always **make a plan** for a text. A good plan shows how many **parts** the text has got and also the main ideas in each part.

Try to **make your text interesting** for the reader. Think of a special way to start the text. Choose good words and phrases that help the reader to see and feel what you describe.

VOCABULARY **5** How to: Make a travel report interesting

→ S13 **a)** *Talk about the first sentence of Dave's report. Do you think this is a good way to start a travel report? Why/why not?*

b) *A travel report needs different kinds of words and phrases. Look at the lists below and find more examples in Dave's report. (Some examples can go in more than one list.)*

1. words that explain 'when': that Saturday morning (line 9) – at last (line 22) – …
2. words that describe places: everything looked green (line 18) – busy streets (line 3) – …
3. words that show feelings: excited (line 11) – we all clapped (line 17) – …
4. words that make a text exciting: a different planet! (line 2) – Oh no! (line 91) – …

How to use a dictionary

> Think! Do you really need a dictionary? What do you do first when you see a new English word? What do you do if you don't know how to translate a German word into English?

1 Talk about different kinds of dictionaries

a) *Match A–E to the right kind of dictionary. (Some sentences are correct for all three kinds.)*

Online … | In a book … | In an electronic dictionary …

A. the words are in a list in alphabetical order.
B. you write in the search box to look up a word.
C. you can see the different meanings of the word.
D. you can hear the word's pronunciation.
E. there are two parts: first words in one language and then words in the other language.

b) *What other information do the different dictionaries give?*

c) *Which kind of dictionary do **you** like to use? Explain why.*

2 Practise with the alphabet → WB 11/20–21

a) *Revision: Take turns to say the alphabet in English.*

b) *Work with the first sentence in part C of Dave's report on page 22. Put all the words in the sentence in alphabetical order. (Be careful with words that start with the same letter – look at the next letters too.) Then check with your partner. Is the order correct?*

3 Find the correct meaning → WB 11/22

a) *English → German: When you find more than one meaning for a word, choose the right meaning for the sentence. Look up the words in* blue *and translate them into German.*

1. Take the second street on the right . That's the right way for the station.
2. I haven't got time to sit and chat today. We can chat when I come next time .
3. This is a very small room . There's room for only one bed.

b) *German → English: Sometimes you need different English words for the same German word. Look up the German words and complete the sentences.*

1. ***tragen***: a) The students … a blue uniform.
   b) They … their books to school in a bag.
2. ***treffen***: a) I often … my friends in the park.
   b) Try to … that tree with your ball.
3. ***Karte***: a) Can you find Wales on the …?
   b) Look at the … for our special lunch.

Our travel report

For your yearbook, work in groups of four and write a short travel report about a class trip. It can be a real trip – or a fantasy trip! It needn't be as long as Dave's report on pages 22–23, but it's important to make it interesting for your readers.

Step 1

Choose an idea for your trip → WB 12/24

a) *What kind of class trip can your group write about? Do you want to use one of these photos? Or have you got your own great idea? Discuss different ideas and then choose* **one** *idea for your travel report.*

1

2

3

> 1. rafting | paddle | current | to capsize
> 2. science fiction | aliens | planet | spaceship
> 3. sightseeing | youth hostel | party | trouble

b) *Work with a placemat to collect ideas for your report. You each think about one of the four topics below. Write down ideas in your part of the placemat.*

1. The place: How did you get there?
2. The people: Who is in the report?
3. Typical activities: What did you do or see during the first part of your trip?
4. A special adventure (e.g. problem, surprise): What happened? What did you do?

c) *Choose which ideas you want to use and write them down in the middle of the placemat.*

> For help with questions in the simple past, look back at **Station 2**.
>
> For help with new words, look at the **Skills page**.
>
> For help with placemats look at page 141 in the **Skills section**.

---

rafting ['rɑːftɪŋ] Schlauchbootfahren | **paddle** ['pædl] Paddel | **current** ['kʌrnt] Strömung | **to capsize** [kæp'saɪz] kentern | **to go sightseeing** ['saɪtˌsiːɪŋ] eine Besichtigungstour machen | **youth hostel** ['juːθ ˌhɒstl] Jugendherberge

Step 2

Plan your travel report → WB 12/25

For help with how to write a plan, look at the **Story** again.

a) *Your report has got four parts.*
Together, write a plan to show the key ideas in each part.

Part 1: The beginning: Here you describe how you got to the place.
Part 2: The first day(s): Here you describe typical activities for this kind of trip.
Part 3: The special adventure: Say what happened, but don't tell the whole story.
This part of the report finishes with a problem or an exciting situation.
Part 4: The ending: Explain how the adventure finished; find a good ending.

b) *Decide who writes which part of the report.*

Do you remember the four kinds of words for travel reports? Look back at the **Story** exercises.

For help with the simple past, look at **Station 1** and **Station 2** again.

Station 3 helps you with adjectives.

Step 3

Write your part of the travel report

a) *Work with the plan from Step 2 and make notes about the information in your part. Don't write sentences – just important words and phrases.*

b) *Read through your notes. Have you got interesting ideas and words?*

c) *Now write your part of the report. Don't forget to use the simple past.*

Step 4

Improve your part of the report → WB 13/26

Work with a partner from your group. Check each other's texts. Help each other to improve the texts.

Look at page 135 in the **Skills section** for tips on how to check texts.

Step 5

Finish your travel report → WB 13/27

a) *Put the four parts together and read the whole report. Are you happy with it? If not, discuss it and improve it.*

b) *Now think of the best way to present your report. Use photos or pictures too.*

The new boy → S21–22

VIEWING

1   Film scenes → WB 14/28

1   **a)** *Watch (00:00-03:01). Look at the headings for Scene A and B and at the phrases in the box. Match the phrases with the right scene.*

> sneaking around   a bad day?
>
> friends again   why lemons?
>
> trouble (between friends)

     Scene A: After school   **Scene B:** The new boy

b) *Jinsoo and Marley want to know why Nick is buying all those things. What do **you** think Nick is up to? What happens next? Talk about your ideas and then watch the last part of the film (03:02-04:45).*

c) *Do you like the film's ending? Explain why / why not. Write two or three sentences.*

     Example: I think the ending is nice / funny / surprising / boring / … because …

VIEWING

2   Film and music

a) *Before you read the box on the right, watch (01:58-04:45) again and listen to the music in the different scenes. What can you say about the music? Why do you think the filmmakers use music that way?*

b) *Now read the box. Then look at the photo. Which adjectives describe the mood and the feelings in the scene? What kind of music would **you** use for the scene?*

Film skills

Films don't work the same way as texts. A film tells a story with words – *and* with **pictures**, **sounds** and **music** too. So you have the story in a film, and you have different ways to tell that story. These are called the audio-visual effects of a film.

Examples: If you want to show that a person is sad, you can use slow and sad music. For an action scene, you can use loud and fast music.

Mood / Feelings:

> excited   sad   tired   happy
>
> angry   unfriendly   hurt   silly
>
> …

Music:

> funny   slow   loud   aggressive
>
> sad   fast   sweet   happy   cool
>
> scary   …

Can you …

1. talk about activities that you did? _ _ _ I went to … | We played / sold …
2. find out what happened? _ _ _ _ _ _ _ _ Did you see …? | Why was he …? | How did she …?
3. say how you felt? _ _ _ _ _ _ _ _ _ _ _ I was / felt embarrassed/… | It was exciting / …
4. compare things? _ _ _ _ _ _ _ _ _ _ _ It's bigger than / as big as … | It's the most exciting …

LANGUAGE

1   The yearbook team

Look at the list of jobs for the yearbook team. Write down what they did yesterday. Make sentences with the correct past forms.

Start: They talked about … They …

– talk about the 'dreams' page
– put the sports pages together
– look at Jay's ideas for the music pages
– collect ideas for the puzzles page
– take a photo of the yearbook team
– make a list of jobs for next week

LANGUAGE

2   Put in the correct past forms

Holly: I **1** (go) swimming in the sea at Southend yesterday.
Dave: Wow! **2** (be) it your mum's idea to go to Southend?
Holly: No, it **3** (not be). Olivia's family **4** (invite) me.
Dave: Lucky you! **5** (you go) on the train?
Holly: Yes, we **6** (do).
Dave: You **7** (be) brave to go in the sea at this time of the year! **8** (be) the water cold?
Holly: Yes, it **9** (be). So we **10** (not stay) in the water for more than a few minutes.

LANGUAGE

3   What are the questions?

Olivia calls home from Ty'n y Berth. Her dad wants to know more. What does he ask?

1. Olivia: We *got up* early this morning.
   Dad: When did you …?
2. Olivia: We *went* for a long walk.
   Dad: Where …?
3. Olivia: We *saw* lots of interesting things.
   Dad: What …?
4. Olivia: My classmates *laughed* at me.
   Dad: Why …?

LANGUAGE

4   Comparative and superlative forms: Pet profiles for the yearbook

1. Luke's dog Sherlock is the (crazy) animal in England. There's nothing (funny) than when he chases his tail. It's always (fast) than he is!
2. The (cute) pets for Holly are her two guinea pigs. Mr Fluff likes to explore. He thinks a trip in a bag is (interesting) than a game on the floor! Honey isn't as (brave) as Mr Fluff.
3. Cats are the (popular) pets in the class. Dave's cat Sid brings presents for the family. Some presents are (good) than others. The (bad) thing for Dave is a mouse in his bed!

S 1/8–12
L 1/16–20

Middle school: How I got lost[1] in London

Rafe Khatchadorian is not very popular with his classmates, and his best friend Leo only exists in Rafe's imagination. A lot of things go wrong for Rafe, especially on a school trip to London to study Living History (when you visit special museums where they show how people lived in the past). When they
5 go to see a famous London wax museum, he makes some silly mistakes, and his popularity score – a sign of how much the others like him – falls and falls.

The big event of the day was a tour around Madame Fifi's House of Wax. Now, of course we were excited about seeing the
10 main attractions – Will and Kate! David Beckham! Rihanna! – but we were *really* excited about the basement[2]. Because in the basement was Madame Fifi's Temple of Terrors, where you could see beheadings[3],
15 people on spikes and other horrible things. In other words, all the blood[4].

Yeah, yeah, we saw all the famous people. But do you *really* want to stand eye to eye with Tom Cruise? *You do?*
20 Not me. I wanted stuff from *my* world. So I stayed longest at Henry VIII (he had six wives[5] and beheaded two of them!), Winston Churchill (he said "We shall never surrender"[6] to Adolf Hitler!), Charles

Darwin (it's thanks to him we know that
25 we come from monkeys[7]!), Guy Fawkes (he tried to blow up[8] Parliament … Wait: should[9] we like him or not?)

I was sad to leave the upper floors. And also …
30

"Scared …?" Leo whispered.

"No, of course I'm not scared," I said.

"Frightened?"

"Frightened is the same as scared," I told him. "And no, I'm not frightened."
35

But, let me tell you a secret: I *was* nervous.

"Is everyone ready?" Gordon, our tour guide, asked.

"Yeah," we all replied.
40

I remembered my popularity score today (-11) and decided to be brave, so my "Yeah" was the loudest. "YEAH!"

"Right, then, let's go," Gordon said. He opened the door but then stopped. "Does
45 anybody in the group have a weak heart[10]?" he asked.

"No," we replied.

"NO!" came my voice, the loudest.

"And everyone knows about the
50 haunting[11]?"

"YEAH!" I shouted, really enjoying myself.

Everyone looked at me – Gordon too.

"What is your name, young man?" he
55 asked.

---

1 **to get lost** [gɛt ˈlɒst] verschwinden; verloren gehen | 2 **basement** [ˈbeɪsmənt] Keller | 3 **beheading** [bɪˈhedɪŋ] Enthauptung | 4 **blood** [blʌd] Blut | 5 **wives** [waɪvz] Ehefrauen | 6 **we shall never surrender** [wi ʃæl ˌnevə srˈendə] wir werden uns nie ergeben | 7 **monkey** [ˈmʌŋki] Affe | 8 **to blow up** [bləʊ ˈʌp] in die Luft sprengen | 9 **should** [ʃʊd] sollten | 10 **weak heart** [wiːk ˈhɑːt] schwaches Herz | 11 **haunting** [ˈhɔːntɪŋ] Spuk

"Rafe," I said in a very small voice.

"And you know about the haunting, do you, Rafe?"

60 "Yes," I said in an even smaller voice.

"You read about it on the Madame Fifi's website?" he asked, with a strange smile.

"Yes, sir," I replied.

Everyone looked at me. They all
65 really wanted to hear the story about the haunting but thanks to me, they didn't get the chance. Gordon just said: "Excellent. Let's go!" – and my popularity score went down again, to -22.

70 He opened the door and we saw the stone steps that went down into the dark. Down and down we went. At the bottom we heard a loud noise. One of the girls cried out[12] but Gordon told her it was just a
75 passing[13] London Underground train. (OK, it wasn't "one of the girls" who cried out, it was me. Like I say, it was dark …)

Slowly, we started to see the wax figures.
80 "Cool," we said when we saw the heads on spikes, the murderers[14], the blood … Really scary stuff. Stuff that had *actually happened*[15].

"Now, Rafe …" Gordon said. "I'm sure
85 you can tell us about the famous Temple of Terrors story?"

NO WAY. I shook my head "no". Gordon smiled. "Well, let me tell you then …"

"Over a hundred years ago, two gentlemen
90 are taking a tour around the famous Madame Fifi's House of Wax. With them is a lady and they both want to impress[16] her.

"Do you know this Temple of Terrors?" the first one says. "They say it's very scary."
95 "Oh yes, very scary," the second man says.

Eleanor (the lady) says: "Oh, Cedric, it sounds terrible."

Both men see their chance to impress their lady friend.

"But I don't believe it," William says.

"Well, William," Cedric says, "let's go down and find out just how scary it is." 100

And the two men take the stone steps down into the Temple of Terrors.

"Well," William says. He looks around in the dark at the scary wax figures and feels very nervous. "I'm not frightened at all!" 105

"Frightened? Not me!" Cedric says, when he suddenly needs to use the bathroom.

"So, let's spend[17] the night here!" William says.

"Good idea!" Cedric says. 110

And so, because the men badly[18] want to impress Eleanor, they both agree[19] to spend the night …

"They couldn't stay the whole night," 115
Gordon continued. "They soon ran out screaming[20], their eyes wide with terror. And the next day, someone found both men at their homes …"

We looked at Gordon in complete silence. "Dead[21]." 120

From: *Middle School: How I Got Lost in London*
by James Patterson

→ WB 16/1–4

12 **to cry out** [kraɪ ˈaʊt] aufschreien | 13 **passing** [ˈpɑːsɪŋ] vorbeifahrend | 14 **murderer** [ˈmɜːdrə]
Mörder | 15 **stuff that had actually happened** [ˌstʌf ðæt həd ˌæktʃuəli ˈhæpnd] Dinge, die
tatsächlich passiert sind | 16 **to impress sb** [ɪmˈpres] jmdn. beeindrucken | 17 **to spend** [spend]
verbringen | 18 **badly** [ˈbædli] unbedingt | 19 **to agree** [əˈɡriː] einwilligen | 20 **screaming** [skriːmɪŋ]
schreiend | 21 **dead** [ded] tot

LISTENING

1 Mr Preston's scary story → WB 17/1

L 1/21

a) *When Mr Preston reads Dave's travel report, he remembers his own class trip to Wales a long time ago. Listen to the story about Mt Snowdon, a castle[1] and ghosts[2] …*

1. **When** did Mr Preston see the ghosts?
2. **Who** were they?

3. **What** did the ghosts do – or not do?
4. **What** does Dave think about the story?

b) *In class, compare Dave's trip to Wales in Unit 1 with his dad's trip. Which trip is more interesting to you? Say why. (Think of the different activities, different feelings, …)*

c) *Look at the two 'ghost scences' in the pictures. Choose one of them and write 6–8 sentences about the ghost in your scene. What do you think is his/her story?*

LANGUAGE

2 Olivia's dream

Last night Olivia had a strange dream. Read her e-mail to Holly. What verbs are missing? Sometimes there's more than one possible answer. Use the simple past.

Holly – I **1** a really strange dream last night …
I **2** at school and **3** the classroom door. But nobody[3] **4** there. Suddenly,
I **5** a strange noise outside. So I **6** out to the playground. That's when I **7**
something in the air: a UFO! Holly, I **8** sooooo scared! The UFO **9** closer and
closer. Then, someone **10** the UFO's door and a green alien **11** out. "Hello Olivia!"
he **12**. "But, how do you know my name?!" I **13**. "Oh, it's me, Jay," he said.
"I always go to school by UFO." Wasn't that a strange dream? Then, when I **14** to
school this morning, I **15** Jay! And: His shirt was GREEN!
xoxo, Olivia 💗

1 castle ['kɑːsl] Burg; Schloss | **2 ghost** [gəʊst] Geist | **3 nobody** ['nəʊbədi] niemand

SPEAKING

3 At Greenwich Market → WB 17/2

a) *Talk about the scene at Greenwich Market. What is everybody doing? Be creative!*

b) *Use different adjectives to talk about the scene. Here are some ideas:*

funny   good   happy   angry   jealous   tired

bored   boring   interesting   typical   big

Examples: A: The boy's ice cream isn't as big as the girl's.
B: I think the scene with the bird is the funniest! What do you think?

VOCABULARY

4 A flyer for Drama Club

a) *Which words can you think of for the gaps? Sometimes there's more than one possible answer.*

b) *Do you think the flyer is a good example for this kind of project? Why / Why not? What can you do differently with this flyer? Find five things.*

We invite all theatre fans to ❶ the TTS Drama Club! We ❷ every Wednesday at 3:30 in Room 0.4.04. Our next play⁴ is William Shakespeare's Romeo and Juliet – and Shakespeare is of course Britain's most ❸ writer⁵! But this isn't just a play: This is a musical of 'R&J', so we ❹ LOTS of boys and girls with a talent for acting and singing! And this isn't a historical 'R&J'! No, we ❺ to show the London of TODAY! So, forget ❻ costumes like in Shakespeare's days. You can wear your own cool ❼! Also, we always need people who⁶ can ❽ posters, sell tickets or ❾ with the sound. For more ❿, just ask Mr Gibbons, the Drama teacher in Years 7 and 9.

4 **play** [pleɪ] Theaterstück | 5 **writer** [ˈraɪtə] Schriftsteller | 6 **people who …** [ˌpiːpl ˈhuː] Leute, die …

Find more online:
48ww9d

London: A special city

London is a huge city, and Greenwich is only a small part of it. On these two pages you can learn more about the British capital and find out what makes it so special.

SPEAKING

1 First facts about London → WB 18/1

a) *What can you find out from the photos? The words on the right can help.*

multi-ethnic city · famous / historical sights

green spaces · royal family · river

underground trains · busy streets

festivals

Example: 1. The Thames goes through the centre of London. It's a big, busy river. You can see famous …

1 The Thames, Big Ben and the London Eye

2 Oxford Street

3 The Tube

4 The Notting Hill Carnival

5 Buckingham Palace

6 Hyde Park

b) *Match the sentence parts to find out more facts about London.*

1. London was originally a Roman town
2. Today London is the
3. It's the capital city of
4. Over eight million people
5. The students in London's schools speak
6. London has got five

a) England and of the UK.
b) international airports.
c) more than 300 different languages.
d) largest city in Europe.
e) with the name 'Londinium'.
f) live in London.

c) *Take turns to tell your partner as much as you can about London in one minute.*

The Tube is over 150 years old. It's the world's oldest underground.

And did you know Big Ben is the name of the clock's bell, and **not** the clock?

VIEWING

2 Royal London → WB 18/2

5 a) *Before you watch: What can you say about Laura's outfit?*

b) *Now watch and choose the correct endings.*

1. Laura's clothes
   a) are for a party.
   b) celebrate royal events.
   c) show what the royal family wear.

2. The Changing of the Guards takes place
   a) in front of Buckingham Palace.
   b) at the Tower of London.
   c) in Hyde Park.

3. Prince Albert was
   a) Queen Victoria's brother.
   b) British.
   c) from Germany.

4. The Royals are part of the British identity
   a) for everyone in the UK.
   b) for some people in the UK.
   c) only for older people.

c) *Your turn: What do you think about royal families? Explain your opinion.*

LISTENING

3 Young Londoners → WB 18/3

L 1/23 a) *A class in London is doing a project about their city. While you listen, work in groups of three. Each group takes different notes under one of these headings.*

b) *Share the information from a) with the other groups with the same question.*

What is good in London? *– exciting things to do* *– …*	*What is not so good?* *– expensive* *– …*	*How is London different?* *– bigger than other cities* *– …*

WRITING

4 What makes London special?

Talk about what you think makes London a special city. Write your ideas in a mind map.

SPEAKING

5 Your turn: Cities in Germany

Talk about German cities. Compare them with London. What is similar and what is different?

Useful phrases

It's also a Roman town / a capital city / …
It isn't as big / … as London.
There aren't as many …
It has / hasn't got famous sights / a river / …

Find more online:
v8kv97

Unit 2

London is amazing!

A | Famous sights: the Houses of Parliament and Big Ben

SPEAKING **1** **Talk about places in London**

Describe the places in the photos. Say what you can see or do there. Find the places on the map at the back of your book.

LISTENING **2** **A video chat with Amir**

L 1/24 ⊙
→ S18–20

a) *Jay is having a video chat with Amir, his cousin. Amir lives in Bradford and has plans to see London with Jay. Listen, and say what kind of things each boy is interested in.*

b) *Listen again and take notes about these places.*

Covent Garden   the British Museum   Brick Lane

the London Wall   Shakespeare's Globe

In Unit 2 you learn

… how to discuss plans and how to describe the way people do things. You learn:

- words for things to do and see in London
- the language of plans (*going-to future*)
- word-building with *some, any, every, no*
- words for getting around by public transport

B Brick Lane: multi-ethnic flair and street art

C The wax figures at Madame Tussauds

D Londoners and tourists at Covent Garden

E The Horse Guards at Whitehall

SPEAKING

 3 Your turn: Choose your London → WB 19/1

→ △ 118/1

Think about what you already know about London. In groups, take turns to tell each other two things that you would really like to see or do there. Explain why. Use your notes from Ex. 2.

VOCABULARY **4 London vocabulary** → WB 19/2

Collect useful words and names for your personal vocabulary. Add more words while you work through Unit 2.

I'm into street art. And great food! So I'd like to see Brick Lane.

It must be fun to walk around Madame Tussauds and see all the famous 'people'!

L 1/25 ◉ **It's going to be fun**

"It was amazing," Amir tells his aunt. He's staying with the Azads and earlier today Jay took him to the Royal Observatory.

"Good. And what are you two going to do
5 tomorrow?" Mrs Azad asks. "Are you going to see more sights in Greenwich?"

"No, we aren't. We're going to visit the British Museum with Olivia and Holly," Jay tells her. "We met them in Greenwich Park this afternoon, and Olivia is like Amir – she 10 loves museums."

Mrs Azad's face shows that she isn't happy with this plan. But Jay can think fast. "Don't worry," he says. "We aren't going to go alone. Shahid is going to take us." His 15 18-year-old brother isn't at home at the moment, so Jay must try to persuade him later.

"Oh, is Shahid going to look after you? That's OK then," says Mrs Azad. 20

"Yes, it's going to be fun. But there's just one thing. The museum is free, but I'm not sure where I'm going to get money for our Oyster cards or for our lunch."

Mrs Azad smiles. "Probably the same 25 place where you *always* get money."

READING

1 **What do you think?** → WB 20/3

1. What is Mrs Azad's problem with the boys' plan?
2. What is Jay's solution to that problem?
3. Where is Jay going to get money?

Across cultures

The cheapest way to travel by public transport in London is with an **Oyster card**. It's a smartcard and you can top it up with credit. What's the cheapest way to travel where you live?

LANGUAGE

 2 **Find the rule for *going to*** → WB 20/4, 21/5 → G6

a) *Find phrases with **going to** in the text. Which part of the time line are they about?*

 b) *How do you make **going to** forms? Write the rule and put it in your folder.*

← yesterday ← today → tomorrow →

LANGUAGE

 **3** **Your turn: What are you going to do?**

a) *First, write down three sentences about your weekend. Walk around and ask a few classmates about their plans.*

→ △ 118/2
→ S24

b) *Take turns to say what you found out about your classmates' plans.*

What are you going to do next weekend?

On Sunday I'm going to visit my grandma.

LANGUAGE **4** **What's going to happen?** → WB 21/6

→ △ 118/3

Write about the people in the picture. Find your own verbs.

Start: 1. The old man and woman **are going to sit down.**
2. The man in the wheelchair **is going to** …

SPEAKING **5** **Play a game: Guess my plans for tomorrow**

→ △ 118/4

Think of a place in London but don't say what it is. Your partner must ask questions and guess the activity. Start the questions with "Are you going to …?"

Example: A: Are you going to listen to music?
B: No, I'm not.
A: Are you going to look at animals?
B: Yes, I am.
A: Are you going to visit London Zoo?
B: Yes, I am. That's right.

look at pictures / …

watch football / street shows / …

visit a historical building / …

listen to street musicians

LISTENING **6** **How to: Get around by Tube** → WB 22/7

L 1/27

→ S18–20

a) *Work with the map of the Tube and DLR at the back of your book. A tourist is at Elephant & Castle station and wants to get to Buckingham Palace. Listen to the dialogue. Which route do you think is best – the man's or the woman's? Why?*

b) *Take turns to describe the routes to the other places above. You can start at Elephant & Castle or go from one sight to another.*

Place / Sight	Station
Buckingham Palace	Victoria
Oxford Street	Oxford Circus
Tower of London	Tower Hill
Transport Museum	Covent Garden
Mudchute Farm	Crossharbour

Useful phrases

You take the … line to … | You change onto the … line. | You go north / south / east / west to … | It's three stops to … | You get off at …

L 1/28 ◉ **Good idea!**

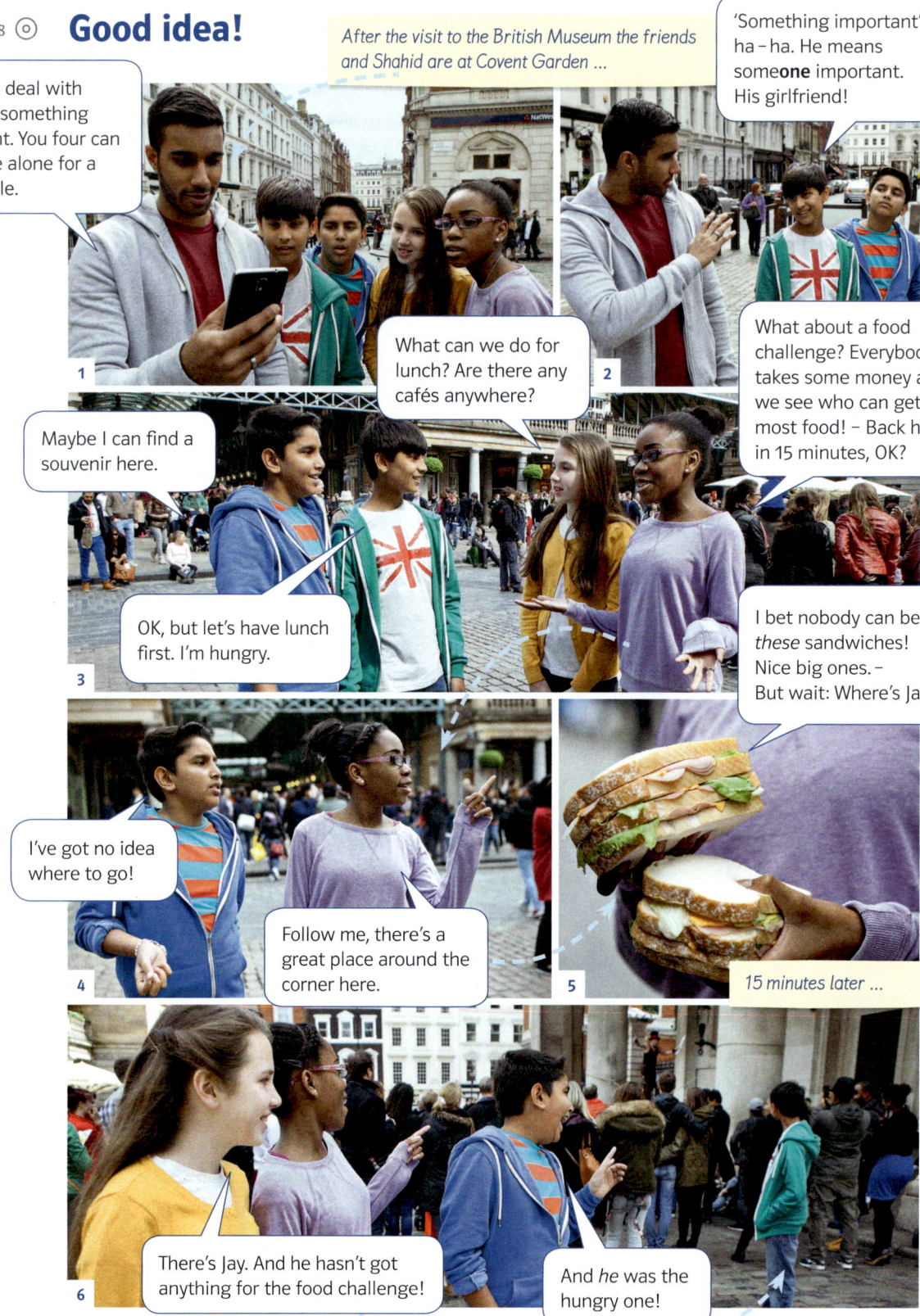

After the visit to the British Museum the friends and Shahid are at Covent Garden …

1 I need to deal with this – it's something important. You four can stay here alone for a little while.

2 'Something important', ha – ha. He means some**one** important. His girlfriend!

What can we do for lunch? Are there any cafés anywhere?

What about a food challenge? Everybody takes some money and we see who can get the most food! – Back here in 15 minutes, OK?

3 Maybe I can find a souvenir here.

OK, but let's have lunch first. I'm hungry.

I bet nobody can beat *these* sandwiches! Nice big ones. – But wait: Where's Jay?

4 I've got no idea where to go!

Follow me, there's a great place around the corner here.

5 *15 minutes later …*

6 There's Jay. And he hasn't got anything for the food challenge!

And *he* was the hungry one!

→ △ 119/5
→ ▲ 119/6

SPEAKING **7** **The photo story** → WB 22/8

*Imagine you're **one** of the people in the story. What can he / she say about it?*

Example: (Jay) I was really hungry. Olivia had a great idea. But then I saw …

LANGUAGE **8** **Revision: Comparison of adjectives**

*What kind of a food challenge would be the best for **you**? Why? Write about it in 5–6 sentences with different forms of adjectives. The examples can help you.*

Examples: I think the **most important thing** is to find **the best food**!
Healthy food is **better than** … food, but **not as** … **as** …

LANGUAGE **9** **Compound words with *some* and *any*** → G7

a) *Match the parts.*

1. I'm hungry. I need	a) anything expensive.
2. I've only got £1. I can't buy	b) some good tricks.
3. Are there public toilets	c) any more time.
4. Let's watch this guy. He's doing	d) something to eat.
5. I can't see the show – I'm behind	e) anyone know?
6. We must go now. We haven't got	f) someone very tall!
7. Where's the Tube station? Does	g) anywhere here?

→ △ 119/7
→ ▲ 120/8

b) *Do you remember the rule for **some** and **any** from last year? Explain it.*

LANGUAGE **10** **Complete the words** → WB 23/9–10, 24/11 → G7   `some` `any` `every` `no`

→ △ 120/9

Holly: What can we do till we meet Shahid later? Has **1** *body* got a good suggestion?
Jay: It must be **2** *thing* that costs **3** *thing* – we haven't got any money left.
Olivia: Let's just walk around. I'm sure that's fun for **4** *one* new in London like Amir. There are lots of interesting things to see **5** *where* you look. What do you think, Amir?
Amir: Well, if **6** *body* wants to make a different suggestion – yes, I'd like that.
Holly: Is there **7** *where* special you'd like to go or **8** *thing* special you'd like to see?
Amir: Well, **9** *thing* is special for me – it's all amazing. But I'd love to walk near the river.
Jay: Is that OK with **10** *body*? – Great, come on, let's go and find the Thames!

SPEAKING  **11** **Your turn: Visitors** → WB 24/12–13

a) *With a partner, think of where you can go or what you can do with young visitors where you live. Make a list of 4–5 different ideas.*

b) *Present your 'Top 3' to the class.*

> **Useful phrases**
>
> **Pros:** good for someone who likes history / … | doesn't cost anything | easy to get there by public transport | something everyone enjoys
>
> **Cons:** (very) expensive | not everyone is into … | boring | too far away | not good in bad weather

L 1/30 ◎ # They can bite *very* hard

If you don't know London well, a bus tour with a guide can be a good idea. You can see and learn much more than if you explore the city alone.

"Now we're going slowly past the Tower of London, one of the city's must-see sights –
5 you can see it clearly on the left. William the Conqueror built the Tower when he became king of England in 1066. In the past it was a castle, a prison and even a royal zoo with big animals like lions and bears! Today
10 it's a must-see sight. Many people come specially to see the Crown Jewels, but the Beefeaters give fantastic tours of the whole Tower – they know its history really well! The Raven Master is a Beefeater too. His
15 job is to look after the ravens carefully and to make sure they stay happily and safely in their home at the Tower. If you visit the Tower, don't go too close to the ravens. They don't always like that – and they can bite *very* hard!"
20

Across cultures

William the Conqueror and his people came from Normandy in France, so after 1066 many French words became part of the English language. Can you give some examples?

SPEAKING **12** A must-see sight for you too?

Would you like to visit the Tower? Why or why not?

LISTENING **13** Rocky's audio tour

L 1/31–33 ◎ **a)** *Listen once. Who is Rocky? What three topics does he tell you about?*

✏ **b)** *Listen again. What does Rocky say about* **food**, **treasure** *and* **ghosts**? *Take notes.*
→ S18–20

→ S17 **c)** *Mediation: There's no 'Rocky' audio tour in German, and a young German tourist wants to know what Rocky says because he doesn't speak English. Give the main information in German.*

Listening skills

When you listen to information, first just try to understand the **gist** (main ideas). Then listen again for **more information**. Collect **key words and phrases** that help you to remember.

VOCABULARY  → WB 24/14, 25/15

14 Talk about the people in the pictures

→ △ 120/10

a) *What are they doing, and how are they doing it? Match the sentences with the photos.*

Example: **1.** He's jumping back **nervously**.

He's jumping back nervously.   She's looking quietly at a tablet PC.

They're clapping their hands loudly.   She's running fast.

He's smiling happily.   She's shouting aggressively.

b) *Discuss what the situation could be.*

Example: **1.** He's jumping back nervously. **Maybe he's scared.**

WRITING  → WB 25/15–16

15 Your turn: My special place in London

Which sight or special place in London do you find really interesting or cool?
In 6–8 sentences, say what the sight is and where it is. Describe it and say why it's special.

I'm going to be famous one day, so my special place is Madame Tussauds! Come and visit me when I'm a wax figure, Lou!

A wax figure?
In a costume like *that*?!

Writing skills

Before you start writing a text, stop and think: Which main points do you want to write about? For example, you can collect your ideas in a mind-map. Or you write down notes under the headings:

Who / What | Where | When | Why

A day out in London → S21–22

→ S21–22

SPEAKING

1 Warm-up

Which places / sights do you think are symbols of London? Write them down and tell the class.

VIEWING

2 Out and about in London → WB 26/17

6 *Watch the film. Which part do **you** really like? Why?*

VIEWING

3 A closer look → WB 26/18

Watch again and answer the questions. These ideas can help.

1. Why do you think Jinsoo's sister, Mina, is with the boys?
2. Where did Jinsoo want to go? Why didn't they go there?
3. What was the problem with Mina at Camden Market?

Jinsoo and Mina's dad

adult / child ticket

sightseeing / normal bus

look after   expensive

VIEWING

4 Setting and atmosphere in film scenes

a) *First, read the skills box. Then watch scenes **A** (01:15 – 01:50) and **B** (01:57 – 02:06) again. Say why you think they're important or interesting for the film.*

A

B

b) *Talk about the setting and atmosphere of your favourite scene in Ex. 2.*

cool   crazy   famous   funny

interesting   international   multi-ethnic

lots to see / discover   people everywhere

c) *Write a short description of what Jinsoo, Marley, Nick and Mina could do in a **different** location in London. Look at your lists from Ex. 1 for ideas.*

Film skills

In a film, the viewer needs to know what the film's **setting** is, so the choice of **locations** in a film is important. A famous place like London really needs to *look* like London!

Atmosphere is important too: crowds, places, views, water, things to look at or buy, cool shops … These things can create a special atmosphere for the viewer.

How to find information on the internet → S5, 9

1 Start with the homepage of a famous attraction's website

Most homepages give basic information and also useful links to other pages. Try to answer these questions with the help of the homepage for the Natural History Museum in London. If the answer is not on the page, which 'quick link' do you think can help?

1. Where is the museum?
2. How do I get there?
3. Is it open every day?
4. Are there any special displays at the moment?
5. Must I pay to visit the museum?

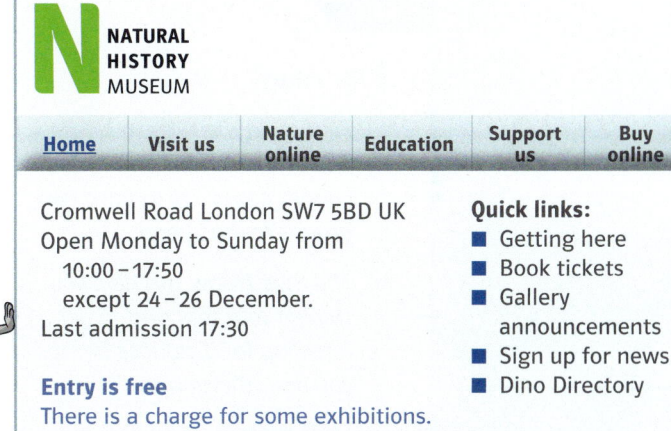

N NATURAL HISTORY MUSEUM

| **Home** | Visit us | Nature online | Education | Support us | Buy online |

Cromwell Road London SW7 5BD UK
Open Monday to Sunday from
  10:00 – 17:50
  except 24 – 26 December.
Last admission 17:30

Entry is free
There is a charge for some exhibitions.

Quick links:
- Getting here
- Book tickets
- Gallery announcements
- Sign up for news
- Dino Directory

2 Skim and scan internet texts → WB 27/20

a) *Skim the text on the right for the **gist**. What is it about? How can the information help visitors?*

b) *Now scan the text for **details** about animals. Make notes.*

> Try to guess new words. Don't worry about words that aren't important.

| Home | **Visit us** | Nature online | Education | Support us | Buy online |

The Galleries at the **Natural History Museum** are in four zones. The **Blue Zone** shows you the amazing diversity of life on Earth, from the smallest to the largest animals. This is also where you can find the popular Dinosaurs gallery. In the **Green Zone** you learn about Earth's ecology and how you can help to look after the planet. Visit the **Red Zone** to go back to the beginning of time and find out how and why our planet changes. Here you can see many of the Earth's minerals and treasures. In the **Orange Zone** you can explore nature in the Wildlife Garden – it features over 2,000 species. Also, see science in action in the spectacular Darwin Centre.

3 Practise with different websites

Partner A: Choose a sight in London (an idea from Unit 2 or your own idea).
Partner B: Find useful or interesting information about your partner's sight and tell him / her about it.

Our London tour

For this task, work in small groups. Each group is going to plan and present a different sightseeing tour for a class trip to London. There are three different tour choices:

| a tour by bus and boat | a tour by Tube | a tour on foot |

Step 1

Tour rules   → WB 28/22

a) First, read the rules in class. Then form groups of 4–5 and choose a tour. Try to have **two** groups for each tour.

b) The map below can help you to plan your tour and to get a feeling for distances before you use other maps.

Rules
- Your tour starts at **Green Park**.
- There must be **enough time** (morning till late afternoon) for everything in your plan.
- Only **one** stop on your tour costs money. The other sights must be **free**.
- You've got sandwiches for **lunch**, so you must plan when and where you can eat them.

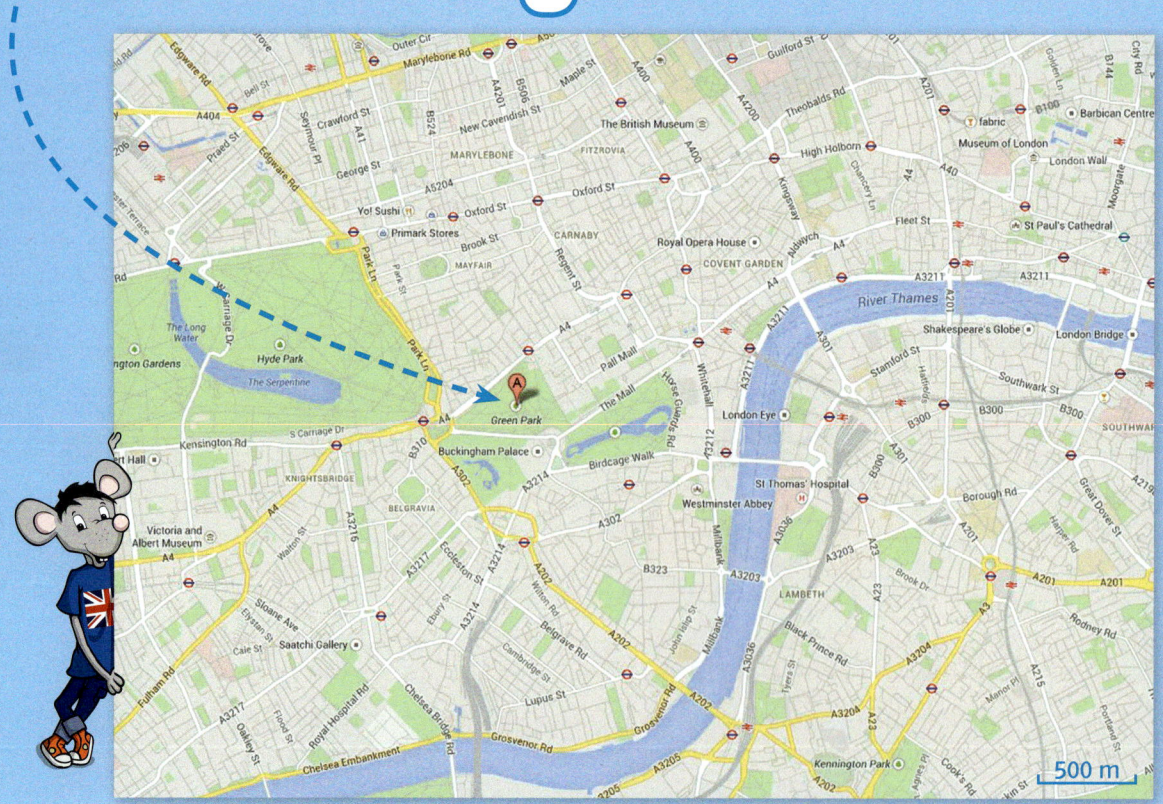

Step 2

Choose the sights on your tour → WB 28/23, 29/24

a) *First think alone for a few minutes about what sights you can visit. Write down your ideas. Which ones would you like to visit in one day? Tick (✔) them.*

b) *Share your ideas. What are your group's favourites? Make your decision about the sights. Look at the map again. Are your plans realistic for the time you have and the distance between activities?*

Start: Good idea – but isn't it a bit far / expensive?
I think we've got enough time / money for …

For help with things to do and see in London, look back at **Across Cultures 2**, at pages 36–44 of **Unit 2** and at your **Workbook**.

For help with how to make and discuss suggestions, look again at **Station 2**.

Step 3

Collect information and write a plan

a) *Collect useful information about each of the sights on your list and work out the best route for your tour. You can look for information on the internet and make notes.*

b) *Use the information to write a plan for the tour (morning → lunch → afternoon). Make sure it's clear where you're going to go and how you're going to get there.*

Step 4

Prepare your presentation

Decide who is going to talk about what. Think what you want to say and make prompt cards. Also prepare some material about your tour. Maybe these ideas can help:

– a poster of the whole tour
– a tour timetable
– a map with your route / sights

Has your tour got a special name? I call my tour 'Tony's Top Tube Tour'. That's a tongue-twister (*Zungenbrecher*). Try it!

Step 5

For help with how to find information on the internet, look at the **Skills page** again.

For help with routes on the Tube, look back at **Station 1**.

Present your tour in class → WB 29/25

a) *Take turns to present your tours.*

Look at page 137 in the **Skills section** for tips on how to give a presentation.

Useful phrases

We'd like to tell you about …
First we're going to …
Then … / After that …
We're / You're going to see / visit …
We can get there on foot / by …
It's a fantastic / an amazing …

b) *Take turns to vote for the best tour. Say why you liked that tour best.*

S 1/16–20
L 2/1–5 ◉

I'm a mudlark

Across cultures

Many London visitors don't know that **the Thames** is a river with two faces – one at high tide, one at low tide. Sometimes, it flows out into the sea like a normal river. But every day at high tide, it flows back towards central London. In the heart of the city there can be a difference of seven metres between high and low tides! At low tide, you can see the muddy banks of the river.

A "Number three is the Wobbly Bridge," Jay told his cousin Amir. The four friends were enjoying their own tour of bridges across the Thames. Now they
5 were walking across their third one, the Millennium Footbridge.

"It isn't wobbly any more. That was just a problem when it was new, but people still use the name," explained
10 Olivia.

Before they got very far, Holly noticed Amir's silver bracelet. "Ooh, that's nice!"

"Yeah, let *me* try it on," Jay said.
15 "Sure, no problem," Amir said. Jay quickly grabbed his cousin's wrist to take the bracelet off. But he wasn't careful enough, dropped it, and the bracelet rolled off the bridge and down
20 into the Thames!

"Jay!" Amir shouted angrily. "That bracelet really meant something to me. And now it's gone!" They all looked down from the bridge. They were lucky.
25 The tide was out and the bracelet was in the mud between the water and the wall.

"Look, there are steps down to the shore," Olivia said. "Come on, let's go
30 and get it. But hm, should we take off our shoes? It's very muddy."

○ **Stop and think:** ○
What could happen next, and why?

B Down on the shore, they found that the mud was very wet. They weren't wearing the right kind of shoes so they needed to walk carefully. They didn't want to fall. 35

"Hi. Are you looking for this?"
The voice came from a man under the bridge.

"Oh, we didn't see you! Yes, that's my bracelet. Thanks! I'm so happy to get it 40 back," Amir told him.

"No problem," the man smiled. "I didn't think it was a present for me! Nice to meet you all. My name is Mike."

Olivia looked at the bucket and trowel 45 which Mike had with him. "Excuse me, but can you please tell us what you're doing here?" she asked politely.

"I'm a mudlark," he said.

C The friends didn't know about mudlarks, 50 so Mike explained. "In the 19th century many children or old people tried to make a little money from things that fell into the Thames. You know – from boats and ships." 55

"And bridges too!" Jay added.
"Yes, from bridges too," Mike laughed. "Anyway, when the tide went out the mudlarks looked on the shore for things to sell. They got their name because they 60 worked in the mud. And at that time, the river was *very* dirty, full of all kinds of pollution. Or worse."

"Worse?" Amir wanted to know.
"Well, dead animals washed up all the 65 time. Human bodies too."

"Yuck!" Holly said. "It's nice to know I've got shoes on my feet!"

"Oh, times are different now – don't
70 worry," Mike explained.

"So you're looking for things to sell?" Holly wanted to know.

"No, no. Mudlarks are different now. We look for history in the mud. Just for
75 fun. There are things in the Thames that go back to Roman times, you know."

"Wow, amazing! Listen to that, Olivia!" said Amir. He knew she loved history too.

"Most things aren't as old as that,"
80 Mike told them. "But look at this glass in my bucket. OK, it's broken, so it doesn't look very good any more. But it's over 100 years old! And when I hold it in my hand I like to think of the story behind it. Who
85 drank from it? How did it get here?"

Mike also showed the friends the other things in his bucket: an old green bottle, a piece of an 18th-century clay pipe, and part of a lucky-charm bracelet. The
90 friends had no idea there was treasure like this in the Thames! They all wanted to help Mike to look for more things. "OK, but please stay near me," he said.

D At first the four new mudlarks found it
95 hard to see anything in the mud, but Mike showed them the best places to look and they started to notice things more easily. Olivia found a euro coin, Amir found an old key, and Holly found a shoe.
100 And then she found something awful, with hair on it.

"Ugh, a HEAD!!!" she screamed.

Mike laughed. "Well, a head from across the sea!" he laughed, as he pulled a coconut from the mud. Then he said, 105
"Sorry, guys, time to go now. The tide is coming in fast and – hey, where's your friend?"

Suddenly they saw that Jay wasn't with them. He wasn't far away, but the water 110
between them was already near the wall.

"Jay! Look, you're going to be cut off!" Mike shouted. "Come on – quick! We need to get to the steps!"

> **Stop and think:**
> What is Jay's problem?
> What could happen next?

E After a few dramatic minutes that felt 115
like *hours*, they all got safely to the top of the steps. The friends said thank you and goodbye to Mike. Then it was time to walk along the south side of the river to the London Eye to meet Shahid. 120

"Mum isn't going to be very happy when she sees our dirty shoes," Jay said to Amir. "Hey, where are you going? That isn't the way to the London Eye!"

Jay, Olivia and Holly watched as Amir 125
ran quickly back onto the bridge and threw something into the river.

"But – that's his bracelet!" Holly said. Jay was surprised too. "The crazy idiot! Why did he do that?" 130

Olivia just smiled. She understood.

SPEAKING

1 **Your reaction** → WB 30/26

Talk about what you found interesting about the story: the people, the history, the things in the river?

READING

2 **Understanding the text** → WB 30/27

a) *Explain the difference between mudlarks in the 19th century and modern mudlarks.*

b) *Why do you think Amir threw his bracelet back into the Thames?*

WRITING

3 **One story, three different perspectives**

a) *Work in groups of three. In your group, each of you (A, B and C) writes about the main ideas of the story in three different ways:*

   A. *Find 6–8 **key words / phrases** from the text. Write down why they're important.*
   B. *Tell the **main ideas** of the story in 6–8 sentences.*
   C. *In 6–8 sentences, talk about **your reaction** to the story.*

b) *Now tell each other your ideas. What ideas are the same or different?*

WRITING

4 **What's the story behind it?** → WB 30/28

→ ▲ 120/11
→ S10–13

*Choose **one** thing from Mike's bucket and create a little story about its history. Who did it belong to? How long ago? How did it get into the Thames? Write at least six sentences.*

Useful phrases

The … belonged to a girl / sailor / tourist / …
He / She lived in the 18th / … century.
He / She visited London last year / …
It was for wine / a treasure box / …
It was his / her favourite …
He / She threw it into the river because …
They / … didn't want it any more because …
It broke (into pieces) when …
One day it fell into the river while …

Example:

> *The wine glass*
>
> *The wine glass belonged to a family over a hundred years ago. They lived in a house next to the Thames. One day …*

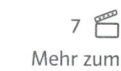

7

Mehr zum
Thema Thames

→ Solutions p. 248

Can you …

1. talk about your plans? _ _ _ _ _ _ _ _ _ _ _ _   I'm / We're going to visit London.
2. use compound words with *some* and *any*? _ _ _ _   I need something to eat. |
   Has anybody got anything nice?
3. understand and give directions for travelling   You take the … line to … | It's three
   by public transport? _ _ _ _ _ _ _ _ _ _ _ _   stops to … | You get off at …

LANGUAGE

1 **What are they going to do tomorrow?**

Use the clues in the pictures and make sentences about their plans.

Start: 1. The Frasers are going to have …

1 · The Frasers

2 · Luke and Sherlock

3 · Mr and Mrs Azad

4 · Holly

5 · Amir

6 · Shahid

LANGUAGE

2 **What do these sellers at Camden Market say?**

A: Does ⟨1⟩ want to buy a cool hat? What about you, young man?
   I'm sure it's just the right thing for ⟨2⟩ cool like you!
B: Come on, ⟨3⟩ ! If you want ⟨4⟩ good to eat, this is the place to get it!
C: A book about London in German? I'm sure I've got one ⟨5⟩ .
   Yes, here you are. Look, ⟨6⟩ is in German.
D: Great souvenirs! You can't find cheaper ones ⟨7⟩ in London –
   ⟨8⟩ costs more than £1!

everything   anybody

something

someone   anywhere

somewhere

nothing   everybody

SPEAKING

3 **Public transport**

*A British visitor to Stuttgart doesn't know how to get around. Tell him how to get from **Bad Cannstatt** to the **Fernsehturm** by public transport.*

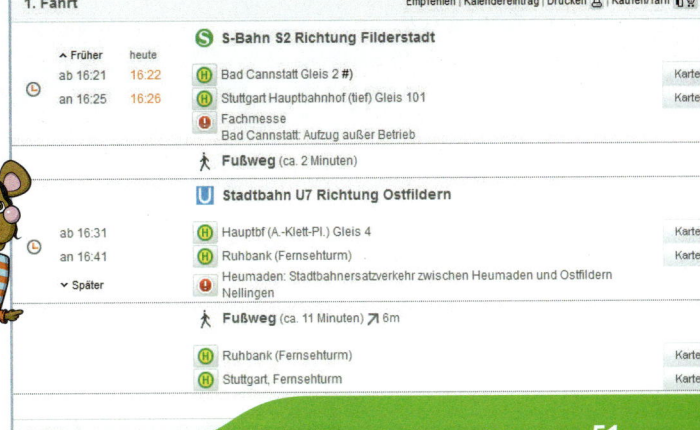

S1/21–24
L2/6–9

The copper[1] treasure

Jamie, Ten Tons and Davies are young mudlarks who live in London in the 1850s. One day, they climb aboard a big ship in the River Thames and start to look for things which they can take away and sell for food; they're all hungry. With them is Patty, a woman who doesn't like Ten Tons very much. This is when
5 they find a real treasure … the copper treasure.

We were moving carefully across the decks and looking for bits and pieces. But there wasn't much so we followed Patty down and started to look for spoons[2] and knives[3]
10 and stuff in the cabins.

I could hear Ten Tons two cabins away. He was talking and shouting to himself as usual. Then I saw Patty at the end of the corridor. She was doing well. You could
15 hear the sound of metal things under her skirts[4]. She looked annoyed[5] when she heard Ten Tons, but I didn't say anything. Yes, Ten Tons was a crazy man, but he was *our* crazy man.

I was crazy too – why was I stealing 20
like this? Davies and Ten Tons didn't have parents – they needed to do this to live. But I had a mother and father and a home. I didn't need to do this. The others laughed each time I looked to check that everything 25
was OK. But it was a good thing I checked so often: I looked up again and … and I saw the dock. It was floating past[6].

I thought … what? There was a man with some cows on the river bank … we 30
were on the other side of the river now! He pointed at us and shouted. The ship started to circle and I suddenly understood … Oh no! The anchor[7] was broken and we were floating away[8] from the bank. 35

"Davies, Tens!" I screamed. "We're moving!"

Ten Tons was up on deck right away. "My God, I've stolen[9] a whole ship this time!" he shouted. Like a captain, he 40
started to march up and down the decks and to give orders[10] to no one. It was so funny! He was very short and he was going up and down the deck like a crazy little engine[11]. 45

Davies came up too. He looked over the side.

"We should[12] get …" he started to say.

Then everything moved. We floated sideways across the river and hit a 50
tugboat[13]. Our ship went up and down and we all fell to the deck floor.

1 **copper** [kɒpə] Kupfer | 2 **spoon** [spuːn] Löffel | 3 **knife** [naɪf] Messer | 4 **skirt** [skɜːt] Rock | 5 **annoyed** [əˈnɔɪd] verärgert | 6 **to float past** [fləʊt ˈpɑːst] vorbeitreiben | 7 **anchor** [ˈæŋkə] Anker | 8 **to float away** [fləʊt əˈweɪ] wegtreiben, abtreiben | 9 **I've stolen** [aɪv ˈstəʊlən] ich habe gestohlen | 10 **order** [ˈɔːdə] Befehl | 11 **engine** [ˈendʒɪn] Lokomotive; Motor | 12 **should** [ʃʊd] sollten | 13 **tugboat** [ˈtʌɡbəʊt] Schlepper *(Schiff)*

Davies almost[14] fell into the river. I saw Ten Tons – he was sliding along on his
55 bum[15] and shouting 'Whhhhhooooah!' I held on to the rail[16]. And then we heard a strange sound, like music. I looked along the deck and saw …

The copper! What a sight! It was rolling
60 along the deck and opening itself up into a shining red sheet. It was like a magician[17] who was slowly opening his cape. The ship moved again and the deck turned to one side. The copper was moving faster and faster … and then it crashed into the
65 rail. The rails broke and the copper hung for a moment, right on the edge[18] of the deck. Then there was another movement. It caught[19] the sun[20], flashed[21] red-golden light[22] at me, went over the edge … and
70 dropped.

I watched it go down. It hummed[23] as it fell. It flashed again in the evening sun and sent a bright[24] red light across the river. Then it hit the water. It was so bright
75 it looked red hot[25]. I was waiting for it to hiss[26]. There was a huge splash in the water … and it was gone. Half a ton or more of new copper, down under the water and lost forever[27].
80

From: *The Copper Treasure* by Melvin Burgess

→ WB 32/1–3

14 almost ['ɔːlməʊst] fast | **15 bum** [bʌm] Hintern | **16 rail** [reɪl] Reling | **17 magician** [mə'dʒɪʃn] Zauberer | **18 edge** [edʒ] Rand | **19 to catch** [kætʃ] einfangen | **20 sun** [sʌn] Sonne | **21 to flash** [flæʃ] blitzen | **22 light** [laɪt] Licht | **23 to hum** [hʌm] summen | **24 bright** [braɪt] leuchtend | **25 red hot** [red 'hɒt] glühend heiß | **26 to hiss** [hɪs] zischen | **27 lost forever** [lɒst fə'revə] für immer verloren

Find more online:
c27n8p

Unit 3

Sport is good for you!

A Camel racing

B Marathon

C BMX

D Rugby

LISTENING **1** On the radio

L 2/10 ⊙
→ S18–20

Gwen is preparing for the TTS sports and health project week. She's listening to sports programmes on the radio. Which sports? Three of them are in the photos; which ones?

SPEAKING **2** Talk about sports

→ S4 **a)** *Use the word cloud from Ex. 1 to describe the sports in the photos. Where and why are these sports popular?*

→ △ 121/1 **b)** *Your turn: Talk about your favourite sports.*

Vocabulary skills

You can use **word clouds** to show how often a word is in a text. The more often a word is in the text, the bigger it is. You can make word clouds on your computer.

In Unit 3 you learn

… how to talk about sports, about your experiences in the past, and about things which have just happened and are still important now. You learn:

- words for sports
- words for health and accidents
- the language of news reports
- the present perfect

E   Wheelchair basketball

LISTENING   **3   TTS sport and health projects**

L 2/11 ⊚   a) *Say which sports Olivia and Gwen are going to use for their projects and why?*

✏   b) *What other sports do they talk about? Make a list.*

c) *Why is sport good for your health?*

Across cultures

The **number one sport** in Britain is football, rugby is number two. Other popular team sports in Britain are cricket and hockey. What team sports are popular in Germany and what do you know about them?

VOCABULARY   **4   Sports words**   → WB 33/1–2

📖
✏   *What sports are you interested in? Make a grid with words and phrases. (Use a dictionary for help.) Use these four headings:*

Sport | Place | Equipment | Team / Individual sport

L 2/12 ◎ **Have you ever run in a marathon?**

"Have you ever seen the London Marathon?" Gwen asked.

"Of course we have!" Holly said. "It starts right here in Greenwich Park."

5 "I want to run in it," Luke said. "But I've checked: You can't until you're 18."

"But haven't you heard of the *mini* marathon?" Gwen asked.

"No, I haven't," Jay said. "What's that?"

10 "It's for 11- to 17-year-olds," Gwen explained. "It's just the last part of the race, and it's before the *real* marathon."

"Are you going to run in it?" Olivia asked Gwen. "I know you like running."

"It isn't that easy," Gwen said. "There are 15 teams for different parts of London, and there are trials to find the fastest runners."

"Where are the trials?" Dave asked.

"For the Greenwich team, here in the park, next Saturday," Gwen said. 20

"Let's do it!" Olivia said. "Who's in?"

"Me," said Gwen. "It was my idea, remember?"

"I'm in too!" Luke said.

Nobody said a word. Then Jay said, "No 25 thanks, I'm out. I've never enjoyed running much. It isn't cool. And Dave has never run in a race. Right, Dave?"

"I've run in races before, but not in a big one like that," Dave said. 30

Holly said, "I've only ever run in short races too, and I'm not very good at running. But I've got an idea: Why don't you run for charity? People often do charity runs to raise money." 35

"That's great," Olivia said. "We can ask our parents, teachers and friends to give money. So it's Gwen, Luke and me."

"Er … just one thing," Gwen said. "Can we run together? You know, my eyes …" 40

"Of course," Olivia said.

"Yeah," Luke said, "we'll be Team Thomas Tallis! The fastest, coolest team in Greenwich. No, in *London*! Look out, here we come!" 45

READING

1 **Are you going to run in it?**

a) *Would you like to run in a marathon? Why / Why not?*

b) *Answer these questions:*
   1. Say who likes / doesn't like running.
   2. What's Holly's idea?
   3. Who isn't going to run in the trials for the mini marathon?

Across cultures

The **London Marathon** is one of the world's biggest races, with over 35,000 runners. It starts in Greenwich Park and finishes at Buckingham Palace. Have you ever watched a marathon? What running events are there in your area?

LANGUAGE

2   Find the rule → WB 34/3–4   → G8

a) *There are examples of a new tense in the text, the present perfect.*
Look at these sentences and the verb forms in the box.
What is different between verbs like **see** *and verbs like* **check**?

I have run in a race before.
Have you ever watched a marathon?

There's a list of
irregular verbs on
page 246.

Infinitive	– Past participle
see	– **seen**
check	– **checked**
hear	– **heard**
enjoy	– **enjoyed**
run	– **run**

b) *Now make two sentences like this about Dave.*

He … … . | … he ever … ?

c) *Write down how you make and answer questions in the present perfect.*

LANGUAGE

3   Say who has done what → WB 35/5

→ ▲ 121/2

… you ever **1** (be) to London? – No, I …, but my sister **2** (be) there.
… you **3** (hear) of the London Marathon? – Yes, I …, I **4** (watch) it three times.
… your parents ever **5** (run) in a marathon? – No, they …, but my dad **6** (play) in an international tennis match.
… your little brother ever **7** (prepare) a meal? – Yes, he … He always helps in the kitchen.
… your grandma ever **8** (give) you extra pocket money? – No, she …

SPEAKING

4   Your turn: Have you ever …? → WB 35/6

→ S24

a) *Write at least three questions for your classmates with* **Have you ever …?**
The words on the right can help.

Examples:
Have you ever seen …?
Have you ever been to …?
Have you ever eaten …?

finished   done   written   fallen
found   broken   asked for   run   been

homework   arm / leg   race
money   book   another country

b) *Ask some of your classmates the questions you wrote.*

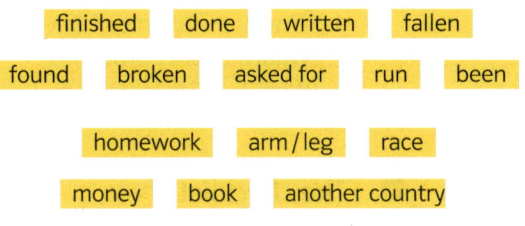

Have you ever been to Austria?

No, I haven't.

c) *Write down what you've found out and tell the class.*

Example: Nicolas and Maria have been
to Austria, but Tom and Lara
haven't.

L 2/15 ◎

Have you been to the doctor's yet?

Gwen: Hi Olivia. Are you still at home?

Olivia: Hi Gwen. Yes, I'm at home. I haven't left for school yet.

Gwen: Good. I've just had an idea. Let's
5   train for the marathon trials. Do you want to go for a run in the park after school today?

Olivia: Great idea, but I've hurt my foot! I think I've twisted my ankle.

Gwen: Oh no! Have you been to the 10 doctor's yet?

Olivia: No, I haven't. I hope it isn't serious. But it hurts when I walk, and I can't run on Saturday with pain like this.

Gwen: But you've already prepared for the 15 trials!

Olivia: I know, it's so unfair! I've done everything I can! I've bought new running shoes, I've stopped eating chocolate, I've found information on 20 the internet about the *best* way to run, I've –

Gwen: Listen, don't worry. I can train with Luke today, and maybe you can join us tomorrow. 25

Olivia: OK. Have you already asked Luke?

Gwen: No, not yet. I can ask him at school today. See you there.

Olivia: Yeah, see you later. Bye!

READING

5 Questions on the text

1. Why does Gwen call Olivia?
2. What's Olivia's problem?
3. What has Olivia done to prepare for the marathon trials?

LANGUAGE

6 The checklist → G8

🧑‍🤝‍🧑 *Ask and answer questions about what the friends have done or haven't done.*

Example: **Has** Gwen **called** Olivia **yet**? – Yes, she **has**.

Things to do	Who?	Done?
1. call Olivia	Gwen	✔
2. make a poster for the charity run	Holly	✘
3. run three miles	Luke	✔
4. read a book about running	Olivia	✔
5. write a chant to cheer the runners	Jay	✘
6. find a good place to watch the marathon	Dave	✘
7. tell their parents about the marathon	Gwen, Luke, Olivia	✔

LANGUAGE

7 **What has just happened?**

→ △ 121/3
→ ▲ 122/4

Example: Mrs Elliot has just cleaned the windows.

Mrs Elliot – clean ✓

Mr Azad – finish

Luke – come back

Jamie – fall off

Amber – buy

Olivia – tidy

Shahid – write

Lucy – go to

VOCABULARY

8 **At the doctor's** → WB 36/7–9

→ S9

Read Olivia's dialogue with the doctor.
Practise your own dialogues with the ideas
in the box.

Doctor: So, what's the problem today?
Olivia: I've had an accident and hurt
my foot.
Doctor: Can you walk on it?
Olivia: No, I can't.
Doctor: Let me have a look. – Oh yes,
you've twisted your ankle.
Olivia: Is it serious, Doctor?
Doctor: No, it isn't. But you need to walk
very carefully for a couple of days.

Useful phrases

I've hurt my hand / foot / arm / head /
shoulder. | I've got a headache /
backache / stomachache. | I feel bad /
sick and I can't … | I've got a cold / a
cough / a fever. | You need to … | You
shouldn't … | You can take pills / …

Olivia: Oh no, so I can't run in the
marathon trials on Saturday …
Doctor: No, you really shouldn't. Here's a
prescription for an ointment.
You can put it on your ankle to stop
the pain.

MEDIATION

9 **Children and accidents** → WB 37/10–11

→ △ 122/5
→ S17

Pia has found a German
survey on the internet and
thinks that Olivia could
use it for her project. What
does the introduction say
about German children's
health? Tell a partner in
English.

Obwohl sie zum größten Teil vermeidbar wären, zählen Unfallver-
letzungen zu den häufigsten gesundheitlichen Beeinträchtigungen
von Kindern und Jugendlichen. Pro Jahr erleiden etwa 15 Prozent
der Kinder und Jugendlichen mindestens eine behandlungsbedürf-
tige Unfallverletzung; Jungen sind öfter betroffen als Mädchen.
Kleinkinder verletzen sich am häufigsten zu Hause. Ältere Kinder
und Jugendliche erleiden Unfälle insbesondere beim Sport und in
der Freizeit sowie in der Schule.

A picnic in the park → S21–22

VIEWING

1 Understanding the story so far

8 *Watch (00:00–03:55). Then match the sentences / the sentence parts below.*

1. Marley's ankle hurts.
2. Laura is going to stay with her grandad in Kent
3. Marley wants to watch the football match
4. Marley thinks it's unfair
5. Jinsoo's mum has made 'kimbap'[1].
6. At first, Jinsoo doesn't like the idea

a) but his dad needs his help in the attic.
b) that everyone is going to watch football and he can't.
c) that Alicia is going to come to Kent too.
d) It's typical Korean snack food.
e) and invites her friends to visit her.
f) He thinks he has twisted it.

SPEAKING

2 How's your ankle?

a) *Watch the rest of the film. What does Marley do? The phrases can help you.*

b) *What does Marley's father say at the end? Do you think he's right? Say why / why not. Think about it from Marley's point of view and from Mr Thompson's too. Look at the box again.*

> **Useful phrases**
>
> to fake an injury / a headache / …
> to teach somebody a lesson
> It's fair / unfair because …
> I think / don't think his father is right …
> Marley deserves it / doesn't deserve it …

c) *Your turn: Have you ever faked anything? Did you get away with it? Tell the class.*

VOCABULARY

3 The picnic → WB 38/12

a) *The friends are having different food for their picnic. Look at the photo and the food words and say what looks good.*

b) *Your turn: In class, talk about **your** 'perfect picnic'. What food from your country / your area / other countries could you have?*

kimbap   sandwiches (egg & cress[2] / cheese & tomato)

Scotch eggs[3]   quiche[4]   pasta salad[5] with tuna[6]

---

1 kimbap ['kɪmbæp] *koreanischer Snack aus Seegras, Reis, Rindfleisch, Käse und Ei* | **2 cress** [kres] Kresse | **3 Scotch egg** [skɒtʃ 'eg] *hart gekochtes Ei in Wurstbrät* | **4 quiche** [kiːʃ] Quiche | **5 pasta salad** [ˌpæstə 'sæləd] Nudelsalat | **6 tuna** ['tjuːnə] Thunfisch

How to understand news reports and take notes → S18–20

For the task on pages 62–63, you need to know what the parts of a radio report are and what language is typical for a radio report. This page can help you.

1 A mountain rescue → WB 39/14

L 2/17 ⊚
✐

a) *Listen to a radio report about an accident in the mountains. Take notes in a grid.*

Time	Place	People	Event

b) *Use your notes and answer the questions.*

1. What was the accident?
2. Why did it happen?
3. What did the mountain rescue team do?
4. Why was the rescue difficult?

5. How serious was the accident?
6. How is the way the news presenter and the reporter speak different to the way the witnesses speak?

2 The language of a radio report → WB 39/15

✐

Read the boxes. Then listen to the report again. Note down which phrases from the bigger box you can hear in the report.
*Also, note down **other** interesting or typical phrases for the news presenter, the reporter, the witness.*
Why do you think they are typical?

Vocabulary skills

The situations are different, but the **language** of radio reports is often the same:

- **News presenters** and **reporters** stay more formal and use a language of facts.
- An **eyewitness** has just seen something dramatic, strange or maybe scary; the language he / she uses often shows more feelings.

Useful phrases

News presenter at radio station:
Hello / Good morning to all our listeners out there. | We've just received news of … | Now we're going to hear from our reporter at the scene: Can you describe the … / Can you tell us about the … | Stay with us for more …

Reporter at the scene:
Where were you when …? | What have you seen? | Has anyone else …? | What else can you tell us?

Eyewitness at the scene:
I couldn't believe my eyes! | This is strange / dramatic / exciting / … | I've never seen anything like it!

The aliens have landed!

Imagine that aliens have landed on Earth – in Greenwich Park! In this Unit task, you and your group write your own radio report about this strange event. For the report, there are five roles: **three witnesses**; a **reporter** (he interviews the witnesses); the **radio news presenter**. Your job is to write – and record – a fun report. Your report should be 3–4 minutes long. Be as creative as possible!

News presenter at radio station

Assistant at sweet shop

Greenwich man in garden

Doctor at hospital

Reporter in Greenwich Park

Step 1

The situation → WB 40/16

In groups of five, look at the scenes above. Talk about what you think is happening / has happened in each scene. Look closely at the words in the box. You need them to talk about the pictures.

Martian | Mars | space | spaceship | UFO | light | sky | star | customer | stomachache | human | to land | to invade | to come in peace | to make friends | to get sick on (too much) chocolate | strange-looking | bright | friendly

Examples:

A: In this scene, you can see that the aliens have landed.
B: What's happening at the hospital? Have the aliens eaten too much chocolate?
C: Look at the park scene: It looks like the aliens want to make friends!

Martian ['mɑːʃn] Marsmensch | **space** [speɪs] Weltraum | **spaceship** ['speɪsʃɪp] Raumschiff | **light** [laɪt] Licht | **sky** [skaɪ] Himmel | **customer** ['kʌstəmə] Kunde / Kundin | **human** ['hjuːmən] Mensch | **to invade** [ɪn'veɪd] eindringen | **in peace** [ɪn 'piːs] in Frieden | **to make friends** [meɪk 'frendz] Freundschaft schließen | **to get sick on sth** [get 'sɪk ɒn] sich an etw. den Magen verderben | **strange-looking** ['streɪndʒ ˌlʊkɪŋ] seltsam aussehend | **bright** [braɪt] hell

Step 2

Choose roles and form expert groups → WB 40/17

a) *In your group, each of you chooses one of the five roles.*

b) *Form expert groups: All students with the same role work together. In your new group, talk about what kind of things **your character** should / could say in a radio report. Make notes – and be creative!*

Examples:

A: *(doctor group)* As a doctor, I want to tell the reporter how the aliens are feeling. The people should know that they got sick on chocolate. They don't speak English, but we know they're feeling better; they're smiling now!

B: *(reporter group)* A reporter should ask how the man in his garden felt when he first saw the UFOs. I'm sure it was a big shock! – Oh, and a reporter should ask how the aliens *paid* for their chocolate at the shop!

> For typical phrases for reporters and witnesses, have another look at the **Skills page** you've just done.

Step 3

Plan and write your report → WB 41/18

a) *Go back to your home group. Each of you is now an expert for one of the roles. Talk about how you all want to put the report together. Think about these points first:*

How should it start? | How should it end: Does the news presenter tell the listeners to listen for more information later? Is the Martians' visit to Earth over? | Which order are the interviews in? | How serious (or silly) should the presenter and the reporter be? | Remember that the presenter needs to say something after every reporter interview.

b) *Now write your report, interview by interview. Each person writes some of it.*

c) *Peer-editing: Trade your part with somebody else and check each other's texts.*

d) *One of you now reads it to the rest of the group. Listen carefully. Does it sound like a radio report? Does it sound interesting enough? Make changes for a better text.*

Step 4

Practise and record your report → WB 41/19

a) *Practice your report a few times, and record yourselves with a smartphone. Does it sound right? Remember: Don't read from the page!*

b) *Now record your final report.*

c) *Play it for the class. Tell the groups what you liked about **their** reports.*

Lou, do you think there are mice on Mars?

Maybe we can go back to Mars with the aliens and find out!

S 1/29–33
L 2/19–23

Hey, don't call *me* silly!

A In Greenwich, it's almost time for the mini marathon to start …

Gwen: It's too bad Olivia can't join us.

Luke: But she can cheer us on with the others and help us to do well today.

Gwen: Yes, for us *and* for 'See with your Heart'. It means a lot to me, as a partially sighted person.

Luke: Your charity means something to *all* of us, Gwen. – But anyway, remember: You mustn't let go of my hand!

Gwen: Luke, that's *my* line: *I'm* the one who can't see well, remember?

Luke: Oh, sorry. I'm just nervous. Do you think I've trained enough?

Gwen: Well, I have! I did lots of extra training. But I can't speak for *you*.

Luke: Great, that really helps.

Gwen: Don't think so much, silly. Just run. And not too fast too soon!

Luke: Hey, don't call *me* silly – look at *them* in their crazy animal costumes. Can you see them?

Gwen: Er, not very well. But there are always people in fancy dress at events like these. They're running for charity too.

Luke: Oh yes: a pet charity, I'm sure; they've got cat and dog costumes. But how can they *run* in them?!

Gwen: No idea. – But hey, look! There are Holly and Olivia! But hm, where are Dave and Jay?

B A few minutes into the race …

Gwen:
This feels GREAT! My big day, after all that training … Now is the moment – MY moment! I can show them how good I am. Just breathe … run … enjoy it! … But what about Luke? Can he keep up? He didn't do any extra training like me. And *he's* worried about *me*? … Oh, those silly runners in the animal costumes in front of us – they aren't really taking this seriously. … What are they doing? Jumping from right to left and getting in the way. Clowns! … I hope they don't get in *our* way.

C Ten minutes later …

Gwen:
Ouch! What's that?! Oh, my stomach; it *really* hurts. … Oh no, I mustn't stop! I'm running for the charity – *and* for Luke! … I don't want to be the new girl with the funny glasses; I want to be the new girl with fast legs! Oh, but my stomach… Come on, just run! … RUN!

D Not far from the finish line …

> **Gwen:**
> I think that stupid cramp is gone. YES! And Luke is still doing fine too. … We're still
> 55 running fast: I think our time is going to be *really* good. … I want to see our photos on the TTS website! "Gwen Parker, the new running star". Sounds great! – OH NO!!!!!!!!! What's happening?!?! Oh no, I don't
> 60 want to fall!

E Just after the race …

Luke:	Gwen, we did it, WE DID IT!
Gwen:	Yes, we did! And it feels GREAT!
Luke:	Well, *now* it feels great. But during
65	the race I had a bad cramp. You started too fast for me!
Gwen:	*You* had a cramp? Oh, now I feel better.
Luke:	I had a cramp and now *you* feel
70	better? I don't understand.
Gwen:	Well, I had a cramp too – but I didn't want to tell you; I didn't want to stop the race.
Luke:	And I didn't want to tell *you* and
75	hear, "You didn't train enough!"
Gwen:	Well, we *both* finished, yippee! And 'See with your Heart' gets some money too!
Luke:	Well, they almost *didn't*: That
80	stupid dog and that stupid cat almost ruined everything for us! I couldn't believe my eyes when they pulled out a smartphone and took a selfie. That one boy fell because
85	of them, and we almost fell too!
Gwen:	They took a *selfie*? In the middle of the race? Oh, I knew those two were trouble!
Olivia:	*(suddenly)* Yes, that's what the race
90	officials thought too so they finally took the dog and the cat out of the race. – Look who I've found!

Luke:	Dave and Jay?!?!
Gwen:	YOU were the dog and the cat?!?! Aaaargh!!! 95
Dave:	Don't be angry, please! We're really sorry. We only wanted to surprise you.
Jay:	Yes, we trained in secret, and ran for the pets' charity! 100
Gwen:	But somebody *fell* because of you two. Luke and I almost fell! I'm sure that boy trained hard. Have you ever thought of that?
Jay:	Well, er … 105
Dave:	We said sorry, Gwen.
Gwen:	Well, don't tell *me*. Have you told the boy yet?
Dave:	Er, no.
Gwen:	Well, *tell* him. *(smiling now)* So we 110 can finally forgive you.
Luke:	But I'm not sure 'sorry' is enough. How about a present for him?
Olivia:	That sounds good. I'm sure we all have nice present ideas. 115
Gwen:	Yes boys, you must do something nice for him. But you can do something nice for me and Luke too. – Luke, where's your phone? Picture time! 120
Luke:	Oh yes – those silly costumes, those faces in the next TTS yearbook! Say CHEESE!

READING

1 **Working with the text** → WB 42/20

a) *Look at the text and talk about these questions.*

1. What different kinds of text are there in parts A–E?
2. Why do people run in a marathon? Find reasons in the text and say who gives them.
3. What can cause problems in a marathon race?
4. What do we learn about Gwen and Luke's hopes and fears?
5. What can you say about their relationship?

→ △ 122/6 b) *Use the text and the pictures to retell what happened.*

READING

2 **What do you think?**

a) *Find adjectives to describe Gwen, Luke, Jay and Dave and their actions.*

→ △ 123/7 b) *Find positive and negative things in the story that they did. Use words from a) to discuss what you think about their actions. Here are some ideas:*

Positive	Negative
On the one hand it was **good** that … I think Gwen was **brave** … …	On the other hand it was really **stupid** … But it was also **dangerous** … …

VOCABULARY

3 **Looking at spoken language**

→ △ 123/8
→ ▲ 123/9

Read the dialogues and Gwen's thoughts out loud. How do Gwen and Luke talk to each other? What language do they use to express their feelings? Which words and phrases would you like to use again? Collect them in a mind map.

WRITING

4 **Another story** → WB 42/21

→ S10–13 *Write about what **isn't** in the story. Choose one of these two topics. You can write a story, a dialogue or a comic. Use your vocabulary from Ex. 2.*

- Just for fun: The race from Jay and Dave's point of view.
- Can you forgive us: Jay and Dave talk to the boy who fell because of them.

Can you . . .

1. talk about experiences in your life / in somebody else's life? _ _ _ _   Have you ever played rugby?
2. talk about things which have (just) happened? _ _ _ _ _ _ _ _ _ _   I've hurt my foot!
3. use *just*, *already* and *yet*? _ _ _ _ _ _ _ _ _ _ _ _ _ _ _ _ _ _ _   I haven't had my dinner yet.

LANGUAGE

1 Match the sentence halves.

1. I think you've broken
2. We've been to
3. I've never eaten
4. Jay has just written
5. Holly hasn't finished
6. I've already asked

a) a new chant.
b) in an Indian restaurant.
c) your ankle.
d) Olivia to help me with my project.
e) Buckingham Palace three times.
f) her homework yet.

LANGUAGE

2 Make dialogues about Luke and Dave

Example: Dave: write | your health report?   → Have you already written your report?
          Luke: no | have | no time | yet   → No, I haven't. I haven't had time yet.

1. Luke: find | information on the internet yet?
   Dave: yes | already | use information in report

2. Luke: Jay | draw | mangas for his report?
   Dave: yes | create | great new characters

3. Dave: see | two new manga comics yet?
   Luke: yes | already | finish one of them

4. Luke: see | Olivia today?
   Dave: no | but I | just | send text

5. Dave: Holly | write about guinea pigs?
   Luke: hope not! | write about guinea pigs | many times before

6. Dave: go | to the park with Sherlock yet?
   Luke: no | but Irina | just | go for a walk with him

VOCABULARY

3 Which word is right?

I love football. I think it's the best in the world! I every of my favourite team, the Wellsey. Do you want to **4** my new poster of the best player ever, Adriano Donaldo? He scores lots of goals with his head because he's very **5** . He even **6** the **7** score of three head goals in one match. My dream is to **8** a football star like him.

highest   match
become   tall
watch   got
see   game

S 2/1–4 ⊙
L 2/24–27

The summer¹ table

August was born² with a genetic defect and has 'facial issues³'. To other people, the highly intelligent boy looks like a monster. Everyone stares at him so he doesn't go to school; his mum teaches him at home. When he is about 10, his parents finally decide to send him to school. On his first day, Auggie has a
5 really hard time. The other children stare at him or ignore him completely. At lunchtime, Auggie feels really bad – his friend Jack Will isn't there, and because of⁴ his face, August has problems eating, too. When a girl, Summer, sits down at his table, he is very surprised.

"Hey, is somebody sitting here?"
10 I looked up, and a girl I never saw before was standing across from my table with a lunch tray⁵ full of food. She had long wavy brown hair, and wore a brown T-shirt with a purple peace sign⁶ on it.
15 "Uh, no," I said.

She put her lunch tray on the table, dropped her rucksack on the floor, and sat down across from me. She started to eat the pasta with cheese sauce on her plate.
20 "Ugh," she said when she took the first bite. "Why didn't I bring a sandwich like you did?"

"Yeah," I said.

"My name is Summer, by the way. What's yours?" 25

"August."

"Cool," she said.

"Summer!"

Another girl who was carrying⁷ a tray came over to the table. "Why are you 30 sitting here? Come back to the table."

"There were too many people," Summer answered her. "Come sit here. There's more room."

The other girl looked confused⁸ for a 35 second. I recognized⁹ her. She was sitting at another table with some friends a few minutes ago: They were looking at me and she had her hand over her mouth and was whispering. I guess Summer was one of the 40 girls at that table too.

"Don't worry," the girl said and went away.

Summer looked at me, smiled, and took another bite of her pasta. 45

"Hey, our names match," she said, as she ate.

I guess she noticed that¹⁰ I didn't know what she meant.

"Summer? August?" she said and 50 smiled, her eyes open wide, as she waited for me to understand.

"Oh, yeah," I said after a second.

"We can make this the 'summer only'

1 **summer** ['sʌmə] Sommer | 2 **to be born** [bi 'bɔːn] geboren werden | 3 **facial issues** [ˌfeɪʃl 'ɪʃuːz] Gesichtsprobleme | 4 **because of** [bɪ'kɒz ˌəv] wegen | 5 **tray** [treɪ] Tablett | 6 **peace sign** ['piːs saɪn] Friedenszeichen | 7 **to carry** ['kæri] tragen | 8 **confused** [kən'fjuːzd] verwirrt | 9 **to recognize** ['rekəgnaɪz] wiedererkennen | 10 **that** [ðæt] dass

lunch table," she said. "Only kids with
55 summer names can sit here. Let's see, is
there anyone here named June or July?"

"There's a Maya," I said.

"Technically, May is spring¹¹," Summer
answered, "but if she wants to sit here, we
60 can make an exception¹²." She said it as
if¹³ she already had a plan. "There's Julian.
That's like the name Julia, which comes
from July."

I didn't say anything.

65 "There's a kid named Reid in my
English class," I said.

"Yeah, I know Reid, but how is Reid a
summer name?" she asked.

"I don't know," I said. "I just imagine …
70 it's like a reed of grass¹⁴ in summer."

"Yeah, OK," she answered and pulled
out her notebook¹⁵. "And Ms.¹⁶ Petosa
could¹⁷ sit here, too. That sounds like the
word 'petal¹⁸', which is a summer thing too,
75 I think."

"She's my tutor," I said.

"I have her for Maths," she answered
and made a face¹⁹.

She started to write the list of names
on a page of her notebook. 80

"So, who else?" she said.

When we finished lunch, we had a
whole list of names of kids and teachers
who could sit at our table if they wanted.
Most of the names weren't really summer 85
names, but they were names that had
some kind of connection to summer. I
even found a way to put Jack Will's name
on the list – I suggested that we could put
his name into a sentence about summer, 90
like "Jack will go to the beach²⁰," and
Summer agreed that that was fine.

"But if someone doesn't have a summer
name and wants to sit with us," she said
very seriously, "they can still sit here if 95
they're nice, OK?"

"OK," I agreed. "Even if it's a winter
name."

"Cool," she answered and gave me a
thumbs-up. 100

Summer looked like her name. She had
a tan²¹, and her eyes were green like the
leaves of a tree.

'The Summer Table' from *WONDER* by R. J. Palacio   → WB 44/1–4

11 **spring** [sprɪŋ] Frühling | 12 **exception** [ɪkˈsepʃn] Ausnahme | 13 **as if** [əzˌˈɪf] als ob | 14 **reed of
grass** [ˌriːd ˌəv ˈgrɑːs] Schilf | 15 **notebook** [ˈnəʊtbʊk] Notizbuch | 16 **Ms.** [mɪz] Frau *(Anrede)* |
17 **could** [kʊd] könnte | 18 **petal** [ˈpetl] Blütenblatt | 19 **to make a face** [meɪkˌə ˈfeɪs] das Gesicht
verziehen | 20 **beach** [biːtʃ] Strand | 21 **tan** [tæn] sonnengebräunte Haut

VOCABULARY

1 On tour on a London pedicab[1]

a) *Choose the right word.*

amazing | quickly | fresh | well | cool | interesting | slowly | cheap | different | easily | important | carefully

The London pedicabs

Do you want to go on a **1** kind of sightseeing tour? Then hop on[2] **2** and enjoy London's sights and attractions from the backseat[3] of a pedicab. Pedicabs are an exciting and environmentally friendly[4] way to travel around the city **3** . Enjoy all the famous sights and get off anywhere you like. Our friendly drivers speak three languages and know all the **4** facts and **5** stories about London. And, of course, they always drive **6** and **7** !

You can start your tour at different places, for example at Covent Garden, with its shops, cafés and restaurants with **8** food from all over the world. You want to take a photo or buy something to drink? – No problem. Our drivers work hard to make your tour an **9** experience. Have a look at Buckingham Palace and see the Changing of the Guard. Stop in front of the Houses of Parliament and listen to the sound of Big Ben. You want to know where you can eat **10** and buy **11** food? Or where you can buy **12** clothes? Just ask our drivers!

Tours:
- ✿ Mini tour: 1 hour | £50 | 1–2 persons
- ✿ Shopping tour: 1 hour | £30 | 1–2 persons

b) *Would you like to see London in a pedicab? Say why / why not.*

c) *Where else could the pedicab tour go? Continue the text.*

LISTENING

2 A radio report: Shopping for souvenirs → WB 45/1

L 2/28 ◎ **a)** *Listen to the radio report and say where the reporter is and what the report is about.*

b) *Listen again. Copy the grid and fill in the missing information.*

	Mr Smith	Amir	American tourist
souvenir			
for			
price			
problem			

c) *What do you think is the best souvenir? What souvenir would you bring? Say why.*

1 **pedicab** [ˈpedɪkæb] Fahrradtaxi, Fahrradrikscha | 2 **to hop on** [hɒpˈɒn] (schnell) einsteigen | 3 **backseat** [ˈbæksiːt] Rücksitz | 4 **environmentally friendly** [ɪnˌvaɪrənˌmentli ˈfrendli] umweltfreundlich

VOCABULARY

3 A sports quiz → WB 45/2

a) *Work with a partner. What sport do you both like? Make notes: where people play, what equipment they need, how many players there are in a team, etc. (For new words, use a dictionary.) Don't show each other your notes!*

b) *Write 5–6 quiz questions with the information in your notes.*

Example: Which of these football teams has never won the World Cup?
   A. England   **B.** Poland   **C.** Italy

c) *Test your partner with your quiz! Who knows the most about the same sport?*

READING

4 Are they crazy?

a) *Skim the text for the gist. Say what it is about in 2–3 sentences.*

BEN NEVIS

You've probably heard of Ben Nevis in Scotland[5]. With its 1344 metres it is the highest mountain in Great Britain. Each year 125,000 people climb this mountain. It usually takes a few hours to get to the peak[6]. But if you go up on the first Saturday in September, you can see people who[7] run up or down the mountain. You think they're crazy? Well, they probably are …

They take part in the Ben Nevis race. It takes place every year in early September. The race starts and finishes in Fort William. The runners do not only run up the mountain but also back down again – that's a distance of 9.9 miles with a height[8] difference of 1,340 metres. And some runners are really fast. In 1984 Kenny Stuart ran up and down the mountain in 1 hour, 25 minutes and 34 seconds – that's still the record[9] today.

To run up and down the mountain you must be really fit. Only runners with a lot of experience can take part in the race. For safety reasons[10] the number of runners is limited to[11] 600. The weather can change quickly in the mountains, so the runners must wear waterproofs[12], a hat, gloves and a whistle[13].

But who had this crazy idea anyway? People say that it was William Swan. On September 27, 1895 he ran from Fort William to the top of the mountain in 2 hours and 41 minutes. He probably didn't know what he started …

b) *Scan the text. What numbers are there in the text and what do they mean? What does it tell you about 1. safety rules 2. the history of the race? Take notes.*

5 **Scotland** [ˈskɒtlənd] Schottland | 6 **peak** [piːk] Gipfel, Bergspitze | 7 **people who …** [ˌpiːpl ˈhuː] Leute, die … | 8 **height** [haɪt] Höhe | 9 **record** [ˈrekɔːd] Rekord | 10 **safety reasons** [ˈseɪfti ˌriːzns] Sicherheitsgründe | 11 **limited to** [ˈlɪmɪtɪd tə] begrenzt auf | 12 **waterproofs** [ˈwɔːtəpruːfs] Regenkleidung | 13 **whistle** [ˈwɪsl] Trillerpfeife

Find more online:
xy4p42

English around the world

Many people in different countries around the world speak English. Learn about where and why, and listen to some different kinds of English.

SPEAKING

1 Which countries speak English?

a) *Which countries do you know where the people speak English?*

b) *On a map or in an atlas, show where these countries are.*

c) *Can you think of a time when you spoke English? Where were you and who did you speak to? The phrases can help.*

> **Useful phrases**
>
> I spoke English …
> with a friend | with a family member |
> on video chat | in a chat room | …
> I was …
> on holiday | at a summer camp |
> in Germany | in another country | …

VIEWING

2 Speaking English

9

a) *Watch the film. What is it about?*

b) *Does Marley talk about any of the countries in your answers to Ex. 1? Which?*

c) *Look at the stills and describe what happens in the two scenes.*

d) *Watch the film again. Say which statements are right. Correct the wrong ones.*

1. The American man works in England.
2. American English is not exactly the same as British English.
3. You can see English signs in China, India and in some other countries.
4. The South Korean man can't help the Romanian woman.

e) *Act out one of these scenes:*

1. You're on holiday and make a new friend from another country.
2. You help an English-speaking person in your town.

> Hi! / Hello! | How are you? |
> I'm … from … | Where are you from? |
> Are you here on holiday? |
> I'm looking for … | Can you …?

READING

3 How English became a world language → WB 46/1

a) *Before you read: Why do you think so many people in the world speak English?*

b) *Read the text. Make a list of the reasons why so many people speak English today. Only take notes! Then use your notes to explain to your partner why English is so important today.*

More than 400 million people in the world today speak English as their first language, and more than 600 million speak it as a second or official language. The first important reason for this is that from about 1600, British sailors and merchants crossed the sea and started colonies. This went on for many years and the British Empire became huge. For example, Australia was a British colony; India and South Africa too. Today, the British king or queen is still head of state in many countries, e. g. Australia.

There's a second important reason why so many people speak English. After World War II, the USA became a superpower and started to influence the world in many new ways. American rock 'n' roll music and Hollywood films became popular almost everywhere. And later, new technology from America (the PC, the internet, the e-mail) made it possible to communicate in every last corner of the world. In English, of course!

LISTENING

4 Where are we from? → WB 46/2

L 2/29

a) *Listen to four people from different English-speaking regions or countries. Which place is each person from? Which ones did you find easy or difficult to understand? Why?*

b) *Listen again. In which place can you hear these words and expressions? Can you remember what they mean?*

> cookie | sunnies | wee | loch |
> lads and lasses | I'm grand | G'day |
> candy | movie | What's the craic? |

VOCABULARY

5 Your turn: English in your language

Collect words in German that are similar to or the same as words in English. Put the words into these categories. (Maybe you can think of more categories too.)

| Clothes | Technology | Food | Sport | … |

Find more online:
tn37pz

Unit 4

Stay in touch

> Special interest forums are a great way to meet friends online. I found 'Pet Paradise', and now Olivia and I have both got profiles.

A

> I see you've got a new friend on Mousebook. Who's Jon?

> He's just a friend, Tony. Don't be jealous!

SPEAKING

1 Media and TTS students: A survey

Read what TTS students say about different media in A–E. Which of the activities have you done this week?

VOCABULARY

2 Media collocations

→ △ 123/1 *Match these verbs and nouns to make phrases to talk about media.*

→ S3 **Example:** I like to change my profile and post new photos. What about you?

change	post	receive	send	read			profile	photo	text message	forum	
talk to	reply to	play	join	check			social network	video game	video chat		
chat	take part in	write	text	have			magazine	discussion	each other	friend	

In Unit 4 you learn

… how to talk and write about communication in your life. You learn:

- media vocabulary and phrases
- the language of giving and getting advice
- modals
- writing skills for letters and replies

I can't live without my smartphone – I check my messages all the time!

B

I usually read magazines online. I love the advice pages! But I buy print magazines too – for the posters.

C

This is my favourite video game. My cousin and I always compare our scores on video chat!

D

E

Social networks are cool. But nasty comments and cyber bullies *aren't* so cool …

LISTENING

3 **More about the survey** → WB 47/1–3

L 2/30–34 ◎

a) *Which media do the TTS students use? Listen and make a list.*

b) *Listen again and take notes. What do the students say about the media?*

Useful phrases

Smartphones / Social networks / … are great because they're fun / practical / easy to use / …

… are great for meeting … / for staying in touch with … / for sharing information about …

Which media?	What's positive?	What's not so positive?
smartphone / mobile	texts / easy to stay in touch	texts from parents!
special interest forums	…	…

c) *Your turn: Talk about how you use the different media.*

L 2/35 ◎ **Dear Ruby**

Holly and Olivia have found an interesting problem in the 'agony aunt' pages of their favourite magazine.

Across cultures

In Britain, the advice pages of teen magazines are often very popular. People write to an **agony aunt** for help with their problems. What kind of agony aunts are there in your country?

JUST ASK RUBY!

Dear Ruby,

I'm writing to you because I don't know what to do. Last week I had a big fight with one of my best friends. Before the fight, we spent all our free time together. But now she has made friends with another girl and they're having a lot of fun. I know this because she posts photos of the two of them on the social network site we use. She acts like she's having a much better time without me! Whenever I see these photos, it really hurts my feelings. Can you please help? I would really like to hear your advice.

Lauren

Dear Lauren,

I'm sorry you're feeling so upset. I understand how hard it is to share a friend; it was the same with me when I was young. As a first step, my advice is to be self-critical: Are you overreacting? Maybe the situation isn't as serious as you think. The next step is to talk to your friend in a friendly way and tell her how you feel. Why don't you invite her to your house after school? Or have you tried texting her? Things usually get better as soon as you talk. Another tip: Please stop looking at your social network site until you've talked to her. The photos only make you feel worse! I hope you two can be friends again very soon.

Ruby

READING   **1**   **Understanding the problem**   → WB 48/4

→ ▲ 124/2   *Answer these questions about Lauren's letter and Ruby's reply.*

1. Why is Lauren writing to Ruby?
2. How does Lauren know about her friend's new friend?
3. When does Lauren feel really bad?
4. Compare how her friend acted before the fight and after (in Lauren's opinion).

LANGUAGE

2 Using linking words → WB 48/5–6 → G9

→ △ 124/3
→ S13

Read what different teens say about how they use different social media websites. Put these words in the gaps. There's sometimes more than one correct answer.

after | before | as soon as | until | whenever | like | because

1. I'm careful. I never give my phone number ___ I've met a new friend face-to-face.
2. ___ somebody starts asking too many personal questions, I just block them.
3. ___ you post photos of yourself online, remember: ___ you post them, they're probably on the internet forever!
4. I'm angry with my cousin ___ she posted that awful photo of me at the lake.
5. My friend doesn't even know some of the people on her friends list! It's ___ she doesn't care about real friends, she just wants a long list of 'friends'.
6. I don't get much attention online ___ I don't post pictures of myself very often!

WRITING

3 Your turn: Media in your life

Write 5–6 sentences about yourself like the ones you see in Ex. 2. Think about these ideas:

- How much information about yourself do you share online? Why? How often?
- Do you and your friends use media differently? How?

VOCABULARY

4 The right vocabulary for advice → WB 49/7

a) *In the letters on page 76, you see some phrases with 'advice vocabulary' in green. In a grid like this one, match the phrases to the three categories.*

Asking for advice	Giving advice	Showing understanding

→ S3

b) *Here are some important advice phrases. Think of them as 'building blocks' for your own sentences about advice. Write a sentence with each phrase. You can write about the same problem as on page 76, or about something different.*

Useful phrases

My advice is to be self-critical / to see it from the other side / to find a compromise.

Why don't you talk to your friend / invite your friend over / text your friend / …

The next step is to talk to / write to / …

It's always a good idea to talk / try / …

I'm sorry you're feel**ing** sad / **you're** hav**ing** trouble with …

I understand how hard / difficult it is to …

Have you tried talk**ing** to him / text**ing** her?

Stop look**ing** at … / think**ing** about / worry**ing** about / …

MEDIATION

5 Learn how to mediate in a fight → WB 49/8

→ S17 *Pia saw a fight between two of her classmates. She decides to join a special club at her school where students learn how to mediate in a fight. She wants to tell Olivia what she found out on the school website, but she doesn't know all the words in English. Help her to describe in her own words what the club is about.*

Mediation skills

If you don't know a word in English, try to **describe it in other words** that you already know.

Example:

"*Zeuge* – He or she saw what happened in an accident or in a fight, for example."

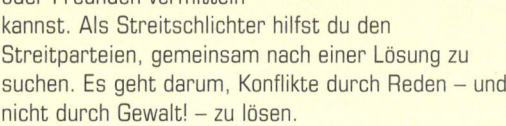

Streitschlichter-AG
Mach dich und andere stark!

In unserer AG lernst du, wie du bei einem Streit zwischen Mitschülern oder Freunden vermitteln kannst. Als Streitschlichter hilfst du den Streitparteien, gemeinsam nach einer Lösung zu suchen. Es geht darum, Konflikte durch Reden – und nicht durch Gewalt! – zu lösen.
Lass dich zum Streitschlichter ausbilden und trage zu einem freundlichen Miteinander an unserer Schule und in deinem Freundeskreis bei!

LISTENING

6 ❬ A song: Friends ❭ Aura Dione

L 3/1 ⊙

→ S9

Free, free to be myself
Free to need some time
Free to need some help
So I'm reaching baby, out
When I'm lonely in the crowd
When the silence[1] gets too loud
I'll be crashing[2] on some couch

And even if I never forget you baby
Tonight I'm gonna let your memory[3] baby
go, oh it's sad I know

But at least[4] I got my friends
Share a raincoat in the wind
They got my back[5] until the end
If I never fall in love again
Well at least I got my friends
Like a lifeboat in the dark
Saving me from the sharks[6]
Even though I got a broken heart
At least I got my friends, got my friends

Text: Aura Dione, Antonina Armato, Tim James, David Jost
© Koolmusic

a) *Which words / lines tell you what kind of a situation the main character is in?*

→ △ 124/4 **b)** *Your turn: What things are symbols of friendship in the song, and for **you**? Why?*

1 silence [ˈsaɪləns] Stille | **2 to crash** [kræʃ] schlafen *(ugs.)* | **3 memory** [ˈmemrɪ] Erinnerung | **4 at least** [ət ˈliːst] wenigstens | **5 They got my back** [ðeɪ ˌɡɒt maɪ ˈbæk] Sie halten mir den Rücken frei; sie passen auf mich auf *(ugs.)* | **6 shark** [ʃɑːk] Hai

L3/2 ⊙ **Forum? What forum?**

Luke: Dad, can I go over to Jay's house? Er, what on earth are you doing? There's water everywhere!

Dad: Really? Where?

5 Luke: Very funny. What's happened?

Dad: There's a problem with one of the pipes. I must fix it before your mum comes home and goes crazy!

Luke: Dad, do you know what you're doing?

10 Dad: Of course! It's just taking longer than I thought.

Luke: You could look at a forum for help.

Dad: Forum? What forum? You mean on the internet? So I can't fix my own

15 washing machine – is that what you think? I don't need the internet. And *you* don't have to look everything up on the internet either!

Luke: But you're wasting so much time!

20 I cannot believe you don't just look online – there's step-by-step advice for everything!

Dad: Well, when I was young, there was no such thing as the internet. But I still

25 learned to do things my way, step-by-step.

Luke: Your way? Hm …

Dad: I've done this a million times before. You should watch me and learn! – Er,

30 what are you doing with my tablet?

Luke: Well, I can use it, right? Anyway, let's see … hm … Oh yes, look: I've found a great website. Hey, over 1,000 people have given it five stars!

35 Dad: You shouldn't believe everything you read online, Luke!

Luke: OK, but … Hey, Dad, what are you doing?! You mustn't remove that pipe! Just listen, please. You see that knob on the right? 40

Dad: Yes, I think I can reach it.

Luke: You have to turn it off, then you …

15 minutes later …

Luke: Yes! It's working! These forums are great! No, please, you needn't say 45 "thanks". Advice is free!

Dad: Fantastic! I fixed it.

Luke: Only because I'm a genius!

Dad: With a very big head. Now, may I have my tablet back, please? 50

READING   **7** **Luke knows best?**

a) *Luke and his dad have different ideas about how to solve the problem. What are they?*

b) *Have you ever had conversations like this one with family or friends? Tell the class.*

LANGUAGE

8   Revision: Modals   → G10

Match the sentence parts.

1. Here are the instructions. If you want, you
2. That pipe isn't the problem. You
3. Look at the mess in the kitchen. We
4. If Mum says yes, you
5. Is that the right knob? I
6. I've found advice on the internet, so you

    a) mustn't remove it.
    b) may use her tablet.
    c) needn't read the instructions.
    d) can't see anything.
    e) can look at them for help.
    f) must clean it up.

LANGUAGE

9   *Must, needn't* and *have to*   → WB 50/9   → G10

a) *Find examples of the forms **must**, **mustn't**, **needn't** and **have to**/ **don't have to** in the text.*

b) *Match the new forms (positive and negative) to the correct German meaning.*

	Modal
müssen / brauchen	
nicht müssen / nicht brauchen	
nicht dürfen	

LANGUAGE

10   Fill in: *must, mustn't, needn't, have to/don't have to*   → WB 50/10   → G10

→ △ 124/5
→ ▲ 125/6

At our school, we have tablet classes, so we `1` bring our tablet to school every day. I think I `2` ask for a new one soon because my tablet is broken. We're lucky that we `3` pay for the tablets ourselves – they're very expensive. I think tablet classes are really cool because we `4` carry so many books to school any more, and we can look up information on the internet. But we `5` follow rules, too: We `6` use the tablets for private communication and we `7` leave our mobiles in our bags!

LANGUAGE

11   *Should, shouldn't* and *could* for advice   → WB 51/11–12   → G11

→ ▲ 125/7
→ △ 125/8

*Tony is having a very bad day. Look at his problems, then write sentences with advice for him. Use **should**, **shouldn't** or **could**. The ideas on the right can help.*

Example: Oh no, that was my dinner for Lou!
    – Maybe you **could** take her to a restaurant.

1. I forgot Lou's birthday yesterday!
2. I've got a new neighbour.
3. I've left my money at home.
4. I want to do something nice for Dad.
5. I want to buy a new phone but haven't got enough money.
6. Someone has taken my bike!

ask a friend   buy flowers

go to the police

take her to a restaurant ✔   say hello

take him to a football game

help your parents at home for pocket money

12 Are you media mad?

→ ▲ 126/9

Take the test and find out how media mad you are!
Do you agree with your results? Why / why not?

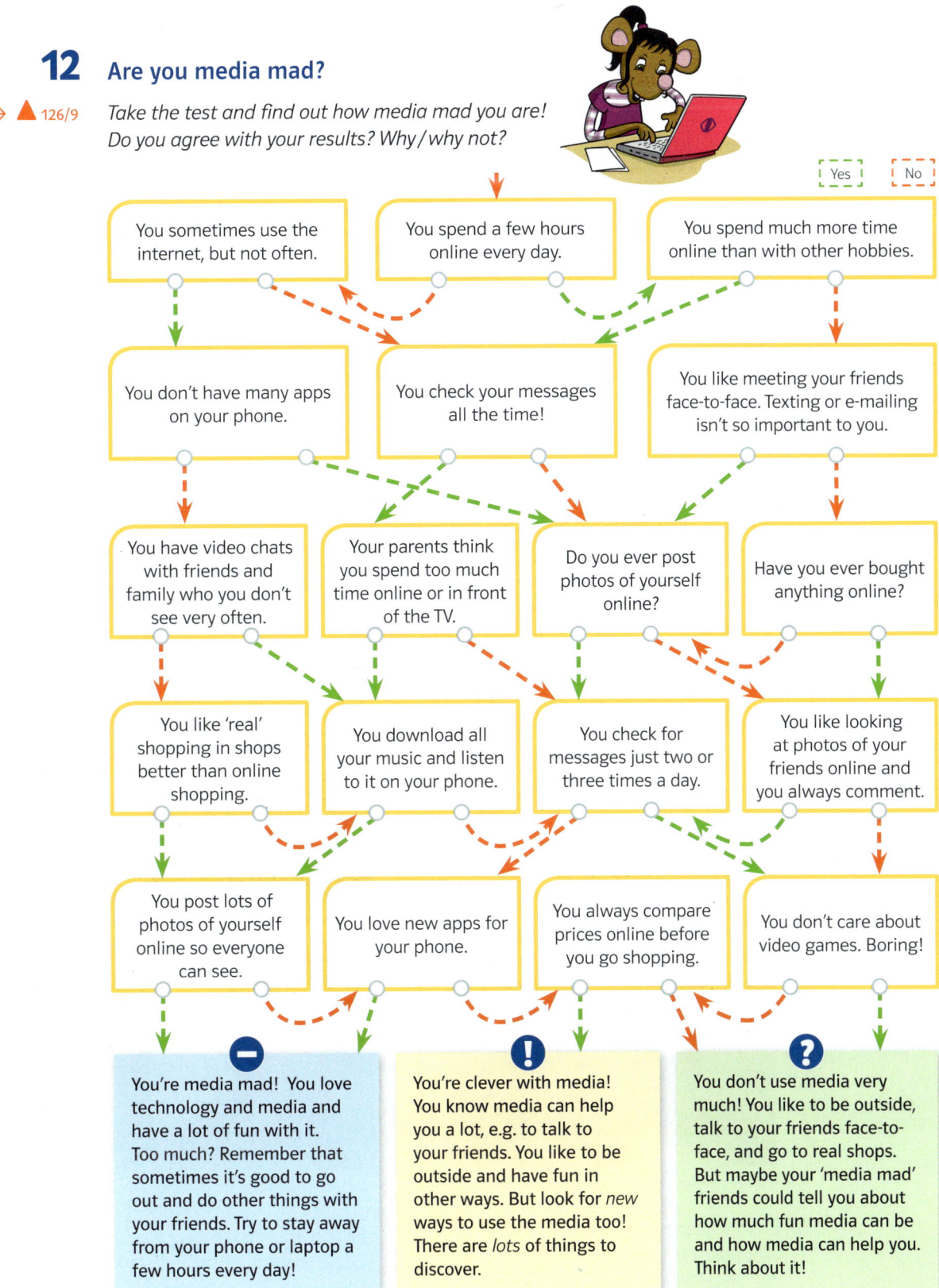

Yes   No

You sometimes use the internet, but not often.

You spend a few hours online every day.

You spend much more time online than with other hobbies.

You don't have many apps on your phone.

You check your messages all the time!

You like meeting your friends face-to-face. Texting or e-mailing isn't so important to you.

You have video chats with friends and family who you don't see very often.

Your parents think you spend too much time online or in front of the TV.

Do you ever post photos of yourself online?

Have you ever bought anything online?

You like 'real' shopping in shops better than online shopping.

You download all your music and listen to it on your phone.

You check for messages just two or three times a day.

You like looking at photos of your friends online and you always comment.

You post lots of photos of yourself online so everyone can see.

You love new apps for your phone.

You always compare prices online before you go shopping.

You don't care about video games. Boring!

⊖ You're media mad! You love technology and media and have a lot of fun with it. Too much? Remember that sometimes it's good to go out and do other things with your friends. Try to stay away from your phone or laptop a few hours every day!

❗ You're clever with media! You know media can help you a lot, e.g. to talk to your friends. You like to be outside and have fun in other ways. But look for *new* ways to use the media too! There are *lots* of things to discover.

❓ You don't use media very much! You like to be outside, talk to your friends face-to-face, and go to real shops. But maybe your 'media mad' friends could tell you about how much fun media can be and how media can help you. Think about it!

Where's Maisie? → S21–22

VIEWING

1 Little dog, big trouble → WB 52/13

a) *Have you ever lost a pet? How did you feel? Tell the class about it.*

10 b) *Watch the film and then talk about the roles of Laura, Nathan and Polly in the story.*

Examples: A: I think Nathan is awful. He's too busy with girls and then …
B: Laura has great friends! They all help …

c) *Now imagine you are Laura. She wants to tell Alicia about what happened with Maisie.*

Start like this: Alicia, I can't believe what Nathan did! He lost Maisie! He was …

SPEAKING

2 Media in the film scenes → WB 52/14–15

Watch the film again. How many different kinds of media can you see in the film?
Say how they helped the friends to find Maisie.

SPEAKING

3 Close-ups

a) *First, read the skills box.*

> **Film skills**
>
> In Unit 1 you learned how music can help to show / describe feelings or atmosphere. Another way to do this in films is with **close-ups**: very close shots of a character's face. In this example, the girl isn't sure: Should she give Nathan her phone number, or not?
>
> With the camera so close, you can 'read' the question in her face!

b) *Look at scenes A and B from the film.*
What do the two close-ups tell us?
The ideas on the right can help you.

> can't believe it | is happy again | loves her dog | wants to look cute / cool for Polly | thinks he's so cool | likes himself a lot | …

How to write a letter and a reply → S10–13

When you write a letter – to an agony aunt, for example – your letter should have different parts. This page shows you how to put a letter and a reply together.

1 The parts of a letter

a) *Read this letter to an agony aunt, and then read the reply. The box on the right shows you which parts of the letters there are. You need to know this for Ex. 2.*

Dear Ruby,

I'm writing to you because I just don't know what to do.
I'm 13, and a new friend has invited me to go on holiday with his family this summer, to Spain. They always go to really cool places, and we just go camping. We never have much money. Before I met my friend, camping was fun. But it doesn't sound fun now. My parents say: "No, you can't go." That isn't fair!
I feel like I'm missing a lot of fun. I'm angry with my parents. What do you think, Ruby?
Thanks for your help!

Yours, Ben

- Begin with a greeting.
- The main idea(s): In an advice letter, the main idea is the problem.
- Ask for advice.
- Say 'Thank you'.
- Your name (often with 'Yours')

Dear Ben,

Yes, I understand that a cool holiday in Spain sounds like fun. But my advice is to ask yourself this: Is your friend really a good friend? Do you care about each other? Why don't you ask him to come with your family on a camping trip. If he's a good friend, you can have fun together anywhere, right? It needn't be on a beach in Spain.
I hope this advice helps!

Ruby

- Begin with a greeting.
- The main idea(s): A reply should show understanding / feelings.
- Give advice.
- Finish your letter.
- Name

> Look back at the phrases box on page 77 for the language of advice.

b) *Say what you think about Ben's problem and Ruby's advice.*

2 Write your own letter and reply → WB 53/16–18

a) *Your partner writes a short letter to an agony aunt, and you write another short letter about a **different** problem. Choose one of the ideas below, or an idea of your own:*

- "My friends say I'm weird because I don't like their music."
- "My two best friends are good at everything and I'm not."

b) *When you're both finished, exchange letters and write a reply to each other with advice.*

Advice letters and replies: Our collection

In this task, you get the chance to talk more about advice for young people's problems. Later, after the different groups have collected and discussed advice for different problems, you're going to write letters and replies for a class advice collection.

Step 1

Choose a topic → WB 54/19

In groups of 4 or 6, choose one of the problems in the list below. Make sure there is at least one group for each question:

A. I want a pet, but my parents say "no".
B. My friends say, "You share too much information about yourself on the internet".
C. My parents never buy cool clothes for me. I look stupid!
D. I never have enough pocket money.
E. I can only watch TV or play video games for an hour on weekday evenings. It isn't enough!

Step 2

Pair work: What do you think? → WB 54/20

*Before you talk to your group about advice for your problem, work **with a partner** in your group for a few minutes. Make notes while you talk about these questions:*

– What places / people could the person go to for help?
– What advice could you give?

Example:

A: As soon as I have a problem, I ask somebody in my family, or maybe a friend at the club I go to / on my football team / …
B: I've never written to an agony aunt, but a friend sometimes writes posts in advice forums.
A: And about the problem: Well, the person should … because it's always a good idea to …

> Look back at the **Stations** and the **Skills page** for help with advice.

> Hey Mick, you always have good advice. What do you think I should do about Lou?

Step 3

Write an 'agony aunt' letter → WB 55/21

a) *Back in your group, discuss the different pairs' ideas about your group's problem. Use your notes from Step 2.*

b) *Now write one letter to an agony aunt about your group's problem. Then put your letter into a class box.*

You know how to write letters. Just look at the **Skills page** again.

Step 4

Exchange questions → WB 55/22

Pick one of the letters from the box. As a group, discuss the problem and write a reply. Everyone in the group should help to check the letter:

– Is the form of the letter correct?
– Is the language for the advice correct?
– Is the advice helpful? How / Why?

That was a great reply. You talked about where you should go for help. That's an important first step!

I thought it was good because your advice was to find a compromise. But I didn't think it was so helpful to say …

Step 5

Present the problem and advice → WB 55/23

What problem did you choose from the class box and what advice did you write? Tell the class. (Speak freely; don't just read from the page!)

The rest of the class should think about these things during the discussion:
– What do you think of the advice?
– Why is it helpful / not so helpful?

Step 6

Organise your letters and replies

As a class, talk about which topics the different problems fit into. Then organise your letters and replies by those topics. Think of how you can make nice pages with pictures, comics, etc.

S 2/7–12
L 3/3–8

It's a disaster!

A Dave's dad, Frank, stopped his car in front of his house. It was raining very hard – he wasn't able to see the house from his car but he was able to see that all the lights
5 were on. The storm was getting worse every minute, with lots of thunder and lightning. He waited for a while and then quickly got out of the car, ran for the house and opened the front door. As he went
10 inside, he nearly fell over all the bags and shoes. "I see Dave's friends are here again!" he thought. He shouted "Hello everyone!" But there wasn't a sound. "Hello-o-o?!" he called again. Nothing. "That's strange," he
15 thought.

Stop and think:
Why do you think the house is so quiet?

He looked in the kitchen – nobody was there. Next, he looked in the living room and saw Gwen, Holly and Olivia. "Hi girls!" he said, but they didn't notice him because
20 they were watching a *loud* music video on Olivia's laptop. Then he saw Jay in the corner.

"How are you, Jay?" he asked, but Jay was busy with text messages and music on his tablet PC. Frank went upstairs. As soon 25
as he opened the door to Dave's bedroom, he saw Dave and Luke. They were sitting on the bed wearing headphones and playing a video game – they didn't notice Frank. "Well, they all look *very* happy to see 30
me, I must say!" he said to himself, as he went back downstairs.

B Jay took off his headphones and tapped the girls' shoulders. "I was thinking," he said. "We should talk about that party we 35
want to have soon."

"Yeah, I was thinking about that too," Olivia answered. "We can have it at my house. My dad and Claire say it's OK. Look, I've already written the invitation." 40

"Great! Let's post a message with the invitation and tell everyone to go to Olivia's house on –"

"No!" Olivia shouted. "We can't just post the invitation like *that*! A lot of people we 45
don't know could see it and come to my house. No, we can only invite people face-to-face. People we *know*."

"Olivia, it's much quicker by internet," Jay said. "Come on, let's just do it! It's fun! 50
He then grabbed Olivia's laptop.

"Jay, what are you doing?!" Olivia cried.

"I'm going to post it, what do you think?" They all started fighting for the laptop. At first they were laughing and 55
joking, but then the girls saw that Jay was *serious*! They were horrified and tried to push him away from the laptop, but Jay was quicker. "Party on Friday 22nd at my house, 52 Begbie Road. Come and have 60
fun!" it said in the invitation text. But just as Jay was pressing 'post', there was a very loud "BANG!" and everything went black.

C Suddenly, the house became very loud
65 and all the friends started shouting at the
same time: "What's happened?" – "I can't
see!" – "My computer has crashed!" – "Oh
no, we're offline too!" – "I can't find my
phone!" – "Help! I don't like the dark!"
70 Frank shouted, "Calm down, it's only
a power cut! Wait a moment while I find
some candles."

"Did you really send that message?"
whispered Holly. "I don't know, I think so!"
75 Jay said.

"To Olivia's friends?" Holly asked.

"No. To *everyone*! But I'm not sure …"
He was really starting to worry now, but he
didn't want to tell the girls. Five minutes
80 later, they were all sitting round the
kitchen table in candlelight.

"Dad, what do we need candles for?"
asked Dave. "Look, our phones have all got
torches!"
85 "Sometimes, the old ways are better!"
smiled Frank. "The only problem we have
right now," Frank went on, "is that we can't
cook – and I'm *really* hungry!"

"How is that a problem?" asked Luke.
90 "Who needs to cook when there are pizza
apps?" Dave and Luke started to show
Mr Preston fantastic apps for his phone.
Mr Preston was impressed! But nobody
noticed that Jay wasn't speaking. "What
95 have I done?" he thought to himself.
"I was just showing off and I went a bit
crazy for a moment. Please tell me the
power cut stopped the message." Then he
said, "Luke, Dave: Can I borrow a phone?
100 I need to check something and I left mine
in the other room." But they were busy
with Mr Preston and his new pizza app.

D Frank was still talking about the old days.
"When I was young, we *talked* to each
105 other, we didn't text all the time."

"Oh no, he *loves* this topic!" Dave
said and, as he spoke, there was a loud
CLICK, and all the lights were back on.

The girls ran to the living room and waited
nervously to get back online. 110

"Come on, come on!" Holly said. And
suddenly they were online again. They
went on to their social network site and …
"Fantastic!" shouted Olivia. "The power cut
stopped the message! But let's teach Jay 115
a lesson." Gwen and Holly smiled at each
other.

E Jay walked slowly back into the living
room.

"You're in *big* trouble now!" Olivia said. 120

"How many messages are there?" he
whispered. His face was white. He felt sick.
"More than 50!" Holly said. "Listen to
these: 'You don't know us but we *love*
parties – see you there!', or 'Party? Cool! I 125
love meeting new people!'"

Now Jay felt *really* sick. "It's a disaster!"
he said. Holly and Olivia were trying very
hard not to laugh.

"What's so funny?" Jay asked. 130

"Don't worry. The power cut stopped
your message. Nobody got it," Olivia said.

"But you're lucky, Jay Azad!" Holly
added. "And you *really* should leave the
party invitations to us next time!" 135

"That," said Jay, "is no problem at all!"

READING

1 Understanding the story → WB 56/24–25

a) *Do you think 'It's a disaster!' is a good title for the story? Say why or why not. What ideas for a different story title do you have?*

b) *There are two main characters in this story: One is Frank, and the other is Jay. Which sentences in the text show that they both feel left out at some point in the story?*

> **Example:** He shouted "Hello everyone!" But there wasn't a sound. (Frank, lines 12–13)

→ △ 126/10
→ S16

c) *Do one of these role plays:*
  – *One of you is Frank, the other is Dave's mum. She asks him what happened.*
    Or:
  – *One of you is Jay, the other is Olivia. They talk about what happened and about their feelings. Use ideas from the text.*

WRITING

2 Writing about pros and cons

→ S8
a) *What can people today do with modern technology and what did people do or use when Frank was very young?*
Make a grid with examples from the text. Then think of more examples and add them to your grid.

New world	Old world
– watch a video	– use candles
– send text messages	…
…	

→ S13
b) *What are the pros and cons of modern technology? First read the skills box. Then write about the two worlds. The phrases box can help you too.*

Writing skills

Use these words / phrases to link ideas and give information:

When things happen (time):
When my parents were young…, then …, now …, today …, before …, after …, as …, when …

Where things happen (place):
in the house, on my phone/PC, everywhere

Why things happen (reasons):
… because …

What else happens:
and …, or …, but …

How things happen:
easily, carefully, dangerously, more quickly, in a friendly way, without thinking, by internet, face-to-face

Useful phrases

Today we've got … | We can … | It's great that … because … | (Not) everything was …, I think … is better than … | But … can be dangerous. We should …

Unsocial Networking

Can you ...

1. talk about media in your life? _ _ _ _   I use ... to send / receive / post / chat / play / read / look up / take part in ...
2. link ideas? _ _ _ _ _ _ _ _ _ _ _ _ _ _ _   I do it when / after / before / because ...
3. talk about rules and instructions?   You must ... / have to ... / needn't ... / mustn't ...
4. give advice to somebody? _ _ _ _ _   Why don't you ...? You should ... You could ...
Have you tried ...ing ...?

VOCABULARY

1   How do people use media?

✐ *Match the sentence parts and make sentences.*

Example: When my grandma wants to chat with her sister, she calls her on the telephone.

1. my dad / want / relax
2. I / want / know / words of a song I've heard
3. my mum / work away from home
4. I / want / tell all my friends how great my holiday is
5. my sister / want / know about the coolest new clothes

a) post / it on my social network profile
b) send / me text messages
c) read / girls' magazines
d) look / it up on the internet
e) watch / football on TV

SPEAKING

2   What can you say to give these people advice?

1. Your brother hurts his foot and doesn't know if it's broken.
2. Your friend missed his favourite TV show.
3. Your sister doesn't know how to fix her bike.
4. Your friend tells you that someone posted really embarrassing photos of her on the internet.
5. Your friend's parents are angry with her: She can't use her smartphone for a week.

LANGUAGE

3   How do you say it in German?

1. My brother's mobile is really old, I think he must buy a new one.
2. He's lucky because he doesn't have to pay for it himself – it's his birthday in two months.
3. I'm even luckier because I needn't wait that long. I can have my dad's new smartphone!
4. But I mustn't tell my brother anything – he can be very jealous!

S 2/13–17
L 3/9–13

Ten-tonne truck

Zoe finds a rat in her room. She wants to train it like she trained her pet hamster (who could break-dance), but she knows she isn't allowed to[1] keep any pets. Raj, a shopkeeper[2] who is the 'agony aunt' of the town, tells her to set Armitage the rat free[3] in the park.

5 "What am I going to do with him, Raj? I'm not allowed to keep him at home; he's the reason why I was suspended[4] from school. My stepmother hated my hamster, she is *never* going to let me keep a rat."

10 Raj thought for a moment. "Maybe you should set him free," he finally said.
"Free?" Zoe said, with a tear[5] in her eye.
"Yes. Rats shouldn't be pets …"
"But this little one is so cute …"
15 "Maybe, but he's going to grow[6]. He can't spend his whole life in your pocket."
"But I love him, Raj, I really do."
"I'm sure you do, Miss Zoe," Raj said. "And if you love him, you should set him 20 free."
So this was goodbye. Zoe knew deep down she would[7] never be able to keep Armitage for long. There were a hundred reasons, but the most important one was: HE WAS A RAT. 25

Children don't have rats as pets. They have cats and dogs and hamsters and mice and rabbits and tortoises. Some kids even have ponies, but never rats. Rats live underground, not in little girls' bedrooms. 30

Zoe walked sadly out of Raj's shop. It was true that sometimes he tried to sell his customers[8] a half-eaten chocolate bar, but all the kids in town knew that when they needed advice, he was the best. 35

And so she had to say goodbye to Armitage. Zoe took the long way back to her flat, through the park. She thought this was the perfect place to set little Armitage free. There were always bits of bread for 40 the ducks – Armitage could[9] eat these. He could drink from the pond and take a bath in it. And maybe there was a squirrel or two he could make friends with.

The little girl carried[10] the little rat in her 45 hand. It was the middle of the afternoon and there were just a few old ladies and their dogs in the park. Armitage wrapped his tail around her thumb – maybe he knew that something was wrong … 50

Zoe walked as slowly as possible. Finally, she reached the middle of the park. She was looking for a nice quiet place. Then she bent down[11] to the ground slowly and opened her hand. But Armitage didn't 55 move. He just stayed in her hand. It was breaking Zoe's heart …

---

1 to be allowed to do sth [bi ə'laʊd tə] dürfen | **2 shopkeeper** [ʃɒpˈkiːpə] Ladenbesitzer | **3 to set sb/sth free** [set 'friː] jmdn./etw. freilassen | **4 to be suspended** [bi səˈspendɪd] (vorübergehend) der Schule verwiesen werden | **5 tear** [tɪə] Träne | **6 to grow** [ɡrəʊ] wachsen | **7 would** [wʊd] würde | **8 customer** [ˈkʌstəmə] Kunde | **9 could** [kʊd] könnte | **10 to carry** [ˈkæri] tragen | **11 to bend down** [bend ˈdaʊn] sich bücken

4

Zoe shook[12] her hand a little, but Armitage only held on tighter[13] to her fingers. She was fighting back tears when she picked the rat up gently[14] and put him carefully on the grass. Once again Armitage didn't move. He just looked up at her sadly. Zoe kissed him gently on his little pink nose.

"Goodbye, little friend," she whispered. "I'm going to miss[15] you."

A tear dropped from her eye.

The little rat turned his little head to one side, like a friend who was trying to understand her. This just made it harder for Zoe.

Finally, Zoe took a big breath and stood up. "Don't look back!" she told herself. But after a few steps she had to look one last time at the place she left him. To Zoe's surprise, Armitage wasn't there.

"He has already run away to the safety of the bushes," she thought. She looked at the grass, but it was long and he was short, and the grass didn't move. Zoe turned round[16] and sadly started to walk home.

She left the park and crossed[17] the road. For a moment, there was no noise of cars, and in the silence, Zoe heard a small 'eek'. She turned round quickly, and in the middle of the road was Armitage.

He was following her!

"Armitage!" she shouted excitedly. He didn't want to be free; he wanted to be with her! She was so happy. Now she didn't have to imagine all kinds of terrible scenes any more: A hungry swan[18] couldn't eat him for dinner, and a ten-tonne truck couldn't run him over[19].

At that moment, she heard a loud thundering noise. Something came along the road towards Armitage, who was still moving slowly to get to Zoe. It was a ten-tonne truck!

Zoe wasn't able to move, she just watched the truck which was speeding[20] closer and closer towards Armitage. How could the driver see a baby rat in the road?

From: *Ratburger* by David Walliams

→ WB 58/1–4

12 **to shake** [ʃeɪk] schütteln | 13 **tight** [taɪt] fest | 14 **gently** ['dʒentli] sanft | 15 **to miss sb/sth** [mɪs] jmdn./etw. vermissen | 16 **to turn round** [tə:n raʊnd] (sich) umdrehen; wenden | 17 **to cross** [krɒs] überqueren | 18 **swan** [swɒn] Schwan | 19 **to run sth over** [rʌn ˈəʊvə] etw. überfahren | 20 **to speed** [spi:d] rasen

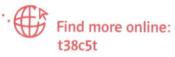
Find more online: t38c5t

Unit 5

Goodbye Greenwich

A A beach in Cornwall, in the south-west of England

B A medieval 'living history' show at Caerphilly Castle in Wales

SPEAKING

1 Parts of the British Isles

→ △ 126/1

Look at the pictures and find the places on the map at the back of your book. Which part of the British Isles do they belong to? Which part of them looks most interesting to you and why?

> The United Kingdom includes Great Britain and Northern Ireland.

> Yes, and most of Ireland is a separate country: the Republic of Ireland.

LISTENING

2 Come on Dave, don't be so negative!

L 3/14 ◉

a) *Dave is talking about his parents' plans and his mum's vet surgery. What is the problem from Dave's point of view? Listen and take notes.*

→ S18–20

b) *Now talk about the different places that Dave and his friends discuss. Make a grid for your answers with these headings:*

Place | Landscape | Things to do | Other information

In Unit 5 you learn

… how to talk about places in the British Isles.
You learn:

• to describe places
• to talk about plans for a journey
• to talk about the future with *will*
• to report what people have just said

C   Pony trekking in Ireland

D   The Edinburgh Festival in the Scottish capital

VOCABULARY   **3**   **Places**   → WB 59/1–2

a) *Collect vocabulary in different categories like landscapes, sights, things to do.*

b) *Each of you does the following: Take four cards and write* **one** *of your words / phrases from a) on each card. Shuffle all the cards and pick four. Choose a place in the British Isles and take turns to talk about it, with the words on your cards.*

c) *Your turn: Find information about a German region (e.g. the North Sea). Write a short text and present it.*

Useful phrases

high mountain | field | forest | sandy /
rocky beach | wide river | deep lake |
island | city | village | harbour | visit
a castle | go hiking / climbing / mountain
biking / (wind) surfing / pony trekking

Across cultures

Did you know that palm trees grow in the
south-west of England? Some call it the
English Riviera. Are there any surprising
facts about the region where you live?

Moving to the middle of nowhere

L 3/15

Dave's parents have found a beautiful house near St Agnes, in the Cornish countryside. Dave is very sad to leave.

Dave: Oh no, why do we have to move to the middle of nowhere? London is
5 just fine. And I'll miss you so much!
Olivia: But the house looks fantastic! And your mum never wanted to live in the city. She'll be happy there with her new surgery and all the farm
10 animals and pets to work with, won't she?
Dave: Yes, but will I be happy? Has anyone ever asked *me*? If I want to see farm animals, I can go to Mudchute Farm.
15 Luke: What about your dad? Will he find work there?
Dave: Well, he travels a lot anyway. He'll stay in London with Aunt Frances when he has to work there. I think
20 it'll be OK for *him*. But me?
Holly: Oh Dave, I'll miss you too! I'm so sorry you won't be able to go to the park with us any longer.
Jay: And we won't be able to play video
25 games together.
Gwen: Come on now, it's not the end of the world. There are games you can play online. Oh, and we'll text you and have lots of video chats together.
30 Olivia: And we'll come to visit you! Cornwall is a great place. Most British people go there for a holiday. I've been there with my mum.

Dave: That's nice for people on holiday – but *I'll* be in a new school, and 35 there'll be nobody I know. It'll be horrible. And I'm sure Sid will hate it too.
Jay: Don't worry, you'll make lots of new friends. But what about Olivia's idea? 40 We could go to Cornwall to visit you.
Holly: All of us together, in Cornwall? Wow! I'll ask my mum.
Luke: Well, maybe. I'll think about it. But we'll have to find the money first, 45 won't we?
Gwen: I'm sure we'll find a way to get there.
Olivia: Will it be OK for us to stay with Dave?
Luke: I'm sure it will. His parents are cool. 50
Dave: That's a wonderful idea. It'll be great to see you all there.

READING

1 Questions about the future → WB 60/3

1. What does Dave say about the Prestons' future in Cornwall?
2. What do his friends say to make him feel better?
3. What will the friends need to do before they go to Cornwall? Think about these things: parents, dates, transport, money.

Examples:

1. He'll miss his friends. His mum will be happy …
2. They'll miss him too. They'll text him …
3. They'll have to ask their parents …

LANGUAGE

2 Rules for the *will* future → WB 60/4 → G12

*Find 4–5 sentences with **will** or **won't** in the text. Say if they're predictions about the future or spontaneous reactions/decisions. You see some examples on the right.*

Prediction	Spontaneous reaction/decision
I'll miss you. She'll be happy there.	I'll ask my mum. We'll text you.

LANGUAGE

3 How will we get there?

Luke goes to a travel agent's to ask about the journey to St Agnes.

→ △ 127/2
→ ▲ 127/3

a) *Complete dialogue A with forms of the **will future** and read it with a partner.*

b) *Now do the same with dialogue B.*

Train + bus: London Paddington to St Agnes
Time: 6 – 7 hours
Prices: £50 – £70
Children under 12 must travel with an adult.

Coach + bus: London Victoria to St Agnes
Time: 8 hours
Prices: £65 – £75
Children under 14 must travel with an adult.

A

Luke: My friends and I want to go to Cornwall, but we're worried that tickets (be) expensive.
Assistant: Don't worry. It (not be) too expensive. But it depends on the date. Give me your dates and I (check) for you.
(a few minutes later)
Yes, on those dates, train tickets per person are £5 cheaper than by coach. – Oh, but now I see better prices for the next day. Between £10 and £15 cheaper by train.
Luke: £15 cheaper per person? Cool! My friends (like) that.

Assistant: Well, I can't promise £15, but it (be) a better price than a day earlier. – Oh, and children under 12 need to travel with a person who is 16 or older.
Luke: Oh, that (not be) a problem. – Anyway, I (talk) to my friends and come back.

B

Olivia: (we go) by train or by coach?
Luke: I think we (go) by train. It (be) cheaper and (not take) so long.
Gwen: And we (not have) to find an adult to go with us.
Holly: There's just one problem: Where (I get) the money?

LISTENING

4 Preparing for the trip → WB 60/5

L 3/18 ◎ *Listen to the dialogue and answer the questions.*

a) *What's Holly's problem? What can she do and who can help her?*

b) *What will these people do? Say one sentence about each person: Dave, Granny Rose, Luke, the girls, the boys, Luke's grandparents, Holly, Amber.*

VOCABULARY

5 How to: Book train tickets on the internet → WB 61/6

Luke wants to book tickets for the five friends and Granny Rose online. They want to leave next Sunday morning and return a week later.

→ △ 127/4
→ S9

a) *Help him to fill in the form (1). He clicks on "Buy train tickets". Then he chooses a connection and clicks on it. A new window shows details for this connection (2).*

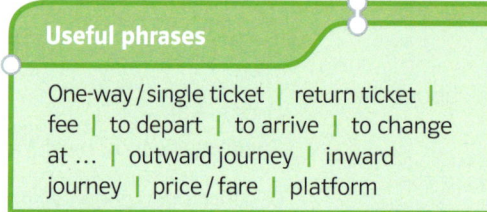

Useful phrases

One-way / single ticket | return ticket | fee | to depart | to arrive | to change at … | outward journey | inward journey | price / fare | platform

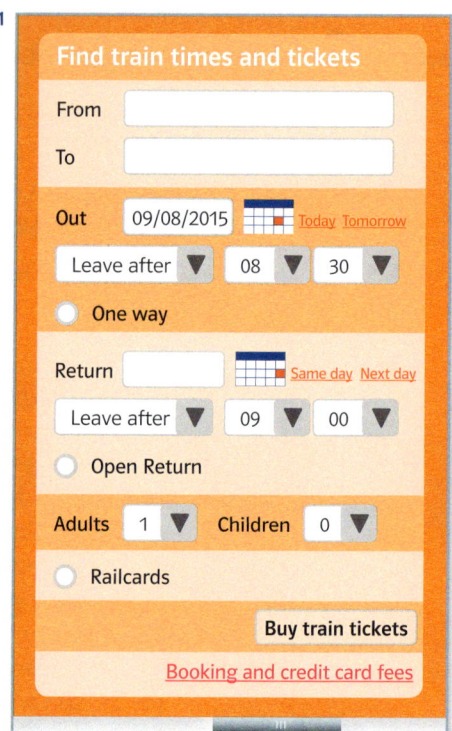

Find train times and tickets

From
To

Out 09/08/2015 Today Tomorrow
Leave after ▼ 08 ▼ 30 ▼
○ One way

Return Same day Next day
Leave after ▼ 09 ▼ 00 ▼
○ Open Return

Adults 1 ▼ Children 0 ▼

○ Railcards

Buy train tickets

Booking and credit card fees

2 Journey Summary — Outward Journey (9 Aug 2015)

Depart		Arrive		Travel by	Duration
09:32	Greenwich	09:43	London Bridge	Train	00h 11 Calling Points
09:53	London Bridge	10:23	London Paddington	Tube	00h 30
10:43	London Paddington	16:46	Redruth	Train	06h 03 Calling Points
17:12	Redruth	17:46	St Agnes	Bus	00h 34

Text me these details   Add to calendar

b) *Match words and phrases from the phrases box with these definitions.*

1. to leave
2. to leave one train and get on another
3. a ticket to go to a place and back
4. going away to a place
5. this tells you what a ticket costs
6. to get to a place
7. a ticket to go to a place
8. going back to your starting place
9. extra money you have to pay

You often hear *will* future in weather forecasts.

MEDIATION

6 The weather forecast → WB 61/7

→ △ 128/5
→ S17

A British tourist wants to do a 5-hour mountain climbing tour. He shows you this weather forecast for tomorrow and asks you if he can go on his tour. What is your advice?

Wettervorhersage Oberallgäu: Während es heute bei Höchsttemperaturen über 30 Grad noch sehr heiß mit viel Sonne ist, zieht morgen eine Schlechtwetterfront von Südwesten herein. Es ist mit starken Unwettern und Hagel zu rechnen, vor allem Samstagnachmittag und -abend. Im Bergland besteht Gefahr durch orkanartige Windböen mit Geschwindigkeiten bis zu 105 km/h. Durch starke Niederschläge kann es zu Überflutungen kommen.

How to get information → S10–13

For the Unit task you'll need information about different parts of the British Isles: England (e.g. Cornwall, or maybe London), Scotland, Wales and Ireland (Northern Ireland or the Republic of Ireland).

1 Where to get information

If you want to collect pictures and facts about interesting places, you can write to a tourist board and ask for free material. What else can you do?

2 Asking for information → WB 62/8–10

Make four groups, one for each of the regions on pages 92–93.
Some organisations have interesting material. Find their e-mail addresses and write a polite e-mail to ask for the material. Some of them don't give you their e-mail addresses but ask you to fill in an internet contact form. Make sure you don't write to the same organisation about the same material more than once!

Writing skills

Before you send off your e-mail or contact form, **remember**:

- Don't forget your greetings.
- Who are you?
- What do you want to do?
- What do you need?
- How do you ask for it politely?
- What information about yourselves do you need to give?

Dear Sir or Madam,

We are students of a German grammar school. We would like to do a project about the British Isles and need information about Scotland for it.
Could you please send us some free material about interesting places in Scotland, Scottish history and things to do in Scotland?
Here is our address:
…-Gymnasium
Class …
…straße (XX)
D-(XXXXX) …

Thank you very much for your help.

Best wishes,
The students of Class (…)

3 Working with the material

When you have enough material, go through it together in your group.
Make notes of interesting ideas for a presentation, and look for the best photos.

L 3/19–20

Dave says he can't wait for us to go there

Dave has been in Cornwall for two days and sends an e-mail to Luke.

Hi Luke! Greetings from sunny Cornwall! It's very hot here today and I've just come back from the beach. Maybe this place is not that bad after all … But I really hope that you aren't having too much fun without me! I miss you all a lot – I even miss my old school! Anyway, I can't wait for you to come here. There's lots to see – the beaches, for example. The coastline is almost 300 miles long. You must bring your swimming things! Look at these photos. This is my favourite beach – I can see it from my bedroom window. I'll send you some more photos soon.

There's lots to do too – all kinds of water sports and other outdoor activities like adventure sports and pony trekking. It feels so different from Greenwich. The landscape here is very wild and dramatic. And there's lots of ancient history – Bodmin Moor with its prehistoric monuments and all the old tin mines and Celtic place names … So, you won't get bored. See you on Sunday!
Love, Dave

A few minutes later Luke gets a call from Olivia.

Olivia: Hi Luke. Have you heard from Dave?

Luke: Yes – he sent me an e-mail a few minutes ago. He writes that it's very hot there today. He's just come back from the beach!

Olivia: Lucky Dave! Is he missing us?

Luke: Oh yes. He says he hopes that we aren't having too much fun without him. And he can't wait for us to go there.

Olivia: Did he send some photos?

Luke: Yes, wait, I'll send you one from my mobile. That's his favourite beach – he can see it from his bedroom window. Isn't it amazing?

Olivia: Wow! I want to go swimming there.

Luke: Well, he tells us that we must take our swimming things. So I'm sure we'll spend some time on the beach.

Olivia: Great! What else does he say?

Luke: Well, he says that the landscape in Cornwall is very wild and dramatic and that there's lots of ancient history too. You'll like that, right?

Olivia: Definitely! I can't wait to go.

Luke: Me neither. Dave promises we won't get bored.

11
Mehr zum
Thema Cornwall

READING **7** **Dave and Cornwall** → WB 63/11

a) *How does Dave feel about his new life in Cornwall compared to his old life in Greenwich?*

b) *What does Dave tell his friend about Cornwall? Talk about:*

    1. activities you can do there   2. the landscape   3. the history

LANGUAGE **8** Find the rule: From direct to indirect speech → G13

Copy the grid and put in the sentences from Dave's e-mail in direct speech. Then add the sentences from Luke's and Olivia's conversation in indirect speech. Underline the words that change and find the rule.

Direct speech	Indirect speech
1. Dave: It's very hot **here** today.	Dave writes that it's very hot **there** today.
2. **I** hope that **you** aren't having too much fun without **me**!	He says **he** hopes that **we** aren't having too much fun without **him**!

3. I can't wait for you to come here.   4. This is my favourite beach. I can see it from my window.   5. You must bring your swimming things!   6. The landscape here is very wild.

LANGUAGE **9** An e-mail from Olivia → WB 63/12 → G13

 128/6
129/7

Olivia sends Dave an e-mail with a selfie. Dave tells his mum what she says.

Start like this: Olivia says it's really wet …

Hi Dave! It's really wet here today. This is me in Greenwich Park in the rain! So we're really excited that we're going to Cornwall soon. Maybe you could even teach us how to surf?! Oh, and we **must** visit all the historical sights near you – I love history and the Celts! And I want to bring typical Cornish food home for my mum. So you mustn't forget the shopping tour! 😊 Bye for now. Olivia.

SPEAKING **10** Languages in Britain

Look at the photo. Which of the Cornish words can you understand?

Across cultures

Everybody in the British Isles speaks English. But Cornwall, Ireland, Scotland, Wales and the Isle of Man still have their own **Celtic languages**. What languages do people in your class speak besides German? Do people speak in a local dialect or with an accent?

LISTENING **11** Announcements

L 3/22–25 ◎

Listen to the dialogues and find out this information for each scene. Take notes:

1. where Mr Preston is   2. where Mr Preston wants to go   3. what sight they talk about
→ S20   4. what the announcement is about.

SPEAKING

12 **Role play: At the travel agent's** → WB 64/13–15

→ S16

One of you is an assistant at a travel agent's. The other chooses one of these roles:
A: A father who wants to travel with his wife and young children; B: A teenager who wants to travel with her mum; or C: a young couple who is interested in sports. They all want to go to Cornwall. Use the useful phrases to make dialogues. (You can also look back at Ex. 3 on p. 95.)

> **Useful phrases**
>
> **Assistant:**
> Hello, what can I do for you?
> How long would you like to stay?
> Do you want to go by car, by train or by
>   coach? Do you need a ticket?
> Would you like to book a room / a flat /
>   a house?
> If you want to …, you can …
>
> **Customer:**
> I'd like to travel to … with …
> Over the weekend / two weeks / …
> We love … / We're into …
> How long does it take?
> We need … tickets.
> How much is it?
> Oh, I think that's too expensive.
> Yes, that's fine. Thank you.

READING

13 **British history: A poem about the Romans**

→ 🔺 129/8

a) *Explain what the poem says about the Romans and what they did in Britain.*

The Romans in Britain
(A history in 40 words)

by Judith Nicholls

The Romans gave us aqueducts
fine buildings and straight[1] roads,
where all those Roman legionaries
marched with heavy loads[2].

They gave us central heating[3],
good laws[4], a peaceful[5] home …
Then after just four centuries
they shuffled back to Rome.

> **Useful phrases**
>
> to build (a bridge, a road, a town) |
> to supply somebody (with water, food) |
> to rule (a country)

b) *Think of how you could complete this little poem about Britain.*

Great Britain is an island.
It is in the North …
It's got green fields and mountains.
It's where I'd like to …

The biggest city is …
It's got a lot to show.
There's always something happening.
It's where I'd like to…

1 **straight** [streɪt] gerade | 2 **heavy load** [ˌhevi ˈləʊd] schwere Last | 3 **central heating** [ˌsentrl ˈhiːtɪŋ]
Zentralheizung | 4 **law** [lɔː] *hier:* Gesetz | 5 **peaceful** [ˈpiːsfl] friedlich

The caves → S21–22

→ S21–22

SPEAKING **1** **Things to do in the country**

Talk about which of these activities are interesting for you.

1. feeding animals
2. milking cows
3. exploring a cave
4. swimming in a lake
5. playing in an adventure playground
6. reading ghost stories
7. walking
8. geocaching

VIEWING **2** **Themes** → WB 65/16

 12 *Watch the film. Then say which themes below play a role in the film. Explain why/why not. Which of them are more important/the most important?*

1. food
2. city and country life
3. school
4. children and adults
5. stories
6. sports
7. love
8. ghosts

VIEWING **3** **Suspense: What's going to happen?**

Watch the film again, find examples of the ideas below and take notes. They can help you to talk about elements that create suspense in a story.

> *Story: What about …*
> – *Laura's grandpa?*
> – *ghosts?*
> – *getting lost?*
> – *phones, maps and torches?*
>
> *Acting: What about …*
> – *people's faces?*
>
> *Audiovisual effects: What about …*
> – *darkness?*
> – *strange sounds, a voice in the caves?*
> – *dramatic music?*

Film skills

Elements that create suspense:
– clues in the story about what could happen
– acting
– music
– light
– sounds

WRITING **4** **Laura and her grandpa**

 Write a sequel to the last scene in the film:
→ S15 *Laura and her grandpa talk about what has really happened and why. Act it and film it.*

Our big British Isles quiz

You're going to work in four groups. You're going to make question cards for a quiz about the British Isles (Wales, England, etc.). You can use information in this book and from other sources. When you're finished, you'll be able to play a quiz game.

Step 1

Get organised → WB 66/18–19

Make four groups of 4–6, one for a different part of the British Isles. In your group, agree on 16 interesting sights or places in your region. Each of you makes 2–4 question cards so you have one for each sight in the end.

For ideas, look at **this unit** and **the other units** in the book. Use information material from **books**, the **internet** and **tourist boards**.

Step 2

Prepare your cards

Make cards like the one below (front and back). But don't finish them until you've done Step 3.

Tower of London

(A question about the sight / place / thing)
Which of these animals never lived at the Tower?

(Three answers, two of which are wrong)
a) a polar bear that loved to fish
b) a raven that was able to talk
c) a zebra that liked beer

(The right answer)

Step 3

Test your cards → WB 67/20

a) *Show the picture of the sight / place / thing on the front of your card. Read the question and the three answers. The others guess which answer is right. Correct them if they're wrong. You can give tips to help them.*

b) *Are the questions, answers and tips OK? If a quiz question is too difficult, make changes or give more tips.*

c) *Now make your cards.*

Useful phrases

Ideas for tips:
In this place you can …
It's famous for …
One of the attractions here is …
If you want to …, you will … here.
If you're interested in history, you should …
It's in the north / east / south / west.
… built it.

Step 4

Play the quiz game in your groups → WB 67/21

- *Shuffle the 16 cards for your group and place them on a table face down.*
- *Each group draws four cards from each group.*
- *In each group, shuffle all the cards again.*
- *Every player draws the same number of cards. One player starts and uses a card for the person next to him / her. If the person gets the answer right, he / she can keep the card.*
- *When you've used all the cards once, the person with the most cards wins!*

Step 5

Your 'British Isles Top 5'

a) *Copy an outline of the map of Britain at the back of this book.*

b) *Mark your 'Top 5' sights / places on the map. Write information about them next to each one.*

c) *Gallery walk: Look at the other posters and try to guess the sights / places.*

I think that's the capital of Scotland. Do you know its name?

Edinburgh?

a polar bear that … [əˌpəʊlə beə ˈðæt] ein Eisbär, der … | **to fish** [fɪʃ] Fische fangen | **zebra** [ˈzebrə] | **beer** [bɪə] Bier

S 2/21–25
L 3/26–30

Things will get better

A Come in, come in!" Mrs Preston said from the hall of the big old house by the sea. "I'll make some tea."

"We can't have tea, Mum," Dave said.
5 "There's no electricity, remember?"

"Oh, yes," she answered. "Well, a glass of water then?"

"Er … OK, yes please, Mrs Preston," Olivia said.

10 "Hi," Dave said to his friends and his granny. "Thanks for coming. Good journey?"

"Yeah, the journey was fine, thanks," Luke answered. "But *you* don't look fine.
15 What's the matter? Is everything OK?"

"No, not really," Dave said. "We've been here a week, and there's no electricity yet. Dad is in London, the cat has run away, I haven't got any friends and I really miss
20 my old life in Greenwich. It's awful here. I hate it."

"Oh, Dave!" Granny Rose said. "Don't be sad. You've only been here a week. Things will get better. You know they will."

B "Here are your glasses of water," Mrs Preston said. Then she looked at one of the glasses. "Oh dear," she said "Why is this water brown? I think we've got a problem with the water now too."

"Let's go out," Dave said to his friends. 30 "We'll go up to the coastal path, to the old mine. Is that OK, Mum?"

"Yes, that's fine," Dave's mum answered. "See you later. I'll call a plumber."

"But it's Sunday", Granny Rose said. 35 "It'll be *really* expensive."

C The friends stood on a hill by an old building. It had a tall chimney, but no roof. There was a strong wind from the sea, and it brought lots of big black clouds. 40

"This old building looks a bit scary," Holly whispered.

"Don't be silly. It's just one of many old mine buildings in this area. Tin was really important here," Olivia said. "Going right 45 back to Celtic times. Tin from Cornwall went all over the world. But now there's almost no tin left."

"Looks like a great place for geocaching!" Luke said excitedly as he 50 grabbed his smartphone. "Let's see if there's a cache somewhere near here. – Yes, there must be a difficult puzzle cache."

"Really?" Dave asked, "Let's solve the puzzle and get to that cache!" 55

Suddenly a deep voice behind them boomed, "Hey you, what are you doing here?! Keep away from MY treasure!"

The friends were scared. They turned around and saw a big man with a serious 60 face and a kind of skirt and trousers. He had wild hair and looked dangerous, not only because of the long spear in his hand.

"I'm sorry, we – we didn't want to steal 65 anything from you. We didn't know the cache was yours," Dave said. He was really scared.

Suddenly the sun came out again and the man's face looked much friendlier. 70

"Hello!" he said to Dave. "It was only a joke. Have you just moved into number 7?"

"Er, yes," Dave said. "And are you a Celtic warrior?"

75 "I'm Bob," the man said. "Your new neighbour."

"Ah," Dave said. "Are you on your way to a fancy dress party?"

The others just looked at Bob's strange 80 clothes and said nothing.

"Oh, don't worry!" Bob laughed. "I don't always wear these clothes. I'm in the local history society. We do shows about the history of Cornwall. These are clothes from 85 Celtic times."

"Right," Dave said. "Nice to meet you."

"I just came up to say hello," Bob said. "Tea at my house anyone?"

D "This is my wife, Helen," Bob said.

90 The friends were in the kitchen of Bob's house. "And these are my children, Jago and Tamara." The boy and girl were both about 13. "Good old Cornish names."

"Hello Dave. I'm Jago," the boy said.

"We're twins," the girl said. "Do you like 95 computers, Dave?"

"Not now, Tamara," Bob said. "I'm sure Dave doesn't want to hear about your new computer games."

Then Olivia saw a big bag of tools on 100 the kitchen floor.

"What do you do, Mr … er …?

"Call me Bob. I'm a plumber. And Helen here's an electrician. We do the plumbing and electrics for half the village. Well, the 105 *whole* village, really."

Then Bob's bag of tools moved. A cat came out of it.

"Oh, there he is! This cat moved in here last week." Bob said.

"Sid!" Dave shouted. "There you are!" 110

E An hour later, there were thirteen people and a cat in Dave's garden. The friends, Bob and his family, Granny Rose and Dave's parents were all at a big table in the garden. There was tea and a cake. 115

"We were on the train before you," Granny Rose said to Dave's dad. "I didn't know that you wanted to come today."

"Change of plan at work," Dave's dad said. "I can be here all this week." 120

"Thanks again for fixing the water," Dave's mum said to Bob. "Are you sure I can't pay you for …"

"No, no," Bob said. "It was a five-minute job, and we're neighbours. But I'll have 125 another piece of Rose's cake, if that's OK."

"And I'll have a look at your electrics tomorrow morning," Helen added.

Dave turned to Luke. "I think it'll be OK here after all," he said. 130

READING

1 **Understanding the text** → WB 68/22

→ S5–7 **a)** *Find headings for parts A–E of the story.*

b) *Answer these questions.*

1. What problems do the Prestons have in their new home?
2. What do the friends think of Bob at first? What do we learn about him?
3. Think of what Granny Rose said at the end of part A. At the end of the story, was she right? Explain.

SPEAKING

2 **Help for Dave**

Talk about what everyone can do to make Dave happier in his new home.

Example: Tamara and Jago can play computer games with him.

WRITING

3 **Creative writing** → WB 68/23

→ S10–13 **a)** *Write a diary entry for one of the characters about what happened on their first day in Cornwall and what he / she felt.*

b) *Write a postcard from one of Dave's friends to his / her parents at home.*

> **Writing skills**
>
> A **diary entry** is a very personal text. Usually nobody else reads it. It's like writing to a close friend. Put the date at the top and start writing about what happened, what was important and how you feel about it. You can also write about your hopes and plans for the future.

Greetings from St Agnes

Dear Mum and Dad,

How are you? We arrived in St Agnes yesterday. There is a beautiful harbour with nice sailboats, and we're camping really close to the sea. The weather is great, and we've spent a lot of time at the beach.

See you soon,

Megan

> **Can you ...**
>
> 1. say what will happen in the future? __ Tomorrow there will be ...
> 2. talk about places and regions? _ _ _ _ It's in ... | It has got ... | There are ... | You can ... there.
> 3. talk about travelling? _ _ _ _ _ _ _ _ We can go by ... | It takes ... | We'll have to change
> 4. report what people have just said? __ He says that ... / They tell us that ...

LANGUAGE

1 Tomorrow's weather forecast

Complete the weather forecast with the correct forms of the verbs in the box.

Tomorrow **1** a nice day. There **2** a lot of sun. There **3** too many clouds. In the morning, it **4** cool, but it **5** nicer in the afternoon. It **6** a fine day for outdoor activities. You can be sure it **7** . But in the evening there **8** more wind, and at night the weather **9** . Clouds **10** and at about 12 o'clock it **11** to rain.

be (5x)

not be

change

get

move in

not rain

start

LANGUAGE

2 What will happen?

Use the ideas to say what will happen.

Example: 1. I really like surfing. – Oh, then you'll love Cornwall!

2. I have to work late today. – No problem. ...
3. I didn't do my homework. – Too bad! ...
4. Hurry up! The train leaves in an hour. – Don't worry, it's not far to the station. ...
5. Let's book the train tickets now. Tomorrow ...

they be more expensive

you love Cornwall ✓   we not be late

we cook dinner for you

Mum say you can't play on your computer

LANGUAGE

3 What people say

Luke has just called his family from Cornwall. Read what they say. What does Luke tell his friends?

Start like this: Jamie says he ...

1. Jamie: I know about the Celts from the Asterix stories. They're my favourite comics.
2. Irina: You must bring some Celtic souvenirs! I love everything Celtic.
3. Mr Elliot: Sherlock is really missing you! He must go with you next time.
4. Mrs Elliot: The whole family will go to Cornwall next year. I'm going to make a list of places to visit when you're back home.

S 2/26–29
L 3/31–34 ◉

A harp[1] on the water – a Welsh legend

Most countries have their legends – stories handed down from generation to generation. These stories talk of kings and queens, of fights between good and bad, rich and poor. Maybe you know the legend of Robin Hood, or of King Arthur? This one from Wales is about what happened to a very cruel[2] king.

5 Long long ago, at the beginning of time on this island, there was a very cruel king who lived in a stone palace where the lake of Bala is now. People said about him: "He kills[3] who he can," and it was true – he
10 killed many.

One day, not long after he became king, and while he was still a young man, he was walking in his garden and thinking about cruelty when he suddenly heard a
15 voice. It sounded like something between a silver bell and a bird's cry[4] and it said: "Vengeance[5] will come. Vengeance will come." Then he heard a second voice, farther away than the first. It asked: "When
20 will it come? When will it come?" Then the first voice replied: "In the third generation.

The third generation." At this he laughed loudly and shouted through the garden: "If it doesn't come before that, why should I care?"
25

And he planned to be crueller than ever.

Years later, the king's three sons[6] were born[7] and they were even crueller than he was. One day he was again walking
30 in the garden when he heard the same voices. They were crying the same words: "Vengeance will come. When will it come? In the third generation, the third generation." Again he laughed loudly.
35 "I laugh in the face of vengeance," he shouted. And he hurried back into the palace to teach his sons more cruelty.

Years passed[8], until the day when the whole palace was celebrating the birth of
40 a son to the king's son and heir[9]. The king sent his guards out into the country. They had to tell everyone who loved the king (and their own lives too) to hurry to the palace to celebrate. One guard had to find
45 a harp player with white hair who lived high up in the hills; he should play music for all the people who came to eat and dance in the palace that night.

The harp player didn't want to come,
50 but he had to. When he saw the silver candlesticks, the golden cups and the beautiful dresses of the ladies, it felt like a strange dream and he couldn't say a word. He wasn't in the mood to play as he
55 watched the faces of the king and his sons

1 **harp** [hɑːp] Harfe | 2 **cruel** ['kruːəl] grausam | 3 **to kill** [kɪl] töten | 4 **cry** [kraɪ] Ruf, Schrei | 5 **vengeance** ['vendʒns] Rache | 6 **son** [sʌn] Sohn | 7 **to be born** [bi 'bɔːn] geboren werden | 8 **to pass** [pɑːs] vorübergehen | 9 **heir** [eə] Thronfolger

silent[16]. The moon moved behind a black cloud. In the dark the harp player couldn't see his hand in front of him and the noise of water below told him that it was dangerous to move. 85

He suddenly thought that he was crazy to follow the voice of a bird, and he remembered sadly that his harp was back at the palace. "I must go back before the dancing starts!" he shouted. But when he thought of those cruel faces he was so horrified that he couldn't move. He was so tired and it was so dark … He fell asleep quickly. 95

In the morning, he got up and rubbed[17] the sleep from his eyes. Then he rubbed them again and again because when he looked towards the palace, there was no palace there! He saw only a huge, calm lake 100 where before there were walls and towers[18]. And his harp was swimming on the water towards him.

with their hard smiles and ice-cold eyes. But the king said: "Play!", and so he had to play.

60 At midnight[10] there was a break between the eating and dancing. The harp player was left alone, with nothing to eat and drink, in a quiet corner. Suddenly he heard a clear voice which said: "Vengeance 65 will come. Vengeance will come." He turned to the window, and in the light of the moon[11] he could see a small brown bird which was flying[12] around in the garden. It seemed[13] to invite him to follow!

70 He was very tired, but he stood up and left the palace. The bird flew in front of him and showed him the path[14] he should take. At the palace wall he stopped for a moment, but "Vengeance, vengeance!" the 75 brown bird cried. Now it seemed as easy to go on as to go back. So they went on and on, until the harp player could see the hill in front of them.

When they reached[15] the top of the 80 hill at last, he was so tired that he had to sit down. For the first time the bird was

'A Harp on the Water' from *Welsh Legends and Folktales* by Gwyn Jones

→ WB 70/1–3

10 **midnight** ['mɪdnaɪt] Mitternacht | 11 **moon** [muːn] Mond | 12 **to fly** [flaɪ] fliegen |
13 **to seem** [siːm] scheinen | 14 **path** [pɑːθ] Pfad | 15 **to reach** [riːtʃ] erreichen | 16 **silent** ['saɪlənt]
still | 17 **to rub** [rʌb] reiben | 18 **tower** [taʊə] Turm

VOCABULARY

1 **Offline for a month**

a) *Sally is a 14-year old blogger from London. Last month she was offline for four weeks. Read about her experience. Fill in the gaps. Put the verbs in the right tense.*

> to spend | to send | face-to-face | to post | to download | to stay in touch | to watch | offline | social networks | to see | challenge | phone | media mad | to get

SALLY'S BLOG

MY MONTH OFFLINE – A REAL CHALLENGE!

I'm **1** ! I use the computer and the internet *very* often. I've got a smartphone, a tablet and a laptop – yes, I **2** a lot of time online. "When I was young we didn't have all those things," my Aunt Elizabeth told me one day. "I bet you can't live for a week **3** ." "Ha," I said. "Of course I can. I can even do it for a month! You'll see!"

Well, that's how it started. I wasn't able to¹ **4** with my friends on my phone or on **5** for four weeks. When my friends met in town they **6** me texts but I wasn't able to read them because I didn't have my **7** anymore. They **8** photos I wasn't able to **9** , and when they **10** videos or **11** new music and then talked about how great it all was, I didn't know what they were talking about. And once, my friend Anne forgot that I was offline. At school, she asked me angrily, "Why didn't you come to my party?!" "*What* party?" I replied. "My birthday party!" Anne answered. Oops, I never **12** her invitation! So that wasn't so great.

But I also discovered that I had more time for other things when I was offline. I read more books, I did more sports and I talked to people **13** more often. But now I'm happy to be online again and tell you about this experience. Try it. It's a real **14** !

b) *Would you be able to stay offline for a month? Say why / why not.*

MEDIATION

2 **A new computer game**

Your little brother has a new computer game, but the instructions are in English and he doesn't understand everything. Explain the main ideas of the game to him.

Welcome to **Jungle World**, where Jolly Joe and his monkey friends swing from tree to tree and try to grab as much fruit as they can! But they have to be careful – the jungle is a dangerous place full of wild animals who want the fruit *and* you! Choose which monkey you want to be and give him / her a name. Then start your adventure through the jungle. With **S-P-A-C-E** your monkey jumps. Press ← → if you want to move left or right and press ↑ ↓ to go up or down. Try to grab as much fruit as you can – the more you get, the more points you get! You find different kinds of small fruit in the trees – but watch out: There are snakes in the trees too! The fruit on the ground is bigger, but be careful there too: Before you can grab some fruit, a tiger or lion could grab *you*! Enjoy **Jungle World**.

1 **I wasn't able to …** [ˌaɪ ˈwɒznt ˈeɪbl̩ tə] ich konnte nicht …

WRITING **3** **A postcard from …**

Have a look at the material you collected for the Task in Unit 5. Imagine you've been to one of the places. Write a postcard to your friend / your grandma / … . Tell them …

Greetings from Scotland –
The Highland Games

– what you did

– what the weather was like

– anything special about the place where you are (landscape, sights, events, etc.)

– anything strange / interesting / exciting that happened to you

– any special food you ate

LISTENING **4** **Travelling around the world: Announcements**

L 3/35 ⊙

a) *Listen to five announcements and say where the people are. Which words helped you to find out about where they are?*

b) *Listen again. Who is the announcement important for? What is the most important information for these people?*

c) *Your turn: Write your own announcement and read it to your partner. Your partner has to guess where you are.*

WRITING **5** **The world 50 years from now**

*In a short text, make predictions about the future. What will life be like 50 (or 100, 200) years from now? Use the **will** future in your text, and think of these ideas:*

how people will live / travel **|** what people will eat / drink **|** what school / nature / technology will be like **|** how people will communicate with each other

forest skyscrapers to live in

robots for cleaning the house

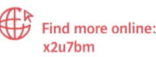
Find more online:
x2u7bm

British stories and legends

Every country has special places where famous historical people lived or important events happened. When we don't know all the facts, we like to hear strange and wonderful stories about them. But how much is really true?

SPEAKING

1 Warm-up

What famous historical people do you know about in your country or in Britain?

READING

2 Typical ingredients of legends

a) *Read the text. Which ingredients do you like in a story or legend? Why?*

Legends are stories about people in history – but usually they aren't completely true. Often, writers have taken historical events and changed them a bit to make the stories more exciting, or maybe to show the difference between right and wrong. Legends have colourful characters like brave kings and cruel queens, or magical characters like wizards. Heroes ('good guys') and villains ('bad guys') have dangerous fights – of course, the good guy usually wins!

Popular heroes are often brave knights, but sometimes they're just normal men and they do brave things to help other people. Villains can be dangerous criminals or very powerful people. They use their power in a bad way. And finally, there are more modern legends from popular books, like Sherlock Holmes. He was a private detective and solved mysterious crimes. He never lived at all, but people all over the world love to think he did!

b) *Look at the stills of Jinsoo and Marley. They're playing the roles of three famous British legends. What do you think the stories are about? What do you know about them?*

Useful phrases

Nouns: king | queen | wizard | hero / heroine | villain | knight | robber | outlaw

Adjectives: colourful | magical | brave | cruel | dangerous | powerful | mysterious

Phrases: to have a fight | to hide in the forest | to use your power | to solve a crime

VIEWING

3 Stories and legends (1)

13 **a)** *Watch the film and take notes about the three legends.*

b) *Match the sentence parts. Find the correct statements for each character.*

1. Sherlock Holmes was a private detective.
2. Robin Hood was a famous outlaw.
3. King Arthur was a powerful king.

a) Dr Watson was his assistant.
b) Many people think Tintagel was his castle.
c) He lived in Sherwood Forest, near Nottingham.
d) He lived in Baker Street in London.
e) His knights sat at the Round Table.
f) He loved Maid Marian.
g) He solved many mysterious crimes.
h) He stole from the rich and gave to the poor.

VIEWING

4 Stories and legends (2) → WB 71/1–2

a) *Watch the film again. Which characters have which props?*

b) *Your turn: Read the skills box. Then find out about another character from a legend or story, maybe a woman like the Celtic queen Boudicca (she fought against the Romans), Vivien, the Lady[6] of the Lake (she gave King Arthur his sword[7] Excalibur) or Miss Marple (a detective in Agatha Christie's crime stories). Which costume, props or set could you give that character in a film? Why?*

c) *Role play: In groups of three, each of you chooses to be one of the characters. Your characters meet. Talk to each other about*

1. where you live
2. what you do
3. what you wear and carry
4. what's good and bad about your life.

Example:
A: Hi there. I'm Robin, I help the poor.
B: And I'm Miss Marple. I love to solve mysterious crimes.
C: …

> bell | castle | bow and arrow[1] |
> gloves | cape[2] | crown[3] |
> lucky charm | magnifying glass[4] | cap[5]

Film skills

A film uses more than pictures, sounds and words to tell a story. It also uses **costumes**, **props** and a **set**. The characters wear **costumes** and they carry or use **props**. We can also see where they live – this is called the **set**.

Example:
If you want to show that a woman is a queen, she can wear a crown and beautiful clothes and live in a castle.

Robin, I hope you don't think you're the *only* hero in this forest!

Of course not, Marian.

1 **bow and arrow** [ˌbəʊ ən ˈærəʊ] Pfeil und Bogen | 2 **cape** [keɪp] Umhang |
3 **crown** [kraʊn] Krone | 4 **magnifying glass** [ˈmæɡnɪfaɪŋ ˌɡlɑːs] Lupe |
5 **cap** [kæp] Kappe; Mütze | 6 **lady** [ˈleɪdi] Herrin; Dame | 7 **sword** [sɔːd] Schwert

Legende

Diese Symbole und Erklärungen zeigen dir, wie du mit den Hilfen, Aufgaben und Aktivitäten auf den *Diff pool*-Seiten arbeiten kannst.

△ Hilfe zur Unit-Aufgabe | oder eine leichtere Variante der Unit-Aufgabe | oder eine zusätzliche Aufgabe

▲ eine zusätzliche Herausforderung

Unit 1

△ **1 Feelings** → Help with Check-in, p. 13/3

How can you feel in these situations? Match the feelings with the sentences. There's often more than one answer.

1. There's a test in English tomorrow.
2. Your team won a football match.
3. You forgot your homework – again.
4. You know all the answers in class today.
5. You're the new student.
6. You're alone, and you don't know what to do.
7. You're at the park and are playing with your friends.
8. You meet your favourite star.
9. You can't find your lucky charm.
10. You have chocolate on your white jeans and everyone can see it.

excited   nervous   happy   sad   shy   bad   good   proud   bored   angry   embarrassed

▲ **2 Charity work** → After Station 1, p. 14/1

*Do you know any children in charity projects? What can **you** do to raise money? Write down some ideas and prepare a short talk for the class.*

△ **3 Irregular simple past forms** → Instead of Station 1, p. 14/2 b)

Put in the correct past forms. Use the verbs below.

Two years ago the students ▢1 (do) fun activities and ▢2 (get) money for Comic Relief. They ▢3 (bring) the money to school. Then the school ▢4 (put) all the money together and ▢5 (give) it to the charity. Red Nose Day ▢6 (be) a non-uniform day, so everyone ▢7 (come) to school in different clothes. But they all ▢8 (wear) something red. Of course they all ▢9 (have) red noses too. Some students ▢10 (take) funny photos for the school website.

got   brought   gave   was   took   wore   had   put   did   came

△ **4** **Sounds** → After Station 1, p. 15/3

How do you say these simple past forms? Put them in the right box, then read them to your partner. Can you hear the difference?

played   stopped   acted   danced   collected   chased

laughed   watched   wanted   started   looked   turned   jumped

[d]	[t]	[ɪd]
played	stopped	acted

△ **5** **The star of the show** → Instead of Station 1, p. 15/5

What does Sherlock tell his dog friends the next day? Write the text again in his words, and use the verbs in the simple past below.

Start: I **did** lots of great tricks in the comedy show yesterday.

1. Sherlock does lots of great tricks in the comedy show.   2. First he jumps over a big box.
3. Then he runs around and chases his tail.   4. After that he dances on a skateboard, and when Olivia starts to play the sax he also sings.   5. The people love it.   6. They laugh and clap and give lots of money to Comic Relief.   7. Luke and his friends try to do their best too, but everyone's eyes are on Sherlock.   8. He feels so happy and proud – he is the real star of the show!

was   did ✔   ran   danced   sang   chased   loved   started

tried   laughed   gave   were   clapped   jumped   felt

△ **6** **A report about a special activity** → Help with Station 1, p. 16/7

What did these people do to raise money for charity? The words below can help you.

| sell old things \| flea market | make cakes and biscuits \| cake sale | run for charity \| find sponsors \| pay money per metre | organise talent show \| sell tickets \| sell drinks |

△ **7** **What they didn't do and what they did** → After Station 2, p. 18/12

Tony was tired last week, but Lou wasn't – so they didn't do things together. What didn't they do? What did they do? Take turns!

Example: You: Tony didn't go skating with Lou, he read a book.
        Your partner: Lou didn't read a book, she went skating in the park.

go skating in the park

swim in the boating lake

play tennis with a friend

buy cheese at Greenwich Market

prepare dinner for her friends

read a book

watch TV

sleep on the sofa

listen to music

play a computer game

▲ **8** **A perfect day** → After Station 2, p. 18/12

Think of something you did on a perfect day. (It needn't be true). Now your partner must find out what it was. He / She can ask questions like these:

Did you do something funny / exciting? Did you do it at home / in the park? Did you do it with friends / parents / alone? Were you nervous / excited / happy?

Think of more questions. Take notes, and then tell your classmates what your partner did on his / her perfect day!

△ **9** **The new forms** → After Station 3, p. 21/20 b)

Tony and Lou are fighting! What do they say?

Tony: I'm **1** (big) than you, Lou!
Lou: OK, I'm not as **2** (big) as you, but I am **3** (nice).
Tony: Maybe. But I'm **4** (popular) than you!
Lou: Oh no, you aren't. That's because I'm **5** (funny) than you.
Tony: You aren't as **6** (funny) as I am. Your jokes are **7** (bad) than my jokes! And I'm **8** (fast) than you.
Lou: That's because you're **9** (tall). But I'm **10** (intelligent). I can use my skates – and then I'm **11** (fast) than you!

△ **10** Say what's different → Instead of Station 3, p. 21/21

Make sentences with comparisons.

Example: 1. Wales is **smaller than** England.

1. Wales is ▮▮ ▮▮ (small) England.
2. The weather today is ▮▮ ▮▮ (bad) yesterday.
3. Route B is ▮▮ ▮▮ (easy) route A.
4. The courses aren't ▮▮ ▮▮ ▮▮ (expensive) most people think.
5. I'm not ▮▮ ▮▮ ▮▮ (nervous) I was about new challenges.

△ **11** Who's the tallest? → After Station 3, p. 21/22

Find out about your classmates! Choose one of the ideas in the box, find two partners and stand next to each other! Who is taller than you? Who has got the most interesting hobby? When you have got a group, shout "Stop!" and present your group to the class. Find the next group.

| tall / short | young / old | boring / interesting hobby | big / small family |

| long / short way to school | young / old parents | silly / nice brother / sister |

▲ **12** The best thing ever → After Station 3, p. 21/22

✏ *Choose two of these things and write a short text about them. Use **than** and **as … as** too.
You can start like this: The tastiest meal I ever had was … It was tastier than…*

| tasty meal[1] | good film | nice teacher | funny book | exciting holiday | bad joke |

△ **13** The secret → Help with Story, p. 24/3 b)

✏ *You can use these ideas and phrases to write your scene.*

1. Look! I think that window … / … help me up?
2. Hey, here's another … / Do you think it's …? / Shshsh, quiet! / Don't … noise!
3. There's a light[2] …! / I think it's … window! / Let's throw …
4. Who's there? / Oh, it's you! / I heard …
5. We can use this to … / I can climb up, and then I can open …

1 tasty meal [ˈteɪsti ˈmiːl] leckeres Essen; leckere Mahlzeit | **2 light** [laɪt] Licht

Unit 2

△ 1 Choose your London → Help with Check-in, p. 37/3

Here are some useful phrases that can help you to discuss where you want to go.

> **Useful phrases**
>
> I'd like to visit … It's free. | I think … is the best place. Let's go there!
>
> We must see …, it's fantastic. | Can we go to …? I hear it's really great.
>
> I'm sure it's fun to …, so I really want to …

△ 2 What are they going to do next week? → After Station 1, p. 38/3

Monday	Tuesday	Wednesday	Thursday	Friday
Amir and Jay – go to the cinema	*Amir – go shopping with Aunt Yasmin, buy a London T-shirt*	*Amir – meet Jay's friends in the afternoon*	*Amir and Shahid – visit Cutty Sark*	*Amir and Jay – have a sleepover at Luke's house*

Amir tells his mum about these plans in an e-mail – what does he write?

Start like this: Dear Mum, I can't call you very often next week because I have so many plans! On Monday, Jay and I are going to go … On Tuesday, Aunt Yasmin is going to …

△ 3 What's going to happen? → Help with Station 1, p. 39/4

These words can help you to write about the people in the picture on p. 53:

open the door   clean the street   take the bus   buy an ice cream

give some money   go to the cinema   play the saxophone

Start: **1.** The old man and woman are going to sit down.   **2.** The man is going to …

△ 4 Guess my plans for tomorrow → Help with Station 1, p. 39/5

What can you do where? These ideas can help you to guess your partner's plans. Match the activities with the right places first.

1. London Dungeon
2. London Eye
3. Royal Observatory
4. Shakespeare's Globe
5. Brick Lane

a) learn about the theatre, watch a Shakespeare play
b) stand on the time line, watch the time ball fall down
c) buy great clothes, see street art
d) get a great view of London
e) hear horror stories, see ghosts

△ **5** **The photo story** → Help with Station 2, p. 41/7

Olivia, Holly, Amir and Jay all have different feelings about the food challenge.
Look at the ideas about what they might say.

Jay	Olivia	Holly	Amir
really like music | fantastic street shows | not so hungry	like a challenge | try something exciting | find cafés boring	doesn't know where the cafés are | try to find something special | everything so expensive	nervous | not know where to look | happy to go with Olivia

▲ **6** **A game: Why didn't you buy any food?** → After Station 2, p. 41/7

One of you is Jay, one of you is Olivia. Olivia starts with the question below. Jay must quickly give
three different answers. Olivia chooses one and writes it down. Then it's her turn to answer
with three different sentences. Jay chooses one, writes it down and goes on with three different
sentences. Go on like this till you have the perfect dialogue.

Start: **Olivia:** Why didn't you buy any food?

> I didn't feel hungry any more.
> I was watching the street shows and they were great.
> I didn't have any money.
> What about your pocket money?
> Why not?
> Maybe someone took it!
> I forgot it at home.
> …

△ **7** **Compound words with *some* and *any*** → After Station 2, p. 41/9

a) *Fill the gaps with **some** or **any**.*

Jay: Let's buy `1` drinks. I have `2` money left.
Olivia: Oh, no! I don't want `3` drinks, and I'm still hungry. Have you got `4` crisps left, Holly?
Holly: No, sorry. I haven't got `5` crisps, but I've got `6` biscuits.

b) *Complete the words with **some** or **any**.*

Amir hasn't bought `1` **thing** for his mum yet, so the friends are looking for souvenir shops. "How much do you want to spend?" Jay wants to know.
"Well, I can't buy `2` **thing** expensive, I've only got a few pounds. But I need `3` **thing** for my mum – maybe there's `4` **thing** in this little shop?" Amir answers.
"I don't think so. Look at the prices! Let's go `5` **where** else," Holly says. "What about Greenwich Market? Or does `6` **one** have a better idea?"

▲ 8 Sherlock, you crazy dog! → After Station 2, p. 41/9

Luke's mum is away at the weekend.
She wrote a note for the family – but
Sherlock found it and now it's in pieces!
Match the parts and write a new note
in the right order.

1. You needn't buy
2. Remember: someone must
3. I wanted to get to the station, so
4. There's something
5. Lots of love for
6. Can someone please
7. I don't want to find
8. Everybody should
9. Hi everyone, I hope

a) clean the windows?
b) in the fridge for you, please check.
c) anything for dinner.
d) clean up a bit.
e) any food on the sofa when I come back.
f) you can manage without me!
g) I didn't do everything before I left.
h) take Sherlock for a walk tomorrow morning.
i) everybody, Mum.

△ 9 Complete the text → Instead of Station 2, p. 41/10

Fill the gaps with these words. Use each word only once.

Holly: What can we do till we meet Shahid later? Has `1` got a good
suggestion?
Jay: It must be `2` that costs `3` – we haven't got any money left.
Olivia: Let's just walk around. I'm sure that's fun for `4` new in London like
Amir. There are lots of interesting things to see `5` you look.
What do you think, Amir?

Amir: Well, if `6` wants to make a different suggestion – yes, I'd like that.
Holly: Is there `7` special you'd like to go or `8` special you'd like to see?
Amir: Well, `9` is special for me – it's all amazing. But I'd love to walk near
the river.
Jay: Is that OK with `10`? – Great, come on, let's go and find the Thames!

`nothing`
`everywhere`
`anybody`
`someone`
`something`
`everybody`
`everything`
`nobody`
`anywhere`
`anything`

△ 10 Act it out! → After Station 3, p. 43/14

Write these activities on cards. One of you
chooses an activity and acts it without words.
The others guess what you're doing, and how.

smile happily | dance slowly | talk quietly |
look around nervously | walk carefully |
write fast | sing loudly | shout aggressively

▲ 11 A treasure in the Thames → Instead of Story, p. 50/4

Think of one thing that the friends find in the Thames: a gold coin, an old ring, a statue,
an oil lamp … Tell the story of how they find it, what they do with it, etc.

3

Unit 3

△ **1 Talk about sports** → Help with Check-In, p. 54/2 b)

Two students made these word clouds. What are their favourite sports? And what sports are **you** *interested in? You can use the words to talk about it.*

▲ **2 Have you really done that?** → After Station 1, p. 57/3

Work with a partner. Each of you writes down six very strange or exciting activities. **One** *of them must be an activity that you have really done. Exchange your activities and find out which one* **your** *partner has done.*

eat worms – take a llama to the park – go water-skiing with my granny – play with a tarantula[1] – sleep in a haunted house[2]

△ **3 Great runners** → After Station 1, p. 59/7

Lisa and Mark help to organise the London Marathon; they need great runners. Put the verbs into the present perfect.

Lisa: We need some great runners this year. Mark, **1** (you write an e-mail to) last year's winners?

Mark: Yes, I have. But I **2** (get) answers from everyone yet. What about the German twins[3], Klara and Lena – I **3** (find) some info about them on the internet.

Lisa: **4** (they win) anything yet? I **5** (never hear) of them.

Mark: They **6** (run) in a few important races. Klara **7** (win) one big marathon, the Frankfurt City Marathon. Lena **8** (win) yet, but she was 'Best European' in the Hamburg Marathon. They always run together.

Lisa: **9** (you check) if they have a website?

Mark: Of course I have. Here, I **10** (copy) their address for you. Let's write them an e-mail. We **11** (not have) famous twins in the Marathon yet.

Lisa: No, it's a good idea to ask them. But wait till I **12** (look) at their website first!

1 **tarantula** [təˈræntjələ] Vogelspinne | 2 **haunted house** [ˌhɔːntɪd ˈhaʊs] Geisterhaus | 3 **twins** [twɪnz] Zwillinge

▲ **4 Write a profile about Brandon** → After Station 2, p. 59/7

*For a magazine, write a short profile about a rich[1] and famous
young young actor, Brandon Fairchild. What has he **already / just / never
done**, or **not yet done**? What is he **going to do** in the future?
Use the ideas below, but also add some of your own ideas.
Be creative! (Use a dictionary for help with new words.)*

already ✔	buy a cool house in Hollywood
never ✘	have a famous girlfriend
just ✔	get award[2] for 'Coolest Actor'
not yet ✘	find a new house in London
future plans ✔	buy his own ship / win an Oscar

△ **5 Children and accidents** → Help with Station 2, p. 59/9

*These words can help you to tell your partner in English
about the German survey.*

Remember, your partner
only needs to understand
the main ideas. You needn't
try to translate everything
word for word!

young people   often   get hurt[3]   have accidents

per cent[4]   every year   injury[5]   see a doctor   small children

△ **6 The London Mini Marathon** → Help with Story, p. 66/1b)

These words and phrases for the three pictures can help you to retell the story.

When the race started,
Gwen was sure … | Olivia
wasn't there, so … | Gwen
was a bit worried about … |
She told Luke, "Don't …" |
Luke saw two people in …

Ten minutes later, Gwen
felt … | She told herself
… | Then there was a
problem with the … |
They got … | But Luke
and Gwen …

Suddenly, … pulled out a
phone and … chaos … |
Another runner … | But
Gwen and Luke finished
… | Olivia found out that
the dog and cat were …

1 rich [rɪtʃ] reich | **2 award** [ə'wɔːd] Auszeichnung; Preis | **3 to get hurt** [get'hɜːt] sich verletzen |
4 per cent [pə'sent] Prozent | **5 injury** ['ɪndʒəri] Verletzung

△ **7 What's the person like?** → Help with Story, p. 66/2

✎ *Which of these words can you use if you want to say something **positive** about someone? Which ones are **negative**? Make two lists. Some of the words can help you to describe the children and their actions.*

> brave | unfriendly | stupid | fast |
> polite | crazy | clever | careful |
> helpful | funny | silly | interesting |
> great | good | boring | confident |
> friendly | popular | awful | nice

△ **8 Useful phrases from the story** → Help with Story, p. 66/3

Complete the phrases; you know them from the story. This can help with your mind map.

1. "My charity does a lot of really important work, so it really ▮ to me."
2. "Olivia can't join us. That's ▮!"
3. "You're silly, not me! So ▮ me silly."
4. "This ▮ great! After all that training, this is the moment, *my* moment!"
5. "There are so many people here, and it's my first marathon! I'm ▮! You too?"

▲ **9 A game: Frozen image⁶!** → After Story, p. 66/3

👥 *Get together in groups of four or five. Choose a scene from the story and practise a frozen image of that scene. (Practise in another room so your classmates can't see you.) Back in the classroom, the others then shout "One… two… freeze⁷!" and your group does its frozen image. Your classmates must guess the scene and explain how they guessed.*

Unit 4

△ **1 Media collocations** → Instead of Check-in, p. 74/2

✎ **a)** *Write down all the media collocations in the text.*

> Tony loves the world of media! He checks his text messages all the time. He loves texting his friends. He sends and receives text messages during lessons too. (Bad boy!) And Tony has joined a popular social network: He's on Mousebook, of course. He regularly posts photos and changes his profile. It's important for Tony to stay in touch with his friends, so he often talks to them on video chat. At weekends, he often plays video games or takes part in discussions. It's easy to forget the time when you're online! Lou isn't so happy about this: Tony doesn't always reply to her text messages quickly enough, and she has to check his profile on Mousebook to see what he's doing!

b) *You can use some of the verbs with more than one noun, e.g., you can **change** your **profile** and you can **check** your **profile** too. How many different media collocations of nouns and verbs can you find?*

6 frozen image [ˌfrəʊzn̩ ˈɪmɪdʒ] erstarrtes Bild | **7 to freeze** [friːz] erstarren

▲ **2** **Ruby's answer** → After Station 1, p. 76/1

Work with a partner. What different bits of advice does Ruby have for Lauren? Write them down on little pieces of paper. Then put the pieces of paper face down on the table. Take turns to pick one up and talk about it. Do you think it's good advice? Why / Why not?

△ **3** **Using linking words: Tony and his phone** → After Station 1, p. 77/2

Read what Tony's friend Robby says about Tony. Use these words to make one sentence out of the two. There's sometimes more than one way!

Example: Tony plays video games too often.
He doesn't call me. → **Whenever** Tony plays video games, he doesn't call me.

| after | before | as soon as |
| whenever | because | when |

1. He got a new smartphone for his birthday. We often saw each other before that.
2. Tony can't leave his phone alone for one minute. He's really into texting.
3. I wanted to go to the cinema with him yesterday. He said "yes".
4. At the cinema, someone said, "You must turn off your phone. The film is starting."
5. Tony heard that. He was shocked.
6. Sometimes a phone rings at the cinema. It always makes the other people angry.

△ **4** **Symbols of friendship** → Help with Station 1, p. 78/6 b)

Here are some phrases and ideas for talking about symbols of friendship.

> **Useful phrases**
>
> A symbol can be **something you do**, like … when you wear the same clothes / colours | when you have a secret together | when you talk about / help each other with problems | …
>
> A symbol can be **a thing**, like … a photo together | a mascot keyring[1] / a mascot toy | special words for things | favourite stickers | …

△ **5** **I've finally got my own smartphone** → After Station 2, p. 80/10

*Make sentences with **must, mustn't, needn't, have to** or **don't have to**.*

1. Now that I've got my own phone I ▭ ask my mum to use hers.
2. But the bad thing now is that I ▭ pay for all my calls myself.
3. My parents are strict[2], so at 9:00 p.m. I ▭ leave my phone with them for the night.
4. But I ▭ give it to them at the weekend.
5. If it costs too much I'll get into trouble[3] so I ▭ spend a lot of time on the internet.
6. Excuse me, I ▭ go now – my best friend is waiting in the chatroom for me!

1 mascot keyring [ˌmæskət ˈkiːrɪŋ] Maskottchen-Schlüsselanhänger | **2** strict [strɪkt] streng |
3 to get into trouble [get ˌɪntə ˈtrʌbl] Ärger bekommen |

▲ 6 VIC – very important chats! → After Station 2, p. 80/10

*Complete the sentences. Use a verb from the box and **must / mustn't**, **have to / don't have to** or **needn't**.*

1. This is a big secret. You …
2. It's 9:00 p.m. so I …
3. Last week I forgot to return[4] the books. This week I …
4. "Have you finished your studies?" – "Yes, I know everything for the test. I …"
5. We're going to the cinema tonight, so you …

> tell   remember   study
>
> text   go

▲ 7 Giving and taking advice → After Station 2, p. 80/11

*On cards, write down situations where **you** might need advice. (The ideas on the right can help you.) Put them face down on the table, between you and your partner. Take turns to choose a card, read the situation to your partner, and say what advice you have for him / her.*

> not good at school
>
> trouble with teacher
>
> fight with friend
>
> not enough pocket money
>
> small room   …

△ 8 You could do that, but I think you should… → After Station 2, p. 80/11

*Read these situations and decide what advice you want to give. Do you need **could** or **should**? (Remember, there's a difference! Check G11 for help.)*

1. Oh no. I left my smartphone at home!
   (use mine)
2. This phone doesn't work at all.
   (buy a new one)
3. Do you like this photo? I want to post it.
   (not post private photos)
4. My computer has been so slow!
   (let me check it)
5. Hmm, 'World of Heroes' or 'Super Talents' – which game is better?
   (try both)
6. Susan is still angry because I sent her that text.
   (tell her you're sorry)
7. I think my profile is boring.
   (write something interesting / exciting)

> Oh, I've got the worst headache!

> I could make some tea, Tony. That always helps you.

---

4 **to return** [rɪˈtɜːn] zurückgeben

▲ **9** **Media mad** → After Station 2, p. 81/12

When you read a flow chart, always start at the top and work down, step by step. First read the text in the middle box in the first line, and then decide if you must follow the red (= no) or green (= yes) flash. Are you surprised abour your results?

Work with a partner. Choose a box for your partner (e.g. 'five / four' is the box with "You don't care about video games"). Your partner must find the box and comment on it. Then it's his / her turn.

Example: A: Two / two. "You check your messages all the time!"

B: I don't know. When I'm bored I often check them. But when I'm with my friends, I don't do that. What about you?

△ **10** **Writing a dialogue** → Help with Story, p. 88/1c)

Here are some ideas to help you write your dialogue.

Mrs Preston:	When did you get … **|** Didn't you ask them what… **|** What happened when … **|** That sounds like a lot of fun, but …
Mr Preston:	When I got home … **|** I was angry because… **|** I found some candles and thought … **|** The kids used their smartphones to …
Jay:	I thought about the party we wanted to have and … **|** It takes so long to write … **|** I'm sorry, it was stupid to … **|** I was so worried when…
Olivia:	Don't you know how dangerous it is to … ? **|** Why didn't you wait for … ? **|** We were really lucky that … **|** I think next time you should … **|** But it's OK, don't worry …

Unit 5

△ **1** **Talking about places** → Help with Check-In, p. 92/1

Where should these people go on holiday?

Start like this: Lou should go to Wales. She can visit …

1. Lou likes stories about the past and she likes to visit old castles.
2. Sandy loves horses and she likes to be outside every day.
3. Andrew is interested in music and traditions.
   He loves watching shows and listening to traditional songs.
4. Ellen is a good swimmer and loves the sea. She thinks it's great to walk along the beach and look for treasures.

2 Frequently asked questions → After Station 1, p. 95/3

Work with a partner and fill in the gaps. Take turns to ask and answer the questions.

1. ▮ rain today?
2. What ▮ do ten years from now?
3. ▮ meet friends after school?
4. Where ▮ spend your holidays?
5. When ▮ do your homework?
6. ▮ watch a scary film with me?
7. ▮ buy me some ice cream?
8. Where ▮ live when you're 30?

3 Mediation: At a German station → After Station 1, p. 95/3

*An English boy is trying to buy a ticket at a German station. He's talking to a man, but the man doesn't speak English. Can you help the boy? Try to use the **will** future where you can.*

Boy: Excuse me, I need to take the next train to Cologne. Will it wait a few more minutes?

Man: *Entschuldigung, ich spreche kein Englisch.*

You: *Dieser Junge muss …*

Man: *Ach so. Nein, der Zug wartet nicht. Aber ich bin sicher, der nächste Zug wird ihm besser gefallen. Es ist ein Express-Zug.*

You: Sorry, the train … But the man is sure …

Boy: Express train? Won't … expensive?

You: …

Man: *Warte kurz, ich schaue nach.*

You: …

Man: *Nein, es wird sogar günstiger! Und er wird früher in Köln ankommen als der frühere Zug!*

You: No, he says it'll … And, he says …

Boy: Cool! I … earlier and I … more money for my visit in Cologne! – Yes, I think I … buy that ticket.

You: Great, but I must go now or my train … leave without me!

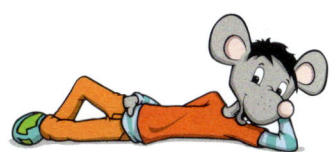

4 Buying train tickets on the internet → After Station 1, p. 96/5

Fill in the new travel words.

| price | inward | arrive | one-way | return | change | fee | depart | outward |

First, Luke forgets to click on ▮1▮, but he doesn't only need the ▮2▮ for a ▮3▮ ticket. So he has to fill in the dates for the ▮4▮ journey and then the ▮5▮ journey. He clicks on ▮6▮, but then he remembers that he doesn't know how long the journey takes. So he chooses the time he wants to ▮7▮. He learns that for St Agnes you have to ▮8▮ at London Bridge and Paddington. Then he wants to know how much the booking[1] ▮9▮ is.

---

1 **booking** ['bʊkɪŋ] Reservierung

△ **5** **What will the weather be like?** → Help with Station 1, p. 96/6

Here are weather pictures and words to help you with exercise 6 on page 96.

Start like this: Today the weather is still … | But tomorrow it'll be… |
Temperatures[1] will … | There will be …

lots of sun

temperatures up to 30 degrees[2]

no wind

partly cloudy

not too much wind

warm   24 degrees

storm   thunder

lots of wind

temperatures fall to 17 degrees

△ **6** **I'm coming soon** → After Station 2, p. 99/9

Change the bold words to put the sentences in indirect speech. Use the words below.

write   say   tell   promise   hope

1. I'll be **there** soon!
2. I'm so excited to see **you** again.
3. I want to see where **you** go to school and meet **your** friends.
4. I'll **bring** some special food. **My** mother gave it to **me**.
5. But it's not for **me** – it's all for **you**!!!
6. I promise **your** brother can have a little bit of it ;-)
7. I hope that **you** and **your** family are excited to see **me**, too.
8. Next year **you** can visit **us**! Love, Jenna

Examples: 1. She says that **she**'ll be **here** soon.
        2. She writes that …

1 **temperature** [ˈtɛmprətʃə] Temperatur | 2 **degree** [dɪˈgriː] Grad

▲ **7** **Where do you want to travel?** → After Station 2, p. 99/9

Work with a partner. Partner A talks about travelling for 20 seconds and Partner B takes notes. Then Partner B reports what Partner A thinks, hopes etc. Take turns.

Start like this: I want to travel to …
I think I can go there …
I'll take my …
But I can't take my …
When I'm there I want to … with …

▲ **8** **A poem about your home town** → After Station 2, 100/13

Write a poem about your town or area. The word groups below rhyme[3]; they can help you with your poem.
Maybe you can think of more words in English that rhyme?

city	be	sea	me	free
village	language	manage		
image	live	give	active	

like	bike	hike	site
bright	night	right	light
run	fun	sun	one

---

3 to rhyme [raɪm] sich reimen

Vocabulary

S1 Vokabelheft

Führe ein dreispaltiges Vokabelheft, in dem du auch neue
Vokabeln notieren kannst, die nicht in der Wortliste stehen.
Die erste Spalte ist für die englische Vokabel bestimmt, die
zweite für die Übersetzung und die dritte für Beispielsätze
oder alles, was dir hilft, dir die Bedeutung zu merken, z. B.
Bilder, *mind maps*, Beziehungen zu anderen Wörtern, auch
in anderen Sprachen.

S2 Vokabelkartei

Es lohnt sich, eine Vokabelkartei anzulegen, um Vokabeln
zu lernen. Sie besteht aus Karteikarten für die Vokabeln und
einem Karton mit fünf Fächern für die Karten.
Schreibe das englische Wort auf die Vorderseite der
Karteikarte und die deutsche Bedeutung auf die Rückseite.
Zusätzlich kannst du weitere Merkhilfen notieren. Stelle
zunächst alle Karten ins erste Fach.
Übe jeden Tag fünf bis zehn Minuten, und zwar so: Nimm
eine Karte nach der anderen heraus und überprüfe, ob du
die Übersetzung weißt (deutsch – englisch, englisch –
deutsch). Wenn ja, stellst du die Karte ins zweite Fach.
Mache weiter, bis das erste Fach leer ist. Das zweite Fach
bearbeitest du dann genauso, allerdings nicht jeden Tag,
sondern nur einmal in der Woche, das dritte Fach alle zwei
Wochen usw.

S3 Wörter im Zusammenhang

Wörter sind die Bausteine der Sprache. Du musst sie
natürlich lernen und jedes für sich verstehen. Zur
Beherrschung einer Sprache gehört aber auch zu wissen,
welche Kombinationen dieser Bausteine möglich sind.
Deshalb ist es wichtig, mit den Wörtern schon die richtigen
Kombinationen mitzulernen. Schreibe Wörter möglichst
immer in typischen Zusammenhängen auf.

Mit Verben kannst du passende Ergänzungen mitlernen, z. B.:

*to **read** a book, a magazine, a comic, a manga*
*to **write** a letter, an e-mail, an invitation, a blog*
*to **go** swimming, shopping, home, away, to the cinema*

Du solltest auch wissen, wann bestimmte grammatische Formen auf bestimmte Wörter folgen. Schreibe dir passende Beispiele zusammen mit der Vokabel auf, z. B.:

*I **would like** to swim, **to** read, **to** go shopping*
*I **like** swimm**ing**, read**ing**, go**ing** shopping*

Welche die richtigen Präpositionen sind, muss man in jeder Sprache auswendig lernen. Notiere auch dafür Beispiele und lerne sie, z.B.:

*The party is **on Friday**, **at seven**, **at the weekend**.*
*My house is **in Dover Street**. We're **on the road to London**.*
*London is **on the Thames**.*

S4 Methoden

Du hast schon mehrere Methoden gelernt, wie du dir Vokabeln besser einprägen kannst:

- Klebezettel mit englischen Wörtern an die entsprechenden Gegenstände in deinem Zimmer kleben

- Wörter als Bildwörter oder mit passenden Bildern aufmalen

- Wörter zusammen mit anderen, die zu einem Thema gehören, in *mind maps* anordnen

- Wörter pantomimisch darstellen und gegenseitig erraten lassen

- Wörter aussprechen, zusammen mit ihrer Übersetzung und vielleicht einem Beispielsatz aufnehmen und immer wieder anhören

- Wörter mit ähnlichen Wörtern in anderen Sprachen notieren

- Wörter, die miteinander in Beziehung stehen, zusammen notieren, z. B. verwandte Wörter, Gegensatzpaare, zusammengehörige Paare

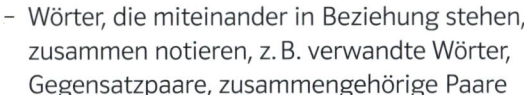

Reading

S5 Schnelllesetechniken

Normalerweise denkst du während des Lesens nicht darüber nach, wie du dabei vorgehst. Wenn du aber eine Aufgabe zu einem Text bekommst oder eine bestimmte Information suchst, liest du bewusster und gezielter. Diese Techniken helfen dir, wenn die Zeit begrenzt ist.

Skimming („den Rahm abschöpfen")	Scanning („maschinell durchsuchen")
Wenn du danach gefragt wirst, worum es in einem Text geht, sollst du ihn nicht einfach nacherzählen, sondern nur das Wichtigste (gist) zusammenfassen. Dazu kannst du den ganzen Text überfliegen und darauf achten, ob bestimmte Wörter (key words) oder Personen häufiger vorkommen. Auch die Überschrift oder Bilder können dir helfen einzuschätzen, was wichtig ist und was nicht. Diese Art des Schnelllesens nennt man *skimming*.	Wenn du nach bestimmten Einzelheiten (details) in einem Text gefragt wirst, musst du ihn überfliegen und die Stellen mit der wichtigen Information finden. Dazu suchst du gezielt nach passenden Stichwörtern (key words). Sie zeigen an, welche Teile du genauer lesen solltest, um die gesuchte Information zu bekommen. Diese Art des Überfliegens nennt man auch *scanning*.

S6 Wichtige Inhalte von Texten herausfinden

Wenn du einen Text liest, solltest du danach immer folgende Fragen beantworten können:

Who ...?	*What ...?*	*When ...?*	*Where ...?*
Wer ist beteiligt?	*Was geschieht?*	*Wann?*	*Wo?*

Dazu kannst du Schnelllesetechniken anwenden, Markierungen im Text machen und dir Fragen und Anmerkungen notieren (S8). Wenn du den Text noch genauer liest, kannst du weitere Fragen beantworten, z. B. Warum geschieht etwas? Wenn es eine Geschichte ist, wer erzählt sie? Für wen wurde der Text geschrieben (Adressat)?

S7 Gliederung als Hilfe

Um einen Text besser zu verstehen, kann es dir helfen, ihn in mehrere Abschnitte zu gliedern. Orientiere dich dabei z. B. an Absätzen und inhaltlichen Punkten, die du dir markiert hast. Überlege anschließend, was in den einzelnen Teilen jeweils das Wichtigste ist und formuliere passende Überschriften. Dies erleichtert es dir, Zusammenfassungen von Texten zu geben oder *Mediation*-Aufgaben zu lösen.

A *Henry hopes to play the lead*

B *Henry is disappointed*

C *Henry sees the positive side of things*

S8 Textbearbeitung mit Markierungen und Notizen

Im geliehenen Buch darfst du das zwar nicht, aber auf Kopien oder in Arbeitsheften solltest du dir angewöhnen, wichtige Stellen in Texten zu markieren und Randnotizen zu machen (z. B. Fragen oder Anmerkungen). Verwende am besten verschiedene Farben: Markiere z. B. wichtige inhaltliche Punkte grün und Informationen zu den Personen blau. Wörter, die du nachschlagen musst, solltest du auch hervorheben. Unterstreiche sie beispielsweise und notiere die richtige Übersetzung am Rand. So fällt dir das erneute Lesen leichter.

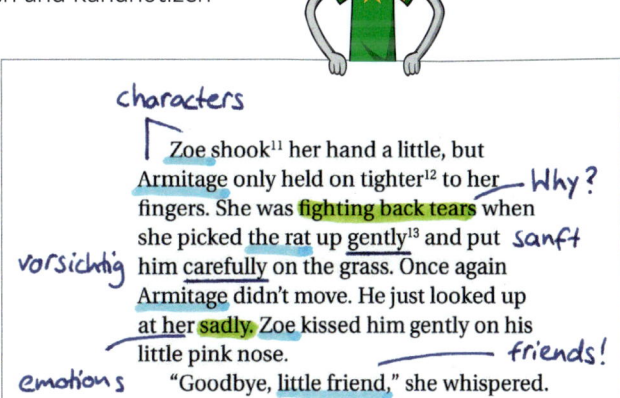

characters

Zoe shook[11] her hand a little, but Armitage only held on tighter[12] to her fingers. — Why?
She was fighting back tears when she picked the rat up gently[13] and put him carefully on the grass. — sanft
vorsichtig
Once again Armitage didn't move. He just looked up at her sadly. Zoe kissed him gently on his little pink nose. — friends!
emotions
"Goodbye, little friend," she whispered. "I'm going to miss[14] you."

S9 Umgang mit neuen Wörtern

Viele Wörter kannst du schon verstehen, obwohl du sie noch nicht gelernt hast.

1. Ähnlichkeit mit Wörtern, die du schon kennst

Oft haben verwandte Wörter den gleichen Stamm, aber andere Vorsilben oder Endungen. Wenn du z. B. *happy* schon kennst, wirst du *unhappy* sicher auch verstehen. Englische Wörter haben oft keine Endungen, aber es gibt sie in verschiedenen Wortarten. Wenn du also das Wort *guide* als Nomen kennst, kannst du dir bestimmt denken, was das Verb *to guide* oder die Zusammensetzung *travel guide* bedeutet.

2. Ähnlichkeit mit Wörtern, die du aus einer anderen Sprache kennst

Viele englische Wörter gibt es genauso oder ähnlich auch im Deutschen, z. B. *computer*, *hobby* oder *pony*. Manchmal hilft dir auch ein Wort, das du aus einer anderen Sprache kennst (Französisch, Latein, …) ein englisches Wort zu verstehen, z. B. weil es ähnlich geschrieben wird oder ähnlich klingt.

3. Verstehen der Wörter im Zusammenhang

Manchmal kannst du dir anhand eines Bildes oder einer Überschrift denken, was ein Wort in einem Text bedeutet. Und wenn du alle Wörter in einem Satz verstehst außer einem, kann dieses oft nur eine bestimmte Bedeutung haben. Was bedeutet z. B. *return* in diesem Satz?
*My dog ran away, and I was really happy when he **returned** after three days.*

Und wenn du doch im Wörterbuch nachschlagen musst, helfen dir die Tipps auf S. 25.

Writing

S10 Planung deines Textes

Überlege, für wen dein Text bestimmt ist (Adressat) und welchen Zweck er erfüllen soll. Vor dem Schreiben machst du dir am besten einen Plan: Notiere in Stichwörtern, was in der Einleitung, dem Hauptteil und dem Schluss deines Textes stehen soll. So vergisst du nichts Wichtiges und findest auch leichter eine schöne Einleitung und einen guten Schluss.

S11 Textsorten und ihre Besonderheiten

Du kennst schon einige wichtige Textsorten und ihre Haupteigenschaften:

E-mail, letter, postcard, invitation	Achte auf die richtige Anrede für den Adressaten, z.B. *Dear …,* Grußformeln am Schluss, z.B. *Yours/Love/Best wishes,* und beachte die Höflichkeitsregeln. Denke bei einem Brief an die Angabe der Empfänger- und Absenderadresse und an das Datum.
Story	Wenn du eine Geschichte vervollständigen sollst, muss dein Teil zum vorgegebenen Text passen. Vermeide also inhaltliche Widersprüche. Außerdem sollten die Erzählperspektive und die Erzählzeit nicht wechseln. Meistens sind Geschichten im *past tense* geschrieben. Gestalte deine Geschichten sprachlich abwechslungsreich und schmücke sie aus.
Dialogue	Wenn du einen Dialog, z.B. für eine Filmszene, schreibst, denke daran, dass du echte mündliche Sprache verwendest, also z.B. *short forms,* verstärkende Ausdrücke usw.
Report	Bei einem Bericht ist die Vollständigkeit und Verständlichkeit der sachlichen Informationen das Wichtigste. Er wird im *past tense* geschrieben.
Prompt cards	Wenn du dich auf eine Präsentation vorbereitest, notiere auf Karteikarten nur Stichwörter, die dich an die einzelnen Punkte des Vortrags erinnern. Schreibe z.B. wichtige Namen, Ereignisse, Orte und Daten unter die Überschriften *Who, What, Where, When.*
Flyer	Ein Flyer sollte gut lesbar sein (Schriftart- und größe) und alle wichtigen Informationen enthalten: *Who?, What?, When?, Where?, Why?* Formuliere außerdem einen ansprechenden Slogan.
Diary entry	Ein Tagebucheintrag erzählt und kommentiert vergangene und erwartete Ereignisse aus der ganz persönlichen Sicht einer Person und ist normalerweise nicht für andere Leser bestimmt.

S12 Überarbeitung deines Textes

Wenn du einen Entwurf erstellt hast, liest du ihn am besten noch einmal gründlich durch. Meistens entdeckst du so noch einige Fehler und kannst holprige Formulierungen verbessern. Nimm dabei eine Checkliste zur Hilfe (siehe rechts), damit du nichts Wichtiges vergisst. Es ist auch eine gute Übung, die Texte mit einem Partner zu tauschen.

Checkliste

Rechtschreibung:
– Wörter richtig geschrieben?
– Am Satzanfang groß?
– Getrennt oder zusammen?

Grammatik:
– Richtige Zeitformen?
– Richtige Formenbildung?

Inhalt:
– Alle wesentlichen Punkte enthalten?
– Keine inhaltlichen Fehler?
– Zusammenhänge erkennbar und logisch?

S13 Sprachliche Verbesserungen

Je größer dein Wortschatz wird, desto mehr Möglichkeiten eröffnen sich dir beim Schreiben von Texten.

Einzelne Sätze kannst du genauer und interessanter gestalten, indem du z. B. Nomen durch Adjektive oder durch weitere Nomen näher beschreibst. Verben kannst du durch adverbiale Bestimmungen ergänzen. Vergleiche die unterschiedliche Information in den beiden folgenden Sätzen:

A *I went to the shop.*

B *I went to the* big pet *shop* in Greenwich with my sister last Saturday.

Deinen gesamten Text kannst du flüssiger gestalten, indem du die Sätze miteinander verknüpfst. So werden logische Zusammenhänge klarer und der Text liest sich leichter. Vergleiche die beiden folgenden Textausschnitte. Der erste wirkt durch die unverbundenen Hauptsätze abgehackt. Der zweite enthält auch Satzgefüge aus Haupt- und Nebensätzen, die mit Hilfe von Bindewörtern *(linking words)* logische Zusammenhänge herstellen. Außerdem geben die vielen Adjektive und Adverbien genauere Informationen und machen den Text interessanter.

A *I went to the shop. I wanted a guinea pig. We looked at all the guinea pigs. I didn't like them. We wanted to leave.*
A girl came in with a box. She brought back a guinea pig. It was cute! I bought it. I'm happy.

B *I went to the big pet shop in Greenwich with my sister last Saturday* **because** *I wanted to buy a nice guinea pig. We looked at all the guinea pigs,* **but** *I didn't like them.* **Just when** *I wanted to leave, a girl came in with a box. She brought back a* **really** *cute guinea pig.* **So** *I bought it* **and** *I'm very happy now.*

Speaking

S14 Sprechen üben

Sprechen lernt man nur durch Sprechen. Du solltest dir angewöhnen, im Englischunterricht immer englisch zu sprechen, ob mit deiner Lehrerin/deinem Lehrer oder in der Partner- und Gruppenarbeit. Um Sprechen zu üben, solltest du allerdings viel mehr sprechen als nur im Unterricht. Vielleicht üben deine Freunde, Eltern oder Geschwister mit dir?

Eine Voraussetzung für das richtige Sprechen ist natürlich, dass du übst, die englischen Wörter richtig auszusprechen. Beim Lernen mit dem Buch kann dir die Lautschrift dabei helfen. Sage sie dir immer wieder laut vor. Einfacher und einprägsamer ist es natürlich, die Vokabeln richtig ausge-sprochen anzuhören und nachzusprechen. Hilfsmittel dafür sind Audio-CDs mit den Schülerbuchtexten, Lernsoftware oder Online-Wörterbücher, in denen du jedes Wort anklicken und anhören kannst.

Übe schwierig auszusprechende Laute, die anders sind als im Deutschen, z.B. das stimmhafte oder stimmlose *th* oder das *w* im Kontrast zum *v* oder ein stimmhaftes *d* oder *g* am Wortende. Dazu kannst du (lustige) Sätze erfinden, sie dir immer wieder vorsprechen und dabei das Tempo steigern, bis die Aussprache zuverlässig klappt.

Wenn du ganze Texte hörst, bekommst du ein Gefühl dafür, wie die Wörter im Textzusammenhang ausgesprochen werden. Die Aussprache unterscheidet sich manchmal stark von der Aussprache der Einzelwörter. Aufeinander treffende Laute werden z.B. häufig miteinander verbunden.

Du hast auch schon gehört, wie die Betonung die Aussprache beeinflussen kann, wenn jemand besonders starke Gefühle ausdrücken will. Das kannst du auch üben.

They **th**ought of **the th**ree **th**ousand **th**ankful **th**ieves.

Why **w**ork **w**ith **v**ocabulary **w**hen you can **v**isit a **w**onderful **v**illage **w**orld?

She wante**d** her ba**g** back and sai**d** what a nice hat she ha**d**.

This is th**e** en**d** o**f** t**h**e story. They know ove**r a** hundred different stories.

It's **so** unfair! Why doesn't anyone **ever** ask **me** what I'm feeling?

S15 Gesprochene Sprache

Auch beim Sprechen kommt es auf die Situation und deinen Gesprächspartner an, wie du dich ausdrückst. Denke z. B. auch an Höflichkeitsregeln.
In der gesprochenen Sprache ist es normal, dass Pausen, unvollständige Sätze, Wiederholungen oder Füllwörter vorkommen:

– Während bei Gleichaltrigen ein *Hi!* als Begrüßung ausreicht, ist Lehrpersonen oder fremden Erwachsenen gegenüber ein *Good morning! / Good morning …* eher angemessen.
– Statt *I want …* sagst du höflicher *I would like …* oder *Could I please have …?*
– Entscheidungsfragen beantwortest du mit Kurzantworten, nicht einfach mit *Yes* oder *No: Yes, I do. No, I'm not.*

Well, I – I really don't know. It's – **er,** *maybe you want to …?*

Es ist wichtig, einem Dialogpartner immer das Gefühl zu geben, dass er einbezogen wird. Dazu dienen *feedback phrases* und Nachfragen.

Then we went to the city farm, Mudchute, **you know.** *And there was this cute little pig –* **you saw it too, right? Guess what Linda did when she saw it!**

S16 Mündliche Aufgaben und ihre Besonderheiten

Es ist viel wichtiger, dass du regelmäßig länger zusammenhängend sprichst, als dass jedes Wort perfekt ausgesprochen und die Grammatik absolut korrekt ist. Wie wäre es, wenn jeder in deiner Klasse in einer Englischstunde eine Minute lang Englisch über ein selbst gewähltes Thema spricht? Hier findest du ein paar Tipps für bestimmte mündliche Aufgaben:

Interview	Sei höflich, aber scheue dich nicht nachzufragen, wenn du etwas nicht sofort verstehst. Achte bei der Fragestellung auf die richtige Zeitform und das richtige Hilfsverb. Antworte auch in der passenden Zeitform.
Asking/ Showing the way	Auch hier ist Höflichkeit wichtig und ganz bestimmte Vokabeln wie *go down X Street, go straight on, go past/turn left/right into Y Lane, it's on the left / right / opposite Z.*
Role play	Versetze dich in deine Rolle und versuche nachzufühlen, was die Person weiß und was sie denkt und fühlt. Verwende typische Merkmale der gesprochenen Sprache und unterstütze deine Worte mit Mimik und Gestik.
Presentation	Bereite deine Präsentation gut vor. Recherchiere die Fakten gründlich. Überlege, was dir wichtig ist und was du sagen möchtest. Besorge Material, das du zeigen willst, und bereite es so auf, dass es gut aussieht und verständlich ist. Mache dir einen Ablaufplan. Schreibe dir Notizen auf *prompt cards*. Versuche frei zu sprechen und nicht abzulesen. Übe deine Präsentation vorher und stoppe die Zeit, die du brauchst.

Mediation

S17 Bearbeitung von Mediationsaufgaben

Mediation ist die Übertragung wichtiger Informationen aus einem gesprochenen oder geschriebenen Text in eine andere Sprache, z.B. aus dem Englischen ins Deutsche oder umgekehrt. Das machst du, wenn du einen Text für jemanden zusammenfassen sollst, der die Sprache des Ausgangstexts nicht versteht. Gelegentlich kann es auch sein, dass du dolmetschen musst, also zwischen Gesprächspartnern vermittelst, die nicht dieselbe Sprache sprechen. Ganz wichtig: Es geht bei der *Mediation* niemals um eine wörtliche Übersetzung *(translation)*!

Lies dir die *Mediation*-Aufgabe gut durch und beachte besonders folgende Dinge:

Adressat:

Für wen ist die Information bestimmt?

➔ Je nachdem, wer die Person ist und wie viel sie schon weiß, sprichst du sie unterschiedlich an.

Ausgangstext

Zweck:

Wozu benötigt die Person die Information?

➔ Du musst nur die Informationen wiedergeben, die für den Adressaten in der jeweiligen Situation wichtig sind. Alles andere kannst du weglassen. Es kann aber auch vorkommen, dass du Dinge zusätzlich erklären musst.

wichtige Info

Beispiel: Dein Ausgangstext ist die Infobroschüre eines Museums, die alle Öffnungszeiten und Eintrittspreise enthält. Wenn dein Gegenüber dich fragt, ob das Museum heute geöffnet ist, musst du nicht unbedingt sagen, wann es sonst noch geöffnet oder geschlossen ist. Will die Person den Eintrittspreis wissen, kommt es auf ihr Alter an und darauf, ob sie allein oder mit einer Gruppe unterwegs ist.

Einen schriftlichen Ausgangstext kannst du in Ruhe durchlesen und die wichtigen Informationen auswählen. Dabei helfen dir alle Techniken, die auf S. 132/133 unter *Reading* beschrieben sind. Formuliere die entsprechenden Inhalte so, dass der Adressat sie gut verstehen kann.

Bei einer Dolmetscheraufgabe wird eine echte mündliche Gesprächssituation simuliert. Deshalb musst du schneller reagieren, um möglichst viel von dem sinngemäß wiederzugeben, was die Gesprächspartner zueinander sagen.

Wenn dir ein Wort in der Zielsprache nicht einfällt, umschreibe es mit anderen Worten *(paraphrasing)*. Beachte bei der schriftlichen und mündlichen Bearbeitung von *Mediation*-Aufgaben außerdem die Tipps unter *Writing* und *Speaking* (siehe S. 134–137)

Listening

S18 Hörverstehen üben

Grundsätzlich ist es zur Übung immer sinnvoll, viele echte englische Texte anzuhören, z. B. Nachrichten oder Kindersendungen in Radio und Fernsehen oder Hörbücher. Dabei ist es nicht schlimm, wenn du nicht jedes Wort verstehst. Dir wird außerdem auffallen, wie unterschiedlich die Aussprache des Englischen je nach Herkunft des Sprechers sein kann.

S19 Techniken des Hörverstehens

Analog zum Lesen gibt es auch beim Hörverstehen unterschiedliche Techniken. Beim *Listening for gist* geht es darum, das Wichtigste in einem Hörtext zu erkennen und zusammenzufassen. Beim *Listening for detail* hingegen sollst du einem Hörtext bestimmte Einzelheiten entnehmen.

Listening for gist	Listening for detail
Welche Wörter und Themen kommen mehrmals vor und spielen deshalb vermutlich eine wichtige Rolle? Höre besonders auf diese und fasse die wichtigsten Inhalte des Textes zusammen.	Nach welchen bestimmten Einzelheiten im Text wirst du gefragt? Höre besonders auf Wörter, die du in der Antwort erwartest, und die Informationen dazu.

Auch beim Hörverstehen hilft eine Tabelle wie beim Leseverstehen. Du kannst darin während des Hörens deine Notizen machen.

Who ...?   What ...?   When ...?   Where ...?

S20 Typische Hörverstehenssituationen

Manchmal hilft dir beim Hörverstehen auch die Kenntnis von typischen Textsorten und Situationen. Wenn du die Textsorte des Hörtextes kennst, überlege dir, worauf es beim Telefonieren, beim Dolmetschen, bei Präsentationen, Durchsagen, Radio- oder Fernsehsendungen ankommt und welche Themen jeweils zu erwarten sind. Gelegentlich geben dir auch Bilder Hinweise zur entsprechenden Situation: Wenn z. B. bestimmte Personen oder Orte dargestellt sind, kannst du leichter einschätzen, worum es in dem Hörtext geht. Achte beim Hören auf Geräusche sowie Stimme und Tonfall des Sprechers. In echten Gesprächssituationen oder Filmen können dir auch Gestik und Mimik das Verständnis erleichtern.

Film skills/Viewing

S21 Inhalt und Gliederung

Ein Film ist auch eine Art Text. Deshalb lassen sich viele ähnliche Fragen dazu stellen:

– Worum geht es?
– Wird eine Geschichte erzählt?
– Welche Personen spielen mit?
– Welches sind die Hauptpersonen?
– Was passiert in welcher Reihenfolge?
– Wann und wo passiert es?

– Welche Gliederung und welche Themen sind zu erkennen?
– Aus wessen Sicht wird die Geschichte erzählt?
– Wer hat den Film gemacht, für welches Publikum und wozu?

Das Anschauen und Verstehen eines Films verlangt dir jedoch nicht nur das Verständnis der Sprache ab, sondern du musst auch auf viele weitere Dinge achten.

S22 Wichtige filmische Aspekte

Wie stellen die Schauspieler den Charakter der Personen dar, die sie verkörpern? Wie drücken sie Gefühle aus?

--➤ Achte vor allem auf Sprache, Mimik und Gestik. Aber auch Kleidung oder Frisuren können eine Rolle spielen.

Wie werden Handlungsort und -zeit dargestellt *(setting)*?
--➤ Achte auf Landschaften, Gebäude und Innenräume, Kleidung und Gegenstände.

Wie wird eine bestimmte Atmosphäre geschaffen *(atmosphere)*?
--➤ Achte auf Licht, Farben, Musik, Geräusche.

Wie unterstützt die Musik den Inhalt des Films?
--➤ Beachte, wann welche Musik ertönt und wann sie wechselt.

Wie helfen bestimmte Kameraeinstellungen den Inhalt deutlicher darzustellen *(shot)*?
--➤ Achte z. B. auf Nahaufnahmen *(close-ups)*.

Wie wird Spannung erzeugt *(suspense)*?
--➤ Achte auf Vorandeutungen, Musik, Licht, Geräusche und natürlich die Gestik und Mimik der Schauspieler.

Mit der Zeit wirst du weitere filmische Mittel kennen lernen, die bestimmte Wirkungen auf den Zuschauer erzeugen.

Kooperative Lernformen

Hier findest du die Erklärung für einige ausgewählte Methoden der kooperativen Arbeit.

S23 Think – Pair – Share

1. *Think:* Du sammelst still mögliche Lösungen zu der Aufgabe. Du kannst deine Ideen in Stichpunkten notieren.
2. *Pair:* Zusammen mit deinem Partner besprichst du leise deine gesammelten Ideen.
3. *Share:* Im Klassengespräch meldet ihr euch und teilt euren Mitschülern die Ergebnisse eurer Partnergespräche mit.

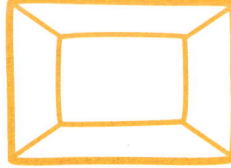

Variante: *Placemat* in Vierergruppen

S24 Milling around (Marktplatz)

Du gehst durch das Klassenzimmer, erfragst von deinen Mitschülern bestimmte Informationen und gibst auch selbst Auskunft. Versuche mit möglichst vielen Mitschülern zu sprechen und verschiedene Informationen zu sammeln. Ihr könnt auch ein Signal vereinbaren, zu dem ihr eure Gesprächspartner wechselt.

S25 Inside outside circle (Kugellager)

1. Bildet zwei Stuhlkreise, einen inneren und einen äußeren.
2. Setzt euch in den Stuhlkreisen so hin, dass immer ein Schüler des äußeren und des inneren Stuhlkreises sich gegenüber sitzen.
3. Stellt euch gegenseitig eure Fragen und beantwortet diese.
4. Rutscht im inneren oder äußeren Kreis nach dem Ende der Gesprächsrunde einen Platz weiter und beginnt ein Gespräch mit einem neuen Mitschüler.

S26 Bus stop (Lerntempoduett)

Sobald du deine Aufgabe fertig bearbeitet hast, gehst du zu einem vereinbarten Treffpunkt, dem *bus stop*. Dort wartest du auf den nächsten Mitschüler, der fertig ist, und zusammen besprecht und vergleicht ihr eure Lösungen. Anschließend verlasst ihr den *bus stop* und bearbeitet die nächste Aufgabe.

S27 Gallery walk (Museumsgang)

1. *Group work:* In der Gruppe erarbeitet ihr ein Thema und haltet euer Ergebnis, z. B. auf einem Poster, fest.
2. *Gallery walk:* Es werden neue Gruppen gebildet. In jeder Gruppe ist ein Schüler jeder Ausgangsgruppe. Jede Gruppe betrachtet die verschiedenen Ergebnisse der Gruppenarbeiten. Jeder präsentiert nun in der neuen Gruppe das Ergebnis seiner Ausgangsgruppe.

Grammar

Liebe Schülerin, lieber Schüler,
jede Sprache besteht aus bestimmten Bausteinen und funktioniert nach bestimmten Regeln.
Die Bausteine sind z.B. einzelne Wörter (Vokabeln). Die Regeln für ihre Zusammensetzung
nennt man Grammatik. Diese musst du außer den Vokabeln lernen, damit du dich verständigen
kannst und damit es nicht zu Missverständnissen kommt.

Jedes Grammatikkapitel (**G**) behandelt Themen, die auf bestimmten Seiten vorne in den *Units*
vorkommen (z.B. Seiten 14–15). Erklärungen, Bilder und Tabellen helfen dir, …
– die Grammatik zu verstehen,
– beim Nachholen, wenn du ein paar Stunden gefehlt hast,
– bei den Hausaufgaben,
– beim Wiederholen,
– bei der Vorbereitung auf Tests und Klassenarbeiten

Regeln sind mit einem blauen Punkt (**o**) gekennzeichnet.
Ein Ausrufezeichen (**!**) bedeutet, dass du hier besonders
aufpassen musst. Mit kleinen Aufgaben (**Test yourself**)
kannst du überprüfen, ob du alles verstanden hast.
Die Lösungen findest du ab Seite 250.

> Hier ist eine Liste aller grammatischen Begriffe aus diesem Buch in alphabetischer Reihenfolge zum Nachschlagen. Links findest du den englischen Begriff, in der Mitte ein Beispiel und rechts den deutschen Ausdruck.

Grammatical terms

English term		Example	Deutsche Bezeichnung
adjective comparison of adjectives comparisons with adjectives	G4, G5 G4 G5	exciting, easy, young After the adventure course I was **more confident**. Wales isn't **as big as** England or Scotland, but it's **bigger than** Northern Ireland.	*Adjektiv* *Steigerung der Adjektive* *Vergleiche mit Adjektiven*
compounds of some, any, every and no	G7	Listen, **everybody**. What can we do for lunch? Are there any cafés **anywhere** near here?	*Zusammensetzungen mit* some, any, every *und* no
going-to future	G6	Jay and Amir **are going to visit** the British Museum.	*Futur mit* going to
indirect speech	G13	He **says** that the landscape in Cornwall **is** very wild.	*indirekte Rede*

English term		Example	Deutsche Bezeichnung
modal auxiliary, modal	G10	can, can't, must, needn't, mustn't, have to	*Modalverb, modales Hilfsverb*
	G11	should(n't), could	
past participle	G8	Gwen and Luke have already **prepared** for the trials. Olivia has **hurt** her foot.	*Partizip Perfekt*
present perfect simple	G8	**Have** you ever **seen** the London Marathon?	*einfache Form des Perfekts*
simple past	G1–G3	Lenny Henry **started** Comic Relief in 1985.	*einfache Form der Vergangenheit*
irregular verb	G1	came, had, met, wore	*unregelmäßiges Verb*
regular verb	G1	answered, played, watched	*regelmäßiges Verb*
negating statements	G2	The man **didn't break** any shop windows.	*Aussagesätze verneinen*
questions	G3	Did the police arrest the man? What did he take from the shop?	*Fragen*
subordinate clauses of comparison, time, reason	G9	The girl wrote to an agony aunt **because** she had a problem. **Before** we had an argument, we spent all our free time together.	*Nebensätze des Vergleichs (Komparativsätze), der Zeit (Temporalsätze), des Grundes (Kausalsätze)*
will future	G12	**I'll miss** you so much!	*Futur mit will*

Unit 1

G1 Two years ago we raised lots of money.

Seiten 14–16

Die einfache Form der Vergangenheit
The simple past

Lenny Henry **started** Comic Relief in 1985 to help people in Africa. On the first Red Nose Day in 1988 people **wore** red noses, **did** fun activities to raise money and **watched** a big comedy show on TV. That **was** many years ago, but today people still do the same things.

> *Das simple past verwendest du, um über eine Handlung oder ein Ereignis zu sprechen, das in der Vergangenheit liegt und abgeschlossen ist.*
> *Du findest es oft in Berichten und Geschichten.*

○ *Bei der Bildung des* simple past *unterscheidest du zwischen regelmäßigen und unregelmäßigen Verben. Anders als bei den Gegenwartsformen sind sie in allen Personen gleich.*

○ *Das* simple past *von* **regelmäßigen Verben** *bildest du aus der* **Grundform des Verbs + -ed.** *Doch bevor du -ed anhängst, musst du folgende Besonderheiten bei der Schreibweise beachten:*

normal	*stummes -e*	*einfacher Konsonant*	*y nach Konsonant*
play – play**ed**	like – lik**ed**	plan – plan**ned**	try – tr**ied**

○ *Beachte, dass -ed auf drei verschiedene Weisen ausgesprochen wird. Sprich …*

[d] *nach Vokalen gefolgt von stimmhaften Konsonanten:*	love – lov**ed**, organise – organis**ed**
[t] *nach stimmlosen Konsonanten:*	help – help**ed**, like – lik**ed**
[ɪd] *nach* **[t]** *oder* **[d]**:	need – need**ed**, paint – paint**ed**

○ *Bei unregelmäßigen Verben musst du die Formen des* simple past *auswendig lernen.*

come – came [keɪm]	have – had [hæd]
do – did [dɪd]	make – made [meɪd]
go – went [went]	put – put [pʊt]
get – got [gɒt]	see – saw [sɔː]
give – gave [geɪv]	take – took [tʊk]

❗ *Das Verb* be *hat im* simple past *zwei Formen:*
I / He / She / It **was** … [wɒz]
We / You / They **were** … [wɜː]
Die verneinten Formen lauten **wasn't** *und* **weren't.**

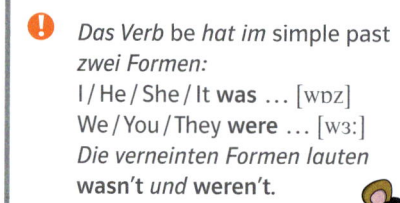

Auf Seite 246 findest du weitere unregelmäßige Verben. Im Dictionary *erkennst du sie am* *.

○ *Im Englischen verwendest du das* simple past, *um eine abgeschlossene Handlung der Vergangenheit wiederzugeben. Im Deutschen kannst du dafür das Präteritum (z. B. er spielte, er ging) oder aber das Perfekt (z. B. er hat gespielt, er ist gegangen) verwenden. Vergleiche:*

Letztes Jahr **haben** wir viel Geld **gesammelt**. – Last year we **raised** lots of money.

Zeitangaben wie yesterday, last week / month / year, in 1985 *oder* two years ago *können dir den Gebrauch des* simple past *signalisieren.*

Test yourself *Complete the e-mail. Use the verbs in the simple past.*

> ✕
>
> Dear Olivia,
> Thank you for your e-mail and the photos. I like them a lot.
> You (want) to know about our charity event. Well, last month we (organise) an event in the park and we (plan) lots of activities. First there (be) games for students, parents and teachers. After that we (sell) cakes. In the afternoon the students in Year 7 (do) some really cool tricks. And then it (be) the turn of the students in Year 8. They (create) a comedy show. The girls (want) to look funny so they (paint) their faces and (wear) some funny costumes too. In the evening the school band (sing) in the park – lots of people (come) to listen. Michael (be) the real star of their show. He (do) some cool moves!
> We (raise) 400 euros in just one day!
> Write soon.
> Pia

G2 How did they know?

Seiten 17–19

Fragen in der einfachen Form der Vergangenheit
Questions in the simple past

Policeman:	**Where were** you last Saturday evening?
Man:	Last Saturday evening? Let me think … Oh yes. On Saturday evening I was at the cinema.
Policeman:	**What** time **did** the film **finish**?
Man:	At about 10 p.m.
Policeman:	**Did** you **go** home right away?
Man:	Well, … **no, I didn't**. I walked along Trafalgar Road before I went home.
Policeman:	Um, … Trafalgar Road?

Bei Fragen unterscheidest du zwischen Entscheidungsfragen und Ergänzungsfragen.
Entscheidungsfragen *beantwortest du im Deutschen mit „ja" oder „nein". **Ergänzungsfragen** enthalten ein Fragewort* (what, who, where, when, why, how).

○ *Du kennst schon die Fragebildung im* simple present:

(Fragewort)	do / does	Subjekt	Vollverb	restlicher Satz	Antwort
	Do	you	go	shopping at the market?	– Yes, I do.
When	do	you	go	shopping at the market?	– I usually go there in the mornings.
	Does	Olivia	go	shopping on Sundays?	– No, she doesn't.
Why	does	Olivia	go	shopping on Saturdays?	– Because she's got time then.

○ *Im* simple past *hat das Hilfsverb do nur eine Form, nämlich* did. *Nach dem Subjekt folgt die Grundform des Vollverbs, weil das Hilfsverb bereits die Vergangenheit ausdrückt.*

(Fragewort)	did	Subjekt	Vollverb	restlicher Satz	Antwort
	Did	the police	arrest	the man?	– Yes, they did.
	Did	the man	take	any money?	– No, he didn't.
What	did	he	take	from the shop?	– He took some T-shirts, sports shoes and a bike.

○ *Enthält die Frage eine Form von* be, *verwendest du im* simple past *bei* I / he / she / it was *und bei* we / you / they were.

(Fragewort)	was / were	Subjekt	restlicher Satz	Antwort
	Was	the man	in Trafalgar Road last Saturday?	– Yes, he was.
	Were	there	any photos of him in Trafalgar Road?	– No, there weren't.
Where	were	you	yesterday evening?	– I was at the cinema.
Who	was		with you?	– My friend was with me.

❗ *Wenn* who *oder* what *Subjekt des Fragesatzes sind, darfst du das Hilfsverb* did *nicht verwenden. Die Fragebildung funktioniert dann genauso wie im Deutschen:*

Who phoned the police?   – *Wer rief die Polizei an?*
What happened on 4th September?   – *Was geschah am 4. September?*

> *Du brauchst ein ‚not' in deiner Frage? Kein Problem! Es schließt sich direkt an das Hilfsverb bzw. die Form von* be *an:* Why did**n't** you go home after the film?, Why were**n't** you at home?

Test yourself *Work in pairs. After somebody broke into a sports shop in Trafalgar Road, the police got a tip from an anonymous caller. What kind of questions did the police ask the caller? Write down four questions and give them to your partner to answer.*

Example: Policeman: What did the man look like?
        Caller: He had brown hair and big ears.

G3 The police didn't know what the man looked like.

Seiten 17–19

Aussagesätze in der einfachen Form der Vergangenheit verneinen
Negating statements in the simple past

Yesterday evening a man broke into a sports shop in Trafalgar Road. He came in through the door, so he **didn't break** any shop windows. He took ten pairs of expensive sports shoes, some T-shirts and a bike. He **didn't take** any money or computers. Luckily, there **weren't** any people in the shop.

Mit didn't, wasn't / weren't *kannst du sagen, dass jemand etwas nicht gemacht hat oder etwas nicht geschehen ist.*

○ *Aussagesätze im* simple present *kennst du schon. Du verneinst sie, indem du ein Hilfsverb einsetzt und es verneinst:*
I / You / We / They   **don't** like dogs.
He / She / It   **doesn't** like dogs.

○ *Im* **simple past** *hat das verneinte Hilfsverb do nur eine Form, nämlich* **didn't**. *Danach folgt die* **Grundform des Vollverbs**, *weil das Hilfsverb bereits die Vergangenheit ausdrückt.*

➕	➖
The man **took** a bike.	The man **didn't take** any money.
The shoes **looked** nice.	The shoes **didn't look** cheap.
He **did** judo on Friday.	He **didn't do** any other sport.

○ *Ist im Satz eine Form von* be *vorhanden, verwendest du bei* I / he / she / it **wasn't** *und bei* we / you / they **weren't**.

➕	➖
The man **was** young.	The man **wasn't** old.
There **were** people in the street.	There **weren't** any people in the shop.

○ *Sätze mit modalen Hilfsverben* (can, can't, must, mustn't, needn't) *kannst du noch nicht in der Vergangenheit verwenden. Das lernst du erst später.*

Test yourself *Complete the article. Use the verbs in the simple past.*

8th September

Man arrested

Greenwich. On 4th September a young man (break into) a sports shop in Trafalgar Road. Yesterday the police (arrest) him. They (not know) what he (look) like at first. But then they (get) an anonymous phone call. The caller (not give) them much information, but she (give) them an address in Greenwich. When the police (get to) the house, two women (be) there but the man (not be). So they (wait) till he (come) home and then they (arrest) him – he (not try) to run away. The police (find) the sports shoes and the T-shirts in the loft, but they (not find) the bike.

G4 An adventure course helps students to be more confident.

Seiten 20–21

Steigerung der Adjektive
Comparison of adjectives

What did you think of the trip to Snowdonia National Park?

I loved it. For me it was **the most exciting** event of the year.

It was really cool. After the adventure course I was **more confident**.

It was good, but I think the centre needs **easier** routes for **younger** students.

I enjoyed the trip but I didn't like climbing. It was **the hardest** challenge for me.

Du verwendest Adjektive und ihre Steigerungsformen, um Lebewesen und Sachen näher zu beschreiben und um sie miteinander zu vergleichen.

○ *Es gibt zwei Möglichkeiten Adjektive zu steigern. Welche du benötigst, hängt von der Anzahl der Silben ab, die die Grundform des Adjektivs (Positiv) hat.*

○ *Einsilbige Adjektive* und *zweisilbige Adjektive, die* auf **-y** *enden, steigerst du, indem du* **-er** *(1. Steigerung / Komparativ) bzw.* **-est** *(2. Steigerung / Superlativ) an die Grundform des Adjektivs anhängst.*

○ *Fast alle anderen **zweisilbigen Adjektive** sowie **alle Adjektive mit mehr als zwei Silben** steigerst du, indem du **more** (1. Steigerung / Komparativ) bzw. **most** (2. Steigerung / Superlativ) **vor** die **Grundform** des Adjektivs setzt.*

	Grundform	1. Steigerung	2. Steigerung	Besonderheiten
	einsilbige Adjektive			
Endungen -er, -est	hard	hard**er**	the hard**est**	–
	big	bi**gg**er	the bi**gg**est	*Endkonsonant wird nach kurzem Vokal verdoppelt*
	nic**e**	nic**er**	the nic**est**	*stummes -e am Ende des Adjektivs fällt weg*
	zweisilbige Adjektive auf -y			
	eas**y**	eas**ier**	the eas**iest**	*y wird zu i, wenn das Adjektiv auf Konsonant + -y endet (außer: shy)*
	funn**y**	funn**ier**	the funn**iest**	
	andere zweisilbige Adjektive sowie mehrsilbige Adjektive			
more, most	awful	**more** awful	the **most** awful	–
	interesting	**more** interesting	the **most** interesting	–

❗ *Beachte, dass **zweisilbige Adjektive**, die **auf -le, -ow oder -er** enden, mit -er / -est gesteigert werden:*
simp**le** *(einfach)* – simpl**er** – the simpl**est** (*e am Ende des Adjektivs fällt weg*)
narr**ow** *(eng, schmal)* – narrow**er** – the narrow**est**
clev**er** *(klug, schlau)* – clever**er** – the clever**est**

❗ *Einige wenige Adjektive werden unregelmäßig gesteigert. Diese musst du auswendig lernen:*
bad – worse – the worst
good – better – the best

Test yourself a) *Copy the grid into your exercise book and fill it in.*

Grundform	1. Steigerung	2. Steigerung
big		
		the worst
	happier	
important		

b) *Write sentences and describe the pictures.*

tall

expensive

Luke is tall.
Holly is … .
But Olivia is the … of the three.

The red car is … .
The blue … .
But … .

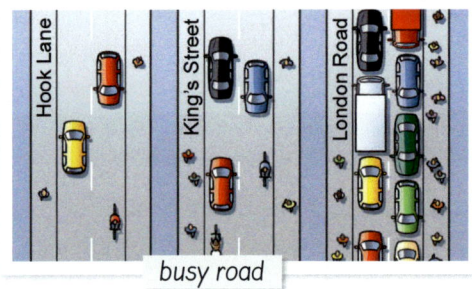

busy road

good idea

Hook Lane is … .
King's Street is … .
But London Road … .

Luke has got a … .
Holly's idea is … .
But Dave has got … .

G5 Outdoor activities are as important as lessons in the classroom.   Seiten 20–21
Gleich oder verschieden: Vergleiche mit Adjektiven
The same or different: Making comparisons with adjectives

DID YOU KNOW …?

1. Wales is part of the UK. It is**n't as big as** England or Scotland, but it's **bigger than** Northern Ireland.
2. Mount Snowdon (1,085 m) is the highest mountain in Wales. But it is**n't higher than** Ben Nevis (1,343 m) in Scotland.
3. The River Severn (362 km) is the longest river in the UK. It is **as long as** the River Neckar in Germany.

Vergleiche mit Adjektiven benutzt du, um Lebewesen oder Sachen miteinander zu vergleichen.

○ *Wenn die Lebewesen oder Sachen in Bezug auf eine Eigenschaft* **gleich** *sind, benutzt du*
   as + *Grundform* + as:
   The River Severn is **as long as** the River Neckar.   *… genauso/so lang wie …*

○ *Wenn die Lebewesen oder Sachen in Bezug auf eine Eigenschaft verschieden sind, benutzt du entweder not as + Grundform + as oder 1. Steigerung + than:*

Wales isn't **as big as** England.	… nicht so groß wie …
Wales is **bigger than** Northern Ireland.	… größer als …
Is climbing **more dangerous than** gorge scrambling?	… gefährlicher als …

❗ *Verwechsle nicht **than** (als) und **then** (dann)!*

Test yourself *Write sentences and compare the rivers, cities, mountains and regions.*

`big`   `small`   `short`   `high`   `long`

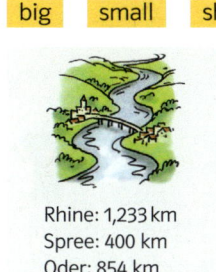

Rhine: 1,233 km
Spree: 400 km
Oder: 854 km

Düsseldorf: 590,000
Stuttgart: 590,000
Cologne: 1 million

Brocken: 1,141 m
Feldberg: 1,493 m
Großer Arber: 1,455 m

the Saarland: 2,570 km²
Hesse: 21,100 km²
Saxony: 18,415 km²

Unit 2

G6 It's going to be fun.   Seiten 38–39
Das Futur mit going to
The going-to future

> What **are** you **going to do** tomorrow? **Are** you **going to see** more sights in Greenwich?

> No, we aren't. We**'re going to visit** the British Museum with Olivia and Holly.

Mit dem going-to future *drückst du feststehende Pläne und Absichten für die nahe Zukunft aus. Du verwendest es auch, wenn es bereits jetzt deutliche Anzeichen dafür gibt, wie die Zukunft werden wird:* A visit to London **is going to be** fun.

○ *Das* going-to future *bildest du aus einer* **Form von** be (am/is/are) + going to + **Grundform des Verbs***:*

Aussage:	The boys **are going to visit** the British Museum with Olivia and Holly.
Verneinung:	Jay **isn't going to go** alone.
Ergänzungsfrage:	What **are** you **going to do** tomorrow, Amir?
Entscheidungsfrage mit Kurzantwort:	**Are** you **going to see** more sights in Greenwich? – Yes, I **am**. / No, I**'m not**.

❗ *Um etwas Zukünftiges auszudrücken, kannst du im Deutschen neben dem Futur oft auch das Präsens verwenden. Im Englischen geht das nicht. Vergleiche:*
We**'re going to visit** London next week.
Wir **werden** *nächste Woche London* **besuchen***.*
Wir **besuchen** *nächste Woche London.*

> *Wörter wie* tomorrow *und* next week *können dir den Gebrauch des* going-to future *anzeigen.*

Test yourself   *What are/aren't the people going to do tomorrow? Look at the pictures and write sentences.*

Jay

Amir

Olivia and Holly

Shahid

Mrs Azad

Mr Azad

G7 It's something important.
Zusammensetzungen mit some, any, every *und* no
The compounds of *some, any, every* and *no*

Seiten 40–41

Listen, **everybody**. What can we do for lunch? Are there any cafés **anywhere** near here?

Mit den Zusammensetzungen von some, any, every *und* no *kannst du allgemein über Dinge, Menschen und Orte sprechen.*

Follow me, there's a great place **somewhere** around the corner here.

○ *Das kennst du schon:*
Some *benutzt du in positiven Aussagen:* Jay has got **some** money.
oder in höflichen Bitten, Angeboten oder Vorschlägen, wenn du eine positive Antwort erwartest: Can you give me **some** money, please? – Yes, sure.

Any *benutzt du in Fragen und zur Verneinung:*
Are there **any** cheap cafés near here? – No, there are**n't any** cheap cafés near here.

○ *Für* some *und* any *gibt es Zusammensetzungen mit* -body/-one *(„jemand"),* -thing *(„etwas") und* -where *(„irgendwo"). Du verwendest sie auf die gleiche Weise wie* some *und* any.

Somebody *und* someone *bzw.* anybody *und* anyone *sind bedeutungsgleich.*

Zusammensetzungen mit some	
somebody / someone:	I can't see the show – **someone** tall is standing in front of me.
something:	I'm hungry. I need **something** to eat.
somewhere:	I know a good café. It's **somewhere** near Covent Garden.
Zusammensetzungen mit any	
anybody / anyone:	Did you ask **anyone**?
anything:	He hasn't got **anything**!
anywhere:	Are there any cheap cafés **anywhere**?

○ *Auch von* no *und* every *gibt es Zusammensetzungen mit* -body/-one, -thing *und* -where. *Sie drücken jeweils das Gegenteil aus:*

Zusammensetzungen mit every	↔	*Zusammensetzungen mit* no
Everybody likes London.		Olivia bets **nobody** can beat her.
jeder, alle		*niemand, keiner*
Everything is OK.		The British Museum costs **nothing**.
alles		*nichts*
There are people **everywhere**.		There's **nowhere** to sit.
überall		*nirgends, nirgendwo*

❗ *Beachte den Unterschied zwischen* everybody/-one *und* anybody/-one*:*

Everybody in my class likes London.   *(ausnahmslos) Jeder …*
Anybody can visit Tate Britain. It's free.   *Jeder (x-beliebige) …*
Mit anybody/-one *ist keine bestimmte Person gemeint, sondern jeder x-beliebige. In dieser Bedeutung kann es auch in positiven Aussagesätzen verwendet werden.*

> Nobody *und* no one *sind bedeutungsgleich. Beachte aber, dass* no one *nicht zusammengeschrieben wird.*

❗ Everybody/-one *und* anybody/-one *sind Singularformen. Die dazugehörigen Pronomen und Possessivbegleiter stehen aber meist im Plural:*
Everybody pays for **their** own Oyster card.
Anybody at the Tube station can tell you where you can buy an Oyster card if you ask **them**.

Test yourself   *Complete the dialogue.*

Amir: Listen, (*alle*). I want to buy a little present for my aunt to say 'thank you'. Is there a good shop (*irgendwo*)?
Olivia: What are you thinking of?
Amir: Well, it must be (*etwas*) special, but it mustn't be (*nichts*) expensive.
Jay: (*Alles*) is expensive in London!
Holly: That's not true! I know a good shop where (*nichts*) costs more than £10.
Amir: OK. Let's go there and see if we can find (*etwas*) for her.

Unit 3

G8 Have you ever run in a marathon?

Seiten 56–59

Die einfache Form des Perfekts
The present perfect simple

> **Have** you ever **seen** the London Marathon?

> Of course, I **have**. It starts right here in Greenwich Park.

> *Mit dem present perfect simple verbindest du die Vergangenheit mit der Gegenwart.*

○ *Mit dem* present perfect simple *kannst du verschiedene Situationen beschreiben:*

a) *Mit* Have you ever … *fragst du, ob jemand etwas schon ein- oder mehrmals gemacht hat.*

Have you ever …?	**Has** Jay **ever run** in a marathon? – No, he **hasn't**. He **has never run** one mile.
In den Antworten auf die Frage findest du oft eines dieser Signalwörter: never, before, only ever, … times.	**Have** Dave and Holly **ever run** in big races? – No, Dave **hasn't run** in big races **before**. And Holly **has only ever run** in short races.
	Have the Elliots **ever watched** the London Marathon? – Yes, they **have**. They**'ve watched** it **three times**.

b) *Mit dem* present perfect simple *kannst du sagen, dass eine Handlung bereits, gerade erst oder noch nicht abgeschlossen wurde:*

> *Die Signalwörter* never, only ever, already *und* just *stehen direkt nach dem Hilfsverb.*

already *(schon, bereits)*	Olivia **has already prepared** for the trials.
just *(gerade erst, eben)*	Gwen **has just had** an idea.
not yet *(noch nicht)*	The girls **haven't left** for school **yet**.

c) *Außerdem kannst du ausdrücken, dass eine Handlung irgendwann in der Vergangenheit stattfand und das Ergebnis dieser Handlung bis in die Gegenwart spürbar bzw. sichtbar ist:*

> I**'ve hurt** my foot. It hurts when I walk.

> Olivia **has bought** new running shoes. They're still clean.

o *Du bildest das* present perfect simple *aus einer Form von* **have (have/has)** *und dem* **past participle***.*

Das past participle *von regelmäßigen Verben entspricht ihrer Form im* simple past (→G1)*. Die Formen von unregelmäßigen Verben musst du lernen. Du findest sie in der 3. Spalte auf den Seiten 244–245.*

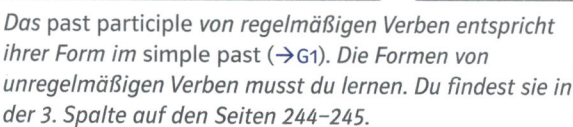

Aussage:	I**'ve run** in races before, but not in a big race like a marathon.
Verneinung:	Jay **hasn't run** one mile.
Ergänzungsfrage:	Who **has heard** of the mini marathon?
Entscheidungsfrage mit Kurzantwort:	**Has** Dave ever **run** in race? – Yes, he **has**. / No, he **hasn't**.

❗ *Beachte die Unterschiede zum Deutschen:*

a) *Das* present perfect simple *bildest du immer mit* have / has + past participle*. Vergleiche:*
I**'ve hurt** my foot. = Ich **habe** mir den Fuß **verletzt.**
I **haven't left** yet. = Ich **bin** noch nicht **losgegangen**.

b) *Auch in Sätzen, die das* present perfect simple *beinhalten, gilt im Englischen die Regel* **S – V – O***. Das* **Objekt** *steht also nach der Verbform.*
Olivia **has hurt** her foot .
Olivia **hat** sich den Fuß **verletzt.**

Test yourself **a)** *You and your classmates are talking about Sports Day. Make questions and write them in your exercise book.*

Have you …	(prepare) (buy) already (start) ever (hurt) (find)	eating healthy food? a name for your team yet? your foot? for Sports Day yet? new sports shoes yet?

b) *Work in small groups. Ask and answer the questions from a).*

Example:
Sabrina: Have you prepared for Sports Day yet?
Martin: Yes, I have. I've already run around the park three times.

Unit 4

G9 **I'm writing to you because I need your advice.** Seiten 76–77
Nebensätze der Zeit, des Grundes und des Vergleichs
Subordinate clauses of time, reason and comparison

> Do you often buy *TeenLife*?

> Well, Claire buys it for me **when** she goes shopping. I like it **because** there are interesting texts and great posters in it.

> *Du kannst Nebensätze verwenden, wenn du deiner Hauptaussage zusätzliche Informationen hinzufügen möchtest. Mit den aus Haupt- und Nebensatz entstehenden Satzgefügen stellst du logische Verbindungen her. Sie sind stilistisch eleganter als hintereinander gereihte Hauptsätze.*

a) *Nebensätze der Zeit (= Temporalsätze):*

after *(nachdem)*	**After** I spoke to my friend, I felt much better.
as soon as *(sobald)*	Things often get better **as soon as** you talk to somebody about it.
before *(bevor, ehe, vor)*	**Before** they had an argument, Lauren spent a lot of her free time with her friend.
until *(bis)*	Never give your address **until** you've really met your new friend face-to-face.
when *(wenn)*	Ask your parents, older sister or brother **when** you need advice.
whenever *(jedes Mal, wenn)*	**Whenever** you want to put photos of other people online, ask them first.

b) *Nebensätze des Grundes (= Kausalsätze):*

because *(weil)*	Lauren wrote to an agony aunt **because** she had a problem.

c) *Nebensätze des Vergleichs (= Komparativsätze):*

like *(als ob)*	My friend acts **like** she's having a much better time without me.

❗ *Beachte, dass die Satzstellung im Deutschen anders ist als im Englischen. Im Englischen bleibt die Reihenfolge* **Subjekt** *–* **Verbform** *–* **Objekt** *sowohl im Haupt- als auch Nebensatz immer erhalten. Vergleiche:*

After **I spoke** to my friend, **I felt** much better.

Nachdem **ich** mit meinem Freund **gesprochen hatte**, **fühlte** **ich** mich besser.

❗ *Wenn du dir die Beispiele in a) – c) einmal genauer anschaust, wirst du feststellen, dass Nebensätze sowohl nach dem Hauptsatz als auch vor dem Hauptsatz stehen können. Steht der* **Hauptsatz vor** *dem* **Nebensatz**, *setzt du* **kein Komma**, *weil die Konjunktion die Sätze trennt. Steht der* **Nebensatz vor** *dem* **Hauptsatz**, *trennst du beide durch* **ein Komma**.*

Test yourself   *Read the posts of some* TeenLife *readers. Complete the sentences with the correct linking word. Add commas where you need them.*

Joe: I like your magazine … it's always got interesting news on my favourite stars in it.
Ginny: I buy *TeenLife* … I get my pocket money from my parents. I love it!
Michael: The concert photos are fantastic. When I look at them it's … I'm there.
Lisa: … I read Ruby's advice I think she really understands our problems.
Sheila: … I tried the make-up in last week's magazine. I'm not going to buy *TeenLife* again! It looked awful on my face.

G10   I must fix it before your mum comes home.   Seite 79–80
Modalverben
Modals

Luke: You could look at a forum for help.
Dad: You mean on the internet? So I **can't fix** my own washing machine – is that what you think? I don't need the internet. And *you* **don't have to** look everything up either!

Mit **can** *oder* **may** *kannst du eine* **Erlaubnis** *einholen oder erteilen.*
Mit **can't** *oder* **mustn't** *drückst du ein* **Verbot** *aus.*
Mit **can** *bzw.* **can't** *sagst du, dass jemand* **(nicht) in der Lage** *ist etwas zu tun.*
Mit **must**, **(not) have to** *und* **needn't** *drückst du* **eine** *oder* **keine** **Notwendigkeit** *aus.*

Erlaubnis:	**Can** I go over to Jay's house? **May** I have my tablet back, please?	*Kann ich …* *Darf ich …*
Verbot:	You **mustn't** remove that pipe. He **can't** use his dad's tools.	*… darfst nicht* *… kann/darf nicht*
(Un)fähigkeit:	I **can** reach the knob. I **can't** fix the washing machine.	*… kann; … bin in der Lage* *… kann nicht;* *… bin nicht in der Lage*
(keine) Notwendigkeit:	I **must** fix the pipe. You **needn't** say "thanks". You **have to** turn the knob off. Luke **doesn't have to** look everything up on the internet.	*… muss* *… musst nicht; … brauchst nicht* *… musst* *… muss nicht; … braucht nicht*

- *Die Modalverben* **can**, **can't**, **may**, **must**, **mustn't** *und* **needn't** *sind in allen Personen gleich. Nur bei* **have to** *musst du in der 3. Person Singular* **has to** *bzw.* **doesn't have to** *verwenden.*

> *May ist höflicher als can und wird meist in Fragen und den Antworten darauf verwendet.*

❗ *Nicht verwechseln:*
Must *benutzt du, um zu sagen, dass etwas aus Sicht des Sprechers notwendig ist.*
Have to *verwendest du, wenn jemand anderes dem Sprecher eine Verpflichtung auferlegt hat oder es um Regeln und Gesetze geht:*
Mr Elliot: I **must** fix the pipe.
Mr Elliot: You **don't have to** look everything up on the internet, Luke.

❗ *Nicht verwechseln:*
You must …   = *Du musst …*
You mustn't …   = *Du darfst nicht …*
You needn't …   = *Du musst nicht … / Du brauchst nicht …*

❗ *Beachte den Unterschied in der Wortstellung:*
He **can't** **use** his dad's tools.
Er **darf** *das Werkzeug seines Vaters* **nicht** **benutzen**.

Test yourself   *You want to take part in a computer course. Write what students can, can't, must, needn't mustn't or (don't) have to do.*

| arrive early | bring own computer | pay before the course starts | wear a uniform |

| do fun things with computers | eat in computer room | keep computer room clean | … |

G11 You could look at a forum for help.

Seite 79–80

Die Modalverben should, shouldn't *und* could
The modals *should*, *shouldn't* and *could*

> Have you got a problem? Well, you **could** look at a forum for help. But you **shouldn't** believe everything you read online.

○ *Die Modalverben* should, shouldn't *und* could *funktionieren wie die Modalverben, die du schon kennst: Du verwendest sie im* simple present, *sie sind in allen Personen gleich und nach ihnen folgt immer ein Vollverb in der Grundform. Vergleiche:*

Mr Elliot **could look** for help on the internet.	*Herr Elliot* **könnte** *im Internet nach Hilfe* **suchen**.
They **should ask** their parents for advice.	*Sie* **sollten** *ihre Eltern um Rat* **fragen**.
You **shouldn't try** to fix everything yourself.	*Du* **solltest nicht versuchen**, *alles selbst zu reparieren*.

Test yourself *What should, could or shouldn't they do? Give advice.*

1. Olivia: In netball I pushed a girl. She fell and hurt her hand.
2. Jay: I've ruined Dave's book.
3. Holly: Mr Fluff often explores under my bed. It's difficult to get him out when he needs to go to bed.
4. Dave: Last weekend I pulled out some flowers in Granny's garden. I thought they were weeds[1].

1 **weeds** [wiːdz] Unkraut

Unit 5

G12 I'll miss you so much!
Das Futur mit will
Will future

Seiten 94–96

> But the house looks fantastic! I'm sure your mum **will be** happy there with all the farm animals to work with.

> I'**ll miss** you so much!

> *Du verwendest das Futur mit* will *für spontane Entscheidungen, Versprechen, Hoffnungen und Vorhersagen, die die Zukunft betreffen.*

○ *Mit dem* will future …

   a) *drückst du spontane Entscheidungen oder Versprechen aus.*

I'**ll text** you.
Holly and I **will visit** you in Cornwall.

   b) *machst du Vorhersagen über zukünftige Ereignisse. (Der Sprecher kann diese nicht beeinflussen.)*

Gwen:	We'**ll miss** you, Dave.
Assistant:	The trip to St Agnes **will take** about seven hours.

> *Diese Wörter können dir den Gebrauch des* will future *anzeigen:* tomorrow, next week/month/year, in a year, probably, perhaps, maybe.

   c) *sagst du, was jemand über ein zukünftiges Ereignis denkt, hofft oder vermutet. Diese Sätze beginnen häufig mit* I hope, I think *oder* I'm sure.

Jay:	I think you'**ll make** lots of new friends quickly.
Dave:	I'm sure Sid **will hate** his new home.

○ *Das* will future *bildest du für alle Personen aus dem Hilfsverb* **will (not) + Grundform des Verbs.** *Die Kurzform lautet* 'll *bzw. bei verneinten Sätzen* won't.

Aussage:	Dave hopes that his friends **will visit** him in St Agnes.
Verneinung:	Aunt Frances **won't come** to Cornwall with them.
Ergänzungsfrage:	What do you think Dave's new school **will be** like?
Entscheidungsfrage mit Kurzantwort:	**Will** your dad **find** work there? – Yes, he **will**. / No, he **won't**.

❗ *Mit dem* going-to *und dem* will future *kennst du zwei Zeitformen der Zukunft. Möchtest du über Zukünftiges sprechen, musst du abwägen:*
Für feststehende **Pläne** *oder* **Absichten** → going-to future (→G6):
The Prestons **are going to move** to Cornwall in summer.
Für **spontane Entscheidungen** → will future:
"I need to put all my things into boxes." – "Don't worry. I**'ll help** you."
Für **Vermutungen, Hoffnungen** *oder* **Vorhersagen** → will future:
I think Dave **will be** OK in Cornwall.

❗ *Verwechsle nicht „Ich will …" (= I want to …) und "I will …" (= Ich werde …).*

Test yourself *What do the friends say when Dave isn't with them? Complete the sentences.*

1. Olivia: I hope Dave … his new school. (love)
2. Holly: I'm sure the Prestons … Granny Rose and Aunt Frances in London soon. (visit)
3. Luke: I don't think the new home … a problem for Sid. He … new cat friends quickly. He … ! (be / make / not get bored)
4. Gwen: I hope Dave … us. (not forget)

G13 He says the landscape in Cornwall is very wild. Seite 98–99
Die indirekte Rede mit Einführungssatz im Präsens
Indirect speech with the reporting verb in the present

Have you heard from Dave?

Yes, he sent me an e-mail a few minutes ago. He **writes** that it**'s** very hot there. He **says** that the landscape in Cornwall **is** very wild.

Mit der indirekten Rede berichtest du, was jemand sagt oder vor kurzem gesagt hat.

Direkte Rede	*Indirekte Rede*
"It**'s** very hot in Cornwall."	Dave **says** **that** it**'s** very hot in Cornwall.
"I**'ve** just **got** back from the beach."	He **tells me** **that** he's just **got** back from the beach.

○ *Die indirekte Rede leitest du durch einen Einleitungssatz mit* say, write, tell sb *oder* promise *ein. Darauf folgt ein Nebensatz, der mit oder ohne* that *eingeleitet werden kann.*

○ *Steht das Verb im Einleitungssatz im* simple present, *wird die Zeitform aus der direkten Rede in den Nebensatz der indirekten Rede übernommen.*

⚠ *Anders als im Deutschen steht nach* that *kein Komma.*

> That *wird oft in der gesprochenen Sprache weggelassen.*

○ *Pronomen, Zeit- und Ortsangaben ändern sich in der indirekten Rede:*
"**I** hope **you** aren't having too much fun without **me**."
→ He says **he** hopes **we** aren't having too much fun without **him**.
"There's a lot of ancient history **here**."
→ He says that there's a lot of ancient history **there**.
"**You** should look at **these** photos."
→ He tells us that **we** should look at **those** photos.
"**This** is my favourite beach. **I** can **see** it from **my** window."
→ He writes that **that**'s his favourite beach. **He** can see it from **his** window.

○ *Auch einige Verben ändern sich in der indirekten Rede:*
"I can't wait for you to **come** here."
→ He says that he can't wait for us to **go** there.
"You must **bring** your swimming things!"
→ He tells us that we must **take** our swimming things.

Test yourself *Look at the pictures and report the statements.*

I love climbing.

My homework is difficult.

We're winning this race.

It's my iPod.

Vocabulary

Vocabulary

Im **Vocabulary** findest du alle wichtigen englischen Wörter und Redewendungen aus *Green Line* 2. Sie stehen in der Reihenfolge, in der sie im Buch vorkommen. Diese Wörter solltest du lernen und anwenden können. Mager gedruckte Einträge musst du **nicht** auswendig lernen. Sie helfen dir, Texte zu verstehen. Weitere nützliche Wörter und Begriffe (z. B. Arbeitsanweisungen), die du **nicht** auswendig lernen musst, findest du ab S. 243. Das *Vocabulary* ist in drei Spalten aufgeteilt:

- Links stehen die englischen Wörter und Sätze. Die Lautschrift in Klammern zeigt dir, wie du das Wort oder den Satz aussprichst.
- In der Mitte steht die deutsche Übersetzung.
- Rechts findest du Beispielsätze, Erklärungen, Bilder oder Hinweise auf Besonderheiten.

An manchen Stellen im Buch stehen neue Wörter in Fußnoten. Sie helfen dir, die Texte zu verstehen, du musst sie aber nicht lernen.

Auf das *Vocabulary* folgt das **Dictionary (English – German, German – English)**. Falls du ein Wort vergessen hast, kannst du in diesen alphabetischen Wortlisten nachsehen.

Englische Begriffe wie *e-mail*, *cool* oder *cornflakes*, die du auch im Deutschen verwendest, stehen nicht im *Vocabulary*. Du kannst ihre Aussprache und Übersetzung aber im *Dictionary* nachschlagen. Das gleiche gilt für Wörter, die auf Englisch und Deutsch fast gleich geschrieben und ausgesprochen werden, wie z. B. *park* oder *partner*.

Abkürzungen und Zeichen

pl	Mehrzahl (Plural)	↔	ist das Gegenteil von
sg	Einzahl (Singular)	→	ist verwandt mit
ugs	umgangssprachlich	=	entspricht
5	In dieser Übung kommen die Wörter vor.	*Fr./Lat.*	verwandte Wörter in anderen Fremdsprachen
!	Achtung!		

Englische Laute

Mitlaute (Konsonanten)

[b]	**b**ed	[p]	**p**icture
[d]	**d**ay	[r]	**r**ed
[ð]	**th**e	[s]	**s**ix
[f]	**f**amily	[ʃ]	**sh**e
[g]	**g**o	[t]	**t**en
[ŋ]	morni**ng**	[tʃ]	**ch**air
[h]	**h**ouse	[v]	**v**ideo
[j]	**y**ou	[w]	**w**e, **o**ne
[k]	**c**an, mil**k**	[z]	ea**s**y
[l]	**l**etter	[ʒ]	revi**s**ion
[m]	**m**an	[dʒ]	**p**a**g**e
[n]	**n**o	[θ]	**th**ank you

Selbstlaute (Vokale)

[ɑː]	c**ar**	[i]	happ**y**
[æ]	**a**pple	[iː]	t**ea**cher
[e]	p**e**n	[ɒ]	d**o**g
[ə]	**a**gain	[ɔː]	b**a**ll
[ɜː]	g**ir**l	[ʊ]	b**oo**k
[ʌ]	b**u**t	[u]	Jan**u**ary
[ɪ]	**i**t	[uː]	t**oo**, tw**o**

Doppellaute

[aɪ]	**I**, m**y**
[aʊ]	n**ow**, m**ou**se
[eɪ]	n**a**me, th**ey**
[eə]	th**ere**, p**air**
[ɪə]	h**ere**, id**ea**
[əʊ]	h**e**ll**o**
[ɔɪ]	b**oy**
[ʊə]	s**ure**

[ː]	der vorangehende Laut ist lang, z. B. *you* [juː]
[‿]	der Bindebogen zeigt, dass zwei Wörter in der Aussprache verbunden werden
[']	die folgende Silbe trägt den Hauptakzent
[ˌ]	die folgende Silbe trägt den Nebenakzent

Across cultures 1 Let's discover TTS!

to **discover** [dɪˈskʌvə]	entdecken	The students *discover* Thomas Tallis School.
subject [ˈsʌbdʒɪkt]	Schulfach	What *subjects* do you like?
exam [ɪɡˈzæm]	Examen; Prüfung	An *exam* is an important test **Fr.** examen *(m)*
dance [dɑːns] *(no pl)*	Tanz	*dance* → to dance
drama [ˈdrɑːmə]	Theater; Drama	In *Drama* class, you can learn how to be an actor.
studies *(pl)* [ˈstʌdiz]	Studium; Lernen; Arbeit für die Schule	My favourite subject is Film *Studies*. **Lat.** studēre
fashion [ˈfæʃn]	Mode	In *Fashion* lessons you learn about clothes.
to **offer** [ˈɒfə]	(an)bieten	Can I *offer* you something to drink? **Fr.** offrir
additional [əˈdɪʃnl]	zusätzlich	
birdwatching [ˈbɜːdˌwɒtʃɪŋ]	Vogelbeobachtung	*Birdwatching* is an additional activity at TTS.
bird [bɜːd]	Vogel	
chess [tʃes]	Schach	
painting [ˈpeɪntɪŋ]	Malerei; Gemälde	*painting* → to paint
assembly [əˈsembli]	Versammlung; Morgenappell	
sign [saɪn]	Zeichen; Schild	In Wales the *signs* are in Welsh. **Lat.** signum *(nt)*
class [klɑːs]	*hier:* Unterricht	In *class*, sometimes you work on your own, sometimes with your classmates.
hall [hɔːl]	Halle; Saal	In the *hall*, the students meet for Assembly.
art [ɑːt]	Kunst	Not every painting is *art*! **Lat.** ars *(f)*
competition [ˌkɒmpəˈtɪʃn]	Wettbewerb; Turnier	There's a painting *competition* at our school this year. **Fr.** compétition *(f)*
to **belong (to)** [bɪˈlɒŋ (tə)]	gehören (zu)	
with special needs [wɪð ˌspeʃl ˈniːdz]	behindert	Students *with special needs* belong to TTS too.

2	**fantastic** [fæn'tæstɪk]	fantastisch; großartig	*fantastic* = great *Fr.* fantastique
	reaction [ri'ækʃn]	Reaktion	
	Maths [mæθs]	Mathematik; Mathe	*Fr.* maths *(f)* (pl)
	Science [saɪəns]	Naturwissenschaften	*Lat.* scientia *(f)*
	Technology [tek'nɒlədʒi]	Technik; Computerunterricht	
3	**partially sighted** [ˌpɑːʃəli 'saɪtɪd]	sehbehindert	Gwen is a new girl at TTS. She's *partially sighted*.
4	**registration** [ˌredʒɪs'treɪʃn]	Anwesenheitskontrolle	*Registration* is before lessons.
	break [breɪk]	Pause	After the first two lessons we always have *break*.
	PE *(= Physical Education)* [ˌpiː'iː; ˌfɪzɪkl_edʒʊ'keɪʃn]	Sportunterricht	In *PE* you do lots of sport.
	RE *(= Religious Education)* [ˌɑːr'iː; rɪˌlɪdʒəs_edʒʊ'keɪʃn]	Religion *(Schulfach)*	
	French [frenʃ]	französisch; Französisch	
	Geography [dʒi'ɒgrəfi]	Geografie; Erdkunde	What do you know about the *geography* of Southern Germany?
	Humanities *(pl)* [hjuː'mænətiz]	Sozialwissenschaften	*Lat.* humanitas *(f)*
	History ['hɪstri]	Geschichte	*Lat.* historia *(f)*

Subjects at school

English	Englisch		**Music**	Musik
German	Deutsch		**Humanities**	Sozialwissenschaften
French	Französisch		**Technology**	Technik
Maths	Mathe		**Science**	Naturwissenschaften
PE	Sport		**RE**	Religion
Art	Kunst		**Geography**	Erdkunde

Make you own fantasy timetable and compare it with your partner's.

5	**Eco** [ɪkəʊ]	Öko-	
	to **join** [dʒɔɪn]	beitreten; sich anschließen; verbinden	Let's *join* the Computer Club!
	to **design** [dɪ'zaɪn]	entwerfen; gestalten	*to design* → design
	should [ʃʊd]	sollte; solltest; sollten; solltet	
	to **welcome** ['welkəm]	willkommen heißen	Let's go and *welcome* our new classmates.
	wildlife ['waɪldlaɪf]	Tierwelt *(in freier Wildbahn)*	The Eco Club did a *wildlife* project.
	to **protect** [prə'tekt]	schützen	
	nature ['neɪtʃə]	Natur	It's important to protect *nature*.
	to **save** [seɪv]	sparen	I want to buy a new smartphone. I need to *save* money for it.

	energy [ˈenədʒi]	Energie; Kraft	*Fr.* énergie *(f)*
	pollution [pəˈluːʃn]	Verschmutzung	*Pollution* makes a river dirty.
	to **make a difference** [ˌmeɪk ə ˈdɪfrns]	etw. verändern	*to make a difference* → to change sth.
6	**as** [æz; əz]	wie	My favourite music is not the same *as* yours. We don't like the same music.
7	**advice** [ədˈvaɪs]	Rat; Ratschlag	What *advice* can you give me?
	actor [ˈæktə]	Schauspieler	*actor* → to act *Lat.* actor *(m)*
	moment [ˈməʊmənt]	Moment; Augenblick	**!** Achtung Betonung.
	to **panic** [ˈpænɪk]	panisch werden	Don't *panic*! *Fr.* paniquer
	to **relax** [rɪˈlæks]	sich entspannen; sich ausruhen; sich beruhigen	Just *relax*!
	confident [ˈkɒnfɪdnt]	selbstsicher; selbstbewusst	*Lat.* confidens
	Take a deep breath. [ˌteɪk ə ˌdiːp ˈbreθ]	Atme(t) tief ein.	
	to **thank** [θæŋk]	danken	*to thank* → Thank you.

Unit 1 My friends and I

Check-in

past [pɑːst]	Vergangenheit	'Today' is now, 'yesterday' is the *past*.
feeling [ˈfiːlɪŋ]	Gefühl	*feeling* → to feel
phrases that … [ˌfreɪzɪz ˈðæt]	Redewendungen, die …	
caught on camera [ˌkɔːt ɒn ˈkæmrə]	ertappt; mit der Kamera festgehalten	
embarrassing [ɪmˈbærəsɪŋ]	peinlich	In the photo Jay is wearing an *embarrassing* outfit.
to **end up** [ˌend ˈʌp]	enden; landen	
yearbook [ˈjɪəbʊk]	Jahrbuch	A book with information about events and students at the school.
round of boxing [ˌraʊnd əv ˈbɒksɪŋ]	Boxrunde	
nose [nəʊz]	Nase	They look funny with their red *noses*.
eye [aɪ]	Auge	
lovebirds *(pl)* [ˈlʌvˌbɜːdz]	Turteltauben	

to **lie** [laɪ]	lügen	The camera never *lies*!
trip [trɪp]	Trip; Reise; Ausflug; Fahrt	Let's go on a fun *trip* at the weekend!
guy [gaɪ]	Typ; Kerl; *(Pl.)* Leute	Our new classmate is a really cool *guy*.
himself [hɪmˈself]	(er) selbst; sich (selbst)	You mustn't help him. He wants to do everything *himself*.
shy [ʃaɪ]	schüchtern	I don't like parties because I'm *shy*.
embarrassed [ɪmˈbærəst]	verlegen	*embarrassed* → embarrassing *Fr.* embarrassé/-e
proud (of) [ˈpraʊd‿əv]	stolz (auf)	Jay is *proud of* himself because he is good at singing.
American [əˈmerɪkən]	Amerikanisch; amerikanisch; aus Amerika; Amerikaner/-in	Yearbooks are an *American* tradition.
report [rɪˈpɔːt]	Bericht; Meldung	Who can write the *report* about the class trip?
during *(+ noun)* [ˈdjʊərɪŋ]	während *(+ Nomen)*	Don't eat *during* lessons.
highlight [ˈhaɪlaɪt]	Highlight; Höhepunkt	

2 appears beside *himself* row, 3 appears beside *shy* row.

Describing a person's character

He's a very **shy** person. It isn't easy for him to give presentations.	schüchtern
She's good at lots of things so she's always **confident** that she can do almost anything.	zuversichtlich; selbstbewusst
He's so **brave**. He's never scared.	tapfer; mutig
She's a **nice / friendly / unfriendly / funny** person.	nett / freundlich / unfreundlich / lustig
He's **lucky** because he's **happy**.	Glück haben / glücklich sein

Describe a person to your partner. Who is it?

Station 1: I love Red Nose Day

(the) best [best]	(der/die/das) Beste	I always try to do *my best* when there's a class test.
ago [əˈgəʊ]	vor *(zeitlich)*	**!** *Ago* steht meistens am Satzende: I did my homework two days *ago*.
to **raise money** [ˌreɪz ˈmʌni]	Geld sammeln	Charities *raise money*.
in need [ɪn ˈniːd]	bedürftig; in Not	*in need* → to need
also [ˈɔːlsəʊ]	auch	I like football and I *also* like basketball. = I like football and I like basketball too.
that's how [ðæts ˈhaʊ]	so	Look at Luke. *That's how* you play football – he's good!
noticeboard [ˈnəʊtɪsbɔːd]	schwarzes Brett	Olivia saw a Red Nose Day poster on the school *noticeboard*.
month [mʌnθ]	Monat	day – week – *month* – year
in the end [ˌɪn ðiˈend]	schließlich; zum Schluss	
real [rɪəl]	echt; richtig; wirklich	Not everything you see on TV is *real*. *real* → really

collection [kə'lekʃn]	Kollektion; Sammlung	collection → to collect *Fr.* collection *(f)*
I can't wait till next time. [aɪ kɑːnt ˌweɪt tɪl nekst 'taɪm]	Ich kann es bis zum nächsten Mal kaum erwarten.	
2 **non-** [nɒn]	nicht-	Red Nose Day is a *non*-uniform day.
5 **the next day** [ðə ˌnekst 'deɪ]	am nächsten Tag	What did Luke tell his friends *the next day*?
yesterday ['jestədeɪ]	gestern	*yesterday* – today – tomorrow
6 **pyjamas** *(pl)* [pɪ'dʒɑːməz]	Schlafanzug; Pyjama	Do you wear *pyjamas* in bed?
to **enjoy** [ɪn'dʒɔɪ]	genießen; sich freuen an	The party was great. I really *enjoyed* it.
comment ['kɒment]	Kommentar	This is a serious problem, so I don't need your funny *comments*!
to **turn off** [ˌtɜːn 'ɒf]	abschalten; ausschalten	Please *turn off* the TV. It's time to go to bed.
hard [hɑːd]	hart; schwer; schwierig	I find German *hard*.
for ... [fɔː; fə]	... lang	Sherlock can swim *for* 30 minutes.
to **think of** ['θɪŋk əv]	(sich) ausdenken; sich etwas einfallen lassen	Can you *think of* other things to do at the weekend?
7 an activity that ... [ən ˌækˌtɪvəti 'ðæt]	eine Aktivität, die ...	
nervous ['nɜːvəs]	nervös; aufgeregt	I felt *nervous* before the class test. *Fr.* nerveux/nerveuse
8 **sale** [seɪl]	Verkauf	*sale* → to sell
to **keep going** [ˌkiːp 'gəʊɪŋ]	aufrechterhalten	A quick answer *keeps* the conversation *going*.

Station 2: How did they know?

coach [kəʊtʃ]	Reisebus	A big bus (for holidays or long trips).
someone ['sʌmwʌn]	jemand	*someone* = somebody
missing ['mɪsɪŋ]	fehlend; verschwunden	What's the *missing* word? "I really ... you."
solution [sə'luːʃn]	Lösung	Let's find a *solution* for your problem. *Fr.* solution *(f)*
anonymous [ə'nɒnɪməs]	anonym	
police [pə'liːs]	Polizei	**!** The *police* <u>are</u> looking for a dangerous man. *Fr.* police *(f)*
to **arrest** [ə'rest]	festnehmen; verhaften	The police *arrested* two men. *Fr.* arrêter
what the man looked like [ˌwɒt ðə mæn 'lʊkt laɪk]	wie der Mann aussah	I didn't see the man. I don't know *what he looks like*.

taxi [ˈtæksi]	Taxi		
driver [ˈdraɪvə]	Fahrer/-in	! My uncle is <u>a</u> taxi *driver*. = Mein Onkel ist Taxifahrer.	
mechanic [məˈkænɪk]	Mechaniker/-in; Kfz-Mechaniker/-in		
farmer [ˈfɑːmə]	Farmer/-in; Landwirt/-in	*farmer* → farm	
postman [ˈpəʊstmən]	Briefträger		
clue [kluː]	Hinweis; Spur	The man's name is the *clue*.	
13	**friendly** [ˈfrendli]	freundlich; nett	I always try to be *friendly* to everyone. *friendly* → friend
14	**all day** [ɔːl ˈdeɪ]	den ganzen Tag	What did you do *all day* on Saturday?
15	**singer** [ˈsɪŋə]	Sänger/-in	Jay thinks he's a *singer*. *singer* → to sing
16	**dream** [driːm]	Traum	In my *dream* I was James Bond.

Station 3: Everyone can enjoy a challenge

challenge [ˈtʃælɪndʒ]	Herausforderung	
course [kɔːs]	Kurs	They organise sports *courses* for school groups. *Lat.* cursus *(m)*
mountain [ˈmaʊntɪn]	Berg	
forest [ˈfɒrɪst]	Wald	There are lots of trees in a *forest*. *Fr.* forêt *(f)*
adventure [ədˈventʃə]	Abenteuer	*Adventure* stories tell about exciting events.
walking [ˈwɔːkɪŋ]	Wandern	! Wenn man *-ing* an ein Verb anhängt, wird es zum Hauptwort (Nomen): walk – *walking*, climb – climbing
climbing [ˈklaɪmɪŋ]	Klettern	! Achtung Aussprache.
gorge scrambling [ˈgɔːdʒ ˌskræmblɪŋ]	Schluchtenklettern	
route [ruːt]	Strecke; Route	*Fr.* route *(f)*
than [ðæn]	als *(bei Vergleichen)*	Her English is better *than* her French.
the worst [ðə ˈwɜːst]	der/die/das schlimmste; der/die/das schlechteste	*the worst* ↔ the best
that's why [ðæts ˈwaɪ]	deshalb	I went to bed late last night. *That's why* I'm tired.

Outdoor activities

to **play** football / tennis	Fußball / Tennis spielen
to **go** skating / swimming / climbing / gorge scrambling	inlineskaten / schwimmen / schluchtenklettern gehen
to **ride** your bike / a horse	Fahrrad fahren / reiten
to **run**	laufen; rennen
to **go for a walk** in a park / in a forest / in the mountains	im Park / im Wald / in den Bergen spazieren gehen
to **climb** a mountain	einen Berg besteigen
to **do** gorge scrambling / mountain climbing	schluchtenklettern / bergsteigen

Tell your partner what you'd like to do in your holidays.

18	**separate** ['seprət]	separat; getrennt; verschieden	Wales is a *separate* country. *Lat.* separatus/-a/-um
	Celtic ['keltɪk; 'seltɪk]	keltisch	*Fr.* celtique
	Welsh [welʃ]	walisisch; Walisisch; Waliser/-in	*Welsh* people are from Wales. Some of them still speak *Welsh*.
22	**low** [ləʊ]	niedrig	
	tall [tɔːl]	groß; hoch	Olivia is *taller* than Lucy.
	high [haɪ]	hoch; groß	*high* ↔ low

Comparing things

Tony: My house is **big**.
Lou: My sister's house is **bigger**.
Tony: I think my house is **the biggest**.

Lou: Your joke is **good**. But my joke is **better**.
Tony: No, my joke is **the best**.

Lou: Football is **exciting**, but tennis is **more exciting**, and inline skating is **the most exciting** sport.

Compare the things in your schoolbag with a partner's things.

Story: It was amazing

amazing [ə'meɪzɪŋ]	unglaublich; toll; erstaunlich	That's an *amazing* story!
planet ['plænɪt]	Planet	
sheep, sheep *(pl)* [ʃiːp]	Schaf	
road [rəʊd]	Straße	I live in King's *Road*.
soon [suːn]	bald	in a short time from now; a short time later
field [fiːld]	Feld; Spielfeld; Wiese; Weide; Acker	On farms there are *fields*.
Welcome! ['welkəm]	Willkommen!	*Welcome* to Wales!
instructor [ɪn'strʌktə]	Lehrer/-in; Betreuer/-in	An *instructor* shows you how to do things. *Lat.* instructor *(m)*
few [fjuː]	wenige	! He's got a *few* friends. = … ein paar Freunde. He's got *few* friends. = … wenige Freunde.
meal [miːl]	Mahlzeit; Essen	Lunch is a *meal*.
a bit [ə 'bɪt]	ein bisschen; ein wenig	
cold [kəʊld]	kalt	The nights in Wales were a bit *cold*.
torch [tɔːtʃ]	Fackel; Taschenlampe	
to go for a walk [ˌgəʊ fər ə 'wɔːk]	spazieren gehen	It's nice today. Let's *go for a walk*.
the dark [ðə 'dɑːk]	Dunkelheit	in *the dark* = im Dunkeln
noise [nɔɪz]	Lärm; Geräusch	What's all the *noise*? I can't sleep!
dark [dɑːk]	dunkel	*dark* → the dark
night walk ['naɪt wɔːk]	Nachtwanderung	
against [ə'genst]	gegen	It was *against* the rules.
to be asleep [ˌbi ə'sliːp]	schlafen	*to be asleep* = to sleep
to tiptoe ['tɪptəʊ]	auf Zehenspitzen gehen	They *tiptoed* back to their rooms.
cloudy ['klaʊdi]	bedeckt; bewölkt	On a *cloudy* night you can't see the stars.
battery ['bætri]	Batterie; Akku	*Fr.* batterie *(f)*
no idea [ˌnəʊ aɪ'dɪə]	keine Ahnung	Which is the right way? – I have *no idea*!
locked [lɒkt]	abgeschlossen	*locked* ↔ open
trouble ['trʌbl]	Ärger; Probleme; Schwierigkeiten	We didn't want *trouble* with our teacher.
secret ['siːkrət]	Geheimnis	Don't tell the others, it's a *secret*. *Fr.* secret *(m)*

memory ['memrɪ]	Erinnerung; Gedächtnis	We all have great *memories* of our school trip. *Lat.* memoria *(f)*
4 **travel report** [ˌtrævl rɪ'pɔːt]	Reisebericht	Do you like Dave's *travel report* about the class trip?
words that … [wɜːdz 'ðæt]	Wörter, die …	

Skills: How to use a dictionary

1 **electronic** [ˌelek'trɒnɪk]	elektronisch	Do you use an *electronic* dictionary?
search [sɜːtʃ]	Suche; Such-	Write the word in the *search* box.
meaning ['miːnɪŋ]	Bedeutung; Sinn	What's the *meaning* of 'to describe'?

Unit task: Our travel report

spaceship ['speɪsʃɪp]	Raumschiff	In science fiction stories there are often *spaceships*.
topic ['tɒpɪk]	Thema	This story is connected with the *topic* of my presentation.
beginning [bɪ'gɪnɪŋ]	Anfang; Beginn	*beginning* ↔ end

Action UK! The new boy

1 to **sneak around** [ˌsniːk‿ə'raʊnd]	herumschleichen	
lemon ['lemən]	Zitrone	
surprising [sə'praɪzɪŋ]	überraschend	*surprising* → surprise
2 **filmmaker** ['fɪlmˌmeɪkə]	Filmemacher/-in	A *filmmaker* makes films.
mood [muːd]	Stimmung; Laune	Can you describe the *mood* in that scene?
unfriendly [ʌn'frendlɪ]	unfreundlich	*unfriendly* ↔ friendly
hurt [hɜːt]	verletzt	He made some really unfriendly comments and now I feel *hurt*.
aggressive [ə'gresɪv]	aggressiv	! Achtung Aussprache. *Fr.* agressif/agressive
scary ['skeərɪ]	unheimlich; gruselig; beängstigend	*scary* → to be scared

Across cultures 2 London: A special city

huge [hjuːdʒ]	riesig; riesengroß; gewaltig	Berlin is a big city. London is a *huge* city.
capital ['kæpɪtl]	Hauptstadt	London is the *capital* of England. *Lat.* capitalis
1 **fact** [fækt]	Fakt; Tatsache	*Lat.* factum *(nt)*
multi-ethnic [ˌmʌltɪ'eθnɪk]	Vielvölker-; international	London is a *multi-ethnic* city.

sight [saɪt]	Sehenswürdigkeit; Anblick	A *sight* is an interesting thing to see in a city.
space [speɪs]	Raum; Fläche; Platz; Ort	Please leave some *space* for my picture on the wall.
underground [ˈʌndəɡraʊnd]	U-Bahn	Let's go by *underground*.
the Tube [ðə ˈtjuːb]	die Londoner U-Bahn	Another name for the London underground is *the Tube*.
carnival [ˈkɑːnɪvl]	Karneval	What costume do you want to wear at the *carnival*?
originally [əˈrɪdʒnli]	ursprünglich	Luke's mother is *originally* from Poland.
Roman [ˈrəʊmən]	Römer/-in; römisch	London was originally a *Roman* town. *Lat.* Romanus/-a/-um
airport [ˈeəpɔːt]	Flughafen	London has got five *airports*. *Fr.* aéroport *(m)*
million [ˈmɪljən]	Million	1,000,000
large [lɑːdʒ]	groß; riesig	London is the *largest* city in Europe.
bell [bel]	Glocke	
2 **guard** [ɡɑːd]	Wache; Wächter/-in	There are always *guards* in front of Buckingham Palace.
queen [kwiːn]	Königin	Elizabeth II is the *Queen* of England.
identity [aɪˈdentəti]	Identität	*Fr.* identité *(f)*

Unit 2 London is amazing!

Check-in

to **get around** [ˌɡet əˈraʊnd]	*hier:* sich fortbewegen	What's the best way to *get around* London? – By Tube.
public transport *(no pl)* [ˌpʌblɪk ˈtrænspɔːt]	öffentliche Verkehrsmittel	*public transport* = the Underground, buses, trains
flair [fleə]	Flair; Atmosphäre	Brick Lane has a multi-ethnic *flair*.
wax figure [ˈwæks ˌfɪɡə]	Wachsfigur	At Madame Tussauds you can see *wax figures* of famous people.
2 to **be interested in** [bɪ ˈɪntrəstɪd ˌɪn]	interessiert sein an; sich interessieren für	*Are* you *interested in* history?
3 **things that …** [θɪŋz ˈðæt]	Dinge, die …	

Station 1: It's going to be fun

to **stay with** [ˈsteɪ wɪð]	wohnen bei	Amir is *staying with* the Azads.
this afternoon [ðɪs ˈɑːftənuːn]	heute Nachmittag	yesterday afternoon – *this afternoon* – tomorrow afternoon
18-year-old [ˌeɪtiːn ˈjɪər ˌəʊld]	18-jährig	My sister is 18. I've got an *18-year-old* sister.
to **persuade** [pəˈsweɪd]	überreden	Jay wants to *persuade* his brother to come with them. *Lat.* persuadēre
probably [ˈprɒbəbli]	möglicherweise; wahrscheinlich	

1	to **travel** [ˈtrævl] fahren; reisen	This year I'd like to *travel* to England.
	smartcard [ˈsmɑːtkɑːd] Chipkarte	
	to **top up** [tɒpˈʌp] aufladen	Jay *topped up* his Oyster card yesterday. Now he must *top up* his phone too.
	credit [ˈkredɪt] Guthaben	I must top up my phone. There's no *credit* on it.
4	**wheelchair** [ˈwiːltʃeə] Rollstuhl	

wheelchair → chair

5	**zoo** [zuː] Zoo; Tierpark	There are lots of animals in a *zoo*.
	musician [mjuːˈzɪʃn] Musiker/-in	*musician* → music **Fr.** musicien *(m)*/musicienne *(f)*
6	to **change (onto)** [tʃeɪndʒ (ˈɒntʊ)] umsteigen (in)	To get to Buckingham Palace from here, you *change onto* the Victoria line.
	north [nɔːθ] Norden; Nord-	
	south [saʊθ] Süden; Süd-	
	stop [stɒp] Haltestelle; Halt	The next *stop* is Elephant & Castle. *stop* → to stop
	to **get off, got off (a bus/ train)** [ˌɡetˈɒf; ˌɡɒtˈɒf] aussteigen (aus einem Bus/ Zug)	Let's *get off* the Underground and take the bus.

Station 2: Good idea!

to **deal, dealt (with)** [diːl; delt (wɪð)] sich befassen (mit); umgehen (mit)	We've got a problem so let's *deal with* it.
a while [ə ˈwaɪl] eine Weile	*a while* = a little time
to **mean, meant** [miːn; ment] meinen; bedeuten	You think the new boy is strange? What do you *mean*? I think he's nice.
girlfriend [ˈɡɜːlfrend] Freundin *(in einer Paarbeziehung)*	Shahid has a *girlfriend*.
souvenir [ˌsuːvnˈɪə] Souvenir; Andenken	I'd like to buy a *souvenir* of London.
anywhere [ˈeniweə] irgendwo; überall (egal, wo)	Are there any souvenir shops *anywhere*?
everybody [ˈevrɪbɒdi] jeder; alle	all the people
... where to go. [ˌweə tə ˈɡəʊ] ... wohin ich gehen kann.	I don't know *where to go*.
to **follow** [ˈfɒləʊ] folgen; hinterhergehen; befolgen	The bird is *following* the man.

corner ['kɔːnə]	Ecke	Most rooms have four *corners*.
I bet [aɪ 'bet]	ich wette	
nobody ['nəʊbədi]	niemand	*nobody* ↔ somebody
to **beat, beat** [biːt; biːt]	schlagen; besiegen	I bet nobody can *beat* Arsenal this year!
one *(sg)*/**ones** *(pl)* [wʌn/wʌnz]	eine/-r/-s	Wenn du im Englischen ein Nomen nicht wiederholen möchtest, kannst du es durch *one/ones* ersetzen: This sandwich is big, that *one* is bigger.
11 **pro** [prəʊ]	Argument dafür	*Lat.* pro
good for someone who … [ˌgʊd fə ˌsʌmwʌn 'huː]	gut für jemanden, der …	
con [kɒn]	Argument dagegen	*Lat.* contra
far [fɑː]	weit	Is Big Ben *far* from Buckingham Palace?

Station 3: They can bite very hard

to **bite, bit** [baɪt; bɪt]	beißen	Does your dog *bite*? It looks a bit scary!
tour [tʊə]	Tour; Fahrt; Rundgang	
guide [gaɪd]	Führer/-in; Reiseführer	A *guide* gives you information (e.g. about a city or a museum). *Fr.* guide *(m)* *(f)*
to **build, built** [bɪld; bɪlt]	bauen	We *built* a new house last year.
to **become, became** [bɪ'kʌm, bɪ'keɪm]	werden	William the Conqueror *became* king of England in 1066.
castle ['kɑːsl]	Schloss; Burg	! Das „t" in *castle* wird nicht gesprochen.
prison ['prɪzn]	Gefängnis	*Fr.* prison *(f)*
lion [laɪən]	Löwe	*Fr.* lion *(m)*
bear [beə]	Bär	
crown jewels [ˌkraʊn 'dʒuːəlz]	Kronjuwelen	The Tower is a museum where you can see the *Crown Jewels*.
Beefeater ['biːfˌiːtə]	königlicher Leibgardist	
raven ['reɪvn]	Rabe	
raven master ['reɪvn ˌmɑːstə]	Herr der Raben	The *raven master* looks after the ravens in the Tower.
careful ['keəfl]	vorsichtig; sorgfältig	
safe [seɪf]	sicher; ungefährlich	*safe* ↔ dangerous
close [kləʊs]	nahe	Don't go too *close* to the ravens.

Describing people, things and actions

I find it **hard** to play tennis.	In tennis, you must hit the ball **hard**.
We're **good** friends.	We know each other **well**.
The bus is **slow**.	It's going **slowly**.
It's a **clear** view.	You can see the hills **clearly**.
The Tower is a **special** sight.	People come **specially** to see the Crown Jewels.
He's a **careful** driver.	He drives **carefully**.
She's a **happy** student.	She always does her homework **happily**.
Don't worry. This place is **safe**.	You can stay here **safely**.
You're so **nervous**.	Why are you jumping back **nervously**?
A library is a **quiet** place.	We have to talk **quietly** there.
It's too **loud** here.	The fans are clapping their hands **loudly**.
Football players are **fast** runners.	They run very **fast**.
These fans are **aggressive**.	They're shouting **aggressively**.

13	**audio tour** [ˈɔːdɪəʊ ˌtʊə]	Audioführung	! Achtung Aussprache. *Fr.* audio-; *Lat.* audire
	treasure [ˈtreʒə]	Schatz	Just look and you can find real *treasures* in the Thames.
	ghost [gəʊst]	Geist; Gespenst	Sometimes there are stories of *ghosts* in old houses.
14	**to jump back** [ˌdʒʌmp ˈbæk]	zurückspringen; *hier:* zurückschrecken	My mum *jumps back* when she sees a mouse.
	could [kʊd]	könnte/-n	
15	**one day** [wʌn ˈdeɪ]	eines Tages	Jay wants to be a famous singer *one day*.

Action UK! A day out in London

	a day out in ... [ə ˌdeɪ ˈaʊt ɪn]	ein Tag in ...	What would you like to do on *a day out in* London?
2	**out and about** [ˌaʊt ən əˈbaʊt]	unterwegs	
3	**adult** [ˈædʌlt]	Erwachsene/-r	*adult* ↔ child
	sightseeing [ˈsaɪtsiːɪŋ]	Sightseeing-; Besichtigungs-	
	normal [ˈnɔːml]	normal	Is it better to take the sightseeing bus or the *normal* one?
4	**choice** [tʃɔɪs]	Wahl; Auswahl	*choice* → to choose *Fr.* choix (f)
	location [ləʊˈkeɪʃn]	Handlungsort; Lage; Standort	The *location* of the film is a famous street in London. *Lat.* locus (m)
	crowd [kraʊd]	Menschenmenge	A lot of people all together in one place.
	view [vjuː]	Aussicht; Sicht; Ausblick; Blick	The house has a fantastic *view* of the Thames.

Out and about in the city

to **take** the bus / the Underground	den Bus / die U-Bahn nehmen
to **go for a walk** in the streets / in a park / along the river	in den Straßen / im Park / am Fluss entlang spazieren gehen
to **sit** in a café / restaurant	in einem Café / Restaurant sitzen
to **have** lunch / dinner	zu Mittag / zu Abend essen
to **go** shopping / to the cinema	einkaufen / ins Kino gehen
to **visit** a sight / a tourist attraction / a museum / a historical building / the zoo	eine Sehenswürdigkeit / eine Touristenattraktion / ein Museum / ein historisches Gebäude / den Zoo besichtigen; besuchen
to **see** famous people / the sights / lots of interesting things	berühmte Leute / die Sehenswürdigkeiten / viele interessante Dinge sehen
to **listen** to street musicians / an audio tour	Straßenmusikern / einer Audioguide-Führung zuhören
to **watch** a football game / a street show	ein Fußballspiel / eine Straßenshow ansehen

What would you like to do in London?

Skills: How to find information on the internet

1	**attraction** [əˈtrækʃn]	Attraktion; Sehenswürdigkeit	The London Eye is one of the city's most popular *attractions*.
	basic [ˈbeɪsɪk]	grundlegend; Grund-	In the first two years of English you learn a lot of *basic* words.
	display [dɪˈspleɪ]	Ausstellung	The Natural History Museum has a great *display* with strange animals at the moment.
	news *(sg)* [njuːz]	Nachricht(en); Neuigkeit(en)	**!** That's good *news*. = Das ist eine gute Nachricht.
2	**life, lives** *(pl)* [laɪf, laɪvz]	Leben	*life* → to live
	earth [ɜːθ]	Erdboden; Erde; die Erde	
	dinosaur [ˈdaɪnəsɔː]	Dinosaurier	

Unit task: Our London tour

on foot [ɒn ˈfʊt]	zu Fuß	**!** by car/train/bus, **but:** *on foot*
distance [ˈdɪstns]	Distanz; Entfernung	What's the *distance* from here to there? *Fr.* distance *(f)*
realistic [ˌrɪəˈlɪstɪk]	realistisch	Are your plans *realistic*?
material [məˈtɪəriəl]	Material	

Story: I'm a mudlark

mudlark [ˈmʌdlɑːk]	jemand, der im Schlamm nach Sachen sucht, die er dann verkaufen kann	
high tide [ˈhaɪ ˌtaɪd]	Flut	
low tide [ˈləʊ ˌtaɪd]	Ebbe	The River Thames has two faces – one at high tide, one at *low tide*.
to flow out [fləʊ ˈaʊt]	hinausfließen	Rivers *flow out* into the sea.
towards [təˈwɔːdz]	in Richtung; auf … zu; darauf zu	Look, that man is coming *towards* us.
central [ˈsentrl]	zentral; Zentral-	*central* → centre *Lat.* centrum *(nt)*
heart [hɑːt]	Herz; *hier:* Zentrum	the *heart* of London = the centre of London
metre [ˈmiːtə]	Meter	
muddy [ˈmʌdi]	schlammig	
bank [bæŋk]	Ufer	A river has two *banks*.
wobbly [ˈwɒbli]	wackelig	
bridge [brɪdʒ]	Brücke	A *bridge* goes over a river.

they were enjoying [ðei wər ɪnˈdʒɔɪɪŋ]	sie genossen gerade	
silver [ˈsɪlvə]	Silber	
to try on [traɪ ˈɒn]	anprobieren	That's a nice T-shirt. Why don't you *try* it *on*, Olivia?
quickly [ˈkwɪkli]	schnell	
to grab [græb]	greifen; ergreifen; schnappen	Holly *grabbed* her bag and left the house quickly.
wrist [rɪst]	Handgelenk	
to drop [drɒp]	fallen (lassen)	Jay *dropped* Amir's bracelet.
to roll off [rəʊl]	hinunterrollen; herunterrollen	The bracelet *rolled* off the bridge.
angrily [ˈæŋgrɪli]	verärgert; zornig; wütend	

It's gone. [ɪts ˈɡɒn]	Es ist weg.	
down [daʊn]	nach unten; herunter; hinunter	They looked *down* from the bridge.
to **be lucky** [bi ˈlʌki]	Glück haben	I'*m lucky*. = Ich habe Glück. I'm happy. = Ich bin glücklich.
mud [mʌd]	Schlamm	*mud* → muddy → mudlark
shore [ʃɔː]	Ufer; Küste	*shore* = bank
wet [wet]	nass	
they weren't wearing [ˌðei wɜːnt ˈweərɪŋ]	sie trugen nicht	
bucket [ˈbʌkɪt]	Eimer	
trowel [ˈtraʊəl]	kleiner Spaten	
a trowel which … [ə ˌtraʊəl ˈwɪtʃ]	ein Spaten, der …	
politely [pəˈlaɪtli]	höflich	
century [ˈsenʃri]	Jahrhundert	We live in the 21st *century*.
anyway [ˈeniweɪ]	trotzdem; jedenfalls; sowieso	
dirty [ˈdɜːti]	dreckig; schmutzig	I can't wear this T-shirt because it's *dirty*.
dead [ded]	tot	
to **wash up** [ˌwɒʃ ˈʌp]	angespült werden	Dead animals *washed up* on the river banks.
all the time [ˌɔːl ðə ˈtaɪm]	die ganze Zeit	I use my phone almost *all the time*.
human body [ˌhjuːmən ˈbɒdi]	menschlicher Körper	
clay pipe [ˈkleɪ paɪp]	Tonpfeife	
at first [ət ˈfɜːst]	zuerst; zunächst	*At first* Luke didn't like Jay very much, but then they became good friends.
to **notice** [ˈnəʊtɪs]	bemerken; wahrnehmen	Did you *notice* anything strange about the woman?
more easily [mɔːr ˌiːzɪli]	leichter	
key [kiː]	Schlüssel	
to **scream** [skriːm]	schreien; kreischen	Holly *screamed* because she found something awful.
coconut [ˈkəʊkənʌt]	Kokosnuss	
to **cut, cut (off)** [kʌt; kʌt (ɒf)]	schneiden; abschneiden	
dramatic [drəˈmætɪk]	dramatisch	*dramatic* → drama *Fr.* dramatique
hour [aʊə]	Stunde	There are 24 *hours* in a day. *Lat.* hora (f)
side [saɪd]	Seite	
to **be surprised** [bi səˈpraɪzd]	überrascht sein	They *were surprised* about all the 'treasure' in the mud!

idiot [ˈɪdiət]	Idiot/-in	**!** Achtung Betonung.	
2	**modern** [ˈmɒdn]	modern	Smartphones are *modern* technology. *Fr.* moderne

Water words

sea – river – lake	Meer – Fluss – See
high tide – low tide – wave	Flut – Ebbe – Welle
to flow out – to flow towards … – to wash up	hinausfließen – in Richtung … fließen – anspülen
bank – shore	Ufer
bridge	Brücke
mud – muddy – wet	Schlamm – schlammig – nass
ship – boat	Schiff – Boot

Unit 3 Sport is good for you!

Check-in

	experience [ɪkˈspɪəriəns]	Erfahrung	What interesting *experiences* can you tell us about?
	things which … [θɪŋz ˈwɪtʃ]	Dinge, die …	
	health [helθ]	Gesundheit	*health* → healthy
	accident [ˈæksɪdnt]	Unfall	My sister had a bike *accident*. *Fr.* accident (m)
	camel racing [ˈkæml ˌreɪsɪŋ]	Kamelrennen	Is *camel racing* really a sport?
	marathon [ˈmærəθn]	Marathon	
1	**radio** [ˈreɪdiəʊ]	Radio	**!** Achtung Aussprache. *Fr.* radio (f)
	programme [ˈprəʊgræm]	Programm; Sendung	There's an interesting *programme* about camel racing on TV now. *Fr.* programme (m)
	runner [ˈrʌnə]	Läufer/-in	*runner* → to run
	race [reɪs]	Wettlauf; Rennen	Can we watch the bike *race* on TV, Mum?
	net [net]	Netz	For tennis, you need a *net*.
	to lose, lost, lost [luːz; lɒst; lɒst]	verlieren	Our team *lost* again!

match [mætʃ]	Spiel; Match	a game (of football/…)
racquet ['rækɪt]	Schläger	
court [kɔːt]	Spielfeld	! a tennis *court* – a football field
to **pass** [pɑːs]	zupassen; zuspielen	
to **kick** [kɪk]	schießen; treten	'Pass' means to throw or *kick* the ball to another player in the same team.
stadium ['steɪdiəm]	Stadion	
score [skɔː]	Punktestand; Spielstand	At the end of the match the *score* was 2-2.
point [pɔɪnt]	Punkt	That's right. One *point* for your team.
to **catch, caught, caught** [kætʃ; kɔːt; kɔːt]	fangen	*to catch* a ball ↔ to throw a ball
pitch [pɪtʃ]	Spielfeld; Platz	You play rugby on a *pitch*.
2 **the … the** [ðə … ðə]	je … desto	*The* quicker you are with your homework, *the* earlier you can meet your friends.
4 **equipment** [ɪ'kwɪpmənt]	Ausstattung; Ausrüstung	*equipment* = things you need for sports activities
individual [ˌɪndɪ'vɪdʒuəl]	individuell; einzeln	Do you do an *individual* sport or a team sport? *Lat.* individuus/-a/-um

Station 1: Have you ever run in a marathon?

ever ['evə]	jemals	It was our funniest project *ever*!
right here [ˌraɪt 'hɪə]	genau hier	The marathon starts *right here*.
until [ʌn'tɪl]	bis; erst wenn	You can't run in a marathon *until* you're 18.
11-year-old [ɪˌlevn'jɪərəʊld]	11-Jährige/-r	The mini marathon is for *11-* to *18-year-olds*.
running ['rʌnɪŋ]	Laufen; Rennen	Gwen loves *running*.
trial [traɪəl]	Qualifikation	There are *trials* in sports to find the best runners or players.
Who's in? [huːz'ɪn]	Wer macht mit?; Wer ist dabei?	
to **be in** [bi'ɪn]	dabei sein; mitmachen	Are you going to run? Well, I'*m in*, and I hope you are too!
run [rʌn]	Rennen; Lauf	*a run* → to run → runner
to **look out** [ˌlʊk'aʊt]	aufpassen	*Look out*, everyone! I'm going to win this race!
1 **area** ['eəriə]	Areal; Gebiet; Fläche	What sports events are there in your *area*?
2 **before** [bɪ'fɔː]	schon einmal; vorher; zuvor	Have you been here *before*? Or is this your first trip?
4 **arm** [ɑːm]	Arm	
leg [leg]	Bein	

Parts of the body

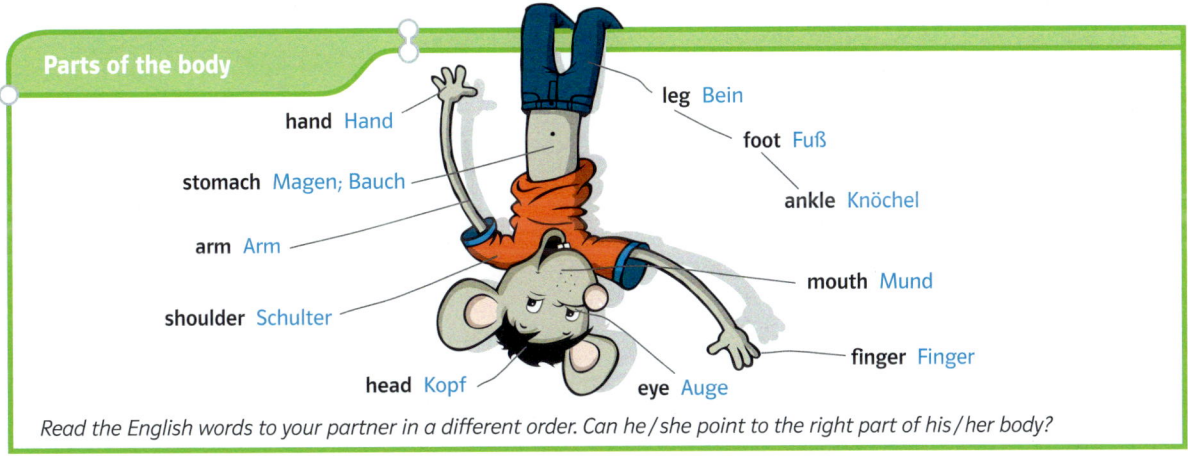

hand Hand

leg Bein

foot Fuß

stomach Magen; Bauch

ankle Knöchel

arm Arm

mouth Mund

shoulder Schulter

finger Finger

head Kopf

eye Auge

Read the English words to your partner in a different order. Can he/she point to the right part of his/her body?

Station 2: Have you been to the doctor's yet?

doctor [ˈdɒktə]	Arzt/Ärztin	**!** Beachte den Unterschied: Have you seen the *doctor* yet? Have you been to the *doctor's* yet? *doctor's* ist die Abkürzung für *doctor's surgery*. *Fr.* docteur *(m)*
yet [jet]	schon; noch	Have you asked your parents about the party *yet*?
to **leave, left, left** [liːv; left; left]	(los)gehen; abfahren; (ver)lassen	Have you *left* the house yet? – No, I'm still at home.
not … yet [nɒt ˈjet]	noch nicht	The friends have*n't* left for the marathon *yet*.
to **train** [treɪn]	trainieren	Luke plays football. He *trains* every day.
to **hurt, hurt, hurt** [hɜːt; hɜːt; hɜːt]	verletzen; weh tun	I *hurt* my leg last month, and it still *hurts* now.
to **twist your ankle** [ˌtwɪst jɔːr ˈæŋkl]	sich den Knöchel verrenken	
pain [peɪn]	Schmerz	I've got a really bad *pain* in my left foot.
unfair [ʌnˈfeə]	unfair	*unfair* ↔ fair
Bye! [baɪ]	Tschüss!	*bye* ↔ hello
6 **mile** [maɪl]	Meile *(brit. Längenmaß)*	1 *mile* = 1,609 metres
chant [tʃɑːnt]	Sprechgesang	*Lat.* cantare
to **cheer** [tʃɪə]	anfeuern; jubeln; zujubeln	Jay is writing a chant to *cheer* the runners in the marathon.
7 to **fall off, fell off, fallen off** [fɔːl ˈɒf; fel ˈɒf; fɔːlən ˈɒf]	herunterfallen; hinunterfallen	I *fell off* my bike and hurt my knee.
8 to **have a look (at)** [ˌhæv ə ˈlʊk]	anschauen	Let's *have a look* at it. = Let's look at it.
shouldn't [ˈʃʊdnt]	sollte(n) nicht	Olivia *shouldn't* run in the marathon with ankle problems.
prescription [prɪˈskrɪpʃn]	Rezept *(für Arzneimittel)*	*Lat.* praescribere

ointment [ˈɔɪntmənt]	Salbe	The doctor gave Olivia a prescription for an *ointment*.
shoulder [ˈʃəʊldə]	Schulter	
headache *(no pl)* [ˈhedeɪk]	Kopfschmerzen; Kopfweh	! *headache* steht immer im Singular: I've got a bad *headache*. *headache* → head
backache [ˈbækeɪk]	Rückenschmerzen; Rückenweh	
stomachache [ˈstʌməkeɪk]	Bauchschmerzen; Bauchweh	
to **feel sick** [ˌfiːl ˈsɪk]	Übelkeit verspüren; sich schlecht fühlen	I *feel sick.* = Mir ist schlecht/übel.
cold [kəʊld]	Erkältung	
cough [kɒf]	Husten	
fever [ˈfiːvə]	Fieber	People with a cold often have a cough and a *fever*. *Fr.* fièvre *(f)*
pill [pɪl]	Pille; Tablette	The doctor wrote a prescription for some *pills*.
9 introduction [ˌɪntrəˈdʌkʃn]	Einführung; Einleitung; Vorstellung	the *introduction* of a report = the first part of a report

Health

to **have an accident**	einen Unfall haben
to **call the emergency service**	den Rettungsdienst rufen
to **hurt your foot / arm / leg/** …	sich den Fuß / Arm / das Bein / … verletzen
to **twist your ankle**	sich den Knöchel verrenken
to **feel a pain in** …	Schmerzen haben in / an …
to **get a prescription**	ein Rezept bekommen
to **put ointment on** …	… einsalben
to **take pills**	Tabletten nehmen
to **have a headache / backache / stomachache**	Kopfweh / Rückenweh / Bauchweh haben
to **feel bad / sick**	sich schlecht / krank fühlen
to **catch a cold / cough / fever**	eine Erkältung / Husten / Fieber bekommen

With a partner, make more doctor dialogues as on p. 73.

I don't feel well today. Maybe I've caught a cold.

Action UK! A picnic in the park

1	**so far** [ˌsəʊ ˈfɑː]	bis jetzt	The players have given the people a great show *so far*.
	attic [ˈætɪk]	Dachboden	
	Korean [kəˈriːən]	koreanisch; Koreanisch; Koreaner/-in	There was *Korean* food at the picnic.
2	to **fake** [feɪk]	vortäuschen; fälschen	
	injury [ˈɪndʒəri]	Verletzung	Who faked an *injury* in the film?
	to **teach somebody a lesson** [ˌtiːtʃ ə ˈlesn]	jmdm. eine Lehre/Lektion erteilen	That wasn't a nice thing to do. Let's *teach him a lesson*.
	to **teach, taught, taught** [tiːtʃ; tɔːt; tɔːt]	unterrichten; lehren; beibringen	*to teach* → teacher
	to **deserve** [dɪˈzɜːv]	verdienen	The others are angry with you, but you *deserved* it. You tricked them!
	point of view [ˌpɔɪnt əv ˈvjuː]	Standpunkt; Ansicht; Perspektive	Who's right and who's wrong from your *point of view*?
	to **get away with** [ˌget əˈweɪ wɪð]	davonkommen mit	Marley didn't *get away with* it.

Skills: How to understand news reports and take notes

1	**rescue** [ˈreskjuː]	Rettung	Here is a report about a *rescue* in the mountains.
	difficult [ˈdɪfɪklt]	schwierig	*difficult* ↔ easy *Fr.* difficil/-e; *Lat.* difficilis/-e
	witness [ˈwɪtnəs]	Zeuge/Zeugin	The police is looking for *witnesses* for the accident.
2	**eyewitness** [ˈaɪwɪtnəs]	Augenzeuge/Augenzeugin	The reporter is talking to an *eyewitness* in front of the camera.
	station [ˈsteɪʃn]	Sender	What's your favourite radio *station*?
	listener [ˈlɪsənə]	Zuhörer/-in	*listener* → to listen
	to **receive** [rɪˈsiːv]	empfangen; erhalten; bekommen	A formal word for 'to get'. *Fr.* recevoir; *Lat.* recipere
	scene [siːn]	Schauplatz	The reporter tried to get to the *scene* of the accident.
	anyone else [ˌeniwʌn ˈels]	irgendjemand; jemand anderes	Don't tell the story to *anyone else*.
	I couldn't believe my eyes. [aɪ ˌkʊdnt bɪˈliːv maɪ ˈaɪz]	Ich traute meinen Augen nicht.	*I couldn't believe my eyes* when I got a dog for my birthday.

Unit task: The aliens have landed!

	to **land** [lænd]	landen	Do you believe that aliens have ever *landed* on Earth?
	to **record** [rɪˈkɔːd]	aufnehmen; aufzeichnen	Let's *record* the scene with a camera.
	assistant [əˈsɪstnt]	Assistent/-in; Verkäufer/-in	! Achtung Schreibung und Aussprache.

hospital [ˈhɒspɪtl]	Krankenhaus; Hospital	*Fr.* hôpital *(m)*
as [æz; əz]	als	
to **end** [end]	enden; beenden	to end ↔ to start to end → end
over [ˈəʊvə]	vorüber; vorbei	School is *over* at 3:15.

Story: Hey, don't call me silly!

almost [ˈɔːlməʊst]	fast; beinahe	It's *almost* 8 o'clock! You're late for school.
to **let go (of)** [ˌlet ˈgəʊ (əv)]	loslassen	Don't *let go of* my hand, Gwen!
I'm the one who … [ˌaɪm ðə ˌwʌn ˈhuː]	ich bin diejenige, die …	
silly [ˈsɪli]	Dummkopf	
fancy dress [ˈfænsi dres]	Verkleidung; Kostüm	
to **breathe** [briːð]	atmen	
to **keep up, kept, up, kept up (with)** [ˌkiːpˈʌp; ˌkeptˈʌp; ˌkeptˈʌp (wɪð)]	mithalten (mit); Schritt halten (mit)	Can Luke *keep up with* Gwen? = Is Luke fast enough?
to **be worried** [bi ˈwʌrid]	beunruhigt sein; besorgt sein	Don't *be worried* = Don't worry
to **take sth seriously** [ˌteɪk ˈsɪəriəsli]	etw. ernst nehmen	If a situation is serious, you must *take it seriously*.
to **get in the way** [ˌget ˌɪn ðə ˈweɪ]	stören; im Weg stehen	The people in the costumes shouldn't *get in the way* of the runners.
stomach [ˈstʌmək]	Magen; Bauch	*Fr.* estomac *(m)*
glasses *(pl)* [ˈglɑːsɪz]	Brille	! *glasses* steht immer im Plural: My *glasses* are broken. I need new ones.
finish line [ˈfɪnɪʃ ˌlaɪn]	Ziellinie	At the end of a run there's always a *finish line*.
stupid [ˈstjuːpɪd]	dumm; blöd	The *stupid* cat and dog almost ruined the race for Gwen and Luke.
cramp [kræmp]	Krampf	
to **be gone** [bi ˈgɒn]	verschwunden sein; weg sein	Near the end of the race, Gwen's cramp *was gone*.
We did it! [ˌwiː ˈdɪd ˌɪt]	Wir haben es geschafft!	*Luke and Gwen did it!*
both [bəʊθ]	beide	Luke and Gwen *both* finished the race.
to **ruin** [ˈruːɪn]	ruinieren; zerstören	Jay and Dave almost *ruined* the race for Luke and Gwen.
official [əˈfɪʃl]	Schiedsrichter/-in	In a race there are always *officials*.

finally [ˈfaɪnli]	schließlich; endlich; zum Schluss; letztlich	first – then – *finally* *Lat.* finis *(m)*
to **surprise** [səˈpraɪz]	überraschen	*to surprise* → surprise
in secret [ɪn ˈsiːkrət]	heimlich	Jay and Dave trained *in secret*. No one knew about it. *in secret* → a secret
because of [bɪˈkɒz̩ əv]	wegen	My feet really hurt *because of* my new shoes.
to **forgive, forgave, forgiven** [fəˈɡɪv; fəˈɡeɪv; fəˈɡɪvn]	vergeben; verzeihen	Can Gwen *forgive* them?
1 **reason** [ˈriːzn]	Grund	Why did you do it? What was the *reason*? *Fr.* raison *(f)*
to **cause** [kɔːz]	verursachen	What or who *caused* the accident?
hope [həʊp]	Hoffnung	*hope* → to hope
fear [fɪə]	Angst; Furcht; Befürchtung	The feeling you have when you are scared.
relationship [rɪˈleɪʃnʃɪp]	Beziehung	Is the *relationship* between you and your neighbours a good one?
2 **positive** [ˈpɒzətɪv]	positiv	*Fr.* positive/positif
negative [ˈneɡətɪv]	negativ; verneint	*negative* ↔ positive
On the one hand …, (but) on the other hand … [ɒn ðə ˈwʌn ˌhænd … (bʌt) ɒn ði ˈʌðə ˌhænd …]	Einerseits …, (aber) andererseits …	*On the one hand* he'd like to be a better runner, *but on the other hand* he doesn't want to train very hard.
4 the boy who … [ðə bɔɪ ˈhuː]	der Junge, der …	

Positive and negative words

		−
What you think of something:	easy, good, great, interesting, useful; amazing, fantastic, perfect	bad, boring, dangerous, difficult; awful, scary
What you think of a person:	creative, cute, fair, friendly, fun, funny, good, polite, popular	aggressive, boring, rude, silly, stupid, unfair, unfriendly
How a person feels:	confident, good, happy, lucky	bad, embarrassed, lonely, sad, shy, unhappy, unlucky

Which of the words are opposites? Write them down together.

Check-out

3 **player** [ˈpleɪə]	Spieler/-in; Mitspieler/-in	*player* → to play

Across cultures 3 English around the world

1	**member** ['membə]	Mitglied	Dave is a *member* of the Preston family. *Fr.* membre *(m)*
	summer camp ['sʌmə kæmp]	Sommerferienlager	I only spoke English when I was at *summer camp* last year.
2	to **mention** ['menʃn]	erwähnen	Did I *mention* that I have a cool new phone? *Fr.* mentionner
	statement ['steɪtmənt]	Aussage; Behauptung; Erklärung	to make a *statement* = to say something
	exactly [ɪg'zæktli]	genau	I don't understand. What *exactly* do you mean? *Lat.* exactus/-a/-um
	South Korean [ˌsaʊθ kə'riːən]	Südkoreaner/-in; südkorea-nisch; Südkoreanisch	
	Romanian [rʊ'meɪniən]	Rumäne/Rumänin; rumänisch; Rumänisch	
3	**first language** [ˌfɜːst 'læŋgwɪdʒ]	Muttersprache	My *first language* is German.
	official language [əˌfɪʃl 'læŋgwɪdʒ]	Amtssprache	In India, English is an *official language*.
	merchant ['mɜːtʃənt]	Kaufmann, Händler	A *merchant* sells and buys things.
	to **cross** [krɒs]	überqueren; kreuzen	You need to *cross* the street to get to the shoe shop.
	colony ['kɒləni]	Kolonie	Many years ago, Germany had *colonies* too. *Fr.* colonie *(f)*; *Lat.* colonia *(f)*
	for example [fər ɪg'zɑːmpl]	zum Beispiel	I speak four languages, *for example* English and French.
	head of state [ˌhed əv 'steɪt]	Staatsoberhaupt	The British queen is *head of state* in Australia.
	superpower ['suːpəˌpaʊə]	Supermacht	Will China and India be the next *superpowers*?
	to **influence** ['ɪnfluəns]	beeinflussen	The USA has *influenced* the world in different ways.
			! Im Englischen verwendet man für „USA" immer die Einzahl (The USA has …), im Deutschen aber die Mehrzahl (Die USA haben …).
	technology [tek'nɒlədʒi]	Technologie	
	to **communicate** [kə'mjuːnɪkeɪt]	kommunizieren; sich verstän-digen	An easy way to *communicate* with people is to speak to them. *Lat.* communicare
4	**region** ['riːdʒn]	Region; Gegend	What *region* in Germany do you come from? *Lat.* regio *(f)*
	expression [ɪk'spreʃn]	Ausdruck; Wendung; Äußerung	We often use English *expressions* in German. *Lat.* expressio *(f)*

Unit 4 Stay in touch

Check-in

to **stay in touch (with)** [ˌsteɪ ɪn ˈtʌtʃ (wɪð)]	in Kontakt bleiben (mit)	E-mails are a good way to *stay in touch* with your friends.
media [ˈmiːdiə]	Medien	Radio, TV and the internet are all *media*. *Fr.* médias *(f) (pl)*; *Lat.* medium *(nt)*
letter [ˈletə]	Brief	 *Lat.* littera *(f)*
interest [ˈɪntrəst]	Interesse	*interest* → interesting → be interested
paradise [ˈpærədaɪs]	Paradies	*Fr.* paradis *(m)*
print [prɪnt]	gedruckt; Druck-	
for [fɔː; fə]	wegen	I buy print magazines *for* the posters.
social network [ˌsəʊʃl ˈnetwɜːk]	soziales Netzwerk	You can chat with all kinds of people in *social networks*.
nasty [ˈnɑːsti]	garstig; gemein	*nasty* ↔ nice
cyber bully [ˌsaɪbə ˈbʊli]	*jemand, der andere in sozialen Netzwerken belästigt oder mobbed*	*Cyber bullies* write nasty comments in social networks.
2 to **change** [tʃeɪndʒ]	wechseln; (sich) ändern	*Fr.* changer
to **post** [pəʊst]	online stellen; posten	Have you *posted* the photos of the class trip?

Media collocations

to check	checken, überprüfen	my e-mails / my profile / my friend's profile	meine E-Mails / mein Profil / das Profil meines Freundes
to change	ändern	my profile	mein Profil
to post to share	posten; hochladen teilen	photos / information about …	Fotos / Informationen über …
to read / to write / to reply to	lesen / schreiben / antworten auf	texts / text messages / e-mails	SMS-Nachrichten / E-Mails
to send / to receive	senden / empfangen	texts / text messages / e-mails / photos / information	SMS-Nachrichten / E-Mails / Fotos / Informationen
to chat with to text to stay in touch with	chatten mit eine SMS schreiben in Kontakt bleiben mit	a friend	einem Freund
to join to take part in	beitreten teilnehmen an	a discussion / a social network / a forum	einer Diskussion / einem sozialen Netzwerk / einem Forum
to have to take part in	führen teilnehmen an	a discussion / a video chat	eine Diskussion / einen Videochat einer Diskussion / einem Videochat
to play	spielen	video games	Computerspiele

to **take part (in)** [ˌteɪk ˈpɑːt (ɪn)]	teilnehmen (an)	Let's *take part in* the new Drama Club at school.
to **text** [tekst]	eine SMS schicken	*to text* → text message
discussion [dɪ'skʌʃn]	Diskussion	*discussion* → to discuss
3 **practical** ['præktɪkl]	praktisch	Smartphones are *practical* to stay in touch with friends. *Fr.* pratique
mobile ['məʊbaɪl]	Handy; Mobiltelefon	*mobile* = phone

Station 1: Dear Ruby

agony aunt ['æɡəniˌɑːnt]	Kummerkastentante	Lauren didn't want to talk about her problem with her friends or her family. So she wrote a letter to her favourite magazine's *agony aunt*.
teen [tiːn]	Jugend-	*teen* → teenager
… what to do. ['wɒt tə duː]	… was ich tun soll.	I don't know *what to do*.
fight [faɪt]	Kampf; Streit	
to **spend, spent, spent** [spend; spent; spent]	verbringen (*Zeit*)	She *spends* all her free time with her dog.
the two of them [ðə 'tuː əv ðəm]	beide	My brothers sent me a photo of *the two of them*.
site [saɪt]	Webseite	
to **act like** ['ækt laɪk]	tun als ob	My sister often *acts like* a baby.
whenever [wen'evə]	wann immer; jedes Mal, wenn; so oft	*Whenever* I ask my brother for something, he says "no".
upset [ʌp'set]	aufgebracht; bestürzt	Why are you so *upset*? – My brother lost my phone!
to **share** [ʃeə]	teilen	Can I have half of your sandwich? Can we *share* it?
self-critical ['selfˌkrɪtɪkl]	selbstkritisch	The agony aunt's advice is to be *self-critical*. I think she's right.
to **overreact** [ˌəʊvəri'ækt]	überreagieren	I know you're angry with him, but don't *overreact* and say bad things about him, OK?
as soon as [əz 'suːnˌəz]	sobald	Things usually get better *as soon as* you talk to the person you're fighting with.
to **make somebody do something** [meɪk]	jmdn. dazu bringen, etw. zu tun	My friend's texts *make* me *feel bad*.
1 **opinion** [ə'pɪnjən]	Meinung	In my *opinion* … = I think … *Lat.* opinio (f)
2 **face-to-face** [ˌfeɪstə'feɪs]	*hier:* persönlich; von Angesicht zu Angesicht	It's fun to meet people *face-to-face* and not just in social networks.
to **block** [blɒk]	blockieren; abblocken	You can *block* messages from people you don't like.

forever [fəˈrevə]	für immer; ewig	When you post photos on the internet, they never go away. They can stay there *forever*.
to **care (about)** [ˈkeər‿əˌbaʊt]	wichtig nehmen; sich kümmern (um); sich interessieren (für)	If you *care about* something then it's important to you.
attention [əˈtenʃn]	Aufmerksamkeit; Beachtung	*Fr.* attention *(f)*; *Lat.* attentio *(f)*
myself [maɪˈself]	ich/mir/mich (selbst); selber	*myself* → yourself → himself
4	**understanding** [ˌʌndəˈstændɪŋ]	Verständnis	What can you say to show *understanding*?
compromise [ˈkɒmprəmaɪz]	Kompromiss	It isn't always easy to find a *compromise*. *Fr.* compromis *(m)*
to **worry** [ˈwʌri]	sich Sorgen machen	Don't *worry* about your friend. Everything is OK now.
5	to **mediate** [ˈmiːdieɪt]	vermitteln	to *mediate* → mediation
6	**friendship** [ˈfrendʃɪp]	Freundschaft	I've got lots of friends. I think *friendship* is very important.

Station 2: Forum? What forum?

to **go over to** [ˌgəʊ ˈəʊvə tə]	hinübergehen zu; zu jmdm. nach Hause gehen	Come on, let's *go over* to your house.
What on earth …? [ˌwɒt‿ɒn‿ˈ3ːθ]	Was um alles in der Welt …?	*What on earth* is this?
pipe [paɪp]	Rohr; Rohrleitung	He broke a *pipe* and now there's water everywhere!
to **fix** [fɪks]	reparieren; befestigen	My bike is broken. Can you *fix* it?
to **go crazy** [ˌgəʊ ˈkreɪzi]	ausflippen; durchdrehen; verrückt werden	I think I'm *going crazy*: I don't understand the Maths homework at all!
to **take, took, taken** [teɪk; tʊk; ˈteɪkn]	dauern; (Zeit) brauchen	It *takes* two hours to get to London by train.
washing machine [ˈwɒʃɪŋ məˌʃiːn]	Waschmaschine	*washing machine* → to wash
to **have to** [ˈhæv tə]	müssen	Our washing machine is broken. We *have to* repair it.
to **waste** [weɪst]	verschwenden	You're *wasting* your time, Dad!
cannot [ˈkænɒt]	kann nicht; können nicht	*cannot* = can't
step-by-step [ˌstepbaɪˈstep]	Schritt-für-Schritt-	On the internet, there's *step-by-step* advice for everything.
no such thing as [ˌnəʊ sʌtʃ θɪŋ‿ˈæs]	nicht so etwas wie	When I was young, there weren't any mobile phones. There was *no such thing*.
still [stɪl]	dennoch	I don't have any money, but I'm *still* going to go to London.
I've done this a million times before. [ˌaɪv dʌn ðɪs ə ˌmɪljən taɪmz bɪˈfɔː]	Ich habe das schon eine Million Mal gemacht.	
knob [nɒb]	Griff	Cupboard doors often have *knobs*.
to **reach** [riːtʃ]	erreichen; dran kommen	My mum put the chocolate on top of the cupboard so my little sister can't *reach* it.
to **work** [wɜːk]	*hier:* funktionieren	Is the washing machine *working* again?

genius [ˈdʒiːniəs]	Genie	*Fr.* génie *(m)*
With a very big head! [ˌwɪð ə ˌveri bɪg ˈhed]	Und ein Angeber!	
may [meɪ]	(vielleicht) können; dürfen	! Wenn du auf Englisch nach etwas fragst oder um etwas bittest, beginne deine Frage mit *may*: *May* I take another piece of cake, please?
8 **mess** [mes]	Unordnung, Durcheinander	What a *mess*! Please tidy your room.
10 **to carry** [ˈkæri]	tragen	Can you *carry* this box for me, please?
11 **flower** [flaʊə]	Blume	
12 **mad** [mæd]	verrückt	My parents think that I'm media *mad*.
result [rɪˈzʌlt]	Ergebnis; Resultat	Have we got the test *results* yet? Who got the most points? *Fr.* résultat *(m)*
to (e-)mail [ˈiːmeɪl]	mailen; per E-Mail schicken	Could you *e-mail* me your part of the class project? I can *mail* you my part too.
friends and family who … [frendz ˌən ˌfæməli ˈhuː]	Freunde und Familienmitglieder, die …	
to download [ˌdaʊnˈləʊd]	herunterladen *(aus dem Internet)*	
to comment (on) [ˈkɒment ˌ(ɒn)]	kommentieren	Please don't *comment* on my test results; I didn't do very well at all! *to comment* → a comment
to stay away from [ˌsteɪ əˈweɪ frəm]	fernbleiben von; meiden	*Stay away from* too much chocolate. It isn't good for your health.
clever [ˈklevə]	schlau; klug	What a *clever* idea!
in other ways [ɪn ˈʌðə weɪz]	auf andere Weise	I don't need my phone all the time. I can have fun *in other ways* too.

Skills: How to write a letter and a reply

1 **camping** [ˈkæmpɪŋ]	Camping; Zelten	We go *camping* every year!
to miss [mɪs]	verpassen; versäumen	Hey, you *missed* a great party! Where were you?
Yours … [jɔːz]	Viele Grüße … *(am Ende von Briefen und Mails)*	! You can end a letter or e-mail like this.
to begin, began, begun [bɪˈgɪn; bɪˈgæn; bɪˈgʌn]	beginnen; anfangen	How do you *begin* a letter or e-mail?
beach [biːtʃ]	Strand	
2 **weird** [wɪəd]	merkwürdig; seltsam; sonderbar	*weird* = strange

Unit task: Advice letters and replies: Our collection

chance [tʃɑːns]	Chance; Gelegenheit; Möglichkeit	Give me another *chance*, please!
weekday ['wiːkdeɪ]	Wochentag	On *weekday* mornings I usually go to school.
to **do about** ['duː ə‚baʊt]	unternehmen wegen	What can I *do about* my teacher? I don't think she likes me.
freely ['friːli]	frei	

Story: It's a disaster!

disaster [dɪ'zɑːstə]	Desaster; Katastrophe; Unglück	Frank's day was a *disaster*. *Fr.* désastre *(m)*
to **rain** [reɪn]	regnen	It's *raining*!
it was raining [‚ɪt wəz 'reɪnɪŋ]	es regnete gerade	
he wasn't able to … [‚hi wɒznt 'eɪbl‚tə]	er konnte nicht …	
he was able to … [‚hi wɒz 'eɪbl‚tə]	er konnte …	
light [laɪt]	Licht; Lampe	At night you need *light*.
to **be on** [bi‚'ɒn]	an sein; laufen	The race *is on*.
thunder *(no pl)* ['θʌndə]	Donner	In a storm there's usually *thunder* and lightning.
lightning *(no pl)* ['laɪtnɪŋ]	Blitz	
to **get out of** [get ‚aʊt‚əv]	aussteigen	He *got out of* the car quickly and ran to the house.
front door [‚frʌnt 'dɔː]	Haustür	Every house has a *front door*.
nearly ['nɪəli]	fast; annähernd	*nearly* = almost
upstairs [ʌp'steəz]	nach oben; im Obergeschoss; oben	
headphones *(pl)* ['hedfəʊnz]	Kopfhörer	Take my *headphones* and listen to this!
downstairs [daʊn'steəz]	nach unten; im Untergeschoss; unten	*downstairs* ↔ upstairs
to **tap** [tæp]	antippen	Jay *tapped* Olivia's shoulder.
I was thinking … [‚aɪ wəz 'θɪŋkɪŋ]	ich dachte gerade …	
to **cry** [kraɪ]	schreien; rufen	*to cry* = to shout *Fr.* crier

to **fight, fought, fought** [faɪt; fɔːt; fɔːt]	kämpfen; (sich) streiten	*to fight* → fight
to **joke** [dʒəʊk]	scherzen	Don't worry, I'm only *joking*! *to joke* → a joke **Lat.** iocus *(m)*
to **push** [pʊʃ]	stoßen; schieben; schubsen	He *pushed* me – and I fell over. That wasn't nice!
to **press** [pres]	drücken; pressen	**Fr.** presser
he was pressing [hi wəz ˈpresɪŋ]	er drückte gerade	
to **go black** [ˌgəʊ ˈblæk]	schwarz werden	After the bang everything *went black*.
to **crash** [kræʃ]	abstürzen	Has your computer ever *crashed*?
to **calm down** [ˌkɑːm ˈdaʊn]	sich beruhigen	**!** Das „l" in *calm* wird nicht ausgesprochen.
power cut [ˈpaʊə ˌkʌt]	Stromausfall	
round [raʊnd]	um … herum	Five minutes later they all sat *round* the table.
candlelight *(no pl)* [ˈkændlaɪt]	Kerzenlicht	
only [ˈəʊnli]	einzige/-r/-s	I'm the *only* girl in my tutor group without glasses.
right now [ˌraɪt ˈnaʊ]	jetzt gleich; sofort; gerade	*Right now* I don't have any problems.
to **cook** [kʊk]	kochen	Have you ever *cooked* an Indian curry?
to **be impressed** [bi ɪmˈprest]	beeindruckt sein	The friends *were impressed* with Jay's dancing and singing.
he wasn't speaking [hi ˌwəznt ˈspiːkɪŋ]	er sprach gerade nicht	
to **show off** [ʃəʊˈɒf]	angeben	My brother always *shows off* with his expensive smartphone.
to **borrow** [ˈbɒrəʊ]	(sich) ausleihen	Can I *borrow* this T-shirt? – OK, but please remember to give it back.
mine [maɪn]	mein/-er/-e/-es	Is this my pizza? = Is it *mine*?
1	to **feel left out** [ˌfiːl left ˈaʊt]	sich ausgeschlossen fühlen	Did Frank *feel left out*?
2	to **link** [lɪŋk]	verbinden	
	dangerously [ˈdeɪndʒrəsli]	gefährlich	
	more quickly [mɔː ˈkwɪkli]	schneller	

Unit 5 Goodbye Greenwich

Check-in

| **journey** [ˈdʒɜːni] | Reise; Fahrt | On our *journey* through England we met a lot of nice people. |
| **future** [ˈfjuːtʃə] | Zukunft | What will the *future* be like? |

	to **report** [rɪˈpɔːt]	berichten; melden	*to report* → report
	medieval [ˌmediˈiːvl]	mittelalterlich	Is every castle *medieval*? – No, of course not. *Fr.* médiéval/-e
	living history show [ˌlɪvɪŋ ˈhɪstəri ˌʃəʊ]	*Show, in der historischer Alltag nachgespielt wird*	
	pony trekking [ˈpəʊni ˌtrekɪŋ]	Ponyreiten im Gelände	You go *pony trekking* in the country.
	Scottish [ˈskɒtɪʃ]	schottisch	Edinburgh is the *Scottish* capital.
1	to **include** [ɪnˈkluːd]	einschließen; beinhalten	The trip will be expensive, but the price *includes* all our meals. *Lat.* includere
2	**places that …** [ˌpleɪsɪz ˈðæt]	Orte, die …	
	landscape [ˈlændskeɪp]	Landschaft	
3	**sandy** [ˈsændi]	sandig; Sand-	
	rocky [ˈrɒki]	felsig; steinig	Not every beach is sandy. Many are *rocky*.
	wide [waɪd]	breit; weit; ausgedehnt	This table is too *wide*, we can't get it through the door.
	deep [diːp]	tief	You mustn't go into *deep* water if you can't swim.
	island [ˈaɪlənd]	Insel	The British Isles are a group of *islands*.
	harbour [ˈhɑːbə]	Hafen	The weather is bad, so the boats are staying in the *harbour*.
	hiking [ˈhaɪkɪŋ]	Wandern	Wales is great for *hiking*.
	mountain biking [ˈmaʊntɪn ˌbaɪkɪŋ]	Mountainbikefahren	
	(wind)surfing [ˈ(wɪnd)sɜːfɪŋ]	(Wind-)Surfen	**!** Beachte: Surfen und Windsurfen sind verschiedene Sportarten.
	palm tree [ˈpɑːm ˌtriː]	Palme	
	to **grow, grew, grown** [grəʊ; gruː; grəʊn]	wachsen	All kinds of flowers *grow* in our garden.

Parts of the British Isles

Places and what you can do there

Places		Activities	
in a city / town	in einer Stadt	to visit a museum / castle to go to a festival	ein Museum / Schloss besichtigen ein Festival besuchen
in the fields	auf den Wiesen und Feldern	to go hiking / mountain biking / pony trekking	wandern / Mountainbike fahren / wanderreiten gehen
in the forest	im Wald	to go for a walk	spazieren gehen
in the mountains	in den Bergen	to go climbing / hiking / mountain biking / pony trekking to go for a walk to climb a mountain	klettern / … spazieren gehen einen Berg besteigen
on an island at the seaside, by the sea, on the coast	auf einer Insel am Meer, an der Küste	to go climbing / hiking / mountain biking / pony trekking to go for a walk to climb a mountain	klettern / …
on the beach, on the shore	am Strand, am Meeresufer		
on the river bank, on the shore	am Flussufer	to go fishing	angeln gehen
in the sea in a river in a lake	im Meer in einem Fluss in einem See	to go swimming / surfing / windsurfing	schwimmen / surfen / windsurfen gehen

Station 1: Moving to the middle of nowhere

to **move (house)** [muːv (haʊs)]	umziehen	When you *move house*, you leave your old home and go to live in a new one. *Lat.* movēre
nowhere [ˈnəʊweə]	nirgendwo; nirgendwohin	*nowhere* → somewhere → everywhere
beautiful [ˈbjuːtɪfl]	schön; hübsch; wunderbar	
Cornish [ˈkɔːnɪʃ]	aus/in Cornwall; kornisch; Kornisch	Dave and his parents are going to move to a *Cornish* town.
countryside [ˈkʌntrɪsaɪd]	Land	in the *countryside* = auf dem Land
to **miss** [mɪs]	vermissen	I *miss* you. = Du fehlst mir.

won't she …? [wəʊnt ˈʃiː]	nicht wahr? stimmts?	
to **stay** [steɪ]	übernachten	We *stayed* at a really nice hotel.
won't be able to … [ˌwəʊnt biˈeɪbl̩ tə]	wirst nicht … können	
(not) any longer [nɒtˌeni ˈlɒŋgə]	(nicht) mehr; (nicht) länger	I don't like it here; I don't want to stay here *any longer*.
to **hate** [heɪt]	hassen; nicht mögen	*to hate* ↔ to love
to **make friends** [ˌmeɪk ˈfrendz]	Freundschaft schließen	I *made* lots of *friends* at my new school.
all of us [ˈɔːl əv ˌʌs]	wir alle	
wonderful [ˈwʌndəfl̩]	wunderbar	*wonderful* = great = fantastic
1 **transport** [ˈtrænspɔːt]	Verkehrsmittel; Transport	*Transport* can be expensive. *Lat.* transportare
3 **travel agent's** [ˈtrævl̩ ˌeɪdʒnts]	Reisebüro	You can buy holidays at the *travel agent's*.
ticket [ˈtɪkɪt]	Fahrschein	*Fr.* ticket *(m)*
to **depend (on)** [dɪˈpend (ɒn)]	abhängen von	The price of the ticket *depends on* the date. *Fr.* dépendre (de)
per [pɜː; pə]	pro	The price for the tickets is £5 *per* person.
to **promise** [ˈprɒmɪs]	versprechen	Can his parents *promise* that Dave will like Cornwall?
with a person who … [wɪð ə ˌpɜːsn ˈhuː]	mit einer Person, die …	
5 to **book** [bʊk]	buchen; reservieren	You can *book* a ticket for a journey, a holiday, a table at a restaurant.
to **return** [rɪˈtɜːn]	zurückkehren; zurückfahren	*to return* = to go or come back *Fr.* retourner
form [fɔːm]	Formular	You often have to fill in *forms* on the internet.
to **click on** [ˈklɪk ɒn]	anklicken	*Click on* 'SEND' to send your e-mail.
connection [kəˈnekʃn]	Verbindung	What *connections* are there from Greenwich to St Agnes today?
one-way ticket [ˈwʌnweɪ ˌtɪkɪt]	einfache Fahrkarte	
single ticket [ˌsɪŋgl̩ ˌtɪkɪt]	einfache Fahrkarte	*single ticket* = one-way ticket
return ticket [rɪˈtɜːn ˌtɪkɪt]	Hin- und Rückfahrkarte	*return ticket* ↔ one-way ticket
fee [fiː]	Gebühr	Is there an extra *fee* on the ticket?
to **depart** [dɪˈpɑːt]	abfahren	When does the train *depart*?
to **arrive** [əˈraɪv]	ankommen	And when does the next train *arrive*? *Fr.* arriver
outward [ˈaʊtwəd]	abfahrend	*Outward* trains leave the station.
inward [ˈɪnwəd]	ankommend	*Inward* trains arrive at the station.

fare [feə]	Fahrpreis	Is there a special *fare* for groups?
platform ['plætfɔːm]	Plattform; Bahnsteig	
to **get on (the bus)** [ˌget ˈɒn]	einsteigen (in den Bus)	*to get on* ↔ to get off
starting place ['stɑːtɪŋ pleɪs]	Startpunkt	

Travel words

to travel	reisen
travel agent's	Reisebüro
to take a journey / trip	eine Reise machen
transport	Transport
by train / coach / car / Underground	mit dem Zug / Bus / Auto / mit der-U-Bahn
station	Bahnhof, Station
airport	Flughafen
on the road	auf der Straße; unterwegs
one way; single / return	einfach / hin und zurück
outward / inward journey	Hinfahrt / Rückfahrt
to depart / arrive	abfahren / ankommen
to change	umsteigen

Tell your partner about a trip you took last summer / last year / …

6	**weather forecast** ['weðə ˌfɔːkɑːst]	Wettervorhersage	It tells you what the weather will be like.

Weather words

It's / The weather is	cold	kalt
	warm	warm
	cloudy	wolkig; bewölkt
	sunny	sonnig
There is / are	clouds	Wolken
	sun	Sonne
	rain	Regen
	wind	Wind
	storm	Sturm
	thunder	Donner
	lightning	Blitz
It's raining.		Es regnet.
The sun is shining.		Die Sonne scheint.

Say what the weather is like today and what it will be like tomorrow.

Skills: How to get information

1	**tourist board** ['tʊərɪst bɔːd]	Touristeninformation	At a *tourist board* you can get information about a country or region.
	contact ['kɒntækt]	Kontakt	**!** Achtung Aussprache.
2	**Dear Sir or Madam** [dɪə ˌsɜːr ɔː 'mædəm]	Sehr geehrte Dame, sehr geehrter Herr	You begin a formal letter like this.
	grammar school ['græmə ˌskuːl]	Gymnasium	A *grammar school* is similar to the German 'Gymnasium'.
	Best wishes [ˌbest 'wɪʃɪz]	Viele Grüße; Herzliche Grüße	You can finish a formal letter like this.
	to **send off** [send 'ɒf]	abschicken	Before you *send off* your e-mail, read it again.
	yourselves [jɔː'selvz]	selber; ihr/euch/Sie/sich (selbst)	Did you enjoy *yourselves*? – Oh yes, the party was really great.

Station 2: Dave says he can't wait for us to go there

	sunny ['sʌni]	sonnig	The weather is really nice today. It's *sunny*.
	hot [hɒt]	heiß	It's very *hot* today.
	coastline ['kəʊstlaɪn]	Küste; Küstenverlauf	Cornwall's *coastline* is almost 300 miles long.
	It feels so different from … [ˌɪt fiːlz səʊ 'dɪfrnt frɒm]	Es ist so anders hier im Vergleich zu …	
	wild [waɪld]	wild	pets – farm animals – *wild* animals
	ancient history [ˌeɪnʃnt 'hɪstri]	antike Geschichte; Frühgeschichte	I love everything Celtic. I'm into *ancient history*.
	prehistoric [ˌpriːhɪ'stɒrɪk]	vorgeschichtlich	
	monument ['mɒnjəmənt]	Monument; Denkmal	In Cornwall you can visit lots of prehistoric *monuments*. *Lat.* monumentum *(nt)*
	tin [tɪn]	Zinn	
	mine [maɪn]	Mine	There's an old tin *mine* near Dave's house.
	to **get bored** [get 'bɔːd]	sich langweilen	This is boring. I'*m getting bored*.
	to **be sure** [bi: 'ʃʊə]	sicher sein	I'*m sure* that this is the right way.
	definitely ['defɪnətli]	bestimmt; definitiv; eindeutig	Are you really sure? – *Definitely*!
	Me neither. [mi: 'naɪðə]	Ich auch nicht.	I don't like it. – *Me neither*!
10	**besides** [bɪ'saɪdz]	neben	Do you speak any languages *besides* German?
	local ['ləʊkl]	örtlich; lokal	The schools in your area are your *local* schools.
	dialect ['daɪəlekt]	Dialekt	Do people speak a *dialect* where you live?
	accent ['æksnt]	Akzent	My granny has a German accent when she speaks English.
11	**announcement** [ə'naʊnsmənt]	Ankündigung; Durchsage	I never understand the *announcements* at the station. *Lat.* annuntiare
12	**a father who …** [ə ˌfɑːðə 'huː]	ein Vater, der …	
	wife, wives *(pl)* [waɪf, waɪvz]	Ehefrau	Mr and Mrs Preston are husband and *wife*.

couple ['kʌpl]	Paar	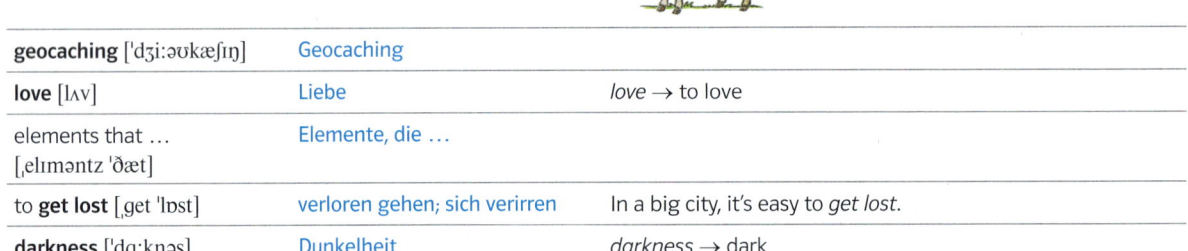 *Fr.* couple *(m)*	
customer ['kʌstəmə]	Kunde/Kundin	A *customer* buys things in a shop. *customer* ↔ assistant	
13 to **supply** [sə'plaɪ]	versorgen	Shops *supply* people with the things they need.	
to **rule** [ru:l]	herrschen; regieren	Elizabeth II *rules* the UK.	

Action UK! The caves

cave [keɪv]	Höhle	*Fr.* caverne *(f)*	
1 to **feed, fed, fed** [fi:d; fed; fed]	füttern; ernähren	Did you *feed* the dog this morning? People must work to *feed* their families.	
to **milk** [mɪlk]	melken		
cow [kaʊ]	Kuh		
geocaching ['dʒi:əʊkæʃɪŋ]	Geocaching		
2 **love** [lʌv]	Liebe	*love* → to love	
3 elements that … [ˌelɪməntz 'ðæt]	Elemente, die …		
to **get lost** [ˌget 'lɒst]	verloren gehen; sich verirren	In a big city, it's easy to *get lost*.	
darkness ['dɑ:knəs]	Dunkelheit	*darkness* → dark	
4 **sequel** ['si:kwl]	Fortsetzung; Folge		

Story: Things will get better

to **get, got, got** [get; gɒt; gɒt]	werden	If you learn more words, your English will *get* better.	
to **come in** [ˌkʌm 'ɪn]	hereinkommen	Mrs Preston invites the friends to *come in*.	
hall [hɔ:l]	Flur; Diele; Korridor		
electricity [ˌelɪk'trɪsəti]	Elektrizität; Strom	If there's no *electricity*, you can't make tea. *Fr.* électricité *(f)*	
What's the matter? [ˌwɒts ðə 'mætə]	Was ist los?; Was hast du?		
Oh dear! [ˌəʊ 'dɪə]	Oje!	I've hurt my leg. – *Oh dear!*	
to **go out** [ˌgəʊ 'aʊt]	ausgehen; hinausgehen	Let's *go out*!	
up [ʌp]	hinauf; nach oben	She looked *up* and down the street.	
coastal path [ˌkəʊstl 'pɑ:θ]	Küstenweg		

plumber [ˈplʌmə]	Installateur/-in; Klempner/-in	A *plumber* can fix your water pipes.
hill [hɪl]	Berg; Hügel	Our house is on a *hill* and we've got a fantastic view.
by [baɪ]	bei; neben; an	*by* = next to
chimney [ˈtʃɪmni]	Kamin; Schornstein	
roof [ruːf]	Dach	a *roof* with a chimney
strong [strɒŋ]	stark	
cloud [klaʊd]	Wolke	
to go right back to [ˌɡəʊ raɪt ˈbæk tə]	zurückgehen auf	Cornwall's mining history *goes right back to* Celtic times.
to solve [sɒlv]	lösen	Dave and his friends want to *solve* the puzzle. *Lat.* solvere
to boom [buːm]	dröhnen	A loud voice *booms*.
to keep away from [ˌkiːp əˈweɪ frəm]	(sich) fernhalten von	*Keep away from* my chocolate!
to turn (a)round [ˌtɜːn (ə)ˈraʊnd]	(sich) umdrehen; wenden	When they heard a voice behind them, they *turned (a)round*.
skirt [skɜːt]	Rock	
trousers (pl) [ˈtraʊzəz]	Hose	! *trousers* steht immer im Plural: You've got cool *trousers*.
spear [spɪə]	Speer	The *spear* is broken.
to steal, stole, stolen [stiːl; stəʊl; stəʊln]	stehlen	The treasure is gone. I think somebody *has stolen* it.
yours [jɔːz]	dein/-er/-e/-es; eure/-r/-s; Ihr/-e	*yours* ↔ mine
sun [sʌn]	Sonne	
to move in/into [ˌmuːv ˈɪn/ˈɪntə]	einziehen in	Dave and his parents *moved into* a new house in Cornwall.
warrior [ˈwɒriə]	Krieger	
society [səˈsaɪəti]	Verein; Gesellschaft	Bob is a member of a local history *society*. *Fr.* société (f)
twin [twɪn]	Zwilling; Zwillings-	
tool [tuːl]	Werkzeug; Gerät	A plumber needs special *tools*.

electrician [ˌelɪkˈtrɪʃn]	Elektriker/-in	*electrician* → electricity
plumbing [ˈplʌmɪŋ]	Sanitärarbeit	*plumbing* → plumber
electrics [ɪˈlektrɪks]	Elektrik	An electrician can fix the *electrics* in your house.
change [tʃeɪndʒ]	Änderung; Veränderung; Wechsel	*change* → to change
to **turn to** [ˈtɜːn tə]	sich wenden an; sich zuwenden	I *turned to* him to say something but he wasn't there any more.

Jobs

Who?		What and where?
mechanic	Mechaniker/-in	to fix, car, tools
plumber	Klempner/-in, Sanitärinstallateur/-in	to fix, plumbing, tools
electrician	Elektriker/-in	to fix, electrics, electricity

3	**diary entry** [ˈdaɪəri entri]	Tagebucheintrag	A *diary entry* is a personal text in which you write about what happened and what you felt.
	nobody else [ˈnəʊbədi els]	niemand anderes	Only you and *nobody else* should read your diary entries.
	postcard [ˈpəʊstkɑːd]	Postkarte	I love it when I get a real *postcard* and not just photos in an e-mail!
	sailboat [ˈseɪlbəʊt]	Segelboot	
	to **camp** [kæmp]	campen; zelten	*to camp* → camping

Across cultures 4 British stories and legends

legend [ˈledʒənd]	Legende; Sage	An old story – maybe true in parts.
2 **ingredient** [ɪnˈɡriːdiənt]	Zutat	Something is missing in this cake; hm, what *ingredient* did I forget?
completely [kəmˈpliːtli]	völlig	What you're saying isn't *completely* true! Some of it is wrong, sorry.
cruel [ˈkruːəl]	grausam	People are sometimes *cruel* to each other. *Fr.* cruel/-le
magical [ˈmædʒɪkəl]	magisch; Zauber-	The world of Harry Potter is a *magical* world.

wizard ['wɪzəd]	Zauberer	
hero, heroes *(pl)* ['hɪərəʊ, 'hɪərəʊz]	Held	The most important character in a book or film, usually good and brave.
villain ['vɪlən]	Bösewicht	*villain ↔* hero
knight [naɪt]	Ritter	
criminal ['krɪmɪnəl]	Kriminelle/-r; Verbrecher/-in	*criminal* = villain *Lat.* criminalis
powerful ['paʊəfl]	stark; mächtig	Who's the most *powerful* person in the world?
power [paʊə]	Kraft; Macht; Stärke	*power →* powerful
private detective [ˌpraɪvət dɪ'tektɪv]	Privatdetektiv/-in	There are lots of books and films about Sherlock Holmes, the famous *private detective*.
mysterious [mɪ'stɪəriəs]	mysteriös; geheimnisvoll	
crime [kraɪm]	Verbrechen; Kriminalität	*crime →* criminal *Lat.* crimen *(nt)*
heroine ['herəʊɪn]	Heldin	Who is your favourite *heroine*?
robber ['rɒbə]	Räuber/-in	A *robber* is a criminal.
outlaw ['aʊtlɔː]	Geächtete/-r; Gesetzlose/-r	Robin Hood was a famous *outlaw*.
to hide, hid, hidden [haɪd; hɪd; 'hɪdn]	(sich) verstecken	My sister sometimes *hides* my things. She thinks it's funny.
3 the Round Table [ðə ˌraʊnd 'teɪbl]	die Tafelrunde	King Arthur and his knights met at the *Round Table*.
the rich [ðə rɪtʃ]	die Reichen	Robin Hood was famous because he stole money from *the rich*.
the poor [ðə pʊə]	die Armen	*the poor ↔* the rich
4 prop [prɒp]	Requisite	You need lots of *props* for a film.
set [set]	Umgebung; Rahmen	A film's *set* shows where the people live, work, etc.

You're my heroine, Lou!

Dictionary

In dieser alphabetischen Wortliste findest du das gesamte Vokabular von *Green Line* 1 und 2.
Namen stehen in einer extra Liste am Ende des **Dictionary**.
Einträge, die aus mehreren Wörtern bestehen, kannst du meist unter verschiedenen
Stichwörtern nachschlagen. So ist z.B. *after all* unter *after* und unter *all* eingetragen.
Die Fundstellen stehen immer hinter dem jeweiligen Wort und zeigen dir an, wo es zum ersten Mal vorkommt, z. B.:
advice [əd'vaɪs] Rat; Ratschlag **II AC1**, 11 kommt zum ersten Mal vor in Band 2, Across cultures 1, Seite 11
adult ['ædʌlt] Erwachsene/-r **II U2**, 44 kommt zum ersten Mal vor in Band 2, Unit 2, Seite 44
U = Unit, AC = Across cultures
Die mit ° gekennzeichneten Verben sind unregelmäßig.
Die mit ° gekennzeichneten Vokabeln sind rezeptiv.

A

a [ə] ein/-e I
 a bit [ə 'bɪt] ein bisschen; ein wenig **II U1**, 22
 a couple of [ə 'kʌplˌəv] ein paar I
 a few [ə 'fju:] ein paar; wenige; einige I
 a girl from Germany [ə ˌgɜːl frəm 'dʒɜːməni] ein Mädchen aus Deutschland I
 a group of three [ə ˌgruːpˌəv 'θriː] eine Dreiergruppe I
 a little [ə 'lɪtl] ein wenig; etwas I
 a lot [ə 'lɒt] viel I
 a lot of [ə 'lɒtˌəv] viel/-e; eine Menge I
 a lot to learn [ə ˌlɒt tə 'lɜːn] viel zu lernen I
a.m. [ˌeɪˈem] vormittags *(Uhrzeit)* I
he was **able** to … [ˌhi wəz 'eɪblˌtə] er konnte … °**II U4**, 86
 he wasn't **able** to … [ˌhi wɒznt 'eɪblˌtə] er konnte nicht … °**II U4**, 86
 won't be **able** to … [ˌwəʊnt biˈeɪblˌtə] wirst nicht … können °**II U5**, 94
aboard [əˈbɔːd] an Bord I
about [əˈbaʊt] ungefähr; circa; etwa I
about [əˈbaʊt] über; von I
 out and **about** [ˌaʊtˌənˌəˈbaʊt] unterwegs **II U2**, 44
 What **about** …? ['wɒtˌəbaʊt] Wie wär's mit …?; Was ist mit …? I
 What is … **about?** [ˌwɒtˌɪz …ˌəˈbaʊt] Worum geht es in/im …? I
above [əˈbʌv] oben °**II U2**, 39
accent ['æksnt] Akzent **II U5**, 99
accident ['æksɪdnt] Unfall **II U3**, 55
across [əˈkrɒs] auf der anderen Seite von; über; hinüber; herüber; quer durch I
 Across cultures [əˌkrɒs 'kʌltʃəz] Interkulturelles I
to **act** [ækt] spielen *(Theater)* I
 to **act** like ['ækt laɪk] tun als ob **II U4**, 76
 to **act** out [ækt 'aʊt] nachspielen °**II AC3**, 72
 acting a scene [ˌæktɪŋˌə 'siːn] eine Theaterszene spielen I
acting ['æktɪŋ] Schauspielen °**II U5**, 101

action ['ækʃn] Handlung; Action; Aktion I
activity [ækˈtɪvəti] Aktivität I
 an **activity** that … [ənˌækˌtɪvəti 'ðæt] eine Aktivität, die … °**II U1**, 16
actor ['æktə] Schauspieler **II AC1**, 11
to **add** [æd] hinzufügen; ergänzen **II AC1**, 11
additional [əˈdɪʃnl] zusätzlich **II AC1**, 8
address [əˈdres] Adresse I
adjective ['ædʒɪktɪv] Adjektiv; Eigenschaftswort °**II U1**, 20
adult ['ædʌlt] Erwachsene/-r **II U2**, 44
adventure [ədˈventʃə] Abenteuer **II U1**, 20
advice [ədˈvaɪs] Rat; Ratschlag **II AC1**, 11
after ['ɑːftə] nach *(zeitlich)* I
 after all [ˌɑːftərˈɔːl] doch; schließlich; immerhin I
 after that [ˌɑːftə 'ðæt] danach I
afternoon [ˌɑːftəˈnuːn] Nachmittag I
 this **afternoon** [ðɪs 'ɑːftənuːn] heute Nachmittag **II U2**, 38
again [əˈgen] wieder; noch einmal; noch mal I
against [əˈgenst] gegen **II U1**, 23
ago [əˈgəʊ] vor *(zeitlich)* **II U1**, 14
agony aunt [ˈægəniˌɑːnt] Kummerkastentante **II U4**, 76
to **agree** (on) [əˈgriː] sich einigen (auf) °**II U5**, 102
 to **agree** (with) [əˈgriː] einer Meinung sein (mit); zustimmen °**II U4**, 81
airport ['eəpɔːt] Flughafen **II AC2**, 34
alien ['eɪliən] Außerirdische/-r; außerirdisches Wesen I
all [ɔːl] alle/-s; ganz I
 after **all** [ˌɑːftərˌɔːl] doch; schließlich; immerhin I
 all day [ɔːl 'deɪ] den ganzen Tag **II U1**, 18
 all night [ɔːl 'naɪt] die ganze Nacht I
 all over [ˌɔːlˌ'əʊvə] überall (in) I
 all the time [ɔːl ðə 'taɪm] die ganze Zeit **II U2**, 48
 all of them [ˈɔːlˌəv ˌðem] alle I
 all of us [ˈɔːlˌəv ˌʌs] wir alle **II U5**, 94

at **all** [ətˌˈɔːl] überhaupt I
bowling **alley** ['bəʊlɪŋˌæli] Bowlingbahn I
almost ['ɔːlməʊst] fast; beinahe **II U3**, 64
alone [əˈləʊn] allein; ohne fremde Hilfe I
along [əˈlɒŋ] entlang I
alphabet ['ælfəbet] Alphabet I
alphabetical [ˌælfəˈbetɪkl] alphabetisch °**II U1**, 25
already [ɔːlˈredi] schon; bereits I
also ['ɔːlsəʊ] auch **II U1**, 14
always ['ɔːlweɪz] immer; ständig I
amazing [əˈmeɪzɪŋ] unglaublich; toll; erstaunlich **II U1**, 22
American [əˈmerɪkən] Amerikanisch; amerikanisch; aus Amerika; Amerikaner/-in **II U1**, 13
an [ən] ein/-e I
ancient history [ˌeɪnʃnt 'hɪstri] antike Geschichte; Frühgeschichte **II U5**, 98
and [ænd; ənd] und I
angrily ['æŋgrɪli] verärgert; zornig; wütend °**II U2**, 48
angry ['æŋgri] wütend; zornig; verärgert; böse I
animal ['ænɪməl] Tier I
ankle ['æŋkl] Fußgelenk; Fußknöchel **II U3**, 58
 to twist your **ankle** [ˌtwɪst jɔːrˌ'æŋkl] sich den Knöchel verrenken **II U3**, 58
announcement [əˈnaʊnsmənt] Ankündigung; Durchsage **II U5**, 99
anonymous [ənˈɒnɪməs] anonym **II U1**, 17
another [əˈnʌðə] ein/-e andere/-r/-s; noch ein/-e; ein/-e andere/-r/-s I
answer ['ɑːnsə] Antwort I
 short **answer** [ˌʃɔːtˌ'ɑːnsə] Kurzantwort I
to **answer** ['ɑːnsə] antworten; beantworten I
 to **answer** the phone [ˌɑːnsə ðə 'fəʊn] einen Anruf entgegennehmen I
 answering machine ['ɑːnsrɪŋ məˌʃiːn] Anrufbeantworter I
any ['eni] irgendein/-e/-er; irgendwelche I
 not **any** more [ˌnɒtˌeni 'mɔː] nicht mehr I
 not … **any** [ˌnɒt … eni] kein/-e/-en I

anyone else [ˌeniwʌn 'els] irgendjemand; jemand anderes II U3, 61

Anything else? [ˌeniθɪŋ 'els] Sonst noch etwas? I

not … **anything** [ˌnɒt 'eniθɪŋ] nichts I

anyway ['eniweɪ] trotzdem; jedenfalls; sowieso II U2, 48

anywhere ['eniweə] irgendwo; überall (egal, wo) II U2, 40

app [æp] App II U4, 81

apple ['æpl] Apfel I

April ['eɪprəl] April I

area ['eəriə] Areal; Gebiet; Fläche II U3, 56

arm [ɑːm] Arm II U3, 57

around [ə'raʊnd] um … herum; umher I

to turn **around** [tɜːn ˌ(ə)'raʊnd] (sich) umdrehen; wenden II U5, 104

to **arrest** [ə'rest] festnehmen; verhaften II U1, 17

to **arrive** [ə'raɪv] ankommen II U5, 96

Art [ɑːt] Kunstunterricht I

art [ɑːt] Kunst II AC1, 9

as [æz; əz] als II U3, 63

as … **as** [əz … əz] so … wie I

as [æz; əz] während; indem I; wie II AC1, 11

as soon **as** [əz 'suːn əz] sobald II U4, 76

to **ask** [ɑːsk] fragen; bitten I

Ask about … ['ɑːsk əˌbaʊt] Frage/Fragt nach … I

to **ask** for ['ɑːsk fə] fragen nach; bitten um I

*to be **asleep** [bi ə'sliːp] schlafen II U1, 23

*to fall **asleep** [fɔːl ə'sliːp] einschlafen I

assembly [ə'sembli] Versammlung; Morgenappell II AC1, 8

assistant [ə'sɪstnt] Assistent/-in; Verkäufer/-in II U3, 62

at [æt; ət] in; auf; bei; an; um (bei Uhrzeitangaben) I

at 7:30 [ət ˌsevn̩'θɜːti] um halb acht I

at all [ət ˌ'ɔːl] überhaupt I

at first [ət 'fɜːst] zuerst; zunächst II U2, 49

at home [ət 'həʊm] zu Hause I

at last [ət 'lɑːst] endlich; schließlich I

at least [ət 'liːst] mindestens; wenigstens °II U2, 50

at the back of [ət ðə 'bæk ˌəv] hinten; am Ende; im hinteren Teil °II U2, 36

at the moment [ət ðə 'məʊmənt] im Moment; gerade I

at the same time [ət ðə ˌseɪm 'taɪm] zur selben Zeit; gleichzeitig I

at the weekend [ət ðə ˌwiːk'end] am Wochenende I

atlas ['ætləs] Atlas II AC3, 72

atmosphere ['ætməsfɪə] Atmosphäre; Stimmung °II U2, 44

attention [ə'tenʃn] Aufmerksamkeit; Beachtung II U4, 77

attic ['ætɪk] Dachboden II U3, 60

attraction [ə'trækʃn] Attraktion; Sehenswürdigkeit II U2, 45

audio ['ɔːdiəʊ] Audio-; Hör- I

audio tour ['ɔːdiəʊ ˌtʊə] Audioführung II U2, 42

audio-visual effect [ˌɔːdiəʊvɪʒuəl ɪ'fekt] audiovisueller Effekt °II U1, 28

August ['ɔːgəst] August I

aunt [ɑːnt] Tante I

agony **aunt** ['ægəniˌɑːnt] Kummerkastentante II U4, 76

away [ə'weɪ] weg I

right **away** [ˌraɪt ə'weɪ] sofort; gleich I

*to run **away** [ˌrʌn ə'weɪ] wegrennen I

*to throw **away** [ˌθrəʊ ə'weɪ] wegwerfen I

awful ['ɔːfl] schrecklich; furchtbar I

B

baby ['beɪbi] Baby; Säugling I

back [bæk] Rückseite; Rücken °II U5, 102

at the **back** of [ət ðə 'bæk ˌəv] hinten; am Ende; im hinteren Teil °II U2, 36

back to **back** [ˌbæk tʊ 'bæk] Rücken an Rücken I

back [bæk] zurück I

*to go right **back** to [ˌgəʊ raɪt 'bæk tə] zurückgehen auf II U5, 104

backache ['bækeɪk] Rückenschmerzen; Rückenweh II U3, 59

background ['bækgraʊnd] Hintergrund I

bacon ['beɪkn] Schinkenspeck; Speck I

bad [bæd] schlecht; böse; schlimm (ugs.) I

Too **bad**! [ˌtuː 'bæd] Zu dumm!; Schade! I

badminton ['bædmɪntən] Badminton I

bag [bæg] Tasche; Tüte I

baked beans (pl) [ˌbeɪkt 'biːnz] weiße Bohnen in Tomatensoße I

ball [bɔːl] Ball I

banana [bə'nɑːnə] Banane I

Bang! [bæŋ] Peng! II U4, 86

bank [bæŋk] Ufer II U2, 48

snack **bar** ['snæk ˌbɑː] Café; Imbissstube I

bargain ['bɑːgɪn] Schnäppchen I

to **bark** [bɑːk] bellen I

basic ['beɪsɪk] grundlegend; Grund- II U2, 45

basketball ['bɑːskɪtbɔːl] Basketball I

bath [bɑːθ] Bad; Badewanne I

bathroom ['bɑːθrʊm] Bad; Badezimmer I

battery ['bætri] Batterie; Akku II U1, 23

*to **be** [biː] sein I

*to **be** about [biː əˈbaʊt] sich handeln um I

*to **be** asleep [ˌbi ə'sliːp] schlafen II U1, 23

*to **be** gone [biː 'gɒn] verschwunden sein; weg sein II U3, 65

*to **be** good at [biː 'gʊd ət] gut sein in I

*to **be** impressed [bi ɪm'prest] beeindruckt sein II U4, 87

*to **be** in [bi 'ɪn] dabei sein; mitmachen II U3, 56

*to **be** in the way [bi ˌɪn ðə 'weɪ] im Weg sein/stehen I

*to **be** interested in [bi 'ɪntrəstɪd ˌɪn] interessiert sein an; sich interessieren für II U2, 36

*to **be** into [bi ˌ'ɪntə] mögen; stehen auf I

*to **be** jealous (of) [bi 'dʒeləs] eifersüchtig sein (auf); neidisch sein (auf) I

*to **be** late [bi 'leɪt] zu spät dran sein; zu spät kommen I

*to **be** lucky [bi 'lʌki] Glück haben II U2, 48

*to **be** on [bi 'ɒn] an sein; laufen II U4, 86

*to **be** right [bi 'raɪt] recht haben I

*to **be** scared (of) [bi 'skeəd ˌəv] Angst haben (vor) I

*to **be** sorry [bi 'sɒri] leid tun I

*to **be** sure [bi 'ʃʊə] sicher sein II U5, 98

*to **be** surprised [bi sə'praɪzd] überrascht sein II U2, 49

*to **be** unlucky [bi: ʌn'lʌki] Pech haben I

*to **be** up to [bi ˌʌp tə] vorhaben °II U1, 28

*to **be** worried [bi 'wʌrid] beunruhigt sein; besorgt sein II U3, 64

*to **be** worth [bi: 'wɜːθ] wert sein I

*to **be** wrong [bi: 'rɒŋ] unrecht haben; sich irren I

Be careful! [bi: 'keəfl] Vorsicht!; Pass/Passt auf! I

Be polite. [bi: pə'laɪt] Sei/Seid höflich. I

Here you are. [ˌhɪə juˈɑː] Bitte schön. I

How much **is/are** …? [ˌhaʊ 'mʌtʃ ɪz/ɑː] Wie viel (kostet/kosten) …? I

I'm from … [ˌaɪm frɒm] Ich bin aus … I

Is this how you (do) …? [ɪz 'ðɪs haʊ jʊ ˌduː] Machst du so …? I

beach [biːtʃ] Strand II U4, 83

baked beans (pl) [ˌbeɪkt 'biːnz] weiße Bohnen in Tomatensoße I

bear [beə] Bär II U2, 42

*to **beat** [biːt] schlagen; besiegen II U2, 40

beautiful ['bjuːtɪfl] schön; hübsch; wunderbar II U5, 94

because [bɪ'kɒz] weil; da I

because of [bɪ'kɒz ˌəv] wegen II U3, 65

*to **become** [bɪ'kʌm] werden II U2, 42

bed [bed] Bett I

*to go to **bed** [ˌgəʊ tə 'bed] ins Bett gehen I

bedroom ['bedrʊm] Schlafzimmer I

Beefeater ['biːfˌiːtə] königlicher Leibgardist II U2, 42

before [bɪ'fɔː] vor (zeitlich); bevor I; schon einmal; vorher; zuvor II U3, 57

*to **begin** [bɪ'gɪn] beginnen; anfangen II U4, 83

beginning [bɪ'gɪnɪŋ] Anfang; Beginn II U1, 27

behind [bɪ'haɪnd] hinter I

to **believe** [bɪ'liːv] glauben I

I couldn't **believe** my eyes. [ai ˌkʊdnt bɪˌliːv maɪˌaɪz] Ich traute meinen Augen nicht. II U3, 61

bell [bel] Glocke II AC2, 34

to **belong** (to) [bɪ'lɒŋ (tə)] gehören (zu) II AC1, 9

below [bɪˈləʊ] unterhalb; unten I

besides [bɪˈsaɪdz] neben II U5, 99

(the) best [best] (der/die/das) Beste II U1, 14

best [best] beste/-r/-s; am besten I
Best wishes [ˌbest ˈwɪʃɪz] Viele Grüße; Herzliche Grüße II U5, 97

I bet [aɪ ˈbet] ich wette II U2, 40

better [ˈbetə] besser; lieber I

between [bɪˈtwiːn] zwischen I

big [bɪɡ] groß I

bike [baɪk] Fahrrad I

mountain biking [ˈmaʊntɪn ˌbaɪkɪŋ] Mountainbikefahren II U5, 93

bilingual [baɪˈlɪŋɡwl] zweisprachig °II U1, 25

bird [bɜːd] Vogel II AC1, 8

birdwatching [ˈbɜːdˌwɒtʃɪŋ] Vogelbeobachtung II AC1, 8

birthday [ˈbɜːθdeɪ] Geburtstag I
Happy Birthday! [ˌhæpi ˈbɜːθdeɪ] Alles Gute zum Geburtstag!; Herzlichen Glückwunsch zum Geburtstag! I

biscuit [ˈbɪskɪt] Keks I

a bit [ə ˈbɪt] ein bisschen; ein wenig II U1, 22

*to bite [baɪt] beißen II U2, 42

black [blæk] schwarz I
*to go black [ˌɡəʊ ˈblæk] schwarz werden II U4, 86

building block [ˈbɪldɪŋ blɒk] Baustein °II U4, 77

to block [blɒk] blockieren; abblocken II U4, 77

*to blow out [ˌbləʊ ˈaʊt] ausblasen; auspusten I

blue [bluː] blau I

BMX [ˌbiːemˈeks] BMX II U3, 54

tourist board [ˈtʊərɪst bɔːd] Touristeninformation II U5, 97

boat [bəʊt] Boot I

boating lake [ˈbəʊtɪŋ ˌleɪk] See zum Rudern I

human body [ˌhjuːmən ˈbɒdi] menschlicher Körper II U2, 48

bonfire [ˈbɒnfaɪə] Lagerfeuer; Freudenfeuer I

book [bʊk] Buch I
exercise book [ˈeksəsaɪz ˌbʊk] Übungsheft I

to book [bʊk] buchen; reservieren II U5, 96

to boom [buːm] dröhnen II U5, 104

bored [bɔːd] gelangweilt I
*to get bored [ɡet ˈbɔːd] sich langweilen II U5, 98

boring [ˈbɔːrɪŋ] langweilig I

to borrow [ˈbɒrəʊ] (sich) ausleihen II U4, 87

both [bəʊθ] beide II U3, 65

bottle [ˈbɒtl] Flasche I

bowl [bəʊl] Schale; Schälchen; Schüssel I

bowling alley [ˈbəʊlɪŋ ˌæli] Bowlingbahn I

box [bɒks] Box; Kasten; Schachtel; Kiste I

boxing [ˈbɒksɪŋ] Boxen II U1, 12
round of boxing [ˌraʊnd əv ˈbɒksɪŋ] Boxrunde II U1, 12

boy [bɔɪ] Junge I
cabin boy [ˈkæbɪn ˌbɔɪ] Schiffsjunge I
the boy who … [ðə bɔɪ ˈhuː] der Junge, der … °II U3, 66

bracelet [ˈbreɪslət] Armband I

brave [breɪv] mutig; tapfer I

bread [bred] Brot I

break [breɪk] Pause II AC1, 10
half-term break [ˌhɑːftɜːm ˈbreɪk] Halbjahresferien I
lunch break [ˈlʌnʃbreɪk] Mittagspause I

*to break [breɪk] brechen; zerbrechen I

broken [ˈbrəʊkn] gebrochen; kaputt I

breakfast [ˈbrekfəst] Frühstück I
*to have breakfast [ˌhæv ˈbrekfəst] frühstücken I

Take a deep breath. [teɪk ə ˌdiːp ˈbreθ] Atme(t) tief ein. II AC1, 11

to breathe [briːð] atmen II U3, 64

bridge [brɪdʒ] Brücke II U2, 48

*to bring [brɪŋ] bringen; mitbringen I

British [ˈbrɪtɪʃ] britisch; Brite/Britin I

brochure [ˈbrəʊʃə] Broschüre; Prospekt I

broken [ˈbrəʊkn] gebrochen; kaputt I

brother [ˈbrʌðə] Bruder I

brown [braʊn] braun I

bucket [ˈbʌkɪt] Eimer II U2, 48

*to build [bɪld] bauen II U2, 42

building [ˈbɪldɪŋ] Gebäude I

building block [ˈbɪldɪŋ blɒk] Baustein °II U4, 77

cyber bully [ˌsaɪbə ˈbʊli] jemand, der andere in sozialen Netzwerken belästigt oder mobbed II U4, 75

*to give the bumps [ˌɡɪv ðə ˈbʌmps] hochleben lassen I

burger [ˈbɜːɡə] Hamburger I

bus [bʌs] Bus I
bus station [ˈbʌs ˌsteɪʃn] Busbahnhof I

busy [ˈbɪzi] belebt; beschäftigt I

but [bʌt] aber I

*to buy [baɪ] kaufen I

buyer [ˈbaɪə] Käufer/-in I

by [baɪ] bei; neben; an II U5, 104

by (bike) [baɪ] mit (dem Fahrrad) I

Bye! [baɪ] Tschüss! II U3, 58

C

cabin boy [ˈkæbɪn ˌbɔɪ] Schiffsjunge I

cache [kæʃ] Cache II U5, 104

café [ˈkæfeɪ] Café I

cafeteria [ˌkæfəˈtɪəriə] Cafeteria I

cake [keɪk] Kuchen; Torte I

(phone) call [ˈfəʊn ˌkɔːl] Anruf; Telefonanruf I

to call [kɔːl] nennen; anrufen; rufen I

caller [ˈkɔːlə] Anrufer/-in I

to calm down [ˌkɑːm ˈdaʊn] sich beruhigen II U4, 87

camel racing [ˈkæml ˌreɪsɪŋ] Kamelrennen II U3, 54

camera [ˈkæmrə] Fotoapparat; Kamera II U1, 12
caught on camera [ˌkɔːt ɒn ˈkæmrə] ertappt; mit der Kamera festgehalten II U1, 12

summer camp [ˈsʌmə kæmp] Sommerferienlager II AC3, 72

to camp [kæmp] campen; zelten II U5, 106

camping [ˈkæmpɪŋ] Camping; Zelten II U4, 83

can [kæn] Dose; Büchse I

can [kæn; kən] können; dürfen I
can't [kɑːnt] kann nicht; können nicht I
Can you name …? [ˈkæn jʊ ˌneɪm] Kannst du … nennen? I

candle [ˈkændl] Kerze I

candlelight (no pl) [ˈkændlaɪt] Kerzenlicht II U4, 87

cannot [ˈkænɒt] kann nicht; können nicht II U4, 79

capital [ˈkæpɪtl] Hauptstadt II AC2, 34

capital letter [ˌkæpɪtl ˈletə] Großbuchstabe I

captain [ˈkæptɪn] Kapitän/-in; Mannschaftsführer/-in I

car [kɑː] Auto I

card [kɑːd] Karte; Spielkarte I

to care (about) [ˈkeər əˌbaʊt] wichtig nehmen; sich kümmern (um); sich interessieren (für) I

careful [ˈkeəfl] vorsichtig; sorgfältig II U2, 42
Be careful! [bi ˈkeəfl] Vorsicht!; Pass/Passt auf! I

carnival [ˈkɑːnɪvl] Karneval II AC2, 34

carrot [ˈkærət] Karotte; Möhre I

to carry [ˈkæri] tragen II U4, 80

castle [ˈkɑːsl] Schloss; Burg II U2, 42

cat [kæt] Katze I

*to catch [kætʃ] fangen II U3, 54

category [ˈkætəɡri] Kategorie; Klasse °II AC3, 73

caught on camera [ˌkɔːt ɒn ˈkæmrə] ertappt; mit der Kamera festgehalten II U1, 12

to cause [kɔːz] verursachen II U3, 66

cave [keɪv] Höhle II U5, 101

to celebrate [ˈseləbreɪt] feiern I

Celtic [ˈkeltɪk; ˈseltɪk] keltisch II U1, 20

cent [sent] Cent (Währung) I

central [ˈsentrl] zentral; Zentral- II U2, 48

centre [ˈsentə] Zentrum; Center I
community centre [kəˈmjuːnəti ˌsentə] Gemeindezentrum I
leisure centre [ˈleʒə ˌsentə] Freizeitzentrum I
tourist information centre [ˌtʊərɪst ɪnfəˈmeɪʃn ˌsentə] Touristeninformation I

century [ˈsentʃri] Jahrhundert II U2, 48

cereal (no pl) [ˈsɪəriəl] Frühstückszerealie; Getreideprodukt (z. B. Cornflakes oder Müsli) I

chair [tʃeə] Stuhl; Sessel I

challenge [ˈtʃælɪndʒ] Herausforderung **II U1**, 20

chance [tʃɑːns] Chance; Gelegenheit; Möglichkeit **II U4**, 84

change [tʃeɪndʒ] Änderung; Veränderung; Wechsel **II U5**, 105

to **change** [tʃeɪndʒ] wechseln; (sich) ändern **II U4**, 74

    to **change** (onto) [tʃeɪndʒ (ˈɒntʊ)] umsteigen (in) **II U2**, 39

chant [tʃɑːnt] Sprechgesang **II U3**, 58

character [ˈkærəktə] Charakter; Figur **I**

charity [ˈtʃærɪti] Wohltätigkeitsverein; wohltätige Zwecke; Wohlfahrt **I**

    charity shop [ˈtʃærɪti ʃɒp] Second-Hand-Laden **I**

lucky **charm** [ˌlʌki ˈtʃɑːm] Glücksbringer; Talisman **I**

to **chase** [tʃeɪs] jagen; nachjagen **I**

chat room [ˈtʃæt rʊm] Chatroom **II AC3**, 72

    video **chat** [ˈvɪdiəʊ ˌtʃæt] Videochat **II U2**, 36

to **chat** [tʃæt] plaudern; chatten *(sich online unterhalten)* **I**

cheap [tʃiːp] billig; preiswert **I**

to **check** [tʃek] überprüfen; prüfen; kontrollieren **I**

Check-in [ˈtʃekɪn] Einchecken **I**

checklist [ˈtʃeklɪst] Checkliste °**II U3**, 58

Check-out [ˈtʃekaʊt] Auschecken **I**

to **cheer** [tʃɪə] anfeuern; jubeln; zujubeln **II U3**, 58

cheese [tʃiːz] Käse **I**

chess [tʃes] Schach **II AC1**, 8

chicken [ˈtʃɪkɪn] Huhn; Hähnchen **I**

    chicken tikka masala [ˌtʃɪkɪn ˌtɪkə məˈsɑːlə] *indisches Hühnchengericht* **I**

child [tʃaɪld], **children** [ˈtʃɪldrən] *(pl)* Kind **I**

    only **child** [ˈəʊnli ˈtʃaɪld] Einzelkind **I**

chimney [ˈtʃɪmni] Kamin; Schornstein **II U5**, 104

chips *(pl) (BE)* [tʃɪps] Pommes frites **I**

chocolate [ˈtʃɒklət] Schokolade **I**

choice [tʃɔɪs] Wahl; Auswahl **II U2**, 44

to **choose** [tʃuːz] auswählen; wählen **I**

Christmas [ˈkrɪsməs] Weihnachten **I**

church [tʃɜːtʃ] Kirche **I**

cinema [ˈsɪnəmə] Kino **I**

circle [ˈsɜːkl] Kreis; Ring **I**

city [ˈsɪti] Stadt; Großstadt **I**

to **clap** [klæp] klatschen **I**

    Clap your hands. [ˌklæp jɔː ˈhændz] Klatsch/Klatscht in die Hände. **I**

class [klɑːs] Klasse; Schulklasse **I**; *hier:* Unterricht **II AC1**, 8

    class display [ˈklɑːs dɪˌspleɪ] Ausstellung in der Klasse **I**

    class poster [ˈklɑːs ˌpəʊstə] Klassenposter **I**

classmate [ˈklɑːsmeɪt] Klassenkamerad/-in; Mitschüler/-in **I**

classroom [ˈklɑːsrʊm] Klassenzimmer **I**

clay pipe [ˈkleɪ paɪp] Tonpfeife **II U2**, 49

to **clean** [kliːn] säubern; reinigen **I**

to **clear** out [klɪərˈaʊt] ausräumen; entrümpeln **I**

clear [klɪə] klar; deutlich **I**

clever [ˈklevə] schlau; klug **II U4**, 81

click [klɪk] Klicken; Klick **II U4**, 87

to **click** on [ˈklɪk ˌɒn] anklicken **II U5**, 96

to **climb** [klaɪm] klettern; besteigen; steigen **I**

climbing [ˈklaɪmɪŋ] Klettern **II U1**, 20

clock [klɒk] Uhr **I**

    o'**clock** [əˈklɒk] Uhr *(Zeitangabe bei vollen Stunden)* **I**

to **close** [kləʊz] schließen; zumachen **I**

close [kləʊs] eng; knapp **I**; nahe **II U2**, 42

    Look **closely** … [ˌlʊk ˈkləʊsli] Schau(t) genau … °**II U3**, 62

    That was **close**! [ˌðæt wəz ˈkləʊs] Das war knapp! **I**

close-up [ˈkləʊsʌp] Nahaufnahme °**II U4**, 82

clothes *(pl)* [kləʊðz] Kleider; Kleidung **I**

cloud [klaʊd] Wolke **II U5**, 104

    word **cloud** [ˈwɜːd ˌklaʊd] Wörterwolke °**II U3**, 54

cloudy [ˈklaʊdi] bedeckt; bewölkt **II U1**, 23

clown [klaʊn] Clown **II U3**, 64

club [klʌb] Klub; Verein; AG **I**

    Cooking **Club** [ˈkʊkɪŋ ˌklʌb] Koch-AG **I**

clue [kluː] Hinweis; Spur **II U1**, 17

coach [kəʊtʃ] Trainer/-in **I**; Reisebus **II U1**, 17

coastal path [ˈkəʊstl ˈpɑːθ] Küstenweg **II U5**, 104

coastline [ˈkəʊstlaɪn] Küste; Küstenverlauf **II U5**, 98

coconut [ˈkəʊkənʌt] Kokosnuss **II U2**, 49

coffee [ˈkɒfi] Kaffee **I**

coin [kɔɪn] Münze **I**

coke [kəʊk] Cola **I**

cold [kəʊld] Erkältung **II U3**, 59

cold [kəʊld] kalt **II U1**, 22

to **collect** [kəˈlekt] sammeln **I**

collection [kəˈlekʃn] Kollektion; Sammlung **II U1**, 14

collocation [ˌkɒləˈkeɪʃn] Wortverbindung °**II U4**, 74

colony [ˈkɒləni] Kolonie **II AC3**, 73

colour [ˈkʌlə] Farbe **I**

    What **colour** is …? [ˌwɒt ˈkʌlər ɪz] Welche Farbe hat …? **I**

colourful [ˈkʌləfl] farbenfroh; bunt **I**

*to **come** [kʌm] kommen **I**

    *to **come** down [kʌm ˈdaʊn] herunterkommen **I**

    *to **come** in [kʌmˈɪn] hereinkommen **II U5**, 104

    Come on! [kʌmˈɒn] Komm schon!; Komm jetzt! **I**

comedian [kəˈmiːdiən] Komiker/-in; Comedian **II U1**, 14

comedy show [ˈkɒmədi ˌʃəʊ] Comedy Show **II U1**, 14

comic [ˈkɒmɪk] Comicheft **II U3**, 66

comment [ˈkɒment] Kommentar **II U1**, 16

to **comment** (on) [ˈkɒment ˌ(ɒn)] kommentieren **II U1**, 81

to **communicate** [kəˈmjuːnɪkeɪt] kommunizieren; sich verständigen **II AC3**, 73

communication [kəˌmjuːnɪˈkeɪʃn] Kommunikation °**II U4**, 75

community centre [kəˈmjuːnəti ˌsentə] Gemeindezentrum **I**

comparative [kəmˈpærətɪv] Komparativ °**II U1**, 20

to **compare** (with/to) [kəmˈpeə] vergleichen (mit) **I**

comparison [kəmˈpærɪsn] Vergleich °**II U2**, 41

competition [ˌkɒmpəˈtɪʃn] Wettbewerb; Turnier **II AC1**, 9

Complete … [kəmˈpliːt] Vervollständige/Vervollständigt … **I**

completely [kəmˈpliːtli] völlig **II AC4**, 112

compound word [ˈkɒmpaʊnd wɜːd] Kompositum *(zusammengesetztes Wort)* °**II U2**, 41

compromise [ˈkɒmprəmaɪz] Kompromiss **II U4**, 77

computer [kəmˈpjuːtə] Computer **I**

con [kɒn] Argument dagegen **II U2**, 41

confident [ˈkɒnfɪdnt] selbstsicher; selbstbewusst **II AC1**, 11

connection [kəˈnekʃn] Verbindung **II U5**, 96

contact [ˈkɒntækt] Kontakt **II U5**, 97

contest [ˈkɒntest] Wettkampf; Wettbewerb **I**

conversation [ˌkɒnvəˈseɪʃn] Konversation; Gespräch; Unterhaltung **I**

to **cook** [kʊk] kochen **II U4**, 87

cooker [ˈkʊkə] Herd **I**

cooking [ˈkʊkɪŋ] Kochen **I**

    Cooking Club [ˈkʊkɪŋ ˌklʌb] Koch-AG **I**

*to leave it to **cool** [liːv ɪt tə ˈkuːl] kalt stellen **I**

cool [kuːl] cool; super **I**

to **copy** [ˈkɒpi] abschreiben; kopieren **I**

corner [ˈkɔːnə] Ecke **II U2**, 40

Cornish [ˈkɔːnɪʃ] aus/in Cornwall; kornisch; Kornisch **II U5**, 94

Correct … [kəˈrekt] Korrigiere/Korrigiert … **I**

correct [kəˈrekt] richtig; korrekt **I**

*to **cost** [kɒst] kosten **I**

costume [ˈkɒstjuːm] Kostüm **I**

cough [kɒf] Husten **II U3**, 59

could [kʊd] könnte/-n **II U2**, 43

to **count** (on) [ˈkaʊnt ˌɒn] zählen (auf) **I**

country [ˈkʌntri], **countries** [ˈkʌntriz] *(pl)* Land **I**

countryside [ˈkʌntrisaɪd] Land **II U5**, 94

couple [ˈkʌpl] Paar **II U5**, 100

    a **couple** of [ə ˈkʌpl ˌəv] ein paar **I**

course [kɔːs] Kurs **II U1**, 20

    of **course** [əv ˈkɔːs] natürlich; selbstverständlich **I**

court [kɔːt] Spielfeld **II U3**, 54

cousin ['kʌzn] Cousin/Cousine I
cow [kaʊ] Kuh II U5, 101
cramp [kræmp] Krampf II U3, 65
to crash [kræʃ] abstürzen II U4, 87
crazy ['kreɪzi] verrückt I
*to go crazy [gəʊ 'kreɪzi] ausflippen; durchdrehen; verrückt werden II U4, 79
cream [kri:m] Creme; Sahne I
ice cream [aɪs 'kri:m] Eis; Eiscreme I
to create [kri'eɪt] schaffen; erschaffen; erfinden I
creative [kri'eɪtɪv] kreativ I
credit ['kredɪt] Guthaben II U2, 38
cricket ['krɪkɪt] Cricket II U3, 55
crime [kraɪm] Verbrechen; Kriminalität II AC4, 112
criminal ['krɪmɪnəl] Kriminelle/-r; Verbrecher/-in II AC4, 112
crisp (BE) [krɪsp] Kartoffelchip I
to cross [krɒs] überqueren; kreuzen II AC3, 73
*to keep your fingers crossed [ˌki:p jɔ: ˌfɪŋgəz 'krɒst] die Daumen drücken I
crowd [kraʊd] Menschenmenge II U2, 44
crown jewels [ˌkraʊn 'dʒu:əlz] Kronjuwelen II U2, 42
cruel ['kru:əl] grausam II AC4, 112
to cry [kraɪ] schreien; rufen II U4, 86
CU (= See you) ['si: ju] Bis dann!; Bis … I
culture ['kʌltʃə] Kultur I
Across cultures [əˌkrɒs 'kʌltʃəz] Interkulturelles I
cupboard ['kʌbəd] Küchenschrank; Schrank I
curry ['kʌri] Curry (Gewürz oder Gericht) I
custard ['kʌstəd] Vanillesoße; Vanillepudding I
customer ['kʌstəmə] Kunde/Kundin II U5, 100
*to cut (off) [kʌt (ɒf)] schneiden; abschneiden II U2, 49
cute [kju:t] niedlich; süß I
cyber bully [ˌsaɪbə 'bʊli] jemand, der andere in sozialen Netzwerken belästigt oder mobbed II U4, 75
cycling ['saɪklɪŋ] Radfahren I

D

dad [dæd] Papa I
dance (no pl) [dɑ:ns] Tanz; Tanzveranstaltung II AC1, 8
to dance [dɑ:ns] tanzen I
I like singing and dancing. [aɪ laɪk ˌsɪŋɪŋ ənd 'dɑ:nsɪŋ] Ich singe und tanze gern. I
dangerous ['deɪndʒrəs] gefährlich I
dangerously ['deɪndzrəsli] gefährlich °II U4, 88
the dark [ðə 'dɑ:k] Dunkelheit II U1, 22
dark [dɑ:k] dunkel II U1, 22
darkness ['dɑ:knəs] Dunkelheit II U5, 101
date [deɪt] Datum I
day [deɪ] Tag I

all day [ɔ:l 'deɪ] den ganzen Tag II U1, 18
one day [wʌn 'deɪ] eines Tages II U2, 43
a day out in … [ə ˌdeɪˌaʊt ɪn] ein Tag in … II U2, 44
the next day [ðə ˌnekst 'deɪ] am nächsten Tag II U1, 15
dead [ded] tot II U2, 48
*to deal (with) [di:l] sich befassen mit; umgehen mit II U2, 40
Oh dear! [əʊ 'dɪə] Oje! II U5, 104
Dear … [dɪə] Lieber …; Liebe … (Anrede in Briefen) I
Dear Sir or Madam [dɪə ˌsɜ:r ɔ: 'mædəm] Sehr geehrte Dame, sehr geehrter Herr II U5, 97
December [dɪ'sembə] Dezember I
to decide [dɪ'saɪd] (sich) entscheiden I
decision [dɪ'sɪʒn] Entscheidung °II U5, 95
*to make a decision [ˌmeɪk ə dɪ'sɪʒn] eine Entscheidung treffen °II U2, 47
deck [dek] Deck I
to decorate ['dekəreɪt] dekorieren; verzieren; schmücken I
decorations (pl) [ˌdekə'reɪʃnz] Dekoration; Schmuck I
deep [di:p] tief II U5, 93
definitely ['definətli] bestimmt; definitiv; eindeutig II U5, 98
definition [ˌdefi'nɪʃn] Definition °II U5, 96
to depart [dɪ'pɑ:t] abfahren II U5, 96
to depend (on) [dɪ'pend (ɒn)] abhängen von II U5, 95
to describe [dɪ'skraɪb] beschreiben I
description [dɪ'skrɪpʃn] Beschreibung °II U2, 44
to deserve [dɪ'zɜ:v] verdienen II U3, 60
to design [dɪ'zaɪn] entwerfen; gestalten II AC1, 11
detail ['di:teɪl] Detail; Einzelheit °II U2, 45
private detective [ˌpraɪvət dɪ'tektɪv] Privatdetektiv/-in II AC4, 112
diagram ['daɪəgræm] Diagramm I
dialect ['daɪəlekt] Dialekt II U5, 99
dialogue ['daɪəlɒg] Dialog; Gespräch I
diary ['daɪəri] Tagebuch II U5, 106
diary entry ['daɪəri entri] Tagebucheintrag II U5, 106
dice [daɪs] Würfel °II U1, 16
Roll two dice. [ˌrəʊl ˌtu: 'daɪs] Würfle/Würfelt mit zwei Würfeln. I
dictionary ['dɪkʃnri] Wörterbuch I
difference ['dɪfrəns] Unterschied I
make a difference [ˌmeɪk ə 'dɪfrns] etw. verändern II AC1, 11
different ['dɪfrnt] anders; unterschiedlich; verschieden I
It feels so different from … [ɪt ˌfi:lz səʊ 'dɪfrnt frɒm] Es ist so anders hier im Vergleich zu … II U5, 98
difficult ['dɪfɪklt] schwierig II U3, 61
dinner ['dɪnə] Abendessen I
dinosaur ['daɪnəsɔ:] Dinosaurier II U2, 45

direct speech [dɪˌrekt 'spi:tʃ] direkte Rede °II U5, 99
direction [dɪ'rekʃn] Richtung I
dirty ['dɜ:ti] dreckig; schmutzig II U2, 48
disappointed [ˌdɪsə'pɔɪntɪd] enttäuscht I
disaster [dɪ'zɑ:stə] Desaster; Katastrophe; Unglück II U4, 86
to discover [dɪ'skʌvə] entdecken II AC1, 8
to discuss [dɪ'skʌs] diskutieren I
discussion [dɪ'skʌʃn] Diskussion II U4, 74
display [dɪ'spleɪ] Ausstellung II U2, 45
class display ['klɑ:s dɪˌspleɪ] Ausstellung in der Klasse I
distance ['dɪstns] Distanz; Entfernung II U2, 46
*to do [du:] machen; tun I
*to do about ['du:ˌəˌbaʊt] unternehmen wegen II U4, 84
*to do our hair ['du:ˌaʊə 'heə] uns frisieren; unsere Haare machen I
Don't translate … [ˌdəʊnt trænz'leɪt] Übersetze/Übersetzt nicht … I
Don't worry! [ˌdəʊnt 'wʌri] Keine Sorge! I
We did it! [ˌwi: 'dɪdˌɪt] Wir haben es geschafft! II U3, 65
doctor ['dɒktə] Arzt/Ärztin II U3, 58
dog [dɒg] Hund I
to walk the dog [ˌwɔ:k ðə 'dɒg] den Hund ausführen; mit dem Hund spazieren gehen I
I'm dog-tired. [ˌaɪm ˌdɒg'taɪəd] Ich bin hundemüde. I
door [dɔ:] Tür I
front door [ˌfrʌnt 'dɔ:] Haustür II U4, 86
down [daʊn] nach unten; herunter; hinunter II U2, 48
*to come down [ˌkʌm 'daʊn] herunterkommen I
*to go down [ˌgəʊ 'daʊn] hinuntergehen; nach unten gehen; entlanggehen I
to note down [ˌnəʊt 'daʊn] notieren; aufschreiben °II U3, 61
*to sit down [ˌsɪt 'daʊn] sich hinsetzen; sich setzen I
*to write down [ˌraɪt 'daʊn] aufschreiben I
to download [ˌdaʊn'ləʊd] herunterladen (aus dem Internet) II U4, 81
downstairs [ˌdaʊn'steəz] nach unten; im Untergeschoss; unten II U4, 86
draft [drɑ:ft] Entwurf; Konzept I
drama ['drɑ:mə] Theater; Drama II AC1, 8
dramatic [drə'mætɪk] dramatisch II U2, 49
*to draw [drɔ:] zeichnen I; ziehen °II U5, 103
drawing ['drɔ:ɪŋ] Zeichnung I
dream [dri:m] Traum II U1, 19
fancy dress ['fænsi dres] Verkleidung; Kostüm II U3, 64
drink [drɪŋk] Getränk I
*to drink [drɪŋk] trinken I
driver ['draɪvə] Fahrer/-in II U1, 17
to drop [drɒp] fallen (lassen) II U2, 48

during (+ noun) [ˈdjʊərɪŋ] während (+ Nomen) II U1, 13
DVD [ˌdiːviːˈdiː] DVD I

E

e.g. (= for example) [ˌiːˈdʒiː] z.B. (= zum Beispiel) I
each [iːtʃ] jede/-r/-s I
  each other [iːtʃˈʌðə] einander; sich; sich gegenseitig I
each [iːtʃ] pro Person; pro Stück I
early [ˈɜːli] früh I
to **earn** [ɜːn] verdienen I
earth [ɜːθ] Erdboden; Erde; die Erde II U2, 45
  What on **earth** …? [ˌwɒtˌɒnˈɜːθ] Was um alles in der Welt …? II U4, 79
more **easily** [mɔːrˈiːzɪli] leichter °II U2, 49
east [iːst] Osten; Ost- I
Easter [ˈiːstə] Ostern I
easy [ˈiːzi] einfach; leicht I
*to **eat** [iːt] essen; fressen I
Eco [ˈiːkəʊ] Öko- II AC1, 11
audio-visual **effect** [ˌɔːdiəʊvɪʒuəl ɪˈfekt] audiovisueller Effekt °II U1, 28
egg [eg] Ei I
eight [eɪt] acht I
electrician [ˌelɪkˈtrɪʃn] Elektriker/-in II U5, 105
electricity [ˌelɪkˈtrɪsəti] Elektrizität; Strom II U5, 104
electrics [ɪˈlektrɪks] Elektrik II U5, 105
electronic [ˌelekˈtrɒnɪk] elektronisch II U1, 25
element [ˈelɪmənt] Element °II U5, 101
  elements that … [ˌelɪməntz ˈðæt] Elemente, die … °II U5, 101
eleven [ɪˈlevn] elf I
nobody **else** [ˈnəʊbədi els] niemand anderes II U5, 106
  what **else** [ˌwɒtˈels] was sonst; was noch I
e-mail [ˈiːmeɪl] E-Mail I
to **e-mail** [ˈiːmeɪl] mailen; per E-Mail schicken II U4, 81
embarrassed [ɪmˈbærəst] verlegen II U1, 13
embarrassing [ɪmˈbærəsɪŋ] peinlich II U1, 12
end [end] Ende; Schluss I
  in the **end** [ˌɪn ðiˈend] schließlich; zum Schluss II U1, 14
to **end** [end] enden; beenden II U3, 63
  to **end** up [ˌendˈʌp] enden; landen II U1, 12
ending [ˈendɪŋ] Ende; Schluss (einer Geschichte) I
energy [ˈenədʒi] Energie; Kraft II AC1, 11
English [ˈɪŋglɪʃ] englisch; Englisch; aus England; Engländer/-in I
  English-speaking [ˈɪŋglɪʃspiːkɪŋ] englischsprachig I
  I'm **English**. [aɪmˈɪŋglɪʃ] Ich bin Engländer/-in. I
to **enjoy** [ɪnˈdʒɔɪ] genießen; sich freuen an II U1, 16

they were **enjoying** [ðeɪ wərɪnˈdʒɔɪɪŋ] sie genossen gerade °II U2, 48
enough [ɪˈnʌf] genug; genügend I
diary **entry** [ˈdaɪəri entri] Tagebucheintrag II U5, 106
equipment [ɪˈkwɪpmənt] Ausstattung; Ausrüstung II U3, 55
er [ɜː] äh I
escalator [ˈeskəleɪtə] Rolltreppe I
etc. (= et cetera) [ɪtˈsetrə] usw. (= und so weiter) °II U4, 85
euro [ˈjʊərəʊ] Euro (Währung) I
even [ˈiːvn] sogar; selbst I
evening [ˈiːvnɪŋ] Abend I
  in the **evenings** [ɪn ðiˈiːvnɪŋz] abends I
event [ɪˈvent] Ereignis; Veranstaltung I
ever [ˈevə] jemals II U3, 56
every [ˈevri] jede/-r/-s I
everybody [ˈevribɒdi] jeder; alle II U2, 40
everyone [ˈevriwʌn] jeder; alle I
everything [ˈevriθɪŋ] alles I
everywhere [ˈevriweə] überall I
exactly [ɪgˈzæktli] genau II AC3, 72
exam [ɪgˈzæm] Examen; Prüfung II AC1, 8
example [ɪgˈzɑːmpl] Beispiel I
  for **example** [fərɪgˈzɑːmpl] zum Beispiel II AC3, 73
to **exchange** [ɪksˈtʃeɪndʒ] austauschen °II AC1, 11
excited [ɪkˈsaɪtɪd] aufgeregt; begeistert I
exciting [ɪkˈsaɪtɪŋ] spannend; aufregend I
Excuse me … [ɪkˈskjuːz mi] Entschuldigung!; Entschuldigen Sie! I
exercise [ˈeksəsaɪz] Übung; Aufgabe I
  exercise book [ˈeksəsaɪz ˌbʊk] Übungsheft I
expensive [ɪkˈspensɪv] teuer I
experience [ɪkˈspɪəriəns] Erfahrung II U3, 55
expert [ˈekspɜːt] Experte/Expertin °II U3, 63
to **explain** [ɪkˈspleɪn] erklären I
to **explore** [ɪkˈsplɔː] auf Entdeckungsreise gehen; sich umschauen; erkunden; erforschen I
to **express** [ɪkˈspres] ausdrücken °II U3, 66
expression [ɪkˈspreʃn] Ausdruck; Wendung; Äußerung II AC3, 73
extra [ˈekstrə] extra; zusätzlich I
eye [aɪ] Auge II U1, 13
  I couldn't believe my **eyes**. [aɪ ˌkʊdnt bɪˌliːv maɪˈaɪz] Ich traute meinen Augen nicht. II U1, 13
eyewitness [ˈaɪwɪtnəs] Augenzeuge/Augenzeugin II U3, 61

F

face [feɪs] Gesicht I
  Put … **face** down. [pʊt ˌfeɪs ˈdaʊn] Lege/Legt … umgedreht hin. I
face-to-face [ˌfeɪstəˈfeɪs] hier: persönlich; von Angesicht zu Angesicht II U4, 77
fact [fækt] Fakt; Tatsache II AC2, 34

fair [feə] gerecht; fair I
to **fake** [feɪk] vortäuschen; fälschen II U3, 60
*to **fall** [fɔːl] fallen; hinfallen I
  *to **fall** asleep [ˌfɔːlˌəˈsliːp] einschlafen I
  *to **fall** off [ˌfɔːlˈɒf] herunterfallen; hinunterfallen II U3, 59
  *to **fall** over [ˌfɔːlˈəʊvə] hinfallen; umkippen I
family [ˈfæmli] Familie I
  family tree [ˈfæmli ˌtriː] Stammbaum I
famous [ˈfeɪməs] berühmt I
fancy dress [ˈfænsi dres] Verkleidung; Kostüm II U3, 64
fantastic [fænˈtæstɪk] fantastisch; großartig II AC1, 9
fantasy [ˈfæntəsi] Fantasie; Traum- I
far [fɑː] weit II U2, 41
  so **far** [ˌsəʊ ˈfɑː] bis jetzt II U3, 60
fare [feə] Fahrpreis II U5, 96
farm [fɑːm] Farm; Bauernhof I
farmer [ˈfɑːmə] Farmer/-in; Landwirt/-in II U1, 17
fashion [ˈfæʃn] Mode II AC1, 8
fast [fɑːst] schnell I
father [ˈfɑːðə] Vater I
  a **father** who … [ə ˌfɑːðə ˈhuː] ein Vater, der … °II U5, 100
favourite [ˈfeɪvrɪt] Lieblings- I
  My **favourite** … [maɪ ˈfeɪvrɪt] Mein/e Lieblings … I
  What's your **favourite** …? [ˈwɒts jə ˌfeɪvrɪt] Was ist dein/-e Lieblings…? I
fear [fɪə] Angst; Furcht; Befürchtung II U3, 66
February [ˈfebruri] Februar I
fee [fiː] Gebühr II U5, 96
*to **feed** [fiːd] füttern; ernähren II U5, 101
*to **feel** [fiːl] fühlen; sich fühlen I
  *to **feel** left out [ˌfiːl left ˈaʊt] sich ausgeschlossen fühlen II U4, 88
  *to **feel** sick [ˌfiːl ˈsɪk] Übelkeit verspüren; sich schlecht fühlen II U3, 59
  It **feels** so different from … [ˌɪt fiːlz səʊ ˈdɪfrnt frɒm] Es ist so anders hier im Vergleich zu … II U5, 98
feeling [ˈfiːlɪŋ] Gefühl II U1, 13
festival [ˈfestɪvl] Festival; Fest I
fever [ˈfiːvə] Fieber II U3, 59
few [fjuː] wenige II U1, 22
  a **few** [ə ˈfjuː] ein paar; wenige; einige I
science **fiction** [ˌsaɪəns ˈfɪkʃn] Science-Fiction (Zukunftsdichtung) II U1, 26
field [fiːld] Feld; Spielfeld; Wiese; Weide; Acker II U1, 22
fifteen [ˌfɪfˈtiːn] fünfzehn I
fight [faɪt] Kampf; Streit II U4, 76
*to **fight** [faɪt] kämpfen; (sich) streiten II U4, 86
figure [ˈfɪgə] Figur; Gestalt II U2, 37
  wax **figure** [ˈwæks ˌfɪgə] Wachsfigur II U2, 37
to **fill** in [ˌfɪlˈɪn] ausfüllen °II U4, 80

film [fɪlm] Film I

to film [fɪlm] filmen; drehen °II U5, 101

filmmaker ['fɪlmˌmeɪkə] Filmemacher/-in II U1, 28

final ['faɪnl] endgültig °II U3, 63

finally ['faɪnli] schließlich; endlich; zum Schluss; letztlich II U3, 65

*to find [faɪnd] finden; herausfinden I

*to find out [ˌfaɪndˈaʊt] herausfinden I

fine [faɪn] gut; in Ordnung; schön I

I'm fine. [ˌaɪm ˈfaɪn] Mir geht's gut. I

finger ['fɪŋgə] Finger I

*to keep your fingers crossed [ˌkiːp jɔː ˌfɪŋgəz ˈkrɒst] die Daumen drücken I

finish line ['fɪnɪʃ ˌlaɪn] Ziellinie II U3, 65

to finish ['fɪnɪʃ] beenden; enden; fertigstellen; aufhören I

finished ['fɪnɪʃt] fertig °II U4, 83

fireworks (pl) ['faɪəwɜːks] Feuerwerk I

first [fɜːst] zuerst; als Erstes; erste/-r/-s I

at first [ət ˈfɜːst] zuerst; zunächst II U2, 49

first language [ˌfɜːst ˈlæŋgwɪdʒ] Muttersprache II AC3, 73

fish [fɪʃ], fish [fɪʃ] (pl) Fisch I

to fit [fɪt] passen °II U4, 85

*to get fit [ˌget ˈfɪt] in Form kommen; fit werden I

five [faɪv] fünf I

to fix [fɪks] reparieren; befestigen II U4, 79

flair [fleə] Flair; Atmosphäre II U2, 37

flat [flæt] Wohnung I

flea market ['fliː ˌmɑːkɪt] Flohmarkt I

floor [flɔː] Fußboden I

to flow out [ˌfləʊ ˈaʊt] hinausfließen II U2, 48

flower ['flaʊə] Blume II U4, 80

flyer ['flaɪə] Flyer I

folder ['fəʊldə] Ordner; Mappe I

to follow ['fɒləʊ] folgen; hinterhergehen; befolgen II U2, 40

the following [ðə ˈfɒləʊɪŋ] folgende/-r/-s °II U5, 93

food [fuːd] Essen; Lebensmittel I

foot [fʊt], feet [fiːt] (pl) Fuß I

on foot [ɒn ˈfʊt] zu Fuß II U2, 46

football ['fʊtbɔːl] Fußball I

for [fɔː; fə] wegen II U4, 75

for example [fər ɪgˈzɑːmpl] zum Beispiel II AC3, 73

for … [fɔː; fə] … lang II U1, 16

weather forecast ['weðə ˌfɔːkɑːst] Wettervorhersage II U5, 96

forest ['fɒrɪst] Wald II U1, 20

forever [fəˈrevə] für immer; ewig II U4, 77

*to forget [fəˈget] vergessen I

*to forgive [fəˈgɪv] vergeben; verzeihen II U3, 65

form [fɔːm] Form I; Formular II U5, 96

negative form ['negətɪv ˌfɔːm] verneinte Form I

past form ['pɑːst ˌfɔːm] Vergangenheitsform °II U1, 14

possessive form [pəˌsesɪv ˈfɔːm] Possessivform I

short form ['ʃɔːt ˌfɔːm] Kurzform I

to form [fɔːm] formen; bilden °II U3, 63

formal ['fɔːml] formal; formell; förmlich °II U3, 61

forum ['fɔːrəm] Forum II U4, 74

four [fɔː] vier I

Four and six is ten. [ˌfɔːr ənd ˌsɪks ɪz ˈten] Vier plus sechs ist zehn. I

free [friː] frei; kostenlos I

free time [ˌfriː ˈtaɪm] Freizeit I

freely ['friːli] frei ⟨II U4, 85⟩

French [frenʃ] französisch; Französisch II AC1, 10

frequently asked [ˌfriːkwəntliˈɑːskt] häufig gefragt I

fresh [freʃ] frisch I

Friday ['fraɪdeɪ] Freitag I

fridge [frɪdʒ] Kühlschrank I

friend [frend] Freund/-in I

*to make friends [ˌmeɪk ˈfrendz] Freundschaft schließen II U5, 94

friends and family who … [ˌfrendz ən ˌfæməli ˈhuː] Freunde und Familienmitglieder, die … °II U4, 81

That's what friends are for. [ˌðæts wɒt ˈfrendz ɑː ˌfɔː] Dafür sind Freunde da. I

friendly ['frendli] freundlich; nett II U1, 18

friendship ['frendʃɪp] Freundschaft II U4, 78

from [frɒm; frəm] aus; von I

from … to [frəm … tə] von … bis I

Where … from? [ˌweə … ˈfrɒm] Woher …? I

front [frʌnt] Vorderseite; Front-; Vorder- °II U5, 102

front door [ˌfrʌnt ˈdɔː] Haustür II U4, 86

in front of [ɪn ˈfrʌnt əv] vor I

fruit [fruːt] Frucht; Obst I

full (of) [fʊl əv] voll (von) I

fun [fʌn] Freude; Spaß I

*to have fun [ˌhæv ˈfʌn] Spaß haben; sich amüsieren I

It's fun. [ˌɪts ˈfʌn] Es macht Spaß. I

fun [fʌn] lustig; witzig; fröhlich I

funny ['fʌni] lustig; witzig I

future ['fjuːtʃə] Zukunft II U5, 93

G

gallery walk ['gæli ˌwɔːk] Museumsrundgang; Vernissage I

game [geɪm] Spiel I

guessing game ['gesɪŋ ˌgeɪm] Ratespiel °II U1, 17

gap [gæp] Lücke; Spalt; Abstand I

garage ['gærɑːʒ] Garage I

garden ['gɑːdn] Garten I

genius ['dʒiːniəs] Genie II U4, 79

geocaching ['dʒiːəʊkæʃɪŋ] Geocaching II U5, 101

Geography [dʒiˈɒgrəfi] Geografie; Erdkunde II AC1, 10

German ['dʒɜːmən] deutsch; Deutsch; aus Deutschland; Deutsche/-r I

*to get [get] holen; bringen; bekommen; besorgen; kaufen I; werden II U5, 104

*to get around [get əˈraʊnd] hier: sich fortbewegen II U2, 37

*to get away with [get əˈweɪ wɪð] davonkommen mit II U3, 60

*to get bored [get ˈbɔːd] sich langweilen II U5, 98

*to get fit [get ˈfɪt] in Form kommen; fit werden I

*to get in the way [get ɪn ðə ˈweɪ] stören; im Weg stehen II U3, 64

*to get into [get ˈɪntə] einsteigen; hineingelangen I

*to get lost [get ˈlɒst] verloren gehen; sich verirren II U5, 101

*to get off (a bus/train) [get ˈɒf] aussteigen (aus einem Bus/Zug) II U2, 39

*to get on (the bus) [get ˈɒn] einsteigen (in den Bus) II U5, 96

*to get on people's nerves [ˌget ɒn ˌsʌmbɒdiz ˈnɜːvz] jemandem auf die Nerven gehen I

*to get organised [get ˈɔːgənaɪzd] sich organisieren °II U5, 102

*to get out of [get ˈaʊt əv] aussteigen; herauskommen aus II U4, 86

*to get right [get ˈraɪt] richtig beantworten °II U5, 103

*to get there ['get ðeə] hinkommen I

*to get to ['get tə] kommen zu; kommen nach; erreichen I

*to get up [get ˈʌp] aufstehen (aus dem Bett) I

Time to get up! [ˌtaɪm tə ˌget ˈʌp] Es ist Zeit aufzustehen! I

ghost [gəʊst] Geist; Gespenst II U2, 42

girl [gɜːl] Mädchen I

a girl from Germany [ə ˌgɜːl frəm ˈdʒɜːməni] ein Mädchen aus Deutschland I

girlfriend ['gɜːlfrend] Freundin (in einer Paarbeziehung) II U2, 40

gist [dʒɪst] das Wesentliche °II U2, 42

*to give [gɪv] geben; schenken I

*to give the bumps [ˌgɪv ðə ˈbʌmps] hochleben lassen I

glass [glɑːs] Glas I

glasses (pl) ['glɑːsɪz] Brille II U3, 64

glove [glʌv] Handschuh I

*to go [gəʊ] gehen; fahren I

*to go black [ˌgəʊ ˈblæk] schwarz werden II U4, 86

*to go crazy [ˌgəʊ ˈkreɪzi] ausflippen; durchdrehen; verrückt werden II U4, 79

*to go down [ˌgəʊ ˈdaʊn] hinuntergehen; nach unten gehen; entlanggehen I *to **go** for a walk [ˌgəʊ fər ə ˈwɔːk] spazieren gehen **II U1**, 22

*to **go** on [ˌgəʊ ˈɒn] weitergehen; weitermachen; weiterführen; fortfahren **I**

*to **go** out [ˌgəʊ ˈaʊt] ausgehen; hinausgehen **II U5**, 104

*to **go** over to [ˌgəʊ ˈəʊvə tə] hinübergehen zu; zu jmdm. nach Hause gehen **II U4**, 79

*to **go** right back to [ˌgəʊ raɪt ˈbæk tə] zurückgehen auf **II U5**, 104

*to **go** shopping [ˌgəʊ ˈʃɒpɪŋ] einkaufen gehen **I**

*to **go** swimming [ˌgəʊ ˈswɪmɪŋ] Schwimmen gehen **I**

*to **go** to bed [ˌgəʊ tə ˈbed] ins Bett gehen **I**

*to **go** together [ˌgəʊ təˈgeðə] zueinander passen; zueinander gehören **I**

*to **go** with [ˈgəʊ wɪð] passen zu; gehören zu **I**

*to **go** wrong [ˌgəʊ ˈrɒŋ] schiefgehen **I**

*to let **go** (of) [ˌlet ˈgəʊ (əv)] loslassen **II U3**, 64

It's **gone**. [ɪts ˈgɒn] Es ist weg. **II U2**, 48

*to be **gone** [bi ˈgɒn] verschwunden sein; weg sein **II U3**, 65

goal [gəʊl] Tor; Ziel **I**

good [gʊd] gut **I**

*to be **good** at [bi ˈgʊd ət] gut sein in **I**

good for someone who … [ˌgʊd fə ˌsʌmwʌn ˈhuː] gut für jemanden, der … °**II U2**, 41

Good morning. [gʊd ˈmɔːnɪŋ] Guten Morgen. **I**

goodbye [gʊdˈbaɪ] auf Wiedersehen **I**

gorge scrambling [ˈgɔːdʒ ˌskræmblɪŋ] Schluchtenklettern **II U1**, 20

to **grab** [græb] greifen; ergreifen; schnappen **II U2**, 48

grammar school [ˈgræmə ˌskuːl] Gymnasium **II U5**, 97

grandad [ˈgrændæd] Opa **I**

grandma [ˈgrænmɑː] Oma **I**

grandparents (pl) [ˈgrænˌpeərənts] Großeltern **I**

granny [ˈgræni] Oma **I**

great [greɪt] großartig; toll; super **I**

It's **great** for … [ɪts ˈgreɪt fə] Es ist super zum/für … **I**

green [griːn] grün **I**

Greenwich Mean Time (= GMT) [ˌgrenɪdʒ ˈmiːn ˌtaɪm] westeuropäische Zeit **I**

greeting [ˈgriːtɪŋ] Gruß **I**

grey [greɪ] grau **I**

grid [grɪd] Gitter; Tabelle; Raster **I**

group [gruːp] Gruppe; Klasse **I**

a **group** of three [ə ˌgruːp əv ˈθriː] eine Dreiergruppe **I**

tutor **group** [ˈtjuːtə ˌgruːp] Klasse (in einer englischen Schule) **I**

*to **grow** [grəʊ] wachsen **II U5**, 93

guard [gɑːd] Wache; Wächter/-in **II AC2**, 35

to **guess** [ges] raten; erraten; vermuten **I**

guessing game [ˈgesɪŋ ˌgeɪm] Ratespiel °**II U1**, 17

guide [gaɪd] Führer/-in; Reiseführer **II U2**, 42

guinea pig [ˈgɪni ˌpɪg] Meerschweinchen **I**

guy [gaɪ] Typ; Kerl; (Pl.) Leute **II U1**, 13

H

*to do our **hair** [ˌduː ˌaʊə ˈheə] uns frisieren; unsere Haare machen **I**

half [hɑːf], **halves** [hɑːvz] (pl) (of) die Hälfte **I**

half [hɑːf] halb **I**

half past [ˌhɑːf ˈpɑːst] halb (bei Uhrzeitangaben) **I**

half-sister [ˈhɑːfˌsɪstə] Halbschwester **I**

half-term break [ˌhɑːftɜːm ˈbreɪk] Halbjahresferien **I**

hall [hɔːl] Halle; Saal **II AC1**, 9; Flur; Diele; Korridor **II U5**, 104

hand [hænd] Hand **I**

Clap your **hands**. [ˌklæp jɔː ˈhændz] Klatsch/Klatscht in die Hände. **I**

On the one **hand** …, (but) on the other **hand** … [ɒn ðə ˌwʌn ˌhænd … (bʌt) ɒn ðiˌʌðə ˌhænd …] Einerseits …, (aber) andererseits … **II U3**, 66

to **happen** [ˈhæpn] geschehen; passieren **I**

happy [ˈhæpi] glücklich; froh; fröhlich **I**

Happy Birthday! [ˌhæpi ˈbɜːθdeɪ] Alles Gute zum Geburtstag!; Herzlichen Glückwunsch zum Geburtstag! **I**

harbour [ˈhɑːbə] Hafen **II U5**, 93

hard [hɑːd] hart; schwer; schwierig **II U1**, 16

hat [hæt] Hut **I**

to **hate** [heɪt] hassen; nicht mögen **II U5**, 94

*to **have** [hæv] haben **I**

*to **have** a look (at) [ˌhæv ə ˈlʊk] anschauen **II U3**, 59

*to **have** breakfast [ˌhæv ˈbrekfəst] frühstücken **I**

*to **have** fun [ˌhæv ˈfʌn] Spaß haben; sich amüsieren **I**

*to **have** got [hæv ˈgɒt] besitzen; haben **I**

*to **have** to [ˈhæv tə] müssen **II U4**, 79

*to **have** (a sweet) [hæv] (ein Bonbon) nehmen; (ein Bonbon) essen **I**

he [hiː] er **I**

head [hed] Kopf **I**

head of state [ˌhed əv ˈsteɪt] Staatsoberhaupt **II AC3**, 73

With a very big **head**! [ˌwɪð ə ˌveri bɪg ˈhed] Und ein Angeber! **II U4**, 79

headache (no pl) [ˈhedeɪk] Kopfschmerzen; Kopfweh **II U3**, 59

heading [ˈhedɪŋ] Überschrift; Titel **I**

headphones (pl) [ˈhedfəʊnz] Kopfhörer **II U4**, 86

health [helθ] Gesundheit **II U3**, 55

healthy [ˈhelθi] gesund **I**

*to **hear** [hɪə] hören **I**

I **hear** … [aɪ ˈhɪə] Ich habe gehört, dass … **I**

heart [hɑːt] Herz; hier: Zentrum **II U2**, 48

*to learn … by **heart** [ˌlɜːn baɪ ˈhɑːt] auswendig lernen **I**

Hello. [helˈəʊ] Hallo. **I**

*to say **hello** (to) [ˌseɪ helˈəʊ tə] grüßen; Grüße ausrichten (an) **I**

help [help] Hilfe **I**

to **help** [help] helfen **I**

helpful [ˈhelpfl] hilfsbereit; hilfreich **I**

helpless [ˈhelpləs] hilflos **I**

her [hɜː] ihr/-e; sie **I**

here [hɪə] hier **I**

right **here** [ˌraɪt ˈhɪə] genau hier **II U3**, 56

Here you are. [ˌhɪə juˈɑː] Bitte schön. **I**

hero [ˈhɪərəʊ], **heroes** [ˈhɪərəʊz] (pl) Held **II AC4**, 112

heroine [ˈherəʊɪn] Heldin **II AC4**, 112

Hey! [heɪ] Hi.; He!; Hallo. **I**

Hi. [haɪ] Hi.; Hallo. **I**

*to **hide** [haɪd] (sich) verstecken **II AC4**, 112

high [haɪ] hoch; groß **II U1**, 21

high tide [ˈhaɪ ˌtaɪd] Flut **II U2**, 48

highlight [ˈhaɪlaɪt] Highlight; Höhepunkt **II U1**, 13

hiking [ˈhaɪkɪŋ] Wandern **II U5**, 93

hill [hɪl] Berg; Hügel **II U5**, 104

him [hɪm] ihn; ihm **I**

himself [hɪmˈself] er/sich (selbst); selber **II U1**, 12

his [hɪz] sein/-e **I**

historical [hɪˈstɒrɪkl] historisch; geschichtlich **I**

History [ˈhɪstri] Geschichte **II AC1**, 10

ancient **history** [ˌeɪnʃnt ˈhɪstri] antike Geschichte; Frühgeschichte **II U5**, 98

living **history** show [ˌlɪvɪŋ ˈhɪstəri ˌʃəʊ] Show, in der historischer Alltag nachgespielt wird **II U5**, 92

*to **hit** [hɪt] schlagen; treffen **I**

hobby [ˈhɒbi], **hobbies** [ˈhɒbiz] (pl) Hobby **I**

hockey [ˈhɒki] Hockey **II U3**, 55

*to **hold** [həʊld] halten; festhalten **I**

holiday [ˈhɒlədeɪ] Urlaub; Feiertag **I**

holidays (pl) [ˈhɒlədeɪz] Ferien **I**

home [həʊm] Zuhause; Heim **I**

at **home** [ət ˈhəʊm] zu Hause **I**

home [həʊm] nach Hause **I**

homepage [ˈhəʊmpeɪdʒ] Homepage **I**

homework [ˈhəʊmwɜːk] Hausaufgabe(n) **I**

hope [həʊp] Hoffnung **II U3**, 66

to **hope** [həʊp] hoffen **I**

hopeful [ˈhəʊpfl] hoffnungsvoll **I**

horrified [ˈhɒrɪfaɪd] entsetzt **I**

horse [hɔːs] Pferd **I**

hospital [ˈhɒspɪtl] Krankenhaus; Hospital **II U3**, 62

hot [hɒt] heiß **II U5**, 98

hour [aʊə] Stunde **II U2**, 49

house [haʊs] Haus **I**

to move (**house**) [muːv (haʊs)] umziehen **II U5**, 94

how [haʊ] wie **I**

How many …? [ˌhaʊ 'meni] Wie viele …? **I**

How are you? [ˌhaʊ ˌ'ɑː jə] Wie geht es dir/euch/Ihnen?; Wie geht es euch?; Wie geht es Ihnen? **I**

How much (is/are) …? [haʊ 'mʌtʃ ɪz/ɑː] Wie viel (kostet/kosten) …? **I**

How old are you? [haʊ ˌ'əʊld ə juː] Wie alt bist du?; Wie alt sind Sie? **I**

How to … ['haʊ tə] Wie man … **I**

Is this **how** you (do) …? [ɪz 'ðɪs haʊ jʊ ˌduː] Machst du so …? **I**

that's **how** [ðæts 'haʊ] so **II U1**, 14

to **hug** [hʌg] umarmen **I**

huge [hjuːdʒ] riesig; riesengroß; gewaltig **II AC2**, 34

human body [ˌhjuːmən 'bɒdi] menschlicher Körper **II U2**, 48

Humanities (pl) [hjuː'mænətiz] Sozialwissenschaften **II AC1**, 10

hungry ['hʌŋgri] hungrig **I**

to **hurry** ['hʌri] eilen; sich beeilen **I**

*to **hurt** [hɜːt] verletzen; weh tun **II U3**, 58

hurt [hɜːt] verletzt **II U1**, 28

I

I [aɪ] ich **I**

I don't know! [aɪ ˌdəʊnt 'nəʊ] Ich weiß (es) nicht! **I**

I don't like … [aɪ 'dəʊnt laɪk] Ich mag … nicht.; Ich mache … nicht gern. **I**

I hear … [aɪ 'hɪə] Ich habe gehört, dass … **I**

I like … [aɪ 'laɪk] Mir gefällt …; Ich mag … **I**

I love you. [aɪ 'lʌv ju] Ich liebe dich.; Ich mag dich. **I**

I love … [aɪ 'lʌv] Ich liebe …; Ich mag … total gern. **I**

I'd like to … (= I would like to) [aɪd 'laɪk tə] Ich möchte …; Ich würde gern … **I**

I'm (not) scared of … [aɪm (nɒt) 'skeəd ˌəv] Ich habe (keine) Angst vor … **I**

I'm dog-tired. [ˌaɪm ˌdɒg'taɪəd] Ich bin hundemüde. **I**

I'm English. [aɪm ˌ'ɪŋglɪʃ] Ich bin Engländer/-in. **I**

I'm fine. [aɪm 'faɪn] Mir geht's gut. **I**

I'm from … [aɪm frɒm] Ich bin aus … **I**

I'm sorry! [aɪm 'sɒri] Tut mir leid! **I**

I'm the one who … [aɪm ðə ˌwʌn 'huː] ich bin diejenige, die … °**II U3**, 64

ice [aɪs] Eis **I**

ice cream [aɪs 'kriːm] Eis; Eiscreme **I**

ice rink ['aɪs ˌrɪŋk] Eisbahn; Schlittschuhbahn **I**

idea [aɪ'dɪə] Idee; Einfall **I**

no **idea** [ˌnəʊ aɪ'dɪə] keine Ahnung **II U1**, 23

identity [aɪ'dentəti] Identität **II AC2**, 35

idiot ['ɪdiət] Idiot/-in **II U2**, 49

if [ɪf] wenn; falls; ob **I**

to **imagine** [ɪ'mædʒɪn] sich (etwas) vorstellen **I**

important [ɪm'pɔːtnt] wichtig **I**

*to be **impressed** [bi ɪm'prest] beeindruckt sein **II U4**, 87

to **improve** [ɪm'pruːv] sich verbessern; verbessern **I**

in [ɪn] in; im; rein; herein **I**

in front of [ɪn 'frʌntˌəv] vor **I**

in need [ɪn 'niːd] bedürftig; in Not **II U1**, 14

in secret [ɪn 'siːkrət] heimlich **II U3**, 65

in the end [ˌɪn ði'end] schließlich; zum Schluss **II U1**, 14

in the evenings [ɪn ði ˌ'iːvnɪŋz] abends **I**

in the mornings [ˌɪn ðə 'mɔːnɪŋz] morgens; vormittags **I**

in the photo(s) [ɪn ðə 'fəʊtəʊ(z)] auf dem Foto/den Fotos **I**

in the street [ˌɪn ðə 'striːt] in der Straße; auf der Straße **I**

to **include** [ɪn'kluːd] einschließen; beinhalten **II U5**, 92

Indian ['ɪndiən] Inder/-in; indisch **I**

indirect speech [ˌɪndɪrekt 'spiːtʃ] indirekte Rede °**II U5**, 99

individual [ˌɪndɪ'vɪdʒuəl] individuell; einzeln **II U3**, 55

infinitive [ɪn'fɪnətɪv] Infinitiv **I**

to **influence** ['ɪnfluəns] beeinflussen **II AC3**, 73

information (no pl) [ˌɪnfə'meɪʃn] Information; Informationen **I**

ingredient [ɪn'griːdiənt] Zutat **II AC4**, 112

injury ['ɪndʒəri] Verletzung **II U3**, 60

inline skating ['ɪnlaɪn ˌskeɪtɪŋ] Inlineskatefahren **I**

inside [ˌɪn'saɪd] innen; im Innern; hinein; nach drinnen; in; drin **I**

instruction [ɪn'strʌkʃn] Instruktion; Anweisung **I**

instructor [ɪn'strʌktə] Lehrer/-in; Betreuer/-in **II U1**, 22

interest ['ɪntrəst] Interesse **II U4**, 74

*to be **interested** in [bi ˌ'ɪntrəstɪd ˌɪn] interessiert sein an; sich interessieren für **II U2**, 36

interesting ['ɪntrəstɪŋ] interessant **I**

international [ˌɪntə'næʃnl] international **I**

internet ['ɪntənet] Internet **I**

interview ['ɪntəvjuː] Interview; Befragung **I**

to **interview** ['ɪntəvjuː] interviewen; befragen **I**

into ['ɪntə] in; in … hinein **I**

*to be **into** [bi ˌ'ɪntə] mögen; stehen auf **I**

Introduce … [ˌɪntrə'djuːs] Stelle/Stellt … vor. **I**

introduction [ˌɪntrə'dʌkʃn] Einführung; Einleitung; Vorstellung **II U3**, 59

invitation [ˌɪnvɪ'teɪʃn] Einladung **I**

to **invite** [ɪn'vaɪt] einladen **I**

inward ['ɪnwəd] ankommend **II U5**, 96

irregular [ɪ'regjələ] unregelmäßig **I**

Is this how you (do) …? [ɪz 'ðɪs haʊ jʊ ˌduː] Machst du so …? **I**

island ['aɪlənd] Insel **II U5**, 93

it [ɪt] es **I**

It's fun. [ɪts 'fʌn] Es macht Spaß. **I**

It's great for … [ɪts 'greɪt fə] Es ist super zum/für … **I**

It's your turn. [ˌɪts 'jɔː tɜːn] Du bist dran. **I**

It's …/They're … [ɪts/ðeə] Es kostet …/Sie kosten … **I**

its [ɪts] sein/-e; ihr/-e **I**

J

January ['dʒænjuri] Januar **I**

*to be **jealous** (of) [bi: 'dʒeləs] eifersüchtig sein (auf); neidisch sein (auf) **I**

jelly ['dʒeli] Tortenguss; Götterspeise; Wackelpudding; Gelee **I**

crown **jewels** [ˌkraʊn 'dʒuːəlz] Kronjuwelen **II U2**, 42

jewellery ['dʒuːəlri] Schmuck **I**

job [dʒɒb] Arbeit; Aufgabe; Job **I**

mouth **jogging** ['maʊθ ˌdʒɒgɪŋ] Training für den Mund **I**

to **join** [dʒɔɪn] beitreten; sich anschließen; verbinden **II AC1**, 11

joke [dʒəʊk] Witz **I**

to **joke** [dʒəʊk] scherzen **II U4**, 86

journey ['dʒɜːni] Reise; Fahrt **II U5**, 93

juice [dʒuːs] Saft **I**

July [dʒʊ'laɪ] Juli **I**

to **jump** [dʒʌmp] springen **I**

to **jump** back [dʒʌmp 'bæk] zurückspringen; hier: zurückschrecken **II U2**, 43

to **jump** the queue [dʒʌmp ðə 'kjuː] sich vordrängeln **I**

June [dʒuːn] Juni **I**

just [dʒʌst] gerade; nur; einfach **I**

K

*to **keep** [kiːp] behalten; aufbewahren; halten **I**

*to **keep** away from [ˌkiːp əˈweɪ frəm] (sich) fernhalten von **II U5**, 104

*to **keep** going [kiːp 'gəʊɪŋ] aufrechterhalten **II U1**, 16

*to **keep** up (with) [kiːp ˌ'ʌp (wɪð)] mithalten (mit); Schritt halten (mit) **II U3**, 64

*to **keep** your fingers crossed [kiːp jɔː ˌfɪŋgəz 'krɒst] die Daumen drücken **I**

key [kiː] Schlüssel **II U2**, 49

key word ['kiː wɜːd] Stichwort; Schlüsselbegriff **I**

to **kick** [kɪk] schießen; treten **II U3**, 54

kind [kaɪnd] Art; Sorte **I**

king [kɪŋ] König **I**

kitchen ['kɪtʃɪn] Küche **I**

knight [naɪt] Ritter II AC4, 112
knob [nɒb] Griff II U4, 79
*to know [nəʊ] kennen; wissen I
  I don't know! [aɪ ˌdəʊnt 'nəʊ] Ich weiß
  (es) nicht! I
  You know how to … [ju: 'nəʊ ˌhaʊ tə]
  Du weißt, wie man …; Ihr wisst, wie
  man … I
Korean [kə'riːən] koreanisch; Koreanisch;
  Koreaner/-in II U3, 60
  South Korean [ˌsaʊθ kə'riːən] Südkore-
  aner/-in; südkoreanisch; Südkoreanisch
  II AC3, 72

L

lake [leɪk] See I
  boating lake ['bəʊtɪŋ ˌleɪk] See zum
  Rudern I
lamb [læm] Lamm; Lämmchen I
land [lænd] Land I
to land [lænd] landen II U3, 62
landscape ['lændskeɪp] Landschaft II U5, 92
language ['læŋgwɪdʒ] Sprache I
  first language [ˌfɜːst 'læŋgwɪdʒ] Muttersprache II AC3, 73
  official language [əˌfɪʃl 'læŋgwɪdʒ] Amtssprache II AC3, 73
laptop ['læptɒp] Laptop II U4, 81
large [lɑːdʒ] groß; riesig II AC2, 34
lassi ['lʌsi] Lassi I
last [lɑːst] letzte/-r/-s I
  at last [ət 'lɑːst] endlich; schließlich I
late [leɪt] spät; zu spät I
  *to be late [bi: 'leɪt] zu spät dran sein; zu
  spät kommen I
later ['leɪtə] später I
to laugh [lɑːf] lachen I
*to learn [lɜːn] lernen I
  *to learn … by heart [ˌlɜːn baɪ 'hɑːt]
  auswendig lernen I
  a lot to learn [ə ˌlɒt tə 'lɜːn] viel zu
  lernen I
at least [ət 'liːst] mindestens; wenigstens
  °II U2, 50
*to leave [liːv] losgehen; abfahren; verlas-
  sen II U3, 58
  *to leave a message [ˌliːv ə 'mesɪdʒ] eine
  Nachricht hinterlassen I
  *to leave it to cool [ˌliːvˌɪt tə 'kuːl] kalt
  stellen I
  *to leave space [liːv 'speɪs] Platz lassen I
left [left] linke/-r/-s; links I
  on the left [ɒn ðə 'left] auf der linken
  Seite; links I
left [left] übrig I
leg [leg] Bein II U3, 57
legend ['ledʒənd] Legende; Sage II AC4, 112
leisure ['leʒə] Freizeit; Freizeit- I
  leisure centre ['leʒə ˌsentə] Freizeitzentrum I
lemon ['lemən] Zitrone II U1, 28

lemonade [ˌlemə'neɪd] Limonade I
lesson ['lesn] Unterrichtsstunde; Schulstunde; Unterricht I
*to let [let] lassen I
  *to let go (of) [ˌlet 'gəʊ (əv)] loslassen
  II U3, 64
  Let's … [lets] Lass/Lasst uns … I
letter ['letə] Buchstabe I; Brief II U4, 75
  capital letter [ˌkæpɪtl 'letə] Großbuchstabe I
to lie [laɪ] lügen II U1, 13
life [laɪf], lives [laɪvz] (pl) Leben II U2, 45
lifeboat ['laɪfbəʊt] Rettungsboot I
lifebuoy ['laɪfbɔɪ] Rettungsring I
light [laɪt] Licht; Lampe II U4, 86
lightning (no pl) ['laɪtnɪŋ] Blitz II U4, 86
to like [laɪk] mögen; gern haben I
  would like [wʊd 'laɪk] würde-/st/-n/-t
  gern; hätte-/st/-n/-t gern I
  I don't like … [aɪ 'dəʊnt laɪk] Ich mag …
  nicht.; Ich mache … nicht gern. I
  I like … [aɪ 'laɪk] Mir gefällt …; Ich
  mag … I
  I like singing and dancing. [aɪ laɪk ˌsɪŋɪŋ
  ənd 'dɑːnsɪŋ] Ich singe und tanze gern. I
  I'd like to … (= I would like to) [aɪd 'laɪk
  tə] Ich möchte …; Ich würde gern … I
  Would you like …? [ˌwʊd jʊ 'laɪk]
  Möchtest du …?; Möchten Sie …?;
  Möchtet ihr …? °II U3, 56
like [laɪk] wie; als ob I
  like that [laɪk 'ðæt] so I
  like this [laɪk 'ðɪs] so I
line [laɪn] Zeile; Linie I
  finish line ['fɪnɪʃ ˌlaɪn] Ziellinie II U3, 65
  time line ['taɪm ˌlaɪn] Zeitstrahl I
link [lɪŋk] Link; Verbindung II U2, 45
to link [lɪŋk] verbinden II U4, 88
  linking word ['lɪŋkɪŋ ˌwɜːd] Bindewort I
lion ['laɪən] Löwe II U2, 42
list [lɪst] Liste I
to listen (to) ['lɪsn] zuhören; anhören I
  Listen again. [ˌlɪsn ə'gen] Hör/Hört noch
  einmal zu. I
  to listen for ['lɪsn fə] horchen auf I
listener ['lɪsənə] Zuhörer/-in II U3, 61
listening ['lɪsnɪŋ] Hören I
little ['lɪtl] klein I
  a little [ə 'lɪtl] ein wenig; etwas I
to live [lɪv] wohnen; leben I
living history show [ˌlɪvɪŋ 'hɪstəri ˌʃəʊ] Show,
  in der historischer Alltag nachgespielt
  wird II U5, 92
  living room ['lɪvɪŋ rʊm] Wohnzimmer I
local ['ləʊkl] örtlich; lokal II U5, 99
location [ləʊ'keɪʃn] Handlungsort; Lage;
  Standort II U2, 44
locked [lɒkt] abgeschlossen II U1, 23
locker ['lɒkə] Schließfach; Spind I
loft [lɒft] Dachboden I
LOL (= laughing out loud) [lɒl] LOL II U1, 12
Londoner ['lʌndənə] Londoner/-in I

lonely ['ləʊnli] einsam I
long [lɒŋ] lang I
  (not) any longer [nɒt ˌeni 'lɒŋgə] (nicht)
  mehr; (nicht) länger II U5, 94
look [lʊk] Blick I
  *to have a look (at) [ˌhævˌə 'lʊk] anschau-
  en II U3, 59
to look [lʊk] schauen; sehen; aussehen I
  to look after [lʊk 'ɑːftə] aufpassen auf;
  hüten; sich kümmern um I
  to look at ['lʊk ət] anschauen; ansehen I
  to look for ['lʊk fɔː] suchen nach I
  to look out [lʊk 'aʊt] aufpassen II U3, 56
  to look up [lʊk 'ʌp] nachschlagen; nachschauen I
  Look! [lʊk] Schau/Schaut mal! I
  Look closely … [ˌlʊk 'kləʊsli] Schau(t)
  genau … °II U3, 62
  what the man looked like [ˌwɒt ðə mæn
  'lʊkt laɪk] wie der Mann aussah II U1, 17
*to lose [luːz] verlieren II U3, 54
*to get lost [get 'lɒst] verloren gehen; sich
  verirren II U5, 101
a lot [ə 'lɒt] viel I
  a lot of [ə 'lɒt əv] viel/-e; eine Menge I
  lots (of) ['lɒts əv] viel/-e; jede Menge I
loud [laʊd] laut I
love [lʌv] Liebe II U5, 101
Love … [lʌv] Liebe Grüße (am Briefende);
  Herzliche Grüße (am Briefende) I
to love [lʌv] lieben; gern mögen I
  would love [wʊd 'lʌv] würde-/st/-n/-t sehr
  gern; hätte-/st/-n/-t sehr gern I
  I love you. [aɪ 'lʌv ju] Ich liebe dich.; Ich
  mag dich. I
  I love … [aɪ 'lʌv] Ich liebe …; Ich
  mag … total gern. I
lovebirds (pl) ['lʌvˌbɜːdz] Turteltauben
  II U1, 13
low [ləʊ] niedrig II U1, 21
  low tide ['ləʊ ˌtaɪd] Ebbe II U2, 48
lucky … ['lʌki] … der/die Glückliche I
  *to be lucky [bi'lʌki] Glück haben II U2, 48
  lucky charm [ˌlʌki 'tʃɑːm] Glücksbringer;
  Talisman I
  … is/are lucky. [ɪz/ɑː 'lʌki] … hat/haben
  Glück. I
lunch [lʌnʃ] Mittagessen I
  lunch break ['lʌnʃbreɪk] Mittagspause I

M

machine [mə'ʃiːn] Automat; Maschine;
  Apparat; Gerät I
  answering machine ['ɑːnsrɪŋ məˌʃiːn]
  Anrufbeantworter I
  washing machine ['wɒʃɪŋ məˌʃiːn] Wasch-
  maschine II U4, 79
mad [mæd] verrückt II U4, 81
Dear Sir or Madam [dɪə ˌsɜːrˌɔː 'mædəm]
  Sehr geehrte Dame, sehr geehrter Herr
  II U5, 97

magazine [ˈmægəˈziːn] Zeitschrift I

magical [ˈmædʒɪkəl] magisch; Zauber- II AC4, 112

to mail [ˈiːmeɪl] mailen; per E-Mail schicken II U4, 81

main [meɪn] Haupt- I

*to make [meɪk] machen; tun; bilden; *hier:* ergeben I

*to make a decision [ˌmeɪk ə dɪˈsɪʒn] eine Entscheidung treffen °II U2, 47

*to make a difference [ˌmeɪk ə ˈdɪfrns] etw. verändern II AC1, 11

*to make a wish [ˌmeɪk ə ˈwɪʃ] sich etwas wünschen I

*to make friends [ˌmeɪk ˈfrendz] Freundschaft schließen II U5, 94

*to make money [ˌmeɪk ˈmʌni] Geld verdienen I

*to make notes [ˌmeɪk ˈnəʊts] Notizen machen I

*to make somebody do something [meɪk] jmdn. dazu bringen, etw. zu tun II U4, 76

*to make sure [ˌmeɪk ˈʃɔː] sich versichern I

*to make trouble [ˌmeɪk ˈtrʌbl] Ärger machen; in Schwierigkeiten bringen I

man [mæn], men [men] *(pl)* Mann I

what the man looked like [ˌwɒt ðə mæn ˈlʊkt laɪk] wie der Mann aussah II U1, 17

mango [ˈmæŋgəʊ] Mango I

many [ˈmeni] viele I

How many …? [ˌhaʊ ˈmeni] Wie viele …? I

map [mæp] Stadtplan; Landkarte I

mind map [ˈmaɪnd mæp] Wörternetz *(eine Art Schaubild)* I

marathon [ˈmærəθn] Marathon II U3, 54

March [mɑːtʃ] März I

to mark [mɑːk] markieren; kennzeichnen °II U5, 103

market [ˈmɑːkɪt] Markt I

flea market [ˈfliː ˌmɑːkɪt] Flohmarkt I

raven master [ˈreɪvn ˌmɑːstə] Herr der Raben II U2, 42

match [mætʃ] Spiel; Match II U3, 54

to match [mætʃ] zuordnen; passen zu; entsprechen I

mate [meɪt] Schiffsoffizier; Maat I

material [məˈtɪəriəl] Material II U2, 47

Maths [mæθs] Mathematik; Mathe II AC1, 9

What's the matter? [ˌwɒts ðə ˈmætə] Was ist los?; Was hast du? II U5, 104

May [meɪ] Mai I

may [meɪ] (vielleicht) können; dürfen II U4, 79

maybe [ˈmeɪbi] vielleicht I

me [miː] ich; mich; mir I

meal [miːl] Mahlzeit; Essen II U1, 22

ready meal [ˌredi ˈmiːl] Fertiggericht I

*to mean [miːn] bedeuten; meinen II U2, 40

meaning [ˈmiːnɪŋ] Bedeutung; Sinn II U1, 25

mechanic [məˈkænɪk] Mechaniker/-in; Kfz-Mechaniker/-in II U1, 17

media [ˈmiːdiə] Medien II U4, 75

to mediate [ˈmiːdieɪt] vermitteln II U4, 78

mediation [ˌmiːdiˈeɪʃn] Sprachmittlung I

medieval [ˌmediˈiːvl] mittelalterlich II U5, 92

*to meet [miːt] treffen; sich treffen I

member [ˈmembə] Mitglied II AC3, 72

memory [ˈmemri] Erinnerung; Gedächtnis II U1, 23

to mention [ˈmenʃn] erwähnen II AC3, 72

merchant [ˈmɜːtʃənt] Kaufmann; Händler II AC3, 73

mess [mes] Unordnung; Durcheinander II U4, 80

message [ˈmesɪdʒ] Botschaft; Nachricht I

*to leave a message [ˌliːv ə ˈmesɪdʒ] eine Nachricht hinterlassen I

*to take a message [ˌteɪk ə ˈmesɪdʒ] eine Nachricht entgegennehmen; jmdm. etw. ausrichten I

text (message) [ˈtekst ˌmesɪdʒ] SMS; Kurznachricht I

metre [ˈmiːtə] Meter II U2, 48

middle [ˈmɪdl] Mitte I

mile [maɪl] Meile *(brit. Längenmaß)* II U3, 58

milk [mɪlk] Milch I

to milk [mɪlk] melken II U5, 101

million [ˈmɪljən] Million II AC2, 34

I've done this a million times before. [ˌaɪv dʌn ðɪs ə ˌmɪljən taɪmz bɪˈfɔː] Ich habe das schon eine Million Mal gemacht. II U4, 79

mind map [ˈmaɪnd mæp] Wörternetz *(eine Art Schaubild)* I

mine [maɪn] Mine II U5, 98

mine [maɪn] mein/-er/-e/-es II U4, 87

mini [ˈmɪni] Mini- II U3, 56

minute [ˈmɪnɪt] Minute I

to miss [mɪs] verpassen; versäumen II U4, 83; vermissen II U5, 94

missing [ˈmɪsɪŋ] fehlend; verschwunden II U1, 17

What is missing? [ˌwɒt ɪz ˈmɪsɪŋ] Was fehlt? I

mistake [mɪˈsteɪk] Fehler I

mobile [ˈməʊbaɪl] Handy; Mobiltelefon II U4, 75

modal [ˈməʊdl] Modalverb °II U4, 75

model [ˈmɒdl] Modell; Tonmodell; Model I

modern [ˈmɒdn] modern II U2, 50

moment [ˈməʊmənt] Moment; Augenblick II AC1, 11

at the moment [ət ðə ˈməʊmənt] im Moment; gerade I

Monday [ˈmʌndeɪ] Montag I

on Mondays [ɒn ˈmʌndeɪz] montags I

money [ˈmʌni] Geld I

*to make money [ˌmeɪk ˈmʌni] Geld verdienen I

pocket money [ˈpɒkɪt ˌmʌni] Taschengeld I

to raise money [ˌreɪz ˈmʌni] Geld sammeln II U1, 14

monster [ˈmɒnstə] Monster; Ungeheuer I

month [mʌnθ] Monat II U1, 14

monument [ˈmɒnjəmənt] Monument; Denkmal II U5, 98

mood [muːd] Stimmung; Laune II U1, 28

more [mɔː] mehr; weitere I

more easily [mɔːr ˈiːzɪli] leichter °II U2, 49

more quickly [mɔː ˈkwɪkli] schneller °II U4, 88

not any more [ˌnɒt ˌeni ˈmɔː] nicht mehr I

more … than [ˈmɔː ðən] mehr … als I

morning [ˈmɔːnɪŋ] Morgen; Vormittag I

in the mornings [ˌɪn ðə ˈmɔːnɪŋz] morgens; vormittags I

Good morning. [ˌgʊd ˈmɔːnɪŋ] Guten Morgen. I

(the) most [ðə ˈməʊst] der/die/das meiste; die meisten I

mother [ˈmʌðə] Mutter I

to motivate [ˈməʊtɪveɪt] motivieren I

mountain [ˈmaʊntɪn] Berg II U1, 20

mountain biking [ˈmaʊntɪn ˌbaɪkɪŋ] Mountainbikefahren II U5, 93

mouse [maʊs], mice [maɪs] *(pl)* Maus/Mäuse I

mouth [maʊθ] Mund I

mouth jogging [ˈmaʊθ ˌdʒɒgɪŋ] Training für den Mund I

move [muːv] Bewegung I

to move [muːv] (sich) bewegen I

to move (house) [muːv haʊs] umziehen II U5, 94

to move in/into [muːv ˈɪn/ˈɪntə] einziehen in II U5, 104

Mr [ˈmɪstə] Herr *(Anrede)* I

Mrs [ˈmɪsɪz] Frau *(Anrede)* I

much [mʌtʃ] viel I

mud [mʌd] Schlamm II U2, 48

muddy [ˈmʌdi] schlammig II U2, 48

mudlark [ˈmʌdlɑːk] *jemand, der im Schlamm nach Sachen sucht, die er dann verkaufen kann* II U2, 48

multi-ethnic [ˌmʌltiˈeθnɪk] Vielvölker-; international II AC2, 34

mum [mʌm] Mama I

museum [mjuːˈziːəm] Museum I

music [ˈmjuːzɪk] Musik I

musician [mjuːˈzɪʃn] Musiker/-in II U2, 39

must [mʌst] müssen I

mustn't [ˈmʌsnt] nicht dürfen I

my [maɪ] mein/-e I

My favourite … [maɪ ˈfeɪvrɪt] Mein/e Lieblings … I

My name is … [maɪ ˈneɪm ɪz] Ich heiße … I

myself [maɪˈself] ich/mir/mich (selbst); selber II U4, 77

mysterious [mɪˈstɪəriəs] mysteriös; geheimnisvoll II AC4, 112

N

name [neɪm] Name I
    name day ['neɪm ˌdeɪ] Namenstag I
    My **name** is … [maɪ 'neɪm ˌɪz] Ich hei-
    ße … I
    What's your **name**? [ˌwɒts jə 'neɪm] Wie
    heißt du?; Wie heißen Sie? I
to **name** [neɪm] nennen; benennen I
nasty ['nɑːsti] garstig; gemein II U4, 75
national ['næʃnl] national; landesweit I
nature ['neɪtʃə] Natur II AC1, 11
near [nɪə] nahe; in der Nähe von I
nearly ['nɪəli] fast; annähernd II U4, 86
in **need** [ɪn 'niːd] bedürftig; in Not II U1, 14
    with special **needs** [wɪð ˌspeʃl 'niːdz]
    behindert II AC1, 9
to **need** (to) [niːd] brauchen; benötigen I
    to **need** (to do) [niːd] (tun) müssen I
    needn't ['niːdnt] nicht brauchen; nicht
    müssen I
negative ['negətɪv] negativ; verneint
    II U3, 66
    negative form ['negətɪv ˌfɔːm] verneinte
    Form I
neighbour (BE) ['neɪbə] Nachbar/-in I
Me **neither**. [mi: 'naɪðə] Ich auch nicht.
    II U5, 98
*to get on people's **nerves** [ˌget ɒn
    ˌsʌmbɒdiz 'nɜːvz] jemandem auf die
    Nerven gehen I
nervous ['nɜːvəs] nervös; aufgeregt II U1, 16
net [net] Netz II U3, 54
netball ['netbɔːl] Korbball I
social **network** [ˌsəʊʃl 'netwɜːk] soziales
    Netzwerk II U4, 75
never ['nevə] nie; niemals I
new [njuː] neu I
news (sg) [njuːz] Nachrichten; Neuigkeiten
    II U2, 45
next [nekst] nächste/-r/-s; der/die
    Nächste(n); als Nächstes I
    next to ['nekst tə] neben I
    the **next** day [ðə ˌnekst 'deɪ] am nächsten
    Tag II U1, 15
nice [naɪs] nett; schön; lieb I
night [naɪt] Nacht I
    all **night** [ˌɔːl 'naɪt] die ganze Nacht I
    night walk ['naɪt wɔːk] Nachtwanderung
    II U1, 23
nine [naɪn] neun I
2nite (= tonight) [təˈnaɪt] heute Abend I
no [nəʊ] kein/-e I
    no idea [ˌnəʊ aɪˈdɪə] keine Ahnung
    II U1, 23
    no such thing as [ˌnəʊ sʌtʃ θɪŋ ˈæz] nicht
    so etwas wie II U4, 79
no [nəʊ] nein I
nobody ['nəʊbədi] niemand II U2, 40
    nobody else ['nəʊbədi els] niemand
    anderes II U5, 106
noise [nɔɪz] Lärm; Geräusch II U1, 22

non- [nɒn] nicht- II U1, 14
normal ['nɔːml] normal II U2, 44
north [nɔːθ] Norden; Nord- II U2, 39
nose [nəʊz] Nase II U1, 12
not [nɒt] nicht I
    not any more [ˌnɒt ˌeni 'mɔː] nicht mehr I
    not … any [ˌnɒt … eni] kein/-e/-en I
    not … anything [ˌnɒt 'eniθɪŋ] nichts I
    not … yet [ˌnɒt 'jet] noch nicht II U3, 58
note [nəʊt] Notiz; Anmerkung I
    *to make **notes** [ˌmeɪk 'nəʊts] Notizen
    machen I
    *to take **notes** [ˌteɪk 'nəʊts] sich Notizen
    machen I
to **note** down [ˌnəʊt 'daʊn] notieren; auf-
    schreiben °II U3, 61
nothing ['nʌθɪŋ] nichts I
to **notice** ['nəʊtɪs] bemerken; wahrnehmen
    II U2, 49
noticeboard ['nəʊtɪsbɔːd] schwarzes Brett
    II U1, 14
noun [naʊn] Nomen; Hauptwort I
November [nəˈvembə] November I
now [naʊ] jetzt; nun I
    right **now** [ˌraɪt 'naʊ] jetzt gleich; sofort;
    gerade II U4, 87
nowhere ['nəʊweə] nirgendwo; nirgendwo-
    hin II U5, 94
number ['nʌmbə] Zahl; Nummer I
nut [nʌt] Nuss I

O

o'clock [əˈklɒk] Uhr (Zeitangabe bei vollen
    Stunden) I
October [ɒkˈtəʊbə] Oktober I
of [ɒv; əv] von I
    of course [əv ˈkɔːs] natürlich; selbstver-
    ständlich I
*to take **off** [ˌteɪk ˈɒf] abnehmen; herunter-
    nehmen; ausziehen I
    to turn **off** [ˌtɜːn ˈɒf] abschalten; ausschal-
    ten II U1, 16
special **offer** [ˌspeʃl ˈɒfə] Sonderangebot I
to **offer** ['ɒfə] anbieten II AC1, 8
office ['ɒfɪs] Büro I
official [əˈfɪʃl] Schiedsrichter/-in II U3, 65
official language [əˌfɪʃl ˈlæŋgwɪdʒ] Amts-
    sprache II AC3, 73
offline ['ɒflaɪn] offline II U4, 87
often ['ɒfn] oft; häufig I
oh [əʊ] null (bei Telefonnummern und
    Uhrzeitangaben) I
Oh! [əʊ] O! I
    Oh dear! [ˌəʊ 'dɪə] Oje! II U5, 104
ointment ['ɔɪntmənt] Salbe II U3, 59
OK [əʊˈkeɪ] o.k.; in Ordnung I
old [əʊld] alt I
    How **old** are you? [haʊ ˌəʊld ə ˈjuː] Wie alt
    bist du?; Wie alt sind Sie? I
11-year-**old** [ɪˌlevnˈjɪərəʊld] 11-Jährige/-r
    II U3, 56

on [ɒn] auf; an; am; in; im I
    *to be **on** [bi ˈɒn] an sein; laufen II U4, 86
    on Mondays [ɒn ˈmʌndeɪz] montags I
    on the left [ɒn ðə ˈleft] auf der linken
    Seite; links I
    on the right [ɒn ðə ˈraɪt] auf der rech-
    ten Seite; rechts I
    on top [ɒn ˈtɒp] oben; obendrauf I
    Come **on**! [ˌkʌm ˈɒn] Komm schon!; Komm
    jetzt! I
once [wʌns] einmal; einst I
one [wʌn] eins I
    one day [wʌn ˈdeɪ] eines Tages II U2, 43
    one-way ticket ['wʌnweɪ ˌtɪkɪt] einfache
    Fahrkarte II U5, 96
one [wʌn], **ones** [wʌnz] (pl) eine/-r/-s
    II U2, 40
online [ɒnˈlaɪn] online II U1, 25
only ['əʊnli] einzige/-r/-s II U4, 87
only ['əʊnli] erst; bloß; nur I
    only child ['əʊnli ˌtʃaɪld] Einzelkind I
Oops! [uːps] Hoppla!; Huch! I
to **open** ['əʊpn] öffnen; aufmachen I
open ['əʊpn] offen; geöffnet; aufgeschla-
    gen I
opinion [əˈpɪnjən] Meinung II U4, 76
opposite ['ɒpəzɪt] gegenüber; auf der ande-
    ren Seite von I
or [ɔː] oder I
orange ['ɒrɪndʒ] Orange I
orange ['ɒrɪndʒ] orange I
order ['ɔːdə] Reihenfolge; Ordnung I
    word **order** ['wɜːd ˌɔːdə] Wortstellung;
    Satzstellung I
organisation [ˌɔːgnaɪˈzeɪʃn] Organisation
    °II U5, 97
to **organise** ['ɔːgənaɪz] organisieren I
*to get **organised** [get ˈɔːgənaɪzd] sich
    organisieren °II U5, 102
originally [əˈrɪdʒnli] ursprünglich II AC2, 34
other ['ʌðə] anders; andere/-r/-s; weitere I
    each **other** [iːtʃ ˈʌðə] einander; sich; sich
    gegenseitig I
    the **others** [ðiˈʌðəz] die anderen I
Ouch! [aʊtʃ] Aua! II U1, 12
our [aʊə; ɑː] unser/-e I
out [aʊt] außerhalb; heraus; hinaus; nach
    draußen I
    to clear **out** [klɪərˈaʊt] ausräumen;
    entrümpeln I
    out and about [ˌaʊt ənˈəˈbaʊt] unterwegs
    II U2, 44
    a day **out** in … [ə ˌdeɪ ˈaʊt ɪn] ein Tag
    in … II U2, 44
outdoor [ˈaʊtdɔː] Freiluft-; Outdoor- II U1, 20
outfit [ˈaʊtfɪt] Outfit; Kleidung II U1, 12
outlaw [ˈaʊtlɔː] Geächtete/-r; Gesetzlose/-r
    II AC4, 112
outline [ˈaʊtlaɪn] Skizze; Umriss °II U5, 103
outside [aʊtˈsaɪd] nach draußen; draußen;
    außerhalb I
outward [ˈaʊtwəd] abfahrend II U5, 96

over ['əʊvə] hinüber; über **I**; vorüber; vorbei **II U3**, 63

*to go **over** to [gəʊ 'əʊvə tə] hinübergehen zu; zu jmdm. nach Hause gehen **II U4**, 79

to **overreact** [ˌəʊvəri'ækt] überreagieren **II U4**, 76

own [əʊn] eigene/-r/-s **I**

P

p.m. [ˌpi:'em] nachmittags *(Uhrzeit)*; abends *(Uhrzeit)* **I**

packet ['pækɪt] Päckchen; Paket; Packung **I**

page [peɪdʒ] Seite **I**

pain [peɪn] Schmerz **II U3**, 58

to **paint** [peɪnt] anmalen; malen **I**

painting ['peɪntɪŋ] Malerei; Gemälde **II AC1**, 8

pair [peə] Paar **I**

  pair work ['peə wɜ:k] Partnerarbeit °**II U4**, 84

palm tree ['pɑ:m ˌtri:] Palme **II U5**, 93

to **panic** ['pænɪk] panisch werden **II AC1**, 11

paper ['peɪpə] Papier **I**

  piece of **paper** [ˌpi:s əv 'peɪpə] Stück Papier **I**

paradise ['pærədaɪs] Paradies **II U4**, 74

parcel ['pɑ:sl] Paket; Päckchen **I**

parents *(pl)* ['peərənts] Eltern **I**

park [pɑ:k] Park **I**

part [pɑ:t] Teil; Stadtteil **I**

  *to take **part** (in) [teɪk 'pɑ:t (ɪn)] teilnehmen (an) **II U4**, 74

partially sighted [ˌpɑ:ʃəli 'saɪtɪd] sehbehindert **II AC1**, 9

past **participle** [ˌpɑ:st pɑ:'tɪsɪpl] Partizip °**II U3**, 57

partner ['pɑ:tnə] Partner/-in **I**

party ['pɑ:ti] Party; Feier **I**

to **pass** [pɑ:s] zupassen; zuspielen **II U3**, 54

  to **pass** (on) [ˌpɑ:s 'ɒn] weitergeben **I**

past [pɑ:st] Vergangenheit **II U1**, 13

  past form ['pɑ:st fɔ:m] Vergangenheitsform °**II U1**, 14

  past participle [ˌpɑ:st pɑ:'tɪsɪpl] Partizip °**II U3**, 57

  simple **past** [ˌsɪmpl 'pɑ:st] Vergangenheitsform °**II U1**, 13

past [pɑ:st] nach *(bei Uhrzeitangaben)*; vorbei (an); vorüber (an) **I**

  half **past** [ˌhɑ:f 'pɑ:st] halb *(bei Uhrzeitangaben)* **I**

  quarter **past**/to ['kwɔ:tə pɑ:st/tə] Viertel nach/vor **I**

pasta ['pæstə] Pasta; Nudeln **I**

coastal **path** [ˌkəʊstl 'pɑ:θ] Küstenweg **II U5**, 104

*to **pay (for)** [peɪ] bezahlen **I**

PC *(= Personal Computer)* [pi:'si:] PC **II AC3**, 73

PE *(= Physical Education)* [ˌpi:'i:; ˌfɪzɪkl̩ edʒʊ'keɪʃn] Sportunterricht **II AC1**, 10

to **peer-edit** ['pɪər ˌedɪt] gegenseitig kontrollieren °**II AC1**, 11

pen [pen] Füller **I**

pencil ['pensl] Bleistift; Buntstift **I**

  pencil-case ['pensl ˌkeɪs] Federmäppchen; Mäppchen **I**

penny ['peni], **pence** [pens] *(pl)* Penny *(brit. Währungseinheit)*; Pence *(brit. Währungseinheit)* **I**

people *(pl)* ['pi:pl] Leute; Menschen **I**

per [pɜ:; pə] pro **II U5**, 95

present **perfect** [ˌpreznt 'pɜ:fɪkt] das Perfekt °**II U3**, 55

perfect ['pɜ:fɪkt] perfekt; vollkommen **I**

person ['pɜ:sn], people ['pi:pl] *(pl)* Person; Mensch **I**

  with a **person** who … [wɪð ə ˌpɜ:sn 'hu:] mit einer Person, die … °**II U5**, 95

personal ['pɜ:snl] persönlich **I**

perspective [pə'spektɪv] Perspektive; Blickwinkel °**II U2**, 50

to **persuade** [pə'sweɪd] überreden **II U2**, 38

pet [pet] Haustier **I**

phone [fəʊn] Telefon; Handy **I**

  to answer the **phone** [ˌɑ:nsə ðə 'fəʊn] einen Anruf entgegennehmen **I**

  phone call ['fəʊn ˌkɔ:l] Anruf; Telefonanruf **I**

photo ['fəʊtəʊ] Foto; Fotografie **I**

  in the **photo**(s) [ˌɪn ðə 'fəʊtəʊ(z)] auf dem Foto/den Fotos **I**

  photo story ['fəʊtəʊ ˌstɔ:ri] Fotostory; Bildgeschichte **I**

  *to take **photos** [ˌteɪk 'fəʊtəʊz] fotografieren; Fotos machen **I**

phrase [freɪz] Redewendung; Ausdruck; Satz **I**

  Useful **phrases** [ˌju:sfl 'freɪzɪz] nützliche Ausdrücke **I**

  phrases that … [ˌfreɪzɪz 'ðæt] Redewendungen, die … °**II U1**, 13

to **pick** [pɪk] auswählen; aussuchen °**II U4**, 85

  pick-up ['pɪkʌp] Pick-up; Wiederaufnehmen **I**

picnic ['pɪknɪk] Picknick **I**

picture ['pɪktʃə] Bild; Foto **I**

pie [paɪ] Kuchen; Pastete **I**

piece [pi:s] Stück **I**

  piece of paper [ˌpi:s əv 'peɪpə] Stück Papier **I**

pier [pɪə] Pier; Hafendamm **I**

pig [pɪg] Schwein **I**

  guinea **pig** ['gɪni ˌpɪg] Meerschweinchen **I**

pill [pɪl] Pille; Tablette **II U3**, 59

pink [pɪŋk] pink; rosa **I**

pipe [paɪp] Pfeife **II U2**, 49; Rohr; Rohrleitung **II U4**, 79

  clay **pipe** ['kleɪ paɪp] Tonpfeife **II U2**, 49

pitch [pɪtʃ] Spielfeld; Platz **II U3**, 54

pizza ['pi:tsə] Pizza **I**

place [pleɪs] Ort; Stelle; Platz **I**

  starting **place** ['stɑ:tɪŋ pleɪs] Startpunkt **II U5**, 96

  *to take **place** [teɪk 'pleɪs] stattfinden **I**

  places that … [ˌpleɪsɪz 'ðæt] Orte, die … °**II U5**, 92

to **place** [pleɪs] legen °**II U5**, 103

placemat ['pleɪsmæt] Placemat; Platzdeckchen **I**

plan [plæn] Plan; Entwurf **I**

to **plan** [plæn] planen **I**

planet ['plænɪt] Planet **II U1**, 22

planner ['plænə] Handbuch; Kalender **I**

platform ['plætfɔ:m] Plattform; Bahnsteig **II U5**, 96

role **play** ['rəʊl pleɪ] Rollenspiel **I**

to **play** [pleɪ] spielen **I**

  to **play** a trick (on) [ˌpleɪ ə 'trɪk ˌɒn] einen Streich spielen **I**

player ['pleɪə] Spieler/-in; Mitspieler/-in **II U3**, 67

Please. [pli:z] Bitte. **I**

plumber ['plʌmə] Installateur/-in; Klempner/-in **II U5**, 104

plumbing ['plʌmɪŋ] Sanitärarbeit **II U5**, 105

plural ['plʊərəl] Plural; Mehrzahl **I**

pocket money ['pɒkɪt ˌmʌni] Taschengeld **I**

poem ['pəʊɪm] Gedicht **I**

point [pɔɪnt] Punkt **II U3**, 54; Zeitpunkt °**II U4**, 88

  point of view [ˌpɔɪnt əv 'vju:] Standpunkt; Ansicht; Perspektive **II U3**, 60

Point. [pɔɪnt] Zeige/Zeigt darauf. **I**

  Point to … ['pɔɪnt tə] Zeige/Zeigt auf … **I**

police [pə'li:s] Polizei **II U1**, 17

polite [pə'laɪt] höflich **I**

  Be **polite.** [bi: pə'laɪt] Sei/Seid höflich. **I**

politely [pə'laɪt] höflich °**II U2**, 48

pollution [pə'lu:ʃn] Verschmutzung **II AC1**, 11

pony ['pəʊni] Pony **I**

  pony trekking ['pəʊni ˌtrekɪŋ] Ponyreiten im Gelände **II U5**, 93

the **poor** [ðə pʊə] die Armen **II AC4**, 113

popular ['pɒpjələ] beliebt; populär **I**

positive ['pɒzətɪv] positiv **II U3**, 66

possessive form [pə'sesɪv ˌfɔ:m] Possessivform **I**

possible ['pɒsəbl] möglich **I**

post [pəʊst] Post *(Eintrag im Internet)* **I**

to **post** [pəʊst] online stellen; posten **II U4**, 74

postcard ['pəʊstkɑ:d] Postkarte **II U5**, 106

poster ['pəʊstə] Poster **I**

  class **poster** ['klɑ:s ˌpəʊstə] Klassenposter **I**

postman ['pəʊstmən] Briefträger **II U1**, 17

pound (£) [paʊnd] Pfund *(brit. Währungseinheit)* **I**

to **pour** [pɔ:] einschenken; eingießen; schütten **I**

power [paʊə] Kraft; Macht; Stärke II **AC4**, 112
  power cut [ˈpaʊə ˌkʌt] Stromausfall II **U4**, 87
  Word **power** [ˈwɜːd ˌpaʊə] die Kraft der Wörter (Wortschatzübung) I
powerful [ˈpaʊəfl] stark; mächtig II **AC4**, 112
practical [ˈpræktɪkl] praktisch II **U4**, 75
to **practise** [ˈpræktɪs] üben; trainieren I
practising [ˈpræktɪsɪŋ] Üben I
prediction [prɪˈdɪkʃn] Vorhersage; Voraussage °II **U5**, 95
prehistoric [ˌpriːhɪˈstɒrɪk] vorgeschichtlich II **U5**, 98
to **prepare** [prɪˈpeə] vorbereiten; zubereiten I
preposition [ˌprepəˈzɪʃn] Präposition I
pre-reading [ˌpriːˈriːdɪŋ] vor dem Lesen I
prescription [prɪˈskrɪpʃn] Rezept (für Arzneimittel) II **U3**, 59
present [ˈpreznt] Geschenk I
present [ˈpreznt] Gegenwart; Präsens °II **U1**, 18
  present perfect [ˌpreznt ˈpɜːfɪkt] das Perfekt °II **U3**, 55
  present progressive [ˌpreznt prəˈgresɪv] Verlaufsform des Präsens/der Gegenwart I
  simple **present** [ˌsɪmpl ˈpreznt] Gegenwart; Präsens I
to **present** [prɪˈzent] präsentieren; vorstellen I
presentation [ˌpreznˈteɪʃn] Präsentation; Vortrag I
presenter [prɪˈzentə] Moderator/-in I
to **press** [pres] drücken; pressen II **U4**, 86
  he was **pressing** [ˌhi wəz ˈpresɪŋ] er drückte gerade °II **U4**, 86
price [praɪs] Preis I
primary school [ˈpraɪmri ˌskuːl] Grundschule I
print [prɪnt] gedruckt; Druck- II **U4**, 75
prison [ˈprɪzn] Gefängnis II **U2**, 42
private detective [ˌpraɪvət dɪˈtektɪv] Privatdetektiv/-in II **AC4**, 112
prize [praɪz] Preis; Gewinn I
pro [prəʊ] Argument dafür II **U2**, 41
probably [ˈprɒbəbli] möglicherweise; wahrscheinlich II **U2**, 38
problem [ˈprɒbləm] Problem; Schwierigkeit I
profile [ˈprəʊfaɪl] Profil; Porträt I
programme [ˈprəʊgræm] Programm; Sendung II **U3**, 54
present **progressive** [ˌpreznt prəˈgresɪv] Verlaufsform des Präsens/der Gegenwart I
project [ˈprɒdʒekt] Projekt I
to **promise** [ˈprɒmɪs] versprechen II **U5**, 95
pronunciation [prəˌnʌnsiˈeɪʃn] Aussprache I
prop [prɒp] Requisite II **AC4**, 113
to **protect** [prəˈtekt] schützen II **AC1**, 11
proud (of) [ˈpraʊd ˌəv] stolz (auf) II **U1**, 13
public [ˈpʌblɪk] öffentlich II **U2**, 37

public transport (no pl) [ˌpʌblɪk ˈtrænspɔːt] öffentliche Verkehrsmittel II **U2**, 37
pudding [ˈpʊdɪŋ] Pudding; Nachtisch I
to **pull** [pʊl] ziehen I
purple [ˈpɜːpl] violett; lila I
to **push** [pʊʃ] stoßen; schieben; schubsen II **U4**, 86
*to **put** [pʊt] setzen; stellen; legen I
  *to **put** through [pʊt ˈθruː] verbinden I
  Put in … [pʊt ˈɪn] Setze/Setzt ein … I
  Put it in … [pʊt ˌɪt ˈɪn] Lege/Legt es in …; Stelle/Stellt es in … I
  Put … face down. [pʊt ˌfeɪs ˈdaʊn] Lege/Legt … umgedreht hin. I
puzzle [ˈpʌzl] Rätsel; Puzzle I
pyjamas (pl) [pɪˈdʒɑːməz] Schlafanzug; Pyjama II **U1**, 16

Q

quality [ˈkwɒləti] Qualität I
quarter past/to [ˈkwɔːtə pɑːst/tə] Viertel nach/vor I
queen [kwiːn] Königin II **AC2**, 35
question [ˈkwestʃən] Frage I
queue [kjuː] Schlange; Warteschlange I
  to jump the **queue** [ˌdʒʌmp ðə ˈkjuː] sich vordrängeln I
quick [kwɪk] schnell I
quickly [ˈkwɪkli] schnell II **U2**, 48
  more **quickly** [mɔː ˈkwɪkli] schneller °II **U4**, 88
quiet [ˈkwaɪət] still; ruhig; leise I
quiz [kwɪz] Quiz; Rätsel I
quote [kwəʊt] Zitat °II **AC1**, 9

R

rabbit [ˈræbɪt] Kaninchen I
race [reɪs] Wettlauf; Rennen II **U3**, 54
camel **racing** [ˈkæml ˌreɪsɪŋ] Kamelrennen II **U3**, 54
racquet [ˈrækɪt] Schläger II **U3**, 54
radio [ˈreɪdiəʊ] Radio II **U3**, 54
raffle [ˈræfl] Tombola I
to **rain** [reɪn] regnen II **U4**, 86
  it was **raining** [ɪt wəz ˈreɪnɪŋ] es regnete °II **U4**, 86
to **raise** money [ˌreɪz ˈmʌni] Geld sammeln II **U1**, 14
rap [ræp] Rap I
to **rap** [ræp] rappen I
rat [ræt] Ratte I
raven [ˈreɪvn] Rabe II **U2**, 42
  raven master [ˈreɪvn ˌmɑːstə] Herr der Raben II **U2**, 42
RE (= Religious Education) [ˌɑːrˈiː; rɪˌlɪdʒəs ˌedʒʊˈkeɪʃn] Religion (Schulfach) II **AC1**, 10
to **reach** [riːtʃ] erreichen; dran kommen II **U4**, 79
reaction [riˈækʃn] Reaktion II **AC1**, 9

*to **read** [riːd] lesen I
reader [ˈriːdə] Leser/-in I
reading [ˈriːdɪŋ] Lesen I
ready meal [ˌredi ˈmiːl] Fertiggericht I
real [rɪəl] echt; richtig; wirklich II **U1**, 14
realistic [rɪəˈlɪstɪk] realistisch II **U2**, 47
really [ˈrɪəli] wirklich I
reason [ˈriːzn] Grund II **U3**, 66
to **receive** [rɪˈsiːv] empfangen; erhalten; bekommen II **U3**, 61
to **record** [rɪˈkɔːd] aufnehmen; aufzeichnen II **U3**, 62
recording [rɪˈkɔːdɪŋ] Aufnahme; Aufzeichnung I
  recording studio [rɪˈkɔːdɪŋ ˌstjuːdiəʊ] Aufnahmestudio; Tonstudio I
to **recycle** [ˌriːˈsaɪkl] recyceln; wiederverwerten II **AC1**, 11
red [red] rot I
to **reef** the sails [ˌriːf ðə ˈseɪlz] die Segel einholen I
region [ˈriːdʒn] Region; Gegend II **AC3**, 73
registration [ˌredʒɪsˈtreɪʃn] Anwesenheitskontrolle II **AC1**, 10
regular [ˈregjələ] regelmäßig; gleichmäßig I
relationship [rɪˈleɪʃnʃɪp] Beziehung II **U3**, 66
to **relax** [rɪˈlæks] sich entspannen; sich ausruhen; sich beruhigen II **AC1**, 11
religious [rɪˈlɪdʒəs] religiös; gläubig I
to **remember** [rɪˈmembə] sich erinnern (an); sich merken; denken an I
  Remember? [rɪˈmembə] Erinnerst du dich?; Erinnert ihr euch? I
reply [rɪˈplaɪ] Antwort; Erwiderung; Entgegnung I
to **reply** [rɪˈplaɪ] antworten; erwidern; entgegnen I
report [rɪˈpɔːt] Bericht; Meldung II **U1**, 13
  travel **report** [ˌtrævl rɪˈpɔːt] Reisebericht II **U1**, 24
to **report** [rɪˈpɔːt] berichten; melden II **U5**, 93
reporter [rɪˈpɔːtə] Reporter/-in II **U3**, 61
rescue [ˈreskjuː] Rettung II **U3**, 61
the **rest** [rest] der Rest I
restaurant [ˈrestrɒnt] Restaurant; Gaststätte I
result [rɪˈzʌlt] Ergebnis; Resultat II **U4**, 81
*to **retell** [ˌriːˈtel] nacherzählen; nochmals erzählen I
return ticket [rɪˈtɜːn ˌtɪkɪt] Hin- und Rückfahrkarte II **U5**, 96
to **return** [rɪˈtɜːn] zurückkehren; zurückfahren II **U5**, 96
revision [rɪˈvɪʒn] Wiederholung °II **U1**, 19
rhyme [raɪm] Reim I
rhythm [ˈrɪðm] Rhythmus I
the **rich** [ðə rɪtʃ] die Reichen II **AC4**, 113
rigging [ˈrɪgɪŋ] Takelage I
right [raɪt] richtig; korrekt; rechts; rechte/-r/-s I
  *to be **right** [bi ˈraɪt] recht haben I

*to get **right** [get 'raɪt] richtig beantworten °**II U5**, 103

on the **right** [ɒn ðə 'raɪt] auf der rechten Seite; rechts **I**

right away [raɪt ə'weɪ] sofort; gleich **I**

right here [raɪt 'hɪə] genau hier **II U3**, 56

right now [raɪt 'naʊ] jetzt gleich; sofort; gerade **II U4**, 87

*to **ring** [rɪŋ] klingeln; läuten **I**

ice **rink** ['aɪs ˌrɪŋk] Eisbahn; Schlittschuhbahn **I**

river ['rɪvə] Fluss **I**

road [rəʊd] Straße **II U1**, 22

robber ['rɒbə] Räuber/-in **II AC4**, 112

rock 'n' roll [rɒk ən 'rəʊl] Rock 'n' Roll **II AC3**, 73

rocky ['rɒki] felsig; steinig **II U5**, 93

role [rəʊl] Rolle **I**

role play ['rəʊl pleɪ] Rollenspiel **I**

to swap **roles** [swɒp 'rəʊlz] Rollen tauschen **I**

rock 'n' roll [rɒk ən 'rəʊl] Rock 'n' Roll **II AC3**, 73

to **roll** off [rəʊl] hinunterrollen; herunterrollen **II U2**, 48

Roll two dice. [rəʊl ˌtuː 'daɪs] Würfle/Würfelt mit zwei Würfeln. **I**

Roman ['rəʊmən] Römer/-in; römisch **II AC2**, 34

Romanian [rʊ'meɪniən] Rumäne/Rumänin; rumänisch; Rumänisch **II AC3**, 72

roof [ruːf] Dach **II U5**, 104

room [ruːm; rʊm] Zimmer; Raum **I**

chat **room** ['tʃæt rʊm] Chatroom **II AC3**, 72

living **room** ['lɪvɪŋ rʊm] Wohnzimmer **I**

roommate ['ruːmmeɪt] Zimmergenosse/Zimmergenossin **I**

round [raʊnd] Runde **II U1**, 12

round of boxing [raʊnd əv 'bɒksɪŋ] Boxrunde **II U1**, 12

the **Round** Table [ðə ˌraʊnd 'teɪbl] die Tafelrunde **II AC4**, 113

round [raʊnd] um … herum **II U4**, 87

to turn **round** [tɜːn (ə)'raʊnd] (sich) umdrehen; wenden **II U5**, 104

route [ruːt] Strecke; Route **II U1**, 20

royal ['rɔɪəl] königlich **I**

rubber ['rʌbə] Radiergummi **I**

rubbish ['rʌbɪʃ] Müll; Gerümpel **I**

rude [ruːd] unhöflich; unverschämt **I**

rugby ['rʌgbi] Rugby **II U3**, 54

to **ruin** ['ruːɪn] ruinieren; zerstören **II U3**, 65

rule [ruːl] Regel **I**

What's the **rule** for …? [wɒts ðə 'ruːl fə] Was ist die Regel für …? **I**

to **rule** [ruːl] herrschen; regieren **II U5**, 100

ruler ['ruːlə] Lineal **I**

run [rʌn] Rennen; Lauf **II U3**, 56

*to **run** [rʌn] rennen; laufen **I**

*to **run** away [rʌn ə'weɪ] wegrennen **I**

runner ['rʌnə] Läufer/-in **II U3**, 54

running ['rʌnɪŋ] Laufen; Rennen **II U3**, 56

S

sad [sæd] traurig **I**

safe [seɪf] sicher; ungefährlich **II U2**, 42

to reef the **sails** [riːf ðə 'seɪlz] die Segel einholen **I**

sailboat ['seɪlbəʊt] Segelboot **II U5**, 106

sailor ['seɪlə] Seemann; Matrose **I**

salad ['sæləd] Salat **I**

sale [seɪl] Verkauf **II U1**, 16

the **same** [ðə 'seɪm] der-/die-/dasselbe; der/die/das gleiche **I**

the **same** way as [ðə seɪm 'weɪ æz] genauso wie °**II U1**, 28

sandwich ['sænwɪdʒ] Sandwich; belegtes Brot **I**

sandy ['sændi] sandig; Sand- **II U5**, 93

Saturday ['sætədeɪ] Samstag **I**

to **save** [seɪv] retten; bergen **I**; sparen **II AC1**, 11

sax ['sæks] Saxofon **I**

saxophone ['sæksəfəʊn] Saxofon **I**

*to **say** [seɪ] sagen; aufsagen; sprechen **I**

*to **say** hello (to) [seɪ hel'əʊ tə] grüßen; Grüße ausrichten (an) **I**

to **scan** [skæn] scannen; nach Details durchsuchen °**II U2**, 45

*to be **scared** (of) [bi: 'skeəd əv] Angst haben (vor) **I**

I'm (not) **scared** of … [aɪm (nɒt) 'skeəd əv] Ich habe (keine) Angst vor … **I**

scary ['skeəri] unheimlich; gruselig; beängstigend **II U1**, 28

scene [siːn] Szene **I**; Schauplatz **II U3**, 61

acting a **scene** [æktɪŋ ə 'siːn] eine Theaterszene spielen **I**

school [skuːl] Schule **I**

grammar **school** ['græmə ˌskuːl] Gymnasium **II U5**, 97

primary **school** ['praɪmri ˌskuːl] Grundschule **I**

schoolbag ['skuːlbæg] Schultasche **I**

Science [saɪəns] Naturwissenschaften **II AC1**, 9

science fiction [saɪəns 'fɪkʃn] Science-Fiction (Zukunftsdichtung) **II U1**, 26

score [skɔː] Punktestand; Spielstand **II U3**, 54

Scottish ['skɒtɪʃ] schottisch **II U5**, 93

gorge **scrambling** ['gɔːdʒ ˌskræmblɪŋ] Schluchtenklettern **II U1**, 20

to **scream** [skriːm] schreien; kreischen **II U2**, 49

sea [siː] Meer **I**

search [sɜːtʃ] Suche; Such- **II U1**, 25

second ['seknd] zweite/-r/-s **I**

secret ['siːkrət] Geheimnis **II U1**, 23

in **secret** [ɪn 'siːkrət] heimlich **II U3**, 65

section ['sekʃn] Abschnitt; Paragraf °**II U1**, 26

*to **see** [siː] sehen **I**

See you! ['siː jə] Bis dann!; Bis … **I**

Wait and **see**! [weɪt ənd 'siː] Warte ab! **I**

self-critical ['selfˌkrɪtɪkl] selbstkritisch **II U4**, 76

self-evaluation [ˌselfɪˌvæljuˈeɪʃn] Selbsteinschätzung **I**

selfie ['selfi] Selfie **II U3**, 65

*to **sell** [sel] verkaufen **I**

seller ['selə] Verkäufer/-in (auf einem Flohmarkt) **I**

*to **send** [send] schicken; senden **I**

*to **send** off [send 'ɒf] abschicken **II U5**, 97

sentence ['sentəns] Satz **I**

separate ['seprət] separat; getrennt; verschieden **II U1**, 20

September [sep'tembə] September **I**

sequel ['siːkwl] Fortsetzung; Folge **II U5**, 101

serious ['sɪəriəs] ernsthaft; ernst **I**

*to take sth **seriously** [teɪk 'sɪəriəsli] etw. ernst nehmen **II U3**, 64

set [set] Umgebung; Rahmen **II AC4**, 113

*to **set** up [set 'ʌp] einrichten; aufbauen **I**

setting ['setɪŋ] Schauplatz; Rahmen °**II U2**, 44

seven ['sevn] sieben **I**

to **share** [ʃeə] teilen **II U4**, 76

she [ʃiː] sie **I**

sheep [ʃiːp], **sheep** [ʃiːp] (pl) Schaf **II U1**, 22

ship [ʃɪp] Schiff **I**

shock [ʃɒk] Schock **II U3**, 63

shoe [ʃuː] Schuh **I**

shop [ʃɒp] Geschäft; Laden **I**

charity **shop** ['tʃærɪti ʃɒp] Second-Hand-Laden **I**

shopping ['ʃɒpɪŋ] Einkaufen; Einkäufe **I**

*to go **shopping** [gəʊ 'ʃɒpɪŋ] einkaufen gehen **I**

shore [ʃɔː] Ufer; Küste **II U2**, 48

short [ʃɔːt] kurz **I**

short answer [ˌʃɔːt 'ɑːnsə] Kurzantwort **I**

short form ['ʃɔːt fɔːm] Kurzform **I**

shot [ʃɒt] Einstellung; Kameraeinstellung °**II U4**, 82

should [ʃʊd] sollte; solltest; sollten; solltet **II AC1**, 11

shouldn't ['ʃʊdnt] sollte(n) nicht **II U3**, 59

shoulder ['ʃəʊldə] Schulter **II U3**, 59

to **shout** [ʃaʊt] schreien; rufen **I**

show [ʃəʊ] Show; Schau; Aufführung **II AC1**, 9

comedy **show** ['kɒmədi ˌʃəʊ] Comedy Show **II U1**, 14

living history **show** [ˌlɪvɪŋ 'hɪstəri ˌʃəʊ] Show, in der historischer Alltag nachgespielt wird **II U5**, 92

talent **show** ['tælənt ˌʃəʊ] Talentwettbewerb **I**

to **show** [ʃəʊ] zeigen **I**

to **show** off [ʃəʊ 'ɒf] angeben **II U4**, 87

shower ['ʃaʊə] Dusche **I**

to **shuffle** ['ʃʌfl] mischen °**II U5**, 93

shy [ʃaɪ] schüchtern **II U1**, 13

sick [sɪk] krank; unwohl **II U3**, 59

*to feel **sick** [ˌfiːl ˈsɪk] Übelkeit verspüren; sich schlecht fühlen II U3, 59

side [saɪd] Seite II U2, 49

sight [saɪt] Sehenswürdigkeit; Anblick II AC2, 34

sightseeing [ˈsaɪtsiːɪŋ] Sightseeing-; Besichtigungs- II U2, 44

sign [saɪn] Zeichen; Schild II AC1, 8

signal word [ˈsɪgnəl ˌwɜːd] Signalwort I

silly [ˈsɪli] Dummkopf II U3, 64

silly [ˈsɪli] dumm; doof; albern I

silver [ˈsɪlvə] Silber II U2, 48

similar [ˈsɪmɪlə] ähnlich °II AC2, 35

simple past [ˌsɪmpl ˈpɑːst] Vergangenheitsform °II U1, 13

simple present [ˌsɪmpl ˈpreznt] Gegenwart; Präsens I

*to **sing** [sɪŋ] singen I

I like **singing** and dancing. [ˌaɪ laɪk ˌsɪŋɪŋ ənd ˈdɑːnsɪŋ] Ich singe und tanze gern. I

singer [ˈsɪŋə] Sänger/-in II U1, 19

single ticket [ˈsɪŋl ˌtɪkɪt] einfache Fahrkarte II U5, 96

Dear **Sir** or Madam [dɪə ˌsɜːrˌɔː ˈmædəm] Sehr geehrte Dame, sehr geehrter Herr II U5, 97

sister [ˈsɪstə] Schwester I

half-**sister** [ˈhɑːfˌsɪstə] Halbschwester I

*to **sit** [sɪt] sitzen I

Sit! [sɪt] Sitz! (Befehl für Hunde); Platz! (Befehl für Hunde) I

*to **sit** down [ˌsɪt ˈdaʊn] sich hinsetzen; sich setzen I

*to **sit** face to face [ˌsɪt feɪs tə ˌfeɪs] sich gegenüber sitzen I

site [saɪt] Webseite II U4, 76

situation [ˌsɪtjuˈeɪʃn] Situation I

six [sɪks] sechs I

Four and **six** is ten. [ˌfɔːr ənd ˌsɪks ɪz ˈten] Vier plus sechs ist zehn. I

size [saɪz] Größe; Kleidergröße I

to **skate** [skeɪt] Inlineskates fahren; Schlittschuh laufen I

skateboard [ˈskeɪtbɔːd] Skateboard II U1, 15

skateboarding [ˈskeɪtbɔːdɪŋ] Skateboardfahren I

skates (pl) [skeɪts] Inlineskates; Rollschuhe; Schlittschuhe I

(inline) **skating** [ˈɪnlaɪn ˌskeɪtɪŋ] Inlineskatefahren I

skill [skɪl] Fertigkeit; Geschick I

to **skim** [skɪm] überfliegen °II U2, 45

skirt [skɜːt] Rock II U5, 104

*to **sleep** [sliːp] schlafen I

sleepover [ˈsliːpˌəʊvə] Übernachtung I

to **slice** [slaɪs] in Scheiben schneiden I

slide [slaɪd] Rutschbahn I

water **slide** [ˈwɔːtə ˌslaɪd] Wasserrutsche I

slogan [ˈsləʊgən] Slogan; Werbespruch II AC1, 11

slow [sləʊ] langsam I

small [smɔːl] klein I

smartcard [ˈsmɑːtkɑːd] Chipkarte II U2, 38

smartphone [ˈsmɑːtfəʊn] Smartphone II U3, 63

smile [smaɪl] Lächeln I

to **smile** [smaɪl] lächeln I

snack [snæk] Snack; Imbiss I

snack bar [ˈsnæk ˌbɑː] Café; Imbissstube I

word **snake** [ˈwɜːd ˌsneɪk] Wortschlange I

to **sneak** around [ˌsniːk əˈraʊnd] herumschleichen II U1, 28

to **snore** [snɔː] schnarchen I

so [səʊ] so; also I

so far [ˌsəʊ ˈfɑː] bis jetzt II U3, 60

social network [ˌsəʊʃl ˈnetwɜːk] soziales Netzwerk II U4, 75

society [səˈsaɪəti] Verein; Gesellschaft II U5, 105

sofa [ˈsəʊfə] Sofa; Couch I

solution [səˈluːʃn] Lösung II U1, 17

to **solve** [sɒlv] lösen II U5, 104

some [sʌm; səm] einige; ein paar; etwas I

somebody [ˈsʌmbədi] jemand I

someone [ˈsʌmwʌn] jemand II U1, 17

something [ˈsʌmθɪŋ] etwas I

sometimes [ˈsʌmtaɪmz] manchmal I

somewhere [ˈsʌmweə] irgendwo II U2, 51

song [sɒŋ] Song; Lied I

soon [suːn] bald II U1, 22

as **soon** as [əz ˈsuːnˌəz] sobald II U4, 76

Sorry! [ˈsɒri] Entschuldigung!; Tut mir leid! I

*to be **sorry** [bi ˈsɒri] leid tun I

I'm **sorry!** [ˌaɪm ˈsɒri] Tut mir leid! I

sound [saʊnd] Ton; Geräusch; Klang I

to **sound** [saʊnd] klingen I

source [sɔːs] Quelle °II U5, 102

south [saʊθ] Süden; Süd- II U2, 39

South Korean [ˌsaʊθ kəˈriːən] Südkoreaner/-in; südkoreanisch; Südkoreanisch II AC3, 72

souvenir [ˌsuːvnˈɪə] Souvenir; Andenken II U2, 40

space [speɪs] Raum; Fläche; Platz; Ort II AC2, 34

*to leave **space** [liːv ˈspeɪs] Platz lassen I

spaceship [ˈspeɪsʃɪp] Raumschiff II U1, 26

*to **speak** [spiːk] sprechen I

he wasn't **speaking** [hi ˌwɒznt ˈspiːkɪŋ] er sprach nicht °II U4, 87

speaker [ˈspiːkə] Redner/-in; Sprecher/-in I

speaking [ˈspiːkɪŋ] Sprechen I

spear [spɪə] Speer II U5, 104

special [ˈspeʃl] besonders; speziell I

special offer [ˌspeʃl ˈɒfə] Sonderangebot I

with **special** needs [wɪð ˌspeʃl ˈniːdz] behindert II AC1, 9

direct **speech** [dɪˌrekt ˈspiːtʃ] direkte Rede °II U5, 99

indirect **speech** [ˌɪndɪrekt ˈspiːtʃ] indirekte Rede °II U5, 99

speech bubble [ˈspiːtʃ ˌbʌbl] Sprechblase I

*to **spell** [spel] buchstabieren I

spelling [ˈspelɪŋ] Rechtschreibung I

*to **spend** [spend] ausgeben (Geld) I; verbringen (Zeit) II U4, 76

spoken [ˈspəʊkn] gesprochen °II U3, 66

sponge [spʌndʒ] Rühr-; Biskuit- I

spontaneous [spɒnˈteɪniəs] spontan °II U5, 95

sport [spɔːt] Sport; Sportart I

squirrel [ˈskwɪrəl] Eichhörnchen I

stadium [ˈsteɪdiəm] Stadion II U3, 54

*to **stand** [stænd] stehen I

*to **stand** up [ˌstænd ˈʌp] aufstehen (von einer Sitzgelegenheit) I

star [stɑː] Star; Stern I

to **stare** [steə] starren; anstarren I

to **start** [stɑːt] anfangen; beginnen; starten I

starting place [ˈstɑːtɪŋ pleɪs] Startpunkt II U5, 96

head of **state** [ˌhed əv ˈsteɪt] Staatsoberhaupt II AC3, 73

statement [ˈsteɪtmənt] Aussage; Behauptung; Erklärung II AC3, 72

station [ˈsteɪʃn] Haltestelle; Bahnhof; Station I; Sender II U3, 61

bus **station** [ˈbʌs ˌsteɪʃn] Busbahnhof I

to **stay** [steɪ] bleiben I; übernachten II U5, 94

to **stay** away from [ˌsteɪ əˈweɪ frəm] fernbleiben von; meiden II U4, 81

to **stay** in touch (with) [ˌsteɪ ɪn ˈtʌtʃ wɪð] in Kontakt bleiben (mit) II U4, 74

to **stay** with [ˈsteɪ wɪð] wohnen bei II U2, 38

steak [steɪk] Steak I

*to **steal** [stiːl] stehlen II U5, 104

step [step] Stufe; Schritt I

step-by-**step** [ˌstepbaɪˈstep] Schritt-für-Schritt- II U4, 79

stepmum [ˈstepmʌm] Stiefmutter I

still [stɪl] Standbild °II AC1, 11

still [stɪl] still I

still [stɪl] noch; immer noch I; dennoch II U4, 79

stomach [ˈstʌmək] Magen; Bauch II U3, 64

stomachache [ˈstʌməkeɪk] Bauchschmerzen; Bauchweh II U3, 59

stop [stɒp] Haltestelle; Halt II U2, 39

to **stop** [stɒp] aufhören (mit); anhalten; stoppen I

Stop and think [ˌstɒp ənd ˈθɪŋk] Warte/Wartet und denk/denkt nach. I

Stop it! [ˈstɒp ˌɪt] Mach/Macht das aus!; Hör/Hört auf! I

storm [stɔːm] Sturm I

story [ˈstɔːri], **stories** [ˈstɔːriz] (pl) Story; Geschichte; Erzählung I

photo **story** [ˈfəʊtəʊ ˌstɔːri] Fotostory; Bildgeschichte I

straight on [streɪt ˈɒn] geradeaus I

strange [streɪndʒ] fremd; seltsam; merkwürdig I

street [striːt] Straße (in der Stadt) I

in the **street** [ˌɪn ðə ˈstriːt] in der Straße; auf der Straße I

strong [strɒŋ] stark II **U5**, 104

student [ˈstjuːdnt] Schüler/-in; Student/-in I

studies (pl) [ˈstʌdiz] Studium; Lernen; Arbeit für die Schule II **AC1**, 8

recording **studio** [rɪˈkɔːdɪŋ ˌstjuːdiəʊ] Aufnahmestudio; Tonstudio I

stuff [stʌf] Zeug I

stupid [ˈstjuːpɪd] dumm; blöd II **U3**, 65

subject [ˈsʌbdʒɪkt] Schulfach II **AC1**, 8

suddenly [ˈsʌdnli] plötzlich; auf einmal I

suggestion [səˈdʒestʃn] Vorschlag; Anregung I

summer [ˈsʌmə] Sommer II **AC3**, 72

summer camp [ˈsʌmə kæmp] Sommerferienlager II **AC3**, 72

sun [sʌn] Sonne II **U5**, 104

Sunday [ˈsʌndeɪ] Sonntag I

sunny [ˈsʌni] sonnig II **U5**, 98

superlative [suːˈpɜːlətɪv] Superlativ °II **U1**, 20

supermarket [ˈsuːpəˌmɑːkɪt] Supermarkt I

superpower [ˈsuːpəˌpaʊə] Supermacht II **AC3**, 73

to **supply** [səˈplaɪ] versorgen II **U5**, 100

sure [ʃʊə; ʃɔː] sicher I

*to be **sure** [bi ˈʃʊə] sicher sein II **U5**, 98

*to make **sure** [ˌmeɪk ˈʃɔː] sich versichern I

surfing [ˈsɜːfɪŋ] Surfen II **U5**, 93

surgery [ˈsɜːdʒəri] Arztpraxis; Praxis; Praxisräume I

surprise [səˈpraɪz] Überraschung I

to **surprise** [səˈpraɪz] überraschen II **U3**, 65

*to be **surprised** [bi səˈpraɪzd] überrascht sein II **U2**, 49

surprising [səˈpraɪzɪŋ] überraschend II **U1**, 28

survey [ˈsɜːveɪ] Umfrage; Studie I

suspense [səˈspens] Spannung °II **U5**, 101

to **swap** roles [ˌswɒp ˈrəʊlz] Rollen tauschen I

sweet [swiːt] süß I

sweets (pl) [swiːts] Süßigkeiten; Bonbons I

*to **swim** [swɪm] schwimmen I

swimming [ˈswɪmɪŋ] Schwimmen I

*to go **swimming** [ˌɡəʊ ˈswɪmɪŋ] Schwimmen gehen I

symbol [ˈsɪmbl] Symbol °II **U2**, 44

T

table [ˈteɪbl] Tisch I

the Round **Table** [ðə ˌraʊnd ˈteɪbl] die Tafelrunde II **AC4**, 113

tablet [ˈtæblət] Tablet II **U4**, 79

tail [teɪl] Schwanz; Schweif I

*to **take** [teɪk] nehmen; mitnehmen; wegnehmen; bringen; mitbringen I; dauern; (Zeit) brauchen II **U4**, 79

*to **take** a message [ˌteɪk ə ˈmesɪdʒ] eine Nachricht entgegennehmen; jmdm. etw. ausrichten I

*to **take** a test [ˌteɪk ə ˈtest] einen Test machen °II **U4**, 81

*to **take** a vote [ˌteɪk ə ˈvəʊt] abstimmen I

*to **take** notes [ˌteɪk ˈnəʊts] sich Notizen machen I

*to **take** off [ˌteɪk ˈɒf] abnehmen; herunternehmen; ausziehen I

*to **take** part (in) [ˌteɪk ˈpɑːt (ɪn)] teilnehmen (an) II **U4**, 74

*to **take** photos [ˌteɪk ˈfəʊtəʊz] fotografieren; Fotos machen I

*to **take** place [ˌteɪk ˈpleɪs] stattfinden I

*to **take** sth seriously [ˌteɪk ˈsɪəriəsli] etw. ernst nehmen II **U3**, 64

Take a deep breath. [ˌteɪk ə ˌdiːp ˈbreθ] Atme(t) tief ein. II **AC1**, 11

Take turns. [ˌteɪk ˈtɜːnz] Wechselt euch ab. I

talent [ˈtælənt] Talent I

talent show [ˈtælənt ˌʃəʊ] Talentwettbewerb I

to **talk** [tɔːk] sprechen; reden I

to **talk** about … [ˈtɔːk əˌbaʊt] sprechen über; erzählen von I

to **talk** to [ˈtɔːk tə] reden mit I

talking [ˈtɔːkɪŋ] Sprechen I

tall [tɔːl] groß; hoch II **U1**, 21

to **tap** [tæp] antippen II **U4**, 86

task [tɑːsk] Aufgabe; Auftrag I

taxi [ˈtæksi] Taxi II **U1**, 17

tea [tiː] Tee I

*to **teach** [tiːtʃ] unterrichten; lehren; beibringen II **U3**, 60

*to **teach** somebody a lesson [ˌtiːtʃ ə ˈlesn] jmdm. eine Lehre/Lektion erteilen II **U3**, 60

teacher [ˈtiːtʃə] Lehrer/-in I

team [tiːm] Team; Gruppe II **U1**, 12

Technology [tekˈnɒlədʒi] Technik; Computerunterricht II **AC1**, 9

technology [tekˈnɒlədʒi] Technologie II **AC3**, 73

teen [tiːn] Jugend- II **U4**, 76

teenager [ˈtiːnˌeɪdʒə] Teenager; Jugendliche/-r I

telephone [ˈtelɪfəʊn] Telefon I

*to **tell** [tel] erzählen; sagen; mitteilen I

Tell me about … [ˈtel miː əˌbaʊt] Erzähle mir von … I

ten [ten] zehn I

ten times [ten ˈtaɪmz] zehnmal I

Four and six is **ten**. [ˌfɔːr ənd ˌsɪks ɪz ˈten] Vier plus sechs ist zehn. I

tennis [ˈtenɪs] Tennis I

tense [tens] Zeit; Zeitform (grammatisch) °II **U3**, 57

test [test] Test; Klassenarbeit; Prüfung I

*to take a **test** [ˌteɪk ə ˈtest] einen Test machen °II **U4**, 81

to **test** [test] testen; prüfen °II **U5**, 103

text [tekst] Text I

text (message) [ˈtekst ˌmesɪdʒ] SMS; Kurznachricht I

to **text** [tekst] eine SMS schicken II **U4**, 74

than [ðæn] als (bei Vergleichen) II **U1**, 20

more … **than** [ˈmɔː ðən] mehr … als I

to **thank** [θæŋk] danken II **AC1**, 11

Thank you. [ˈθæŋk juː] Danke. I

thankful [ˈθæŋkfl] dankbar I

Thanks. [θæŋks] Danke. I

that [ðæt; ðət] dass I

that [ðæt] das; jenes I

after **that** [ˌɑːftə ˈðæt] danach I

like **that** [laɪk ˈðæt] so I

That's … [ðæts] Das macht … I

that's how [ðæts ˈhaʊ] so II **U1**, 14

that's why [ðæts ˈwaɪ] deshalb II **U1**, 20

That was close! [ˌðæt wəz ˈkləʊs] Das war knapp! I

That's what friends are for. [ˌðæts wɒt ˈfrendz ˌɑː ˌfɔː] Dafür sind Freunde da. I

an activity **that** … [ən ækˌtɪvəti ˈðæt] eine Aktivität, die … °II **U1**, 16

elements **that** … [ˌelɪmənts ˈðæt] Elemente, die … °II **U5**, 101

phrases **that** … [ˌfreɪzɪz ˈðæt] Redewendungen, die … °II **U1**, 13

places **that** … [ˌpleɪsɪz ˈðæt] Orte, die … °II **U5**, 92

things **that** … [ˌθɪŋz ˈðæt] Dinge, die … °II **U2**, 37

words **that** … [ˌwɜːdz ˈðæt] Wörter, die … °II **U1**, 24

the [ðə; ði] der; die (auch Pl.); das I

the others [ðiˈ ʌðəz] die anderen I

the same [ðə ˈseɪm] der-/die-/dasselbe; der/die/das gleiche I

the … **the** [ðə … ðə] je … desto II **U3**, 54

theatre [ˈθɪətə] Theater I

their [ðeə] ihr/-e (Pl.) I

them [ðem] sie (Pl.); ihnen I

theme [θiːm] Thema; Motto I

then [ðen] dann; danach I

there [ðeə] da; dort; dahin; dorthin I

there is/are [ðərˈɪz/ˈɑː] da ist/sind; es gibt I

these [ðiːz] diese (hier) I

they [ðeɪ] sie (Pl.) I

It's …/**They're** … [ɪts/ðeə] Es kostet …/ Sie kosten … I

thing [θɪŋ] Ding; Sache I

things that … [ˌθɪŋz ˈðæt] Dinge, die … °II **U2**, 37

things which … [ˌθɪŋz ˈwɪtʃ] Dinge, die … °II **U3**, 55

*to **think** [θɪŋk] denken; nachdenken; glauben I

*to **think** of [ˈθɪŋk əv] halten von; denken über I; (sich) ausdenken; sich etwas einfallen lassen II **U1**, 16

Stop and **think** [ˌstɒp ənd ˈθɪŋk] Warte/ Wartet und denk/denkt nach. I

Think of … [ˈθɪŋk‿əv] Denke/Denkt
an … I

I was **thinking** [aɪ wəz ˈθɪŋkɪŋ] ich dachte
gerade °II U4, 86

third [θɜːd] dritte/-r/-s I

thirteen [ˌθɜːˈtiːn] dreizehn I

this [ðɪs] dies; diese/-r/-s I

   this afternoon [ðɪs ˈɑːftənuːn] heute
Nachmittag II U2, 38

   This is … [ˈðɪs ɪz] Das (hier) ist … I

those [ðəʊz] diese dort; jene I

thought [θɔːt] Gedanke °II U3, 66

thousands of [ˈθaʊzndz‿əv] tausende
(von) I

three [θriː] drei I

through [θruː] durch I

*to **throw** (at) [θrəʊ] werfen (nach) I

   *to **throw** away [ˌθrəʊ‿əˈweɪ] wegwerfen I

thunder (no pl) [ˈθʌndə] Donner II U4, 86

Thursday [ˈθɜːzdeɪ] Donnerstag I

to tick [tɪk] abhaken °II U2, 47

ticket [ˈtɪkɪt] Los; Ticket; Eintrittskarte I;
Fahrschein II U5, 95

   one-way **ticket** [ˈwʌnweɪ ˌtɪkɪt] einfache
Fahrkarte II U5, 96

   return **ticket** [rɪˈtɜːn ˌtɪkɪt] Hin- und Rückfahrkarte II U5, 96

   single **ticket** [ˈsɪŋgl ˌtɪkɪt] einfache Fahrkarte II U5, 96

high tide [ˈhaɪ ˌtaɪd] Flut II U2, 48

   low **tide** [ˈləʊ ˌtaɪd] Ebbe II U2, 48

to tidy (a room) [ˈtaɪdi] aufräumen; in Ordnung bringen I

till [tɪl] bis I

time [taɪm] Zeit I; Mal II U1, 14

   all the **time** [ˌɔːl ðə ˈtaɪm] die ganze Zeit
II U2, 48

   at the same **time** [ət ðə ˌseɪm ˈtaɪm] zur
selben Zeit; gleichzeitig I

   free **time** [ˌfriː ˈtaɪm] Freizeit I

   ten **times** [ten ˈtaɪmz] zehnmal I

   time line [ˈtaɪm ˌlaɪn] Zeitstrahl I

   I can't wait till next **time**. [aɪ kɑːnt ˌweɪt
tɪl nekst ˈtaɪm] Ich kann es bis zum
nächsten Mal kaum erwarten. II U1, 14

   Time to get up! [ˌtaɪm tə ˌgetˈʌp] Es ist
Zeit aufzustehen! I

   What **time**? [ˌwɒt ˈtaɪm] Um wie viel Uhr? I

   What's the **time**? [ˌwɒts ðə ˈtaɪm] Wie spät
ist es?; Wie viel Uhr ist es? I

timetable [ˈtaɪmˌteɪbl] Stundenplan; Fahrplan I

tin [tɪn] Zinn II U5, 98

tinned [tɪnd] Dosen-; aus der Dose I

tip [tɪp] Tipp; Ratschlag I

to tiptoe [ˈtɪptəʊ] auf Zehenspitzen gehen
II U1, 23

tired [taɪəd] müde I

title [ˈtaɪtl] Titel; Überschrift °II U4, 88

to [tʊ; tə] zu; nach; auf; in; vor (bei Uhrzeitangaben) I

   from … **to** [frəm … tə] von … bis I

quarter past/**to** [ˈkwɔːtə pɑːst/tə] Viertel
nach/vor I

toast [təʊst] Toast I

today [təˈdeɪ] heute I

together [təˈgeðə] zusammen; miteinander;
gemeinsam I

toilet [ˈtɔɪlət] Toilette I

tomato [təˈmɑːtəʊ], tomatoes [təˈmɑːtəʊz]
(pl) Tomate I

tomorrow [təˈmɒrəʊ] morgen I

too [tuː] auch; zu I

   Too bad! [tuː ˈbæd] Zu dumm!; Schade! I

   You **too**? [juː ˈtuː] Du auch? I

tool [tuːl] Werkzeug; Gerät II U5, 105

top [tɒp] Spitze; oberer Teil; oberes Ende I

   on **top** [ɒn ˈtɒp] oben; obendrauf I

to top up [ˌtɒpˈʌp] aufladen II U2, 38

topic [ˈtɒpɪk] Thema II U1, 26

torch [tɔːtʃ] Fackel; Taschenlampe II U1, 22

to stay in touch (with) [ˌsteɪ ɪn ˈtʌtʃ wɪð] in
Kontakt bleiben (mit) II U4, 74

tour [tʊə] Tour; Fahrt; Rundgang II U2, 42

   audio **tour** [ˈɔːdiəʊ ˌtʊə] Audioführung
II U2, 42

tourist [ˈtʊərɪst] Tourist/-in I

   tourist board [ˈtʊərɪst bɔːd] Touristeninformation II U5, 97

   tourist information centre [ˌtʊərɪst
ɪnfəˈmeɪʃn ˌsentə] Touristeninformation I

towards [təˈwɔːdz] in Richtung; auf … zu;
darauf zu II U2, 48

town [taʊn] Stadt I

toy [tɔɪ] Spielzeug I

to trace [treɪs] verfolgen; nachspüren I

to trade [treɪd] austauschen °II U3, 63

tradition [trəˈdɪʃn] Tradition I

train [treɪn] Zug I

to train [treɪn] trainieren II U3, 58

training [ˈtreɪnɪŋ] Training II U3, 64

to translate [trænzˈleɪt] übersetzen I

   Don't **translate** … [ˌdəʊnt trænzˈleɪt]
Übersetze/Übersetzt nicht … I

translation [trænzˈleɪʃn] Übersetzung I

transport [ˈtrænspɔːt] Verkehrsmittel; Transport II U5, 94

   public **transport** (no pl) [ˌpʌblɪk
ˈtrænspɔːt] öffentliche Verkehrsmittel
II U2, 37

travel [ˈtrævl] (das) Reisen; Reise II U1, 24

   travel agent's [ˈtrævlˌeɪdʒnts] Reisebüro
II U5, 95

   travel report [ˌtrævl rɪˈpɔːt] Reisebericht
II U1, 24

to travel [ˈtrævl] fahren; reisen II U2, 38

treasure [ˈtreʒə] Schatz II U2, 42

tree [triː] Baum I

   family **tree** [ˈfæmli ˌtriː] Stammbaum I

   palm **tree** [ˈpɑːm ˌtriː] Palme II U5, 93

pony trekking [ˈpəʊni ˌtrekɪŋ] Ponyreiten im
Gelände II U5, 93

trial [traɪəl] Qualifikation II U3, 56

trick [trɪk] Trick; Streich I

to play a **trick** (on) [ˌpleɪ‿ə ˈtrɪk‿ɒn] einen
Streich spielen I

trifle [ˈtraɪfl] Trifle (englischer Nachtisch) I

trip [trɪp] Trip; Reise; Ausflug; Fahrt II U1, 13

trouble [ˈtrʌbl] Ärger; Probleme; Schwierigkeiten II U1, 23

   *to make **trouble** [ˌmeɪk ˈtrʌbl] Ärger
machen; in Schwierigkeiten bringen I

trousers (pl) [ˈtraʊzəz] Hose II U5, 104

trowel [ˈtraʊəl] kleiner Spaten II U2, 48

   a **trowel** which … [ə ˈtraʊəl wɪtʃ] ein
Spaten, der … °II U2, 48

true [truː] wahr °II U1, 18

to try [traɪ] versuchen; probieren I

   to **try** on [ˌtraɪˈɒn] anprobieren II U2, 48

   Try … [traɪ] Versuch es mal mit …; Probier mal … I

T-shirt [ˈtiːʃɜːt] T-Shirt I

the Tube [ðə ˈtjuːb] die Londoner U-Bahn
II AC2, 34

Tuesday [ˈtjuːzdeɪ] Dienstag I

tunnel [ˈtʌnl] Tunnel I

It's your turn. [ɪts jɔː ˈtɜːn] Du bist dran. I

   Take **turns**. [ˌteɪk ˈtɜːnz] Wechselt euch
ab. I

   Your **turn**. [ˈjɔː ˌtɜːn] Du bist dran. I

to turn [tɜːn] einbiegen; abbiegen I

   to **turn** (a)round [ˌtɜːn‿(ə)ˈraʊnd] (sich)
umdrehen; wenden II U5, 104

   to **turn** off [ˌtɜːn‿ˈɒf] abschalten; ausschalten II U1, 16

   to **turn** to [ˈtɜːn tə] sich wenden an; sich
zuwenden II U5, 105

tutor [ˈtjuːtə] Klassenlehrer/-in I

   tutor group [ˈtjuːtə ˌgruːp] Klasse (in einer
englischen Schule) I

TV (= television) [tiːˈviː (ˈtelɪvɪʒn)] Fernsehen; Fernseher I

   to watch **TV** [ˌwɒtʃ tiːˈviː] fernsehen I

twelve [twelv] zwölf I

twin [twɪn] Zwilling; Zwillings- II U5, 105

to twist your ankle [ˌtwɪst jɔːr ˈæŋkl] sich
den Knöchel verrenken II U3, 58

two [tuː] zwei I

   the **two** of them [ðə ˈtuː‿əv ðəm] beide
II U4, 76

   two of which [ˈtuː‿əv wɪtʃ] zwei von ihnen
°II U5, 102

typical [ˈtɪpɪkl] typisch I

U

u (= you) [juː; jə] du; Sie; ihr I

UFO [ˈjuːefəʊ] UFO II U3, 62

uncle [ˈʌŋkl] Onkel I

under [ˈʌndə] unter I

underground [ˈʌndəgraʊnd] U-Bahn
II AC2, 34

*to understand [ˌʌndəˈstænd] verstehen I

understanding [ˌʌndəˈstændɪŋ] Verständnis
II U4, 77

unfair [ʌnˈfeə] unfair II U3, 58

unfriendly [ʌnˈfrendli] unfreundlich **II U1**, 28

uniform [ˈjuːnɪfɔːm] Uniform **I**

unit [ˈjuːnɪt] Lektion; Kapitel; Einheit **I**

*to be **unlucky** [biː ʌnˈlʌki] Pech haben **I**

until [ʌnˈtɪl] bis; erst wenn **II U3**, 56

to **unwrap** [ʌnˈræp] auswickeln; auspacken **I**

up [ʌp] hinauf; (nach) oben **II U5**, 104

to end **up** [ˌend ˈʌp] enden; landen **II U1**, 12

*to get **up** [ˌget ˈʌp] aufstehen *(aus dem Bett)* **I**

to look **up** [ˌlʊk ˈʌp] nachschlagen; nachschauen **I**

upset [ʌpˈset] aufgebracht; bestürzt **II U4**, 76

upstairs [ʌpˈsteəz] nach oben; im Obergeschoss; oben **II U4**, 86

us [ʌs] uns **I**

to **use** [juːz] benutzen; verwenden; gebrauchen **I**

useful [ˈjuːsfl] nützlich; hilfreich **I**

Useful phrases [ˈjuːsfl ˈfreɪsɪz] nützliche Ausdrücke **I**

usually [ˈjuːʒli] normalerweise; gewöhnlich; meistens **I**

V

verb [vɜːb] Verb **I**

very [ˈveri] sehr **I**

very much [ˌveri ˈmʌtʃ] sehr **I**

vet [vet] Tierarzt/Tierärztin **I**

video [ˈvɪdiəʊ] Video **II U4**, 75

video chat [ˈvɪdiəʊ ˌtʃæt] Videochat **II U2**, 36

view [vjuː] Aussicht; Sicht; Ausblick; Blick **II U2**, 44

point of **view** [ˌpɔɪnt əv ˈvjuː] Standpunkt; Ansicht; Perspektive **II U3**, 60

viewer [ˈvjuːə] Zuschauer/-in °**II U2**, 44

viewing [ˈvjuːɪŋ] Hör-/Sehverstehen **I**

village [ˈvɪlɪdʒ] Dorf **I**

villain [ˈvɪlən] Bösewicht **II AC4**, 112

visit [ˈvɪzɪt] Besuch **I**

to **visit** [ˈvɪzɪt] besichtigen; besuchen **I**

visitor [ˈvɪzɪtə] Besucher/-in **I**

vocabulary [vəˈkæbjəlri] Vokabular; Wortschatz **I**

voice [vɔɪs] Stimme **I**

volleyball [ˈvɒlibɔːl] Volleyball **I**

*to take a **vote** [ˌteɪk ə ˈvəʊt] abstimmen **I**

to **vote** [vəʊt] abstimmen; wählen **I**

W

to **wait** (for) [weɪt] warten (auf) **I**

I can't **wait** till next time. [aɪ kɑːnt ˌweɪt tɪl nekst ˈtaɪm] Ich kann es bis zum nächsten Mal kaum erwarten. **II U1**, 14

Wait and see! [weɪt ənd ˈsiː] Warte ab! **I**

gallery **walk** [ˈgælri ˌwɔːk] Museumsrundgang; Vernissage **I**

*to go for a **walk** [ˌgəʊ fər ə ˈwɔːk] spazieren gehen **II U1**, 22

night **walk** [ˈnaɪt wɔːk] Nachtwanderung **II U1**, 23

to **walk** [wɔːk] gehen; laufen **I**

to **walk** the dog [ˌwɔːk ðə ˈdɒg] den Hund ausführen; mit dem Hund spazieren gehen **I**

walking [ˈwɔːkɪŋ] Wandern **II U1**, 20

wall [wɔːl] Wand; Mauer **I**

to **want** (to) [ˈwɒnt tə] wollen; mögen **I**

wardrobe [ˈwɔːdrəʊb] Kleiderschrank **I**

to **warm** up [ˌwɔːm ˈʌp] aufwärmen; sich aufwärmen **I**

warm-up [ˈwɔːm ˌʌp] Aufwärmübung **I**

warrior [ˈwɒriə] Krieger **II U5**, 105

to **wash** [wɒʃ] waschen; sich waschen **I**

to **wash** up [ˌwɒʃ ˈʌp] angespült werden **II U2**, 48

washing machine [ˈwɒʃɪŋ məˌʃiːn] Waschmaschine **II U4**, 79

to **waste** [weɪst] verschwenden **II U4**, 79

to **watch** [wɒtʃ] beobachten; (sich) ansehen; zuschauen **I**

to **watch** TV [ˌwɒtʃ tiːˈviː] fernsehen **I**

water [ˈwɔːtə] Wasser **I**

water slide [ˈwɔːtə ˌslaɪd] Wasserrutsche **I**

wave [weɪv] Welle **I**

wax [wæks] Wachs **II U2**, 37

wax figure [ˈwæks ˌfɪgə] Wachsfigur **II U2**, 37

way [weɪ] Weg; Art und Weise **I**

*to be in the **way** [biː ɪn ðə ˈweɪ] im Weg sein/stehen **I**

*to get in the **way** [ˌget ɪn ðə ˈweɪ] stören; im Weg stehen **II U3**, 64

in other **ways** [ɪn ˈʌðə weɪz] auf andere Weise **II U4**, 81

the same **way** as [ðə seɪm ˈweɪ æz] genauso wie °**II U1**, 28

we [wiː; wi] wir **I**

We're from … [ˈwɪə frəm] Wir sind aus … **I**

*to **wear** [weə] anhaben; tragen *(Kleidung)* **I**

they weren't **wearing** [ˌðeɪ wɜːnt ˈweərɪŋ] sie trugen nicht °**II U2**, 48

weather [ˈweðə] Wetter **I**

weather forecast [ˈweðə ˌfɔːkɑːst] Wettervorhersage **II U5**, 96

website [ˈwebsaɪt] Website; Internetauftritt **I**

wedding [ˈwedɪŋ] Hochzeit **I**

Wednesday [ˈwenzdeɪ] Mittwoch **I**

week [wiːk] Woche **I**

weekday [ˈwiːkdeɪ] Wochentag **II U4**, 84

weekend [ˌwiːkˈend] Wochenende **I**

at the **weekend** [ət ðə ˌwiːkˈend] am Wochenende **I**

weird [wɪəd] merkwürdig; seltsam; sonderbar **II U4**, 83

Welcome! [ˈwelkəm] Willkommen! **II U1**, 22

to **welcome** [ˈwelkəm] willkommen heißen **II AC1**, 11

You're **welcome**. [jɔː ˈwelkəm] Bitte schön.; Nichts zu danken.; Gern geschehen. **I**

well [wel] tja; nun **I**

Welsh [welʃ] walisisch; Walisisch; Waliser/-in **II U1**, 20

west [west] Westen; West- **I**

wet [wet] nass **II U2**, 48

what [wɒt] was; welche/-r/-s; was für ein **I**

What about … ? [ˈwɒt əbaʊt] Wie wär's mit …?; Was ist mit …? **I**

What are …? [ˈwɒt ɑː] Welche … sind es? **I**

What colour is …? [ˌwɒt ˈkʌlər ɪz] Welche Farbe hat …? **I**

what else [ˌwɒt ˈels] was sonst; was noch **I**

What is missing? [ˌwɒt ɪz ˈmɪsɪŋ] Was fehlt? **I**

What is … about? [ˌwɒt ɪz …əˈbaʊt] Worum geht es in/im …? **I**

What on earth …? [ˌwɒt ɒn ˈɜːθ] Was um alles in der Welt …? **II U4**, 79

What time? [ˌwɒt ˈtaɪm] Um wie viel Uhr? **I**

what to … [ˈwɒt tə] was man … **I**

What's that? [ˌwɒts ˈðæt] Was ist das? **I**

What's the matter? [ˌwɒts ðə ˈmætə] Was ist los?; Was hast du? **II U5**, 104

What's the rule for …? [ˌwɒts ðə ˈruːl fə] **I**

What's the time? [ˌwɒts ðə ˈtaɪm] Wie spät ist es?; Wie viel Uhr ist es? Was ist die Regel für …? **I**

What's your favourite …? [ˈwɒts jə ˌfeɪvrɪt] Was ist dein/-e Lieblings…? **I**

What's your name? [ˌwɒts jə ˈneɪm] Wie heißt du?; Wie heißen Sie? **I**

… **what** to do. [ˈwɒt tə duː] … was ich tun soll. **II U4**, 76

what the man looked like [ˌwɒt ðə mæn ˈlʊkt laɪk] wie der Mann aussah **II U1**, 17

wheel [wiːl] Rad; Steuerrad; Steuer **I**

wheelchair [ˈwiːltʃeə] Rollstuhl **II U2**, 39

when [wen] wenn; wann; als **I**

whenever [wenˈevə] wann immer; jedes Mal, wenn; so oft **II U4**, 76

where [weə] wo; wohin **I**

Where … from? [ˌweə … ˈfrɒm] Woher …? **I**

… **where** to go. [ˌweə tə ˈgəʊ] … wohin ich gehen kann. **II U2**, 40

which [wɪtʃ] welche/-r/-s **I**

a trowel **which** … [ə ˈtraʊəl wɪtʃ] ein Spaten, der … °**II U2**, 48

things **which** … [θɪŋz ˈwɪtʃ] Dinge, die … °**II U3**, 55

a **while** [ə ˈwaɪl] eine Weile **II U2**, 40

while [waɪl] während **I**

to **whip** [wɪp] schlagen **I**

to **whisper** [ˈwɪspə] flüstern **I**

white [waɪt] weiß **I**

who [huː] wer; wem; wen **I**

Who … for? [ˌhuː ˈfɔː] Für wen …? **I**

Who is it? [ˌhuː ˈɪz ɪt] Wer ist es? **I**

Who's in? [huːz ˈɪn] Wer macht mit?; Wer ist dabei? **II U3**, 56

a father **who** … [ə ˌfɑːðə ˈhuː] ein Vater, der … °**II U5**, 100

friends and family **who** … [frendz ən ˌfæməli ˈhuː] Freunde und Familienmitglieder, die … °**II U4**, 81

good for someone **who** … [ˌɡʊd fə ˌsʌmwʌn ˈhuː] gut für jemanden, der … °**II U2**, 41

I'm the one **who** … [aɪm ðə ˌwʌn ˈhuː] ich bin diejenige, die … °**II U3**, 64

the boy **who** … [ðə bɔɪ ˈhuː] der Junge, der … °**II U3**, 66

with a person **who** … [wɪð ə ˌpɜːsn ˈhuː] mit einer Person, die … °**II U5**, 95

whole [həʊl] ganz **I**

whoosh [wʊʃ] wusch **I**

why [waɪ] warum **I**

that's **why** [ðæts ˈwaɪ] deshalb **II U1**, 20

wide [waɪd] breit; weit; ausgedehnt **II U5**, 93

wife [waɪf], **wives** [waɪvz] (pl) Ehefrau **II U5**, 100

wild [waɪld] wild **II U5**, 98

wildlife [ˈwaɪldlaɪf] Tierwelt (in freier Wildbahn) **II AC1**, 11

*to **win** [wɪn] gewinnen; siegen **I**

wind [wɪnd] Wind **II U5**, 104

window [ˈwɪndəʊ] Fenster **I**

windsurfing [ˈwɪndsɜːfɪŋ] Windsurfen **II U5**, 93

wine [waɪn] Wein **I**

winner [ˈwɪnə] Gewinner/-in; Sieger/-in **I**

wish [wɪʃ] Wunsch **I**

*to make a **wish** [ˌmeɪk ə ˈwɪʃ] sich etwas wünschen **I**

Best **wishes** [ˌbest ˈwɪʃɪz] Viele Grüße; Herzliche Grüße **II U5**, 97

with [wɪð] mit; bei **I**

without [wɪˈðaʊt] ohne **I**

witness [ˈwɪtnəs] Zeuge/Zeugin **II U3**, 61

wizard [ˈwɪzəd] Zauberer **II AC4**, 112

wobbly [ˈwɒbli] wackelig **II U2**, 48

woman [ˈwʊmən], **women** [ˈwɪmɪn] (pl) Frau **I**

won't she [wəʊnt ˈʃiː] nicht wahr?; stimmts? °**II U5**, 94

wonderful [ˈwʌndəfl] wunderbar **II U5**, 94

Woof! [wʊf] Wau! **I**

word [wɜːd] Wort **I**

compound **word** [ˈkɒmpaʊnd wɜːd] Kompositum (zusammengesetztes Wort) °**II U2**, 41

key **word** [ˈkiː wɜːd] Stichwort; Schlüsselbegriff **I**

linking **word** [ˈlɪŋkɪŋ wɜːd] Bindewort **I**

signal **word** [ˈsɪɡnəl wɜːd] Signalwort **I**

word cloud [ˈwɜːd klaʊd] Wörterwolke °**II U3**, 54

word order [ˈwɜːd ˌɔːdə] Wortstellung; Satzstellung **I**

Word power [ˈwɜːd ˌpaʊə] die Kraft der Wörter (Wortschatzübung) **I**

word snake [ˈwɜːd sneɪk] Wortschlange **I**

word-building [ˈwɜːdˌbɪldɪŋ] Wortbildung °**II U2**, 37

words that … [ˌwɜːdz ˈðæt] Wörter, die … °**II U1**, 24

work [wɜːk] Arbeit **I**

pair **work** [ˈpeə wɜːk] Partnerarbeit °**II U4**, 84

to **work** [wɜːk] arbeiten **I**; funktionieren **II U4**, 79

to **work** out [ˌwɜːk ˈaʊt] herausfinden; ausarbeiten °**II U2**, 47

workshop [ˈwɜːkʃɒp] Workshop **I**

world [wɜːld] Erde; Welt **I**

worm [wɜːm] Wurm **I**

*to be **worried** [bi ˈwʌrid] beunruhigt sein; besorgt sein **II U3**, 64

to **worry** [ˈwʌri] sich Sorgen machen **II U4**, 77

Don't **worry!** [ˌdəʊnt ˈwʌri] Keine Sorge! **I**

the **worst** [ðə ˈwɜːst] der/die/das schlimmste; der/die/das schlechteste **II U1**, 20

*to be **worth** [bi ˈwɜːθ] wert sein **I**

would like [wʊd ˈlaɪk] würde/-st/-n/-t gern; hätte/-st/-n/-t gern **I**

would love [wʊd ˈlʌv] würde/-st/-n/-t sehr gern; hätte/-st/-n/-t sehr gern **I**

Would you like …? [ˌwʊd jʊ ˈlaɪk] Möchtest du …?; Möchten Sie …?; Möchtet ihr …? °**II U3**, 56

Wow! [waʊ] Wow! **I**

to **wrap** [ræp] einwickeln; einpacken **I**

wrapping [ˈræpɪŋ] Verpackung; Hülle **I**

wrist [rɪst] Handgelenk **II U2**, 48

*to **write** [raɪt] schreiben **I**

*to **write** down [raɪt ˈdaʊn] aufschreiben **I**

writing [ˈraɪtɪŋ] Schreiben **I**

wrong [rɒŋ] falsch **I**

*to be **wrong** [bi ˈrɒŋ] unrecht haben; sich irren **I**

*to go **wrong** [ˌɡəʊ ˈrɒŋ] schiefgehen **I**

X

XOXO [ˌhʌɡz ən ˈkɪsɪz] Umarmungen und Küsse (am Ende von E-Mails und SMS) **I**

Y

yeah (infml) [jeə] ja **I**

year [jɪə] Jahr; Schuljahr **I**

11-**year**-old [ɪˌlevnˈjɪərəʊld] 11-Jährige/-r **II U3**, 56

18-**year**-old [eɪtiːn ˈjɪərˌəʊld] 18-jährig **II U2**, 38

yearbook [ˈjɪəbʊk] Jahrbuch **II U1**, 12

yellow [ˈjeləʊ] gelb **I**

yes [jes] ja **I**

yesterday [ˈjestədeɪ] gestern **II U1**, 15

yet [jet] schon; noch **II U3**, 58

not … **yet** [nɒt ˈjet] noch nicht **II U3**, 58

yoghurt [ˈjɒɡət] Joghurt **I**

you [juː; jə] du; ihr; Sie **I**

You know how to … [juː ˈnəʊ ˌhaʊ tə] Du weißt, wie man …; Ihr wisst, wie man … **I**

You too? [juː ˈtuː] Du auch? **I**

You're into … [ˈjɔːrˌɪntə] Du magst …; Du stehst auf … **I**

You're welcome. [jɔː ˈwelkəm] Bitte schön.; Nichts zu danken.; Gern geschehen. **I**

young [jʌŋ] jung **I**

your [jɔː; jə] dein/-e; euer/eure; Ihr/-e **I**

What's **your** name? [ˌwɒts jə ˈneɪm] Wie heißt du?; Wie heißen Sie? **I**

Your turn. [ˈjɔː tɜːn] Du bist dran. **I**

yours [jɔːz] dein/-er/-e/-es; eure/-r/-s; Ihr/-e **II U5**, 104

Yours … [jɔːz] Viele Grüße … (am Ende von Briefen und Mails) **II U4**, 83

yourself [jɔːˈself] du/dir/dich/Sie/sich (selbst); selber **I**

yourselves [jɔːˈselvz] selber; ihr/euch/Sie/sich (selbst) **II U5**, 97

Z

zero [ˈzɪərəʊ] null **I**

zoo [zuː] Zoo; Tierpark **II U2**, 39

Boys' names

Amir [ɑˈmiːr] II U2, 36
Ben [ben] I
Bob [bɒb] I
Damian [ˈdeɪmiən] I
Dave [deɪv] I
David [ˈdeɪvɪd] I
Desmond [ˈdezmənd] I
Filip [ˈfɪlɪp] I
Frank [fræŋk] II U4, 86
Henry [ˈhenri] I
Jack [dʒæk] I
Jago [ˈdʒeɪɡəʊ] II U5, 105
Jahangir [dʒəˈhʌŋɡɪə] I
Jamie [ˈdʒeɪmi] I
Jay [dʒeɪ] I
Jinsoo [ˈdʒɪnzuː] II U2, 44
John [dʒɒn] II U1, 17
Jon [dʒɒn] II U4, 74
Luke [luːk] I
Marley [ˈmɑːli] II U2, 44
Mick [mɪk] II U4, 84
Mike [maɪk] II U2, 48
Nathan [ˈneɪθn] II U4, 82
Nick [nɪk] II U2, 44
Peter [ˈpiːtə] II U1, 17
Shahid [ʃɑˈhiːd] I
Steve [stiːv] I
Tony [ˈtəʊni] I
Tyler [ˈtaɪlə] I
Will [wɪl] II U1, 22

Girls' names

Alicia [əˈlɪsiə; əˈlɪʃə] I
Amber [ˈæmbə] I
Anna [ˈænə] I
Anne [æn] I
Beata [biˈɑːtə] I
Carol [ˈkærəl] I
Ceri [ˈkeri] II U1, 22
Claire [ˈkleə] I
Emily [ˈemɪli] I
Frances [ˈfrɑːnsɪs] I
Gwen [ɡwen] II AC1, 9
Helen [ˈhelɪn] II U5, 105
Holly [ˈhɒli] I
Irina [ɪˈriːnə] I
Judith [ˈdʒuːdɪθ] II U5, 100
Julie [ˈdʒuːli] I
Laura [ˈlɔːrə] I
Lauren [ˈlɔːrən] II U4, 76
Lou [luː] I
Lucy [ˈluːsi] I
Maisie [ˈmeɪzi] II U4, 82
Megan [ˈmeɡən] II U5, 106
Mila [ˈmiːlə] I
Mina [ˈmiːnə] II U2, 44
Olivia [ɒlˈɪviə] I
Pia [ˈpiːə] I
Polly [ˈpɒli] II AC1, 11

Rose [rəʊz] I
Ruby [ˈruːbi] II U4, 76
Sally [ˈsæli] I
Seeta [ˈsiːtə] I
Tamara [təˈmɑːrə] II U5, 105
Vivien [ˈvɪvjən] II AC4, 113

Surnames

Azad [əˈzɑːd] I
Elliot [ˈeliət] I
Fraser [ˈfreɪzə] I
Green [ɡriːn] I
Nicholls [ˈnɪkəlz] II U5, 100
Parker [ˈpɑːkə] II U3, 65
Preston [ˈprestən] I
Richardson [ˈrɪtʃədsn] I
Swindon [ˈswɪndən] I
Thompson [ˈtɒmsən] II U3, 60
Walker [ˈwɔːkə] I
Zajac [ˈzeɪdʒæk] I

Place names

Baker Street [ˈbeɪkə ˌstriːt] II AC4, 113
Begbie Road [ˌbegbi ˈrəʊd] II U4, 86
Bradford [ˈbrædfəd] II U2, 36
Brick Lane [brɪk ˈleɪn] II U2, 37
Brook Lane [brʊk ˈleɪn] I
Caerphilly [keəˈfili] walisische Stadt II U5, 92
Camden Market [ˈkæmdən ˌmɑːkɪt] II U2, 44
College Way [ˌkɒlɪdʒ ˈweɪ] I
Cologne [kəˈləʊn] Köln I
Covent Garden [ˌkɒvnt ˈɡɑːdn] II U2, 37
Cracow [ˈkrækɒv; ˈkrɑːkaʊ] Krakau I
Edinburgh [ˈedɪnbrə] II U5, 93
Enfield [enˈfiːld] I
Greenwich Park [ˌɡrenɪdʒ ˈpɑːk] I
Greenwich Pier [ˌɡrenɪdʒ ˈpɪə] I
Hollywood [ˈhɒliwʊd] II AC3, 73
Hyde Park [ˌhaɪd ˈpɑːk] II AC2, 34
Isle of Man [aɪl əv ˈmæn] II U5, 99
Kidbrooke Gardens [ˌkɪdbrʊk ˈɡɑːdnz] I
King William Walk [ˌkɪŋ ˈwɪljəm ˌwɔːk] I
London [ˈlʌndən] I
Nelson Road [ˌnelsn ˈrəʊd] I
Nottingham [ˈnɒtɪŋəm] II AC4, 113
Oxford Street [ˈɒksfəd ˌstriːt] II AC2, 34
Paddington [ˈpædɪŋtən] II U5, 95
South Street [ˈsaʊθ ˌstriːt] I
Southend [saʊθˈend] II U1, 29
St Agnes [seɪnt ˈæɡnəs] II U5, 94
Tintagel [tɪnˈtædʒl] II AC4, 113
Tower Hill [ˌtaʊə ˈhɪl] II U2, 39
Ty'n y Berth [tiːn ə ˈbɜːθ] II U1, 20
Victoria Park [ˌvɪktɔːriə ˈpɑːk] I
Village Way [ˌvɪlɪdʒ ˌweɪ] I
Wimbledon [ˈwɪmbldən] I

Geographical names

America [əˈmerɪkə] II AC3, 73
Australia [ɒsˈtreɪliə] Australien II AC3, 73
Austria [ˈɔːstriə] Österreich II U3, 57
Bodmin Moor [ˌbɒdmɪn ˈmɔː] Hochmoorlandschaft im nordöstlichen Cornwall II U5, 98
Britain [ˈbrɪtn] Großbritannien I
British Empire [ˌbrɪtɪʃ ˈempaɪə] britisches Königreich II AC3, 73
British Isles [ˌbrɪtɪʃ ˈaɪlz] Britische Inseln II U5, 93
Canada [ˈkænədə] Kanada I
China [ˈtʃaɪnə] China I
Cornwall [ˈkɔːnwɔːl] II U5, 92
England [ˈɪŋɡlənd] England I
Europe [ˈjʊərəp] Europa II AC2, 34
France [frɑːns] Frankreich II U2, 42
Germany [ˈdʒɜːməni] Deutschland I
Great Britain (GB) [ˌɡreɪt ˈbrɪtn] Großbritannien II U5, 92
India [ˈɪndiə] Indien II AC3, 72
Isle of Dogs [aɪl əv ˈdɒɡz] I
Kent [kent] Grafschaft im Südosten Englands II U3, 60
Normandy [ˈnɔːməndi] die Normandie II U2, 42
North Sea [ˌnɔːθ ˈsiː] Nordsee II U5, 93
Northern Ireland [ˌnɔːðn ˈaɪələnd] Nordirland II U5, 92
Pakistan [ˌpɑːkɪˈstɑːn] I
Poland [ˈpəʊlənd] Polen I
Republic of Ireland [rɪˌpʌblɪk əv ˈaɪələnd] Republik Irland II U5, 92
Riviera [rɪvˈjeɪrə] Landschaft in Italien II U5, 93
Scotland [ˈskɒtlənd] Schottland II U5, 97
Sherwood Forest [ˌʃɜːwʊd ˈfɒrɪst] II AC4, 113
Snowdonia National Park [snəʊˌdəʊniə ˌnæʃnl ˈpɑːk] II U1, 20
South Africa [ˌsaʊθ ˈæfrɪkə] Südafrika II AC3, 73
Spain [speɪn] Spanien II U4, 83
Thames [temz] I
United Kingdom (UK) [juːˌnaɪtɪd ˈkɪŋdəm (juːˈkeɪ)] Vereinigtes Königreich von Großbritannien und Nordirland I
USA (United States of America) [juːesˈeɪ (juːˌnaɪtɪd ˌsteɪts əv əˈmerɪkə)] USA (Vereinigte Staaten von Amerika) II AC3, 73
Wales [weɪlz] II U1, 20

Other names

Big Ben [ˌbɪɡ ˈben] II AC2, 34
British Museum [ˌbrɪtɪʃ mjuːˈziːəm] II U2, 36
Buckingham Palace [ˌbʌkɪŋəm ˈpælɪs] II AC2, 34
Changing of the Guards [ˌtʃeɪndʒɪŋ əv ðə ˈɡɑːdz] Wachwechsel vor dem Buckingham Palace II AC2, 35

Comic Relief [ˌkɒmɪk rɪ'li:f] *wohltätige Organisation* **II U1**, 14

Croeso i Gymru [ˌkrɔɪsəʊ_i: 'gʌmri] **II U1**, 22

Crossharbour ['krɒsˌhɑ:bə] **II U2**, 39

Cutty Sark [ˌkʌti 'sɑ:k] **I**

Diwali [dɪ'wɑ:li] **I**

Docklands Light Railway *(DLR)* [ˌdɒklændz ˌlaɪt 'reɪlweɪ] *Regionalbahn im Osten Londons* **I**

Eid [i:d] **I**

Elephant & Castle ['elɪfənt ənd kɑ:sl] **II U2**, 39

Excalibur [ek'skælɪbə] **II AC4**, 113

For he's a jolly good fellow [fə ˌhi:z_ə ˌdʒɒli gʊd 'feləʊ] *Volkslied* **I**

Greenwich Foot Tunnel [ˌgrenɪdʒ 'fʊt ˌtʌnl] **I**

Guy Fawkes Night ['gaɪ fɔ:ks ˌnaɪt] **I**

Halloween [ˌhæləʊ'i:n] *Tag vor Allerheiligen* **I**

Hanukkah ['hɑ:nəkə] **I**

the Houses of Parliament [ðə ˌhaʊzɪz_əv 'pɑ:ləmənt] *britisches Parlamentsgebäude* **II U2**, 36

London Eye [ˌlʌndən_'aɪ] **II AC2**, 34

London Wall [ˌlʌndən 'wɔ:l] **II U2**, 36

London Zoo [ˌlʌndən 'zu:] **II U2**, 39

Madame Tussauds [ˌmædəm tʊ'sɔ:dz] **II U2**, 37

Meridian Line [məˌrɪdiən 'laɪn] Nullmeridian **I**

Mickey Mouse [ˌmɪki 'maʊs] **I**

Millennium Footbridge [mɪˌleniəm 'fʊtbrɪdʒ] **II U2**, 48

Mother's Day ['mʌðəz ˌdeɪ] **I**

Mousebook ['maʊsbʊk] **II U4**, 74

Mudchute Farm [ˌmʌdʃu:t 'fɑ:m] **I**

Natural History Museum [ˌnætʃrl 'hɪstri mju:ˌzi:əm] **II U2**, 45

Notting Hill Carnival [ˌnɒtɪŋ hɪl 'kɑ:nɪvl] **I**

Oyster card ['ɔɪstə ˌkɑ:d] **II U2**, 38

Red Nose Day [ˌred nəʊz 'deɪ] **II U1**, 12

Rocky ['rɒki] **II U2**, 42

Royal Observatory [ˌrɔɪəl_əb'zɜ:vətri] **I**

Sherlock ['ʃɜ:lɒk] **I**

Shrove Tuesday [ˌʃrəʊv 'tju:zdeɪ] Fastnachtsdienstag **I**

Sid [sɪd] **I**

Tandoori [tæn'dʊəri] **I**

Thomas Tallis School *(= TTS)* [ˌtɒməs 'tælɪs ˌsku:l] **I**

the Tower of London [ðə ˌtaʊər_əv 'lʌndən] **II AC2**, 35

Transport Museum [ˌtrænspɔ:t mju:'zi:əm] **II U2**, 39

TTS planner [ˌti:ti:ˌes 'plænə] Handbuch für TTS-Schülerinnen und -Schüler **I**

Valentine's Day ['væləntaɪnz ˌdeɪ] **I**

Victoria [vɪk'tɔ:riə] **II U2**, 39

Whitehall ['waɪthɔ:l] *Straße in London* **II U2**, 37

World War II [ˌwɜ:ld ˌwɔ: 'tu:] Zweiter Weltkrieg **II AC3**, 73

Famous names

Agatha Christie [ˌægəθə 'krɪsti] **II AC4**, 113

Boudicca ['bu:dɪkə] **II AC4**, 113

Daniel Craig [ˌdænjəl 'kreɪg] **II U1**, 19

Dr Watson [ˌdɒktə 'wɒtsən] **II AC4**, 113

James Bond [ˌdʒeɪmz 'bɒnd] **II U1**, 19

King Arthur [ˌkɪŋ_'ɑ:θə] König Artus **II AC4**, 113

Lenny Harry [ˌleni 'hæri] *britischer Comedian* **II U1**, 14

Maid Marian [ˌmeɪd 'mæriən] **II AC4**, 113

Miss Marple [mɪs 'mɑ:pl] **II AC4**, 113

Prince Albert [ˌprɪns 'ælbət] **II AC2**, 35

Queen Victoria [ˌkwi:n vɪk'tɔ:riə] **II AC2**, 35

Robin Hood [ˌrɒbɪn 'hʊd] **II AC4**, 113

Sherlock Holmes [ˌʃɜ:lɒk 'həʊmz] **II AC4**, 112

William the Conqueror [ˌwɪljəm ðə 'kɒŋkrə] **II U2**, 42;

A

abbiegen to turn I
abblocken to block II U4, 77
Abend evening I
  heute Abend 2nite (= tonight) I
Abendessen dinner I
abends in the evenings I
abends (Uhrzeit) p.m. I
Abenteuer adventure II U1, 20
aber but I
abfahren *to leave II U3, 58; to depart II U5, 96
abfahrend outward II U5, 96
abgeschlossen locked II U1, 23
abhängen von to depend (on) II U5, 95
abnehmen *to take off I
abschalten to turn off I
  Schalt/Schaltet es ab! Turn it off! I
abschicken *to send off II U5, 97
abschneiden *to cut (off) II U2, 49
abschreiben to copy I
Abstand gap I
abstimmen *to take a vote; to vote I
abstürzen to crash II U4, 87
acht eight I
Acker field II U1, 22
Action action I
Adresse address I
AG club I
aggressiv aggressive II U1, 28
äh er I
keine Ahnung no idea II U1, 23
Akku battery II U1, 23
Aktion action I
Aktivität activity I
Akzent accent II U5, 99
albern silly I
alle all of them; everyone I; everybody II U2, 40
  wir alle all of us II U5, 94
alle/-s all I
allein alone I
alles everything I
Alphabet alphabet I
als as II U3, 63
  als ob like I
als (bei Vergleichen) than II U1, 20
als when I
also so I
alt old I
  Wie alt bist du? How old are you? I
  Wie alt sind Sie? How old are you? I
am on I
  am besten best I
  am Wochenende at the weekend I
aus Amerika American II U1, 13
Amerikaner/-in American II U1, 13
amerikanisch American II U1, 13
Amtssprache official language II AC3, 73
sich amüsieren *to have fun I
an on; at I; by II U5, 104

an Bord aboard I
an sein *to be on II U4, 86
anbieten to offer II AC1, 8
Anblick sight II AC2, 34
Andenken souvenir II U2, 40
andere/-r/-s other I
  die anderen the others I
  ein-/e andere/-r/-s another I
Einerseits …, (aber) andererseits … On the one hand …, (but) on the other hand … II U3, 66
(sich) ändern to change II U4, 74
anders different; other I
Änderung change II U5, 105
Anfang beginning II U1, 27
anfangen to start I; *to begin II U4, 83
anfeuern to cheer II U3, 58
angeben to show off II U4, 87
Und ein Angeber! With a very big head! II U4, 79
von Angesicht zu Angesicht face-to-face II U4, 77
angespült werden to wash up II U2, 48
Angst fear II U3, 66
  Angst haben (vor) *to be scared (of) I
  Ich habe (keine) Angst vor … I'm (not) scared of … I
anhaben *to wear I
anhalten to stop I
anhören to listen (to) I
anklicken to click on II U5, 96
ankommen to arrive II U5, 96
ankommend inward II U5, 96
Ankündigung announcement II U5, 99
anmalen to paint I
Anmerkung note I
annähernd nearly II U4, 86
anonym anonymous II U1, 17
anprobieren to try on II U2, 48
Anregung suggestion I
Anruf phone call I
  einen Anruf entgegennehmen to answer the phone I
Anrufbeantworter answering machine I
anrufen to call I
Anrufer/-in caller I
anschauen to look at I; *to have a look (at) II U3, 59
sich anschließen to join II AC1, 11
ansehen to look at I
(sich) ansehen to watch I
Ansicht point of view II U3, 60
anstarren to stare I
antike Geschichte ancient history II U5, 98
antippen to tap II U4, 86
Antwort answer; reply I
antworten to answer; to reply I
Anweisung instruction I
Anwesenheitskontrolle registration II AC1, 10
Apfel apple I
App app II U4, 81

Apparat machine I
April April I
Arbeit job; work I
Arbeit für die Schule studies (pl) II AC1, 8
arbeiten to work I
Areal area II U3, 56
Ärger trouble II U1, 23
  Ärger machen *to make trouble I
Argument dafür pro II U2, 41
  Argument dagegen con II U2, 41
Arm arm II U3, 57
die Armen the poor II AC4, 113
Art kind I
  Art und Weise way I
Arzt/Ärztin doctor II U3, 58
Arztpraxis surgery I
Assistent/-in assistant II U3, 62
Atlas atlas II AC3, 72
atmen to breathe II U3, 64
  Atme(t) tief ein. Take a deep breath. II AC1, 11
Atmosphäre flair II U2, 37
Attraktion attraction II U2, 45
Aua! Ouch! II U1, 12
auch too I; also II U1, 14
  Du auch? You too? I
Audio- audio I
Audioführung audio tour II U2, 42
auf on; at; to I
  auf dem Foto/den Fotos in the photo(s) I
  auf der anderen Seite von across; opposite I
  auf der Straße in the street I
  auf einmal suddenly I
  auf Wiedersehen goodbye I
  auf … zu towards II U2, 48
aufbauen *to set up I
aufbewahren *to keep I
Aufführung show II AC1, 9
Aufgabe task; exercise; job I
aufgebracht upset II U4, 76
aufgeregt excited I; nervous II U1, 16
aufgeschlagen open I
aufhören to finish I
  Hör/Hört auf! Stop it! I
aufhören (mit) to stop I
aufladen to top up II U2, 38
aufmachen to open I
Aufmerksamkeit attention II U4, 77
Aufnahme recording I
Aufnahmestudio recording studio I
aufnehmen to record II U3, 62
aufpassen to look out II U3, 56
  aufpassen auf to look after I
  Pass/Passt auf! Be careful! I
aufräumen to tidy (a room) I
aufrechterhalten *to keep going II U1, 16
aufregend exciting I
aufsagen *to say I
aufschreiben *to write down I
aufstehen (aus dem Bett) *to get up I
  Es ist Zeit aufzustehen! Time to get up! I

aufstehen *(von einer Sitzgelegenheit)* *to stand up I
Auftrag task I
aufwärmen to warm up I
   sich **aufwärmen** to warm up I
Aufwärmübung warm-up I
aufzeichnen to record II U3, 62
Aufzeichnung recording I
Auge eye II U1, 13
   Ich traute meinen **Augen** nicht. I couldn't believe my eyes. II U3, 61
Augenblick moment II AC1, 11
Augenzeuge/Augenzeugin eyewitness II U3, 61
August August I
aus from I
   aus Cornwall Cornish II U5, 94
ausblasen *to blow out I
Ausblick view II U2, 44
Auschecken Check-out I
(sich) ausdenken *to think of II U1, 16
Ausdruck phrase I; expression II AC3, 73
   nützliche **Ausdrücke** Useful phrases I
ausflippen *to go crazy II U4, 79
Ausflug trip II U1, 13
den Hund ausführen to walk the dog I
ausgeben *(Geld)* *to spend I
ausgedehnt wide II U5, 93
ausgehen *to go out II U5, 104
sich ausgeschlossen fühlen *to feel left out II U4, 88
(sich) ausleihen to borrow II U4, 87
auspacken to unwrap I
auspusten *to blow out I
ausräumen to clear out I
jmdm. etw. ausrichten *to take a message I
sich ausruhen to relax II AC1, 11
Ausrüstung equipment II U3, 55
Aussage statement II AC3, 72
ausschalten to turn off I
   Schalt/Schaltet es aus! Turn it off! I
aussehen to look I
   wie der Mann **aussah** what the man looked like II U1, 17
außerhalb outside; out I
Außerirdische/-r alien I
Äußerung expression II AC3, 73
Aussicht view II U2, 44
Aussprache pronunciation I
Ausstattung equipment II U3, 55
aussteigen *to get out of II U4, 86
   aussteigen (aus einem Bus/Zug) *to get off (a bus/train) II U2, 39
Ausstellung display II U2, 45
   Ausstellung in der Klasse class display I
Auswahl choice II U2, 44
auswendig lernen *to learn … by heart I
auswickeln to unwrap I
ausziehen *to take off I
Auto car I
Automat machine I

B

Baby baby I
Bad bath I
Badewanne bath I
Badezimmer bathroom I
Badminton badminton I
Bahnhof station I
Bahnsteig platform II U5, 96
bald soon II U1, 22
Ball ball I
Banane banana I
Bär bear II U2, 42
Basketball basketball I
Batterie battery II U1, 23
Bauch stomach II U3, 64
Bauchschmerzen stomachache II U3, 59
Bauchweh stomachache II U3, 59
bauen *to build II U2, 42
Bauernhof farm I
Baum tree I
Beachtung attention II U4, 77
beängstigend scary II U1, 28
beantworten to answer I
bedeckt cloudy II U1, 23
bedeuten *to mean II U2, 40
Bedeutung meaning II U1, 25
bedürftig in need II U1, 14
sich beeilen to hurry I
beeindruckt sein *to be impressed II U4, 87
beeinflussen to influence II AC3, 73
beenden to finish I; to end II U3, 63
sich befassen mit *to deal (with) II U2, 40
befestigen to fix II U4, 79
befolgen to follow II U2, 40
befragen to interview I
Befragung interview I
Befürchtung fear II U3, 66
begeistert excited I
Beginn beginning II U1, 27
beginnen to start I; *to begin II U4, 83
behalten *to keep I
Behauptung statement II AC3, 72
behindert with special needs II AC1, 9
bei with; at I; by II U5, 104
beibringen *to teach II U3, 60
beide both II U3, 65
beide the two of them II U4, 76
Bein leg II U3, 57
beinahe almost II U3, 64
beinhalten to include II U5, 92
Beispiel example I
   zum **Beispiel** for example II AC3, 73
beißen *to bite II U2, 42
beitreten to join II AC1, 11
bekommen *to get I; to receive II U3, 61
belebt busy I
beliebt popular I
bellen to bark I
bemerken to notice II U2, 49
benötigen to need (to) I
benutzen to use I

beobachten to watch I
bereits already I
Berg mountain II U1, 20; hill II U5, 104
bergen to save I
Bericht report II U1, 13
berichten to report II U5, 93
sich beruhigen to relax II AC1, 11; to calm down II U4, 87
berühmt famous I
beschäftigt busy I
beschreiben to describe I
besichtigen to visit I
Besichtigungs- sightseeing II U2, 44
besiegen *to beat II U2, 40
besitzen *to have got I
besonders special I
besorgen *to get I
besorgt sein *to be worried II U3, 64
besser better I
(der/die/das) Beste (the) best II U1, 14
besteigen to climb I
beste/-r/-s best I
   am **besten** best I
bestimmt definitely II U5, 98
bestürzt upset II U4, 76
Besuch visit I
besuchen to visit I
Besucher/-in visitor I
Betreuer/-in instructor II U1, 22
Bett bed I
   ins **Bett** gehen *to go to bed I
beunruhigt sein *to be worried II U3, 64
bevor before I
(sich) bewegen to move I
Bewegung move I
bewölkt cloudy II U1, 23
bezahlen *to pay (for) I
Beziehung relationship II U3, 66
bieten to offer II AC1, 8
Bild picture I
bilden *to make I
Bildgeschichte photo story I
billig cheap I
Bindewort linking word I
bis till I; until II U3, 56
   Bis … CU *(= See you)*; See you! I
   Bis dann! CU *(= See you)*; See you! I
   bis jetzt so far II U3, 60
   von … **bis** from … to I
Biskuit- sponge I
ein bisschen a bit II U1, 22
Bitte. Please. I
   Bitte schön. Here you are.; You're welcome. I
bitten to ask I
   bitten um to ask for I
blau blue I
bleiben to stay I
Bleistift pencil I
Blick look I; view II U2, 44
Blitz lightning *(no pl)* II U4, 86
blockieren to block II U4, 77

blöd stupid **II U3**, 65
bloß only **I**
Blume flower **II U4**, 80
BMX BMX **II U3**, 54
weiße **Bohnen** in Tomatensoße baked
 beans (pl) **I**
Bonbons sweets (pl) **I**
Boot boat **I**
an **Bord** aboard **I**
böse angry; bad **I**
Bösewicht villain **II AC4**, 112
Botschaft message **I**
Bowlingbahn bowling alley **I**
Box box **I**
Boxen boxing **II U1**, 12
Boxrunde round of boxing **II U1**, 12
brauchen to need (to) **I**
 nicht **brauchen** needn't **I**
 (Zeit) **brauchen** *to take **II U4**, 79
braun brown **I**
brechen *to break **I**
breit wide **II U5**, 93
schwarzes **Brett** noticeboard **II U1**, 14
Brief letter **II U4**, 75
Briefträger postman **II U1**, 17
Brille glasses (pl) **II U3**, 64
bringen *to bring; *to get; *to take **I**
 in Schwierigkeiten **bringen** *to make
 trouble **I**
 jmdn. dazu **bringen**, etw. zu tun *to make
 somebody do something **II U4**, 76
Brite/**Britin** British **I**
britisch British **I**
Broschüre brochure **I**
Brot bread **I**
 belegtes **Brot** sandwich **I**
Brücke bridge **II U2**, 48
Bruder brother **I**
Buch book **I**
buchen to book **II U5**, 96
Büchse can **I**
Buchstabe letter **I**
buchstabieren *to spell **I**
bunt colourful **I**
Buntstift pencil **I**
Burg castle **II U2**, 42
Büro office **I**
Bus bus **I**
Busbahnhof bus station **I**

C

Cache cache **II U5**, 104
Café café; snack bar **I**
Cafeteria cafeteria **I**
campen to camp **II U5**, 106
Camping camping **II U4**, 83
Cent (Währung) cent **I**
Center centre **I**
Chance chance **II U4**, 84
Charakter character **I**
Chatroom chat room **II AC3**, 72

chatten (sich online unterhalten) to chat **I**
Chipkarte smartcard **II U2**, 38
circa about **I**
Clown clown **II U3**, 64
Cola coke **I**
Comedian comedian **II U1**, 14
Comedy Show comedy show **II U1**, 14
Comic comic **II U3**, 66
Comicheft comic **II U3**, 66
Computer computer **I**
Computerunterricht Technology **II AC1**, 9
cool cool **I**
aus **Cornwall** Cornish **II U5**, 94
Couch sofa **I**
Cousin/**Cousine** cousin **I**
Creme cream **I**
Cricket cricket **II U3**, 55
Curry (Gewürz oder Gericht) curry **I**

D

da because **I**
da there **I**
 da ist/sind there is/are **I**
dabei sein *to be in **II U3**, 56
Dach roof **II U5**, 104
Dachboden loft **I**; attic **II U3**, 60
dahin there **I**
Sehr geehrte **Dame,** sehr geehrter Herr
 Dear Sir or Madam **II U5**, 97
danach then; after that **I**
dankbar thankful **I**
Danke. Thank you.; Thanks. **I**
danken to thank **II AC1**, 11
 Nichts zu **danken.** You're welcome. **I**
dann then **I**
darauf zu towards **II U2**, 48
das the **I**
das that **I**
 Das (hier) ist … This is … **I**
 Das macht … That's … **I**
 Das war knapp! That was close! **I**
dass that **I**
Datum date **I**
dauern *to take **II U4**, 79
die **Daumen** drücken *to keep your fingers
 crossed **I**
davonkommen mit *to get away with
 II U3, 60
Deck deck **I**
definitiv definitely **II U5**, 98
dein/-e your **I**
dein/-er/-e/-es yours **II U5**, 104
Dekoration decorations (pl) **I**
dekorieren to decorate **I**
denken *to think **I**
 Denke/**Denkt** an … Think of … **I**
 denken an to remember **I**
 denken über *to think of **I**
Denkmal monument **II U5**, 98
dennoch still **II U4**, 79
der the **I**

der-/**die-**/**dasselbe** the same **I**
Desaster disaster **II U4**, 86
deshalb that's why **II U1**, 20
deutlich clear **I**
Deutsch German **I**
deutsch German **I**
Deutsche/-r German **I**
aus **Deutschland** German **I**
Dezember December **I**
Diagramm diagram **I**
Dialekt dialect **II U5**, 99
Dialog dialogue **I**
die (auch Pl.) the **I**
Diele hall **II U5**, 104
Dienstag Tuesday **I**
dies this **I**
diese (hier) these **I**
 diese dort those **I**
diese/-r/-s this **I**
Ding thing **I**
Dinosaurier dinosaur **II U2**, 45
Diskussion discussion **II U4**, 74
diskutieren to discuss **I**
Distanz distance **II U2**, 46
doch after all **I**
Donner thunder (no pl) **II U4**, 86
Donnerstag Thursday **I**
doof silly **I**
Dorf village **I**
dort there **I**
dorthin there **I**
Dose can **I**
 aus der **Dose** tinned **I**
Dosen- tinned **I**
Drama drama **II AC1**, 8
dramatisch dramatic **II U2**, 49
dran kommen to reach **II U4**, 79
Du bist **dran.** Your turn.; It's your turn. **I**
draußen outside **I**
 nach **draußen** out **I**
dreckig dirty **II U2**, 48
drei three **I**
eine **Dreiergruppe** a group of three **I**
dreizehn thirteen **I**
drin inside **I**
dritte/-r/-s third **I**
dröhnen to boom **II U5**, 104
Druck- print **II U4**, 75
drücken to press **II U4**, 86
 die Daumen **drücken** *to keep your
 fingers crossed **I**
du you; u (= you) **I**
 Du auch? You too? **I**
 Du bist **dran.** Your turn.; It's your turn. **I**
 Du bist … You're … **I**
 Du weißt, wie man … You know how
 to … **I**
du/dir/dich/Sie/sich (selbst) yourself **I**
dumm silly **I**; stupid **II U3**, 65
 Zu **dumm!** Too bad! **I**
Dummkopf silly **II U3**, 64
dunkel dark **II U1**, 22

Dunkelheit the dark **II U1**, 22; darkness **II U5**, 101
durch through **I**
durchdrehen *to go crazy **II U4**, 79
Durcheinander mess **II U4**, 80
Durchsage announcement **II U5**, 99
dürfen can **I**; may **II U4**, 79
    nicht **dürfen** mustn't **I**
Dusche shower **I**
DVD DVD **I**

E

Ebbe low tide **II U2**, 48
echt real **II U1**, 14
Ecke corner **II U2**, 40
Ehefrau wife, wives (pl) **II U5**, 100
Ei egg **I**
Eichhörnchen squirrel **I**
eifersüchtig sein (auf) *to be jealous (of) **I**
eigene/-r/-s own **I**
eilen to hurry **I**
Eimer bucket **II U2**, 48
ein/-e a; an **I**
    ein paar a couple of **I**
    ein wenig a little **I**
    ein/-e andere/-r/-s another **I**
    noch **ein/-e** another **I**
einander each other **I**
einbiegen to turn **I**
Einchecken Check-in **I**
eindeutig definitely **II U5**, 98
eine/-r/-s one, ones (pl) **II U2**, 40
Einerseits …, (aber) andererseits … On the
    one hand …, (but) on the other hand …
    II U3, 66
einfach easy **I**
    einfache Fahrkarte one-way ticket; single
    ticket **II U5**, 96
einfach just **I**
Einfall idea **I**
sich etwas **einfallen** lassen *to think of
    II U1, 16
Einführung introduction **II U3**, 59
eingießen to pour **I**
Einheit unit **I**
die Segel **einholen** to reef the sails **I**
einige some; a few **I**
Einkäufe shopping **I**
Einkaufen shopping **I**
einkaufen gehen *to go shopping **I**
einladen to invite **I**
Einladung invitation **I**
Einleitung introduction **II U3**, 59
einmal once **I**
einpacken to wrap **I**
einrichten *to set up **I**
eins one **I**
einsam lonely **I**
einschenken to pour **I**
einschlafen *to fall asleep **I**
einschließen to include **II U5**, 92

einst once **I**
einsteigen *to get into **I**
    einsteigen (in den Bus) *to get on (the
    bus) **II U5**, 96
Eintrittskarte ticket **I**
einwickeln to wrap **I**
Einzelkind only child **I**
einzeln individual **II U3**, 55
einziehen in to move in/into **II U5**, 104
einzige/-r/-s only **II U4**, 87
Eis ice; ice cream **I**
Eisbahn ice rink **I**
Eiscreme ice cream **I**
Elektrik electrics **II U5**, 105
Elektriker/-in electrician **II U5**, 105
Elektrizität electricity **II U5**, 104
elektronisch electronic **II U1**, 25
elf eleven **I**
Eltern parents (pl) **I**
E-Mail e-mail **I**
    per **E-Mail** schicken to mail **II U4**, 81
empfangen to receive **II U3**, 61
Ende ending; end **I**
enden to finish **I**; to end up **II U1**, 12; to end
    II U3, 63
endlich at last **I**; finally **II U3**, 65
Energie energy **II AC1**, 11
eng close **I**
aus **England** English **I**
Engländer/-in English **I**
    Ich bin **Engländer/-in.** I'm English. **I**
Englisch English **I**
englisch English **I**
englischsprachig English-speaking **I**
entdecken to discover **II AC1**, 8
auf **Entdeckungsreise** gehen to explore **I**
Entfernung distance **II U2**, 46
eine Nachricht **entgegennehmen** *to take a
    message **I**
    einen Anruf **entgegennehmen** to answer
    the phone **I**
entgegnen to reply **I**
Entgegnung reply **I**
entlang along **I**
entlanggehen *to go down **I**
entrümpeln to clear out **I**
(sich) **entscheiden** to decide **I**
Entschuldigen Sie! Excuse me … **I**
Entschuldigung! Sorry!; Excuse me … **I**
entsetzt horrified **I**
sich **entspannen** to relax **II AC1**, 11
entsprechen to match **I**
enttäuscht disappointed **I**
entwerfen to design **II AC1**, 11
Entwurf plan; draft **I**
er he **I**
Erdboden earth **II U2**, 45
Erde world **I**; earth **II U2**, 45
    die **Erde** earth **II U2**, 45
Erdkunde Geography **II AC1**, 10
Ereignis event **I**
Erfahrung experience **II U3**, 55

erfinden to create **I**
erforschen to explore **I**
ergänzen to add **I**
Ergebnis result **II U4**, 81
ergreifen to grab **II U2**, 48
erhalten to receive **II U3**, 61
sich **erinnern** (an) to remember **I**
    Erinnerst du dich? Remember? **I**
    Erinnert ihr euch? Remember? **I**
Erinnerung memory **II U1**, 23
Erkältung cold **II U3**, 59
erklären to explain **I**
Erklärung statement **II AC3**, 72
erkunden to explore **I**
ernähren *to feed **II U5**, 101
ernst serious **I**
    etw. **ernst** nehmen *to take sth seriously
    II U3, 64
ernsthaft serious **I**
erraten to guess **I**
erreichen *to get to **I**; to reach **II U4**, 79
erschaffen to create **I**
erst only **I**
    erst wenn until **II U3**, 56
erstaunlich amazing **II U1**, 22
erste/-r/-s first **I**
    als **Erstes** first **I**
ertappt caught on camera **II U1**, 12
Erwachsene/-r adult **II U2**, 44
erwähnen to mention **II AC3**, 72
erwidern to reply **I**
Erwiderung reply **I**
erzählen *to tell **I**
    erzählen von to talk about … **I**
    nochmals **erzählen** *to retell **I**
    Erzähle mir von … Tell me about … **I**
Erzählung story, stories (pl) **I**
es it **I**
    Es ist super zum/für … It's great for … **I**
Essen food **I**; meal **II U1**, 22
essen *to eat **I**
    (ein Bonbon) **essen** *to have (a sweet) **I**
etwa about **I**
etwas some; something; a little **I**
euer/eure your **I**
eure/-r/-s yours **II U5**, 104
Euro (Währung) euro **I**
ewig forever **II U4**, 77
Examen exam **II AC1**, 8
extra extra **I**

F

Fackel torch **II U1**, 22
fahren *to go **I**; to travel **II U2**, 38
Fahrer/-in driver **II U1**, 17
einfache **Fahrkarte** one-way ticket; single
    ticket **II U5**, 96
Fahrplan timetable **I**
Fahrpreis fare **II U5**, 96
Fahrrad bike **I**
Fahrschein ticket **II U5**, 95

Fahrt trip II U1, 13; tour II U2, 42; journey II U5, 93
fair fair I
Fakt fact II AC2, 34
fallen *to fall I
  fallen (lassen) to drop II U2, 48
falls if I
falsch wrong I
fälschen to fake II U3, 60
Familie family I
fangen *to catch II U3, 54
Fantasie fantasy I
fantastisch fantastic II AC1, 9
Farbe colour I
  Welche **Farbe** hat …? What colour is …? I
farbenfroh colourful I
Farm farm I
Farmer/-in farmer II U1, 17
fast almost II U3, 64; nearly II U4, 86
Fastnachtsdienstag Shrove Tuesday I
Februar February I
Federmäppchen pencil-case I
Was **fehlt?** What is missing? I
fehlend missing II U1, 17
Fehler mistake I
Feier party I
feiern to celebrate I
Feiertag holiday I
Feld field II U1, 22
felsig rocky II U5, 93
Fenster window I
Ferien holidays (pl) I
fernbleiben von to stay away from II U4, 81
(sich) **fernhalten** von *to keep away from II U5, 104
Fernsehen TV (= television) I
fernsehen to watch TV I
Fernseher TV (= television) I
Fertiggericht ready meal I
Fertigkeit skill I
fertigstellen to finish I
Fest festival I
fest(e) hard II U2, 42
festhalten *to hold I
Festival festival I
festnehmen to arrest II U1, 17
Feuerwerk fireworks (pl) I
Fieber fever II U3, 59
Figur character I; figure II U2, 37
Film film I
Filmemacher/-in filmmaker II U1, 28
finden *to find I
Finger finger I
Fisch fish, fish (pl) I
fit werden *to get fit I
Fläche space II AC2, 34; area II U3, 56
Flair flair II U2, 37
Flasche bottle I
Flohmarkt flea market I
Flughafen airport II AC2, 34
Flur hall II U5, 104
Fluss river I

flüstern to whisper I
Flut high tide II U2, 48
Flyer flyer I
Folge sequel II U5, 101
folgen to follow II U2, 40
Form form I
  in **Form** kommen *to get fit I
  verneinte **Form** negative form I
Formular form II U5, 96
hier: sich **fortbewegen** *to get around II U2, 37
fortfahren *to go on I
Fortsetzung sequel II U5, 101
Forum forum II U4, 74
Foto photo; picture I
  auf dem **Foto**/den **Fotos** in the photo(s) I
  Fotos machen *to take photos I
Fotoapparat camera II U1, 12
Fotografie photo I
fotografieren *to take photos I
Fotostory photo story I
Frage question I
fragen to ask I
  Frage/Fragt nach … Ask about … I
  fragen nach to ask for I
Französisch French II AC1, 10
französisch French II AC1, 10
Frau woman, women (pl) I
Frau (Anrede) Mrs I
frei free I
frei freely (II U4, 85)
Freiluft- outdoor II U1, 20
Freitag Friday I
Freizeit free time; leisure I
Freizeitzentrum leisure centre I
fremd strange I
fressen *to eat I
Freude fun I
Freudenfeuer bonfire I
sich **freuen** an to enjoy II U1, 16
Freund/-in friend I
  Dafür sind **Freunde** da. That's what friends are for. I
Freundin (in einer Paarbeziehung) girlfriend II U2, 40
freundlich friendly II U1, 18
Freundschaft friendship II U4, 78
  Freundschaft schließen *to make friends II U5, 94
frisch fresh I
uns **frisieren** *to do our hair I
froh happy I
fröhlich happy; fun I
Frucht fruit I
früh early I
Frühgeschichte ancient history II U5, 98
Frühstück breakfast I
frühstücken *to have breakfast I
Frühstückszerealie cereal (no pl) I
fühlen *to feel I
  sich **fühlen** *to feel I

sich ausgeschlossen **fühlen** *to feel left out II U4, 88
sich schlecht **fühlen** *to feel sick II U3, 59
Führer/-in guide II U2, 42
Füller pen I
fünf five I
fünfzehn fifteen I
funktionieren to work II U4, 79
Für wen …? Who … for? I
Furcht fear II U3, 66
furchtbar awful I
Fuß foot, feet (pl) I
  zu **Fuß** on foot II U2, 46
Fußball football I
Fußboden floor I
Fußgelenk ankle II U3, 58
Fußknöchel ankle II U3, 58
füttern *to feed II U5, 101

G

ganz all I; whole I
  den **ganzen** Tag all day II U1, 18
Garage garage I
garstig nasty II U4, 75
Garten garden I
Gaststätte restaurant I
Geächtete/-r outlaw II AC4, 112
Gebäude building I
geben *to give I
  es **gibt** there is/are I
Gebiet area II U3, 56
gebrauchen to use I
gebrochen broken I
Gebühr fee II U5, 96
Geburtstag birthday I
  Alles Gute zum **Geburtstag!** Happy Birthday! I
  Herzlichen Glückwunsch zum **Geburtstag!** Happy Birthday! I
Gedächtnis memory II U1, 23
Gedicht poem I
gedruckt print II U4, 75
Sehr **geehrte** Dame, sehr **geehrter** Herr
  Dear Sir or Madam II U5, 97
gefährlich dangerous I
Mir **gefällt** … I like … I
Gefängnis prison II U2, 42
Gefühl feeling II U1, 13
gegen against II U1, 23
Gegend region II AC3, 73
sich **gegenseitig** each other I
gegenüber opposite I
Geheimnis secret II U1, 23
geheimnisvoll mysterious II AC4, 112
gehen *to go; to walk I; *to leave II U3, 58
  ins Bett **gehen** *to go to bed I
  nach unten **gehen** *to go down I
  zu jmdm. nach Hause **gehen** *to go over to II U4, 79
  Wie **geht** es dir/euch/Ihnen? How are you? I

gehören (zu) to belong (to) **II AC1**, 9
  gehören zu *to go with **I**
  zueinander **gehören** *to go together **I**
Geist ghost **II U2**, 42
gelangweilt bored **I**
gelb yellow **I**
Geld money **I**
  Geld sammeln to raise money **II U1**, 14
  Geld verdienen *to make money **I**
Gelee jelly **I**
Gelegenheit chance **II U4**, 84
Gemälde painting **II AC1**, 8
gemein nasty **II U4**, 75
Gemeindezentrum community centre **I**
gemeinsam together **I**
genau exactly **II AC3**, 72
  genau hier right here **II U3**, 56
Genie genius **II U4**, 79
genießen to enjoy **II U1**, 16
genug enough **I**
genügend enough **I**
Geocaching geocaching **II U5**, 101
geöffnet open **I**
Geografie Geography **II AC1**, 10
gerade just; at the moment **I**; right now **II U4**, 87
geradeaus straight on **I**
Gerät machine **I**; tool **II U5**, 105
Geräusch sound **I**; noise **II U1**, 22
gerecht fair **I**
Gern geschehen. You're welcome. **I**
  gern haben to like **I**
  gern mögen to love **I**
  hätte/-st/-n/-t **gern** would like **I**
  hätte/-st-/-n/-t sehr **gern** would love **I**
  würde/-st/-n/-t **gern** would like **I**
  würde/-st/-n/-t sehr **gern** would love **I**
Gerümpel rubbish **I**
Geschäft shop **I**
geschehen to happen **I**
Geschenk present **I**
Geschichte story, stories (pl) **I**; History **II AC1**, 10
  antike **Geschichte** ancient history **II U5**, 98
geschichtlich historical **I**
Geschick skill **I**
Gesellschaft society **II U5**, 105
Gesetzlose/-r outlaw **II AC4**, 112
Gesicht face **I**
Gespenst ghost **II U2**, 42
Gespräch dialogue; conversation **I**
Gestalt figure **II U2**, 37
gestalten to design **II AC1**, 11
gestern yesterday **II U1**, 15
gesund healthy **I**
Gesundheit health **II U3**, 55
Getränk drink **I**
getrennt separate **II U1**, 20
gewaltig huge **II AC2**, 34
Gewinn prize **I**
gewinnen *to win **I**
Gewinner/-in winner **I**

gewöhnlich usually **I**
Gitter grid **I**
Glas glass **I**
glauben *to think; to believe **I**
gläubig religious **I**
der/die/das **gleiche** the same **I**
gleich right away **I**
  jetzt **gleich** right now **II U4**, 87
gleichmäßig regular **I**
gleichzeitig at the same time **I**
Glocke bell **II AC2**, 34
Glück haben *to be lucky **II U2**, 48
  … hat/haben **Glück**. … is/are lucky. **I**
glücklich happy **I**
Glücksbringer lucky charm **I**
Götterspeise jelly **I**
grau grey **I**
grausam cruel **II AC4**, 112
greifen to grab **II U2**, 48
Griff knob **II U4**, 79
groß big **I**; tall; high **II U1**, 21; large **II AC2**, 34
großartig great **I**; fantastic **II AC1**, 9
Großbuchstabe capital letter **I**
Größe size **I**
Großeltern grandparents (pl) **I**
Großstadt city **I**
grün green **I**
Grund reason **II U3**, 66
Grund- basic **II U2**, 45
grundlegend basic **II U2**, 45
Grundschule primary school **I**
Gruppe group **I**; team **II U1**, 12
gruselig scary **II U1**, 28
Gruß greeting **I**
  Grüße ausrichten (an) *to say hello (to) **I**
  Herzliche **Grüße** Best wishes **II U5**, 97
  Herzliche **Grüße** (am Briefende) Love … **I**
  Liebe **Grüße** (am Briefende) Love … **I**
  Viele **Grüße** Best wishes **II U5**, 97
  Viele **Grüße** … (am Ende von Briefen und Mails) Yours … **II U4**, 83
grüßen *to say hello (to) **I**
gut good; fine **I**
  gut sein in *to be good at **I**
  Guten Morgen. Good morning. **I**
  Mir geht's **gut**. I'm fine. **I**
Guthaben credit **II U2**, 38
Gymnasium grammar school **II U5**, 97

H

unsere **Haare** machen *to do our hair **I**
haben *to have got; *to have **I**
  hätte/-st/-n/-t gern would like **I**
  hätte/-st-/-n/-t sehr gern would love **I**
Hafen harbour **II U5**, 93
Hafendamm pier **I**
Hähnchen chicken **I**
halb (bei Uhrzeitangaben) half past **I**
halb half **I**
Halbjahresferien half-term break **I**
Halbschwester half-sister **I**

die **Hälfte** half, halves (pl) (of) **I**
Halle hall **II AC1**, 9
Hallo. Hello.; Hi.; Hey! **I**
Halt stop **II U2**, 39
halten *to hold; *to keep **I**
  halten von *to think of **I**
Haltestelle station **I**; stop **II U2**, 39
Hamburger burger **I**
Hand hand **I**
  Klatsch/Klatscht in die **Hände**. Clap your hands. **I**
Handbuch planner **I**
  Handbuch für TTS-Schülerinnen und -Schüler TTS planner **I**
sich **handeln** um *to be about **I**
Handgelenk wrist **II U2**, 48
Händler merchant **II AC3**, 73
Handlung action **I**
Handlungsort location **II U2**, 44
Handschuh glove **I**
Handy phone **I**; mobile **II U4**, 75
hart hard **II U1**, 16
hassen to hate **II U5**, 94
häufig often **I**
  häufig gefragt frequently asked **I**
Haupt- main **I**
Hauptstadt capital **II AC2**, 34
Hauptwort noun **I**
Haus house **I**
  nach **Hause** home **I**
  zu **Hause** at home **I**
  zu jmdm. nach **Hause** gehen *to go over to **II U4**, 79
Hausaufgabe(n) homework **I**
Haustier pet **I**
Haustür front door **II U4**, 86
He! Hey! **I**
Heim home **I**
heimlich in secret **II U3**, 65
heiß hot **II U5**, 98
Ich **heiße** … My name is … **I**
  Wie **heißen** Sie? What's your name? **I**
  Wie **heißt** du? What's your name? **I**
Held hero, heroes (pl) **II AC4**, 112
Heldin heroine **II AC4**, 112
helfen to help **I**
heraus out **I**
herausfinden *to find; *to find out **I**
Herausforderung challenge **II U1**, 20
herauskommen aus *to get out of **II U4**, 86
Herd cooker **I**
herein in **I**
hereinkommen *to come in **II U5**, 104
Herr (Anrede) Mr **I**
  Herr der Raben raven master **II U2**, 42
  Sehr geehrte Dame, sehr geehrter **Herr** Dear Sir or Madam **II U5**, 97
herrschen to rule **II U5**, 100
um … **herum** around **I**
herumschleichen to sneak around **II U1**, 28
herunter down **II U2**, 48
herunterfallen *to fall off **II U3**, 59

herunterkommen *to come down I

herunterladen *(aus dem Internet)* to download II U4, 81

herunternehmen *to take off I

herunterrollen to roll off II U2, 48

Herz heart II U2, 48

Herzliche Grüße Best wishes II U5, 97

    Herzliche Grüße *(am Briefende)* Love … I

heute today I

    heute Abend 2nite *(= tonight)* I

    heute Nachmittag this afternoon II U2, 38

Hi. Hi.; Hey! I

hier here I

    genau hier right here II U3, 56

    Hier ist … Here's … I

Highlight highlight II U1, 13

Hilfe help I

    ohne fremde Hilfe alone I

hilflos helpless I

hilfreich useful; helpful I

hilfsbereit helpful I

hinauf up II U5, 104

hinaus out I

hinausfließen to flow out II U2, 48

hinausgehen *to go out II U5, 104

hinein inside I

hineingelangen *to get into I

Hin- und Rückfahrkarte return ticket II U5, 96

hinfallen *to fall over; *to fall I

hinkommen *to get there I

sich hinsetzen *to sit down I

hinter behind I

Hintergrund background I

hinterhergehen to follow II U2, 40

hinüber over; across I

hinübergehen zu *to go over to II U4, 79

hinunter down II U2, 48

hinunterfallen *to fall off II U3, 59

hinuntergehen *to go down I

hinunterrollen to roll off II U2, 48

Hinweis clue II U1, 17

hinzufügen to add I

historisch historical I

Hobby hobby, hobbies *(pl)* I

hoch tall; high II U1, 21

hochleben lassen *to give the bumps I

Hochzeit wedding I

Hockey hockey II U3, 55

hoffen to hope I

Hoffnung hope II U3, 66

hoffnungsvoll hopeful I

höflich polite I

    Sei/Seid höflich. Be polite. I

Höhepunkt highlight II U1, 13

Höhle cave II U5, 101

holen *to get I

Homepage homepage I

Hoppla! Oops! I

Hör- audio I

horchen auf to listen for I

Hören listening I

hören *to hear I

    Ich habe gehört, dass … I hear … I

Hör-/Sehverstehen viewing I

Hose trousers *(pl)* II U5, 104

Hospital hospital II U3, 62

hübsch beautiful II U5, 94

Huch! Oops! I

Hügel hill II U5, 104

Huhn chicken I

Hülle wrapping I

Hund dog I

    den Hund ausführen to walk the dog I

    mit dem Hund spazieren gehen to walk the dog I

Ich bin hundemüde. I'm dog-tired. I

hungrig hungry I

Husten cough II U3, 59

Hut hat I

hüten to look after I

I

ich I; me I

    Ich bin aus … I'm from … I

    Ich bin Engländer/-in. I'm English. I

    Ich bin … I'm … I

    Ich heiße … My name is … I

    Ich mache … nicht gern. I don't like … I

    Ich mag … nicht. I don't like … I

    Ich möchte … I'd like to … *(= I would like to)* I

    Ich weiß (es) nicht! I don't know! I

    Ich würde gern … I'd like to … *(= I would like to)* I

Idee idea I

Identität identity II AC2, 35

Idiot/-in idiot II U2, 49

ihm him I

ihn him I

ihnen them I

ihr you; u *(= you)* I

Ihr/-e your I; yours II U5, 104

ihr/-e her; its I

ihr/-e *(Pl.)* their I

    Ihr wisst, wie man … You know how to … I

im in; on I

    im Innern inside I

    im Moment at the moment I

    im Weg sein/stehen *to be in the way I

Imbiss snack I

Imbissstube snack bar I

immer always I

    für immer forever II U4, 77

    immer noch still I

immerhin after all I

in in; on; at; to; into; inside I

    in Cornwall Cornish II U5, 94

    in der Nähe von near I

    in der Straße in the street I

    in Not in need II U1, 14

    in … hinein into I

    in Ordnung OK; fine I

indem as I

Inder/-in Indian I

indisch Indian I

individuell individual II U3, 55

Infinitiv infinitive I

Information information *(no pl)* I

Informationen information *(no pl)* I

Inlineskates fahren to skate I

Inlineskatefahren inline skating I

Inlineskates skates *(pl)* I

innen inside I

Insel island II U5, 93

Installateur/-in plumber II U5, 104

Instruktion instruction I

interessant interesting I

Interesse interest II U4, 74

sich interessieren (für) to care (about) II U4, 77

    sich interessieren für *to be interested in II U2, 36

interessiert sein an *to be interested in II U2, 36

Interkulturelles Across cultures I

international international I; multi-ethnic II AC2, 34

Internet internet I

Internetauftritt website I

Interview interview I

interviewen to interview I

irgendein/-e/-er any I

irgendjemand anyone else II U3, 61

irgendwelche any I

irgendwo anywhere II U2, 40; somewhere II U2, 51

sich irren *to be wrong I

J

ja yes; yeah *(infml)* I

jagen to chase I

Jahr year I

Jahrbuch yearbook II U1, 12

Jahrhundert century II U2, 48

18-jährig 18-year-old II U2, 38

11-Jährige/-r 11-year-old II U3, 56

Januar January I

je … desto the … the II U3, 54

jedenfalls anyway II U2, 48

jede/-r/-s every; each I

    jede Menge lots (of) I

    jedes Mal, wenn whenever II U4, 76

jeder everyone I; everybody II U2, 40

jemals ever II U3, 56

jemand somebody I; someone II U1, 17

    jemand anderes anyone else II U3, 61

jene those I

jenes that I

jetzt now I

    jetzt gleich right now II U4, 87

Job job I

Joghurt yoghurt I

jubeln to cheer **II U3**, 58
Jugend- teen **II U4**, 76
Jugendliche/-r teenager **I**
Juli July **I**
jung young **I**
Junge boy **I**
Juni June **I**

K

Kaffee coffee **I**
Kalender planner **I**
kalt cold **II U1**, 22
   kalt stellen *to leave it to cool **I**
Kamelrennen camel racing **II U3**, 54
Kamera camera **II U1**, 12
   mit der **Kamera** festgehalten caught on
   camera **II U1**, 12
Kamin chimney **II U5**, 104
Kampf fight **II U4**, 76
kämpfen *to fight **II U4**, 86
Kaninchen rabbit **I**
Kapitän/-in captain **I**
Kapitel unit **I**
kaputt broken **I**
Karneval carnival **II AC2**, 34
Karotte carrot **I**
Karte card **I**
Kartoffelchip crisp *(BE)* **I**
Käse cheese **I**
Kasten box **I**
Katastrophe disaster **II U4**, 86
Katze cat **I**
kaufen *to buy; *to get **I**
Käufer/-in buyer **I**
Kaufmann merchant **II AC3**, 73
keine Ahnung no idea **II U1**, 23
Keine Sorge! Don't worry! **I**
kein/-e no **I**
kein/-e/-en not … any **I**
Keks biscuit **I**
keltisch Celtic **II U1**, 20
kennen *to know **I**
Kerl guy **II U1**, 13
Kerze candle **I**
Kerzenlicht candlelight *(no pl)* **II U4**, 87
Kfz-Mechaniker/-in mechanic **II U1**, 17
Kind child, children *(pl)* **I**
Kino cinema **I**
Kirche church **I**
Kiste box **I**
Klang sound **I**
klar clear **I**
Klasse group; class **I**
   Ausstellung in der **Klasse** class display **I**
Klasse *(in einer englischen Schule)* tutor
   group **I**
Klassenarbeit test **I**
Klassenkamerad/-in classmate **I**
Klassenlehrer/-in tutor **I**
Klassenposter class poster **I**
Klassenzimmer classroom **I**

klatschen to clap **I**
   Klatsch/Klatscht in die Hände. Clap your
   hands. **I**
Kleider clothes *(pl)* **I**
Kleidergröße size **I**
Kleiderschrank wardrobe **I**
Kleidung clothes *(pl)* **I**; outfit **II U1**, 12
klein small; little **I**
Klempner/-in plumber **II U5**, 104
Klettern climbing **II U1**, 20
klettern to climb **I**
Klick click **II U4**, 87
Klicken click **II U4**, 87
klingeln *to ring **I**
klingen to sound **I**
Klub club **I**
klug clever **II U4**, 81
knapp close **I**
   Das war **knapp**! That was close! **I**
sich den **Knöchel** verrenken to twist your
   ankle **II U3**, 58
Koch-AG Cooking Club **I**
Kochen cooking **I**
kochen to cook **II U4**, 87
Kokosnuss coconut **II U2**, 49
Kollektion collection **II U1**, 14
Kolonie colony **II AC3**, 73
Komiker/-in comedian **II U1**, 14
kommen *to come **I**
   kommen nach *to get to **I**
   kommen zu *to get to **I**
   Komm jetzt! Come on! **I**
   Komm schon! Come on! **I**
Kommentar comment **II U1**, 16
kommentieren to comment (on) **II U4**, 81
kommunizieren to communicate **II AC3**, 73
Kompromiss compromise **II U4**, 77
König king **I**
Königin queen **II AC2**, 35
königlich royal **I**
   königlicher Leibgardist Beefeater **II U2**, 42
können can **I**
   kann nicht can't **I**; cannot **II U4**, 79
   können nicht can't **I**; cannot **II U4**, 79
   (vielleicht) **können** may **II U4**, 79
   Kannst du … nennen? Can you
   name …? **I**
könnte/-n could **II U2**, 43
Kontakt contact **II U5**, 97
   in **Kontakt** bleiben (mit) to stay in touch
   (with) **II U4**, 74
kontrollieren to check **I**
Konversation conversation **I**
Konzept draft **I**
Kopf head **I**
Kopfhörer headphones *(pl)* **II U4**, 86
Kopfschmerzen headache *(no pl)* **II U3**, 59
Kopfweh headache *(no pl)* **II U3**, 59
kopieren to copy **I**
Korbball netball **I**
Koreaner/-in Korean **II U3**, 60
Koreanisch Korean **II U3**, 60

koreanisch Korean **II U3**, 60
menschlicher **Körper** human body **II U2**, 48
korrekt correct; right **I**
Korridor hall **II U5**, 104
Korrigiere/Korrigiert … Correct … **I**
kosten *to cost **I**
   Es **kostet** …/Sie **kosten** … It's …/
   They're … **I**
   Wie viel **kostet/kosten** …? How much is/
   are …? **I**
kostenlos free **I**
Kostüm costume **I**; fancy dress **II U3**, 64
Kraft energy **II AC1**, 11; power **II AC4**, 112
   die **Kraft** der Wörter *(Wortschatzübung)*
   Word power **I**
kräftig hard **II U2**, 42
Krampf cramp **II U3**, 65
krank sick **II U3**, 59
Krankenhaus hospital **II U3**, 62
kreativ creative **I**
Kreis circle **I**
kreischen to scream **II U2**, 49
kreuzen to cross **II AC3**, 73
Krieger warrior **II U5**, 105
Kriminalität crime **II AC4**, 112
Kriminelle/-r criminal **II AC4**, 112
Kronjuwelen crown jewels **II U2**, 42
Küche kitchen **I**
Kuchen cake; pie **I**
Küchenschrank cupboard **I**
Kuh cow **II U5**, 101
Kühlschrank fridge **I**
Kultur culture **I**
Kummerkastentante agony aunt **II U4**, 76
sich **kümmern** (um) to care (about) **II U4**, 77
   sich **kümmern** um to look after **I**
Kunde/Kundin customer **II U5**, 100
Kunst art **II AC1**, 9
Kunstunterricht Art **I**
Kurs course **II U1**, 20
kurz short **I**
Kurzantwort short answer **I**
Kurzform short form **I**
Kurznachricht text (message) **I**
Küste shore **II U2**, 48; coastline **II U5**, 98
Küstenverlauf coastline **II U5**, 98
Küstenweg coastal path **II U5**, 104

L

Lächeln smile **I**
lächeln to smile **I**
lachen to laugh **I**
Laden shop **I**
Lage location **II U2**, 44
Lagerfeuer bonfire **I**
Lamm lamb **I**
Lämmchen lamb **I**
Lampe light **II U4**, 86
Land country, countries *(pl)*; land **I**; country-
   side **II U5**, 94
landen to end up **II U1**, 12; to land **II U3**, 62

landesweit national I
Landkarte map I
Landschaft landscape II U5, 92
Landwirt/-in farmer II U1, 17
lang long I
  (nicht) **länger** (not) any longer II U5, 94
… **lang** for … II U1, 16
langsam slow I
sich **langweilen** *to get bored II U5, 98
langweilig boring I
Laptop laptop II U4, 81
Lärm noise II U1, 22
lassen *to let I; *to leave II U3, 58
  Lass/Lasst uns … Let's … I
Lassi lassi I
Lauf run II U3, 56
Laufen running II U3, 56
laufen *to run; to walk I; *to be on II U4, 86
Läufer/-in runner II U3, 54
Laune mood II U1, 28
laut loud I
läuten *to ring I
Leben life, lives (pl) II U2, 45
leben to live I
Lebensmittel food I
legen *to put I
  Lege/Legt es in … Put it in … I
Legende legend II AC4, 112
jmdm. eine **Lehre/Lektion** erteilen *to teach
  somebody a lesson II U3, 60
lehren *to teach II U3, 60
Lehrer/-in teacher I; instructor II U1, 22
königlicher **Leibgardist** Beefeater II U2, 42
leicht easy I
leid tun *to be sorry I
  Tut mir **leid**! Sorry!; I'm sorry! I
leise quiet I
Lektion unit I
  jmdm. eine Lehre/**Lektion** erteilen *to
  teach somebody a lesson II U3, 60
Lernen studies (pl) II AC1, 8
lernen *to learn I
  viel zu **lernen** a lot to learn I
  auswendig **lernen** *to learn … by heart I
Lesen reading I
  vor dem **Lesen** pre-reading I
lesen *to read I
Leser/-in reader I
letzte/-r/-s last I
letztlich finally II U3, 65
Leute people (pl) I
(Pl.) **Leute** guy II U1, 13
Licht light II U4, 86
lieb nice I
  Lieber … Dear … I
  Liebe … (Anrede in Briefen) Dear … I
  Liebe Grüße (am Briefende) Love … I
Liebe love II U5, 101
lieben to love I
  Ich **liebe** dich. I love you. I
  Ich **liebe** … I love … I
lieber better I

Lieblings- favourite I
  Mein/e **Lieblings** … My favourite … I
  Was ist dein/e **Lieblings**…? What's your
  favourite …? I
Lied song I
lila purple I
Limonade lemonade I
Lineal ruler I
Linie line I
Link link II U2, 45
linke/-r/-s left I
links on the left; left I
  auf der **linken** Seite on the left I
Liste list I
lokal local II U5, 99
LOL LOL (= laughing out loud) II U1, 12
Londoner/-in Londoner I
Los ticket I
lösen to solve II U5, 104
losgehen *to leave II U3, 58
loslassen *to let go (of) II U3, 64
Lösung solution II U1, 17
Löwe lion II U2, 42
Lücke gap I
lügen to lie II U1, 13
lustig funny; fun I

M

Maat mate I
machen *to do; *to make I
  Fotos **machen** *to take photos I
  sich Notizen **machen** *to take notes I
  Machst du so …? Is this how you
  (do) …? I
Macht power II AC4, 112
mächtig powerful II AC4, 112
Mädchen girl I
  ein **Mädchen** aus Deutschland a girl from
  Germany I
Magen stomach II U3, 64
magisch magical II AC4, 112
Mahlzeit meal II U1, 22
Mai May I
mailen to mail II U4, 81
Mal time II U1, 14
malen to paint I
Malerei painting II AC1, 8
Mama mum I
manchmal sometimes I
Mango mango I
Mann man, men (pl) I
  wie der **Mann** aussah what the man
  looked like II U1, 17
Mannschaftsführer/-in captain I
Mäppchen pencil-case I
Mappe folder I
Marathon marathon II U3, 54
Markt market I
März March I
Maschine machine I
Match match II U3, 54

Material material II U2, 47
Mathe Maths II AC1, 9
Mathematik Maths II AC1, 9
Matrose sailor I
Mauer wall I
Maus/Mäuse mouse, mice (pl) I
Mechaniker/-in mechanic II U1, 17
Medien media II U4, 75
Meer sea I
Meerschweinchen guinea pig I
mehr more I
  (nicht) **mehr** (not) any longer II U5, 94
  mehr … als more … than I
Mehrzahl plural I
meiden to stay away from II U4, 81
Meile (brit. Längenmaß) mile II U3, 58
mein/-e my I
  Mein/e Lieblings… My favourite … I
mein/-er/-e/-es mine II U4, 87
meinen *to mean II U2, 40
Meinung opinion II U4, 76
die **meisten** (the) most I
der/die/das **meiste** (the) most I
meistens usually I
melden to report II U5, 93
Meldung report II U1, 13
melken to milk II U5, 101
eine **Menge** a lot of I
  jede **Menge** lots (of) I
Mensch person, people (pl) I
Menschen people (pl) I
Menschenmenge crowd II U2, 44
menschlicher Körper human body II U2, 48
sich **merken** to remember I
merkwürdig strange I; weird II U4, 83
Meter metre II U2, 48
mich me I
Milch milk I
Million million II AC2, 34
Mine mine II U5, 98
Mini- mini II U3, 56
Minute minute I
mir me I
  Mir geht's gut. I'm fine. I
mit with I
mit (dem Fahrrad) by (bike) I
mitbringen *to bring; *to take I
miteinander together I
Mitglied member II AC3, 72
mithalten (mit) *to keep up (with) II U3, 64
mitmachen *to be in II U3, 56
mitnehmen *to take I
Mitschüler/-in classmate I
Mitspieler/-in player II U3, 67
Mittagessen lunch I
Mittagspause lunch break I
Mitte middle I
mitteilen *to tell I
mittelalterlich medieval II U5, 92
Mittwoch Wednesday I
Mobiltelefon mobile II U4, 75
Mode fashion II AC1, 8

Model model I
Modell model I
Moderator/-in presenter I
modern modern II U2, 50
mögen to like; *to be into; to want (to) I
  gern mögen to love I
  nicht mögen to hate II U5, 94
  Du magst … You're into … I
  Ich mag dich. I love you. I
  Ich mag … I like … I
  Ich mag … nicht. I don't like … I
  Ich mag … total gern. I love … I
  Ich möchte … I'd like to … (= I would like to) I
möglich possible I
möglicherweise probably II U2, 38
Möglichkeit chance II U4, 84
Möhre carrot I
Moment moment II AC1, 11
  im Moment at the moment I
Monat month II U1, 14
Monster monster I
Montag Monday I
montags on Mondays I
Monument monument II U5, 98
Morgen morning I
  Guten Morgen. Good morning. I
morgen tomorrow I
morgens in the mornings I
motivieren to motivate I
Motto theme I
Mountainbikefahren mountain biking II U5, 93
müde tired I
Müll rubbish I
Mund mouth I
Münze coin I
Museum museum I
Museumsrundgang gallery walk I
Musik music I
Musiker/-in musician II U2, 39
müssen must I; *to have to II U4, 79
  (tun) müssen to need (to do) I
  nicht müssen needn't I
mutig brave I
Mutter mother I
Muttersprache first language II AC3, 73
mysteriös mysterious II AC4, 112

N

nach to I
  nach draußen outside; out I
  nach drinnen inside I
  nach Hause home I
  nach unten downstairs II U4, 86
  nach oben upstairs II U4, 86
  (nach) oben up II U5, 104
  nach unten down II U2, 48
nach (bei Uhrzeitangaben) past I
nach (zeitlich) after I
Nachbar/-in neighbour (BE) I

nachdenken *to think I
  Warte/Wartet und denk/denkt nach. Stop and think I
nacherzählen *to retell I
nachjagen to chase I
Nachmittag afternoon I
  heute Nachmittag this afternoon II U2, 38
nachmittags (Uhrzeit) p.m. I
Nachricht message I
  eine Nachricht entgegennehmen *to take a message I
  eine Nachricht hinterlassen *to leave a message I
Nachrichten news (sg) II U2, 45
nachschauen to look up I
nachschlagen to look up I
nachspüren to trace I
nächste/-r/-s next I
  der/die Nächste(n) next I
  als Nächstes next I
  am nächsten Tag the next day II U1, 15
Nacht night I
  die ganze Nacht all night I
Nachtisch pudding I
Nachtwanderung night walk II U1, 23
in der Nähe von near I
nahe near I; close II U2, 42
Name name I
Namenstag name day I
Nase nose II U1, 12
nass wet II U2, 48
national national I
Natur nature II AC1, 11
natürlich of course I
Naturwissenschaften Science II AC1, 9
neben next to I; besides II U5, 99; by II U5, 104
negativ negative II U5, 92
nehmen *to take I
  (ein Bonbon) nehmen *to have (a sweet) I
  etw. ernst nehmen *to take sth seriously II U3, 64
neidisch sein (auf) *to be jealous (of) I
nein no I
nennen to name; to call I
jemandem auf die Nerven gehen *to get on people's nerves I
nervös nervous II U1, 16
nett nice I; friendly II U1, 18
Netz net II U3, 54
soziales Netzwerk social network II U4, 75
neu new I
Neuigkeiten news (sg) II U2, 45
neun nine I
nicht not I
  nicht mehr not any more I
  nicht mögen to hate II U5, 94
  noch nicht not … yet II U3, 58
  Ich auch nicht. Me neither. II U5, 98
nicht- non- II U1, 14
nichts nothing; not … anything I
  Nichts zu danken. You're welcome. I

nie never I
niedlich cute I
niedrig low II U1, 21
niemals never I
niemand nobody II U2, 40
  niemand anderes nobody else II U5, 106
nirgendwo nowhere II U5, 94
nirgendwohin nowhere II U5, 94
noch still I; yet II U3, 58
  noch ein/-e another I
  noch einmal again I
  noch mal again I
  noch nicht not … yet II U3, 58
Nomen noun I
Nord- north II U2, 39
Norden north II U2, 39
normal normal II U2, 44
normalerweise usually I
in Not in need II U1, 14
Notiz note I
  Notizen machen *to make notes I
  sich Notizen machen *to take notes I
November November I
Nudeln pasta I
null zero I
null (bei Telefonnummern und Uhrzeitangaben) oh I
Nullmeridian Meridian Line I
Nummer number I
nun now I
nun well I
nur only; just I
Nuss nut I
nützlich useful I
  nützliche Ausdrücke Useful phrases I

O

O! Oh! I
o.k. OK I
ob if I
oben on top I; upstairs II U4, 86
  (nach) oben up II U5, 104
obendrauf on top I
oberer Teil top I
  oberes Ende top I
im Obergeschoss upstairs II U4, 86
Obst fruit I
oder or I
offen open I
öffentlich public II U2, 37
offline offline II U4, 87
öffnen to open I
oft often I
  so oft whenever II U4, 76
ohne without I
  ohne fremde Hilfe alone I
Oje! Oh dear! II U5, 104
Öko- Eco II AC1, 11
Oktober October I
Oma grandma; granny I
Onkel uncle I

online stellen to post II U4, 74
online online II U1, 25
Opa grandad I
Orange orange I
orange orange I
Ordner folder I
Ordnung order I
  in Ordnung fine I
  in Ordnung bringen to tidy (a room) I
organisieren to organise I
Ort place I; space II AC2, 34
örtlich local II U5, 99
Ost- east I
Osten east I
Ostern Easter I
Outdoor- outdoor II U1, 20
Outfit outfit II U1, 12

P

Paar pair I; couple II U5, 100
ein paar some; a few; a couple of I
Päckchen packet; parcel I
Packung packet I
Paket packet; parcel I
Palme palm tree II U5, 93
panisch werden to panic II AC1, 11
Papa dad I
Papier paper I
  Stück Papier piece of paper I
Paradies paradise II U4, 74
Park park I
Partner/-in partner I
Party party I
passen zu *to go with; to match I
  zueinander passen *to go together I
passieren to happen I
Pasta pasta I
Pastete pie I
Pause break II AC1, 10
PC PC (= Personal Computer) II AC3, 73
Pech haben *to be unlucky I
peinlich embarrassing II U1, 12
Pence (brit. Währungseinheit) penny, pence
  (pl) I
Peng! Bang! II U4, 86
Penny (brit. Währungseinheit) penny, pence
  (pl) I
perfekt perfect I
Person person, people (pl) I
  pro Person each I
hier: persönlich face-to-face II U4, 77
persönlich personal I
Perspektive point of view II U3, 60
Pfeife pipe II U2, 49
Pferd horse I
Pfund (brit. Währungseinheit) pound (£) I
Picknick picnic I
Pick-up pick-up I
Pier pier I
Pille pill II U3, 59
pink pink I

Pizza pizza I
Placemat placemat I
Platzdeckchen placemat I
Plan plan I
planen to plan I
Planet planet II U1, 22
Plattform platform II U5, 96
Platz place I; space II AC2, 34; pitch II U3, 54
Platz! (Befehl für Hunde) Sit! I
plaudern to chat I
plötzlich suddenly I
Plural plural I
Polen Poland I
Polizei police II U1, 17
Pommes frites chips (pl) (BE) I
Pony pony I
Ponyreiten im Gelände pony trekking
  II U5, 93
populär popular I
Porträt profile I
Possessivform possessive form I
Post (Eintrag im Internet) post I
Poster poster I
Postkarte postcard II U5, 106
praktisch practical II U4, 75
Präposition preposition I
Präsentation presentation I
präsentieren to present I
Praxis surgery I
Praxisräume surgery I
Preis price; prize I
preiswert cheap I
pressen to press II U4, 86
Privatdetektiv/-in private detective
  II AC4, 112
pro per II U5, 95
  pro Person each I
  pro Stück each I
probieren to try I
  Probier mal … Try … I
Problem problem I
Probleme trouble II U1, 23
Profil profile I
Programm programme II U3, 54
Projekt project I
Prospekt brochure I
prüfen to check I
Prüfung test I; exam II AC1, 8
Pudding pudding I
Punkt point II U3, 54
Punktestand score II U3, 54
Puzzle puzzle I
Pyjama pyjamas (pl) II U1, 16

Q

Qualifikation trial II U3, 56
Qualität quality I
quer durch across I
Quiz quiz I

R

Rabe raven II U2, 42
  Herr der Raben raven master II U2, 42
Rad wheel I
Radfahren cycling I
Radiergummi rubber I
Radio radio II U3, 54
Rahmen set II AC4, 113
Rap rap I
rappen to rap I
Raster grid I
Rat advice II AC1, 11
raten to guess I
Ratschlag tip I; advice II AC1, 11
Rätsel puzzle; quiz I
Ratte rat I
Räuber/-in robber II AC4, 112
Raum room I; space II AC2, 34
Raumschiff spaceship II U1, 26
Reaktion reaction II AC1, 9
realistisch realistic II U2, 47
recht haben *to be right I
rechte/-r/-s right I
rechts on the right; right I
  auf der rechten Seite on the right I
Rechtschreibung spelling I
recyceln to recycle II AC1, 11
reden to talk I
  reden mit to talk to I
Redewendung phrase I
Redner/-in speaker I
Regel rule I
  Was ist die Regel für …? What's the rule
  for …? I
regelmäßig regular I
regieren to rule II U5, 100
Region region II AC3, 73
regnen to rain II U4, 86
die Reichen the rich II AC4, 113
Reihenfolge order I
Reim rhyme I
rein in I
reinigen to clean I
Reise trip II U1, 13; travel II U1, 24; journey
  II U5, 93
Reisebericht travel report II U1, 24
Reisebüro travel agent's II U5, 95
Reisebus coach II U1, 17
Reiseführer guide II U2, 42
(das) Reisen travel II U1, 24
reisen to travel II U2, 38
Religion (Schulfach) RE (= Religious Education) II AC1, 10
religiös religious I
Rennen race II U3, 54; running; run II U3, 56
rennen *to run I
reparieren to fix II U4, 79
Reporter/-in reporter II U3, 61
Requisite prop II AC4, 113
reservieren to book II U5, 96
der Rest the rest I

Restaurant restaurant **I**
Resultat result **II U4**, 81
retten to save **I**
Rettung rescue **II U3**, 61
Rettungsboot lifeboat **I**
Rettungsring lifebuoy **I**
Rezept *(für Arzneimittel)* prescription
  II U3, 59
Rhythmus rhythm **I**
richtig correct; right **I**; real **II U1**, 14
Richtung direction **I**
  in **Richtung** towards **II U2**, 48
riesengroß huge **II AC2**, 34
riesig huge; large **II AC2**, 34
Ring circle **I**
Ritter knight **II AC4**, 112
Rock skirt **II U5**, 104
Rock 'n' Roll rock 'n' roll **II AC3**, 73
Rohr pipe **II U4**, 79
Rohrleitung pipe **II U4**, 79
Rolle role **I**
  Rollen tauschen to swap roles **I**
Rollenspiel role play **I**
Rollschuhe skates *(pl)* **I**
Rollstuhl wheelchair **II U2**, 39
Rolltreppe escalator **I**
Römer/-in Roman **II AC2**, 34
römisch Roman **II AC2**, 34
rosa pink **I**
rot red **I**
Route route **II U1**, 20
Rücken an **Rücken** back to back **I**
Rückenschmerzen backache **II U3**, 59
Rückenweh backache **II U3**, 59
Hin- und **Rückfahrkarte** return ticket
  II U5, 96
rufen to shout; to call **I**; to cry **II U4**, 86
Rugby rugby **II U3**, 54
ruhig quiet **I**
Rühr- sponge **I**
ruinieren to ruin **II U3**, 65
Rumäne/Rumänin Romanian **II AC3**, 72
Rumänisch Romanian **II AC3**, 72
rumänisch Romanian **II AC3**, 72
Runde round **II U1**, 12
Rundgang tour **II U2**, 42
Rutschbahn slide **I**

S

Saal hall **II AC1**, 9
Sache thing **I**
Saft juice **I**
Sage legend **II AC4**, 112
sagen *to say; *to tell **I**
Sahne cream **I**
Salat salad **I**
Salbe ointment **II U3**, 59
sammeln to collect **I**
  Geld **sammeln** to raise money **II U1**, 14
Sammlung collection **II U1**, 14
Samstag Saturday **I**

Sand- sandy **II U5**, 93
sandig sandy **II U5**, 93
Sandwich sandwich **I**
Sänger/-in singer **II U1**, 19
Sanitärarbeit plumbing **II U5**, 105
Satz phrase; sentence **I**
Satzstellung word order **I**
säubern to clean **I**
Säugling baby **I**
Saxofon saxophone; sax **I**
Schach chess **II AC1**, 8
Schachtel box **I**
Schade! Too bad! **I**
Schaf sheep, sheep *(pl)* **II U1**, 22
schaffen to create **I**
  Wir haben es **geschafft**! We did it!
  II U3, 65
Schälchen bowl **I**
Schale bowl **I**
Schatz treasure **II U2**, 42
Schau show **II AC1**, 9
schauen to look **I**
  Schau/**Schaut** mal! Look! **I**
Schauplatz scene **II U3**, 61
in **Scheiben** schneiden to slice **I**
schenken *to give **I**
scherzen to joke **II U4**, 86
schicken *to send **I**
schieben to push **II U4**, 86
Schiedsrichter/-in official **II U3**, 65
schiefgehen *to go wrong **I**
schießen to kick **II U3**, 54
Schiff ship **I**
Schiffsjunge cabin boy **I**
Schiffsoffizier mate **I**
Schild sign **II U1**, 22
Schinkenspeck bacon **I**
Schlafanzug pyjamas *(pl)* **II U1**, 16
schlafen *to sleep **I**; *to be asleep **II U1**, 23
Schlafzimmer bedroom **I**
schlagen *to hit; to whip **I**; *to beat **II U2**, 40
Schläger racquet **II U3**, 54
Schlamm mud **II U2**, 48
schlammig muddy **II U2**, 48
Schlange queue **I**
schlau clever **II U4**, 81
schlecht bad **I**
  der/die/das **schlechteste** the worst
  II U1, 20
  sich **schlecht** fühlen *to feel sick **II U3**, 59
schließen to close **I**
Schließfach locker **I**
schließlich at last; after all **I**; in the end
  II U1, 14; finally **II U3**, 65
schlimm *(ugs.)* bad **I**
  der/die/das **schlimmste** the worst
  II U1, 20
Schlittschuh laufen to skate **I**
Schlittschuhbahn ice rink **I**
Schlittschuhe skates *(pl)* **I**
Schloss castle **II U2**, 42

Schluchtenklettern gorge scrambling
  II U1, 20
Schluss end **I**
  zum **Schluss** in the end **II U1**, 14; finally
  II U3, 65
Schluss *(einer Geschichte)* ending **I**
Schlüssel key **II U2**, 49
Schlüsselbegriff key word **I**
Schmerz pain **II U3**, 58
Schmuck jewellery; decorations *(pl)* **I**
schmücken to decorate **I**
schmutzig dirty **II U2**, 48
Schnäppchen bargain **I**
schnappen to grab **II U2**, 48
schnarchen to snore **I**
schneiden *to cut (off) **II U2**, 49
  in Scheiben **schneiden** to slice **I**
schnell fast; quick **I**
schnell quickly **II U2**, 48
Schock shock **II U3**, 63
Schokolade chocolate **I**
schön nice; fine **I**; beautiful **II U5**, 94
schon already **I**; yet **II U3**, 58
  schon einmal before **II U3**, 57
Schornstein chimney **II U5**, 104
schottisch Scottish **II U5**, 93
Schrank cupboard **I**
schrecklich awful **I**
Schreiben writing **I**
schreiben *to write **I**
schreien to shout **I**; to scream **II U2**, 49; to
  cry **II U4**, 86
Schritt step **I**
  Schritt halten (mit) *to keep up (with)
  II U3, 64
  Schritt-für-**Schritt**- step-by-step **II U4**, 79
schubsen to push **II U4**, 86
schüchtern shy **II U1**, 13
Schuh shoe **I**
Schule school **I**
Schüler/-in student **I**
Schulfach subject **II AC1**, 8
Schuljahr year **I**
Schulklasse class **I**
Schulstunde lesson **I**
Schultasche schoolbag **I**
Schulter shoulder **II U3**, 59
Schüssel bowl **I**
schütten to pour **I**
schützen to protect **II AC1**, 11
Schwanz tail **I**
schwarz black **I**
  schwarz werden *to go black **II U4**, 86
  schwarzes Brett noticeboard **II U1**, 14
Schweif tail **I**
Schwein pig **I**
schwer hard **II U1**, 16
Schwester sister **I**
schwierig hard **II U1**, 16; difficult **II U3**, 61
Schwierigkeit problem **I**
Schwierigkeiten trouble **II U1**, 23

in **Schwierigkeiten** bringen *to make trouble I
Schwimmen swimming I
Schwimmen gehen *to go swimming I
schwimmen *to swim I
Science-Fiction (*Zukunftsdichtung*) science fiction II U1, 26
sechs six I
Vier plus **sechs** ist zehn. Four and six is ten. I
Second-Hand-Laden charity shop I
See lake I
See zum Rudern boating lake I
Seemann sailor I
die **Segel** einholen to reef the sails I
Segelboot sailboat II U5, 106
sehbehindert partially sighted II AC1, 9
sehen *to see; to look I
Sehenswürdigkeit sight II AC2, 34; attraction II U2, 45
sehr very; very much I
Sehr geehrte Dame, **sehr** geehrter Herr Dear Sir or Madam II U5, 97
Hör-/**Sehverstehen** viewing I
sein *to be I
beeindruckt **sein** *to be impressed II U4, 87
Sei/Seid höflich. Be polite. I
sein/-e his; its I
Seite page I; side II U2, 49
auf der anderen **Seite** von across; opposite I
selber yourself I; himself II U1, 12; myself II U4, 77; yourselves II U5, 97
selbst even I
du/dir/dich/Sie/sich (**selbst**) yourself I
ihr/euch/Sie/sich (**selbst**) yourselves II U5, 97
er/sich (**selbst**) himself II U1, 12
ich/mir/mich (**selbst**) myself II U4, 77
selbstbewusst confident II U1, 20
Selbsteinschätzung self-evaluation I
selbstkritisch self-critical II U4, 76
selbstsicher confident II U1, 20
selbstverständlich of course I
Selfie selfie II U3, 65
seltsam strange I; weird II U4, 83
senden *to send I
Sender station II U3, 61
Sendung programme II U3, 54
separat separate II U1, 20
September September I
Sessel chair I
setzen *to put I
sich **setzen** *to sit down I
Show show II AC1, 9
Comedy **Show** comedy show II U1, 14
sich each other I
sicher sure I; safe II U2, 42
sicher sein *to be sure II U5, 98
Sicht view II U2, 44
Sie you; u (*= you*) I

Sie sind … You're … I
sie her; she I
sie (*Pl.*) them I; they I
sieben seven I
siegen *to win I
Sieger/-in winner I
Sightseeing- sightseeing II U2, 44
Signalwort signal word I
Silber silver II U2, 48
singen *to sing I
Ich **singe** und tanze gern. I like singing and dancing. I
Sinn meaning II U1, 25
Situation situation I
sitzen *to sit I
Sitz! (*Befehl für Hunde*) Sit! I
sich gegenüber **sitzen** *to sit face to face I
Skateboard skateboard II U1, 15
Skateboardfahren skateboarding I
Slogan slogan II AC1, 11
Smartphone smartphone II U3, 63
SMS text (message) I
eine **SMS** schicken to text II U4, 74
Snack snack I
so like this; so; like that I; that's how II U1, 14
so oft whenever II U4, 76
so … wie as … as I
sobald as soon as II U4, 76
Sofa sofa I
sofort right away I; right now II U4, 87
sogar even I
sollte should II AC1, 11
sollte(n) nicht shouldn't II U3, 59
Sommer summer II AC3, 72
Sommerferienlager summer camp II AC3, 72
Sonderangebot special offer I
sonderbar weird II U4, 83
Song song I
Sonne sun II U5, 104
sonnig sunny II U5, 98
Sonntag Sunday I
Sonst noch etwas? Anything else? I
Keine **Sorge**! Don't worry! I
sich **Sorgen** machen to worry II U4, 77
sorgfältig careful II U2, 42
Sorte kind I
Souvenir souvenir II U2, 40
sowieso anyway II U2, 48
soziales Netzwerk social network II U4, 75
Sozialwissenschaften Humanities (*pl*) II AC1, 10
Spalt gap I
Spanien Spain II U4, 83
spannend exciting I
sparen to save II AC1, 11
Spaß fun I
Spaß haben *to have fun I
Es macht **Spaß**. It's fun. I
spät late I
zu **spät** late I
zu **spät** kommen *to be late I
Wie **spät** ist es? What's the time? I

zu **spät** dran sein *to be late I
kleiner **Spaten** trowel II U2, 48
später later I
spazieren gehen *to go for a walk II U1, 22
mit dem Hund **spazieren** gehen to walk the dog I
Speck bacon I
Speer spear II U5, 104
speziell special I
Spiel game I; match II U3, 54
spielen to play I
einen Streich **spielen** to play a trick (on) I
spielen (*Theater*) to act I
eine Theaterszene **spielen** acting a scene I
Spieler/-in player II U3, 67
Spielfeld field II U1, 22; court; pitch II U3, 54
Spielkarte card I
Spielstand score II U3, 54
Spielzeug toy I
Spind locker I
Spitze top I
Sport sport I
… ist ein toller **Sport**. … is a great sport. I
Sportart sport I
Sportunterricht PE (*= Physical Education*) II AC1, 10
Sprache language I
Sprachmittlung mediation I
Sprechblase speech bubble I
Sprechen speaking; talking I
sprechen *to say; to talk; *to speak I
sprechen über to talk about … I
Sprecher/-in speaker I
Sprechgesang chant II U3, 58
springen to jump I
Spur clue II U1, 17
Staatsoberhaupt head of state II AC3, 73
Stadion stadium II U3, 54
Stadt city; town I
Stadtplan map I
Stadtteil part I
Stammbaum family tree I
ständig always I
Standort location II U2, 44
Standpunkt point of view II U3, 60
Star star I
stark strong II U5, 104; powerful II AC4, 112
Stärke power II AC4, 112
starren to stare I
starten to start I
Startpunkt starting place II U5, 96
Station station I
stattfinden *to take place I
Steak steak I
stehen *to stand I
stehen auf *to be into I
Du **stehst** auf … You're into … I
stehlen *to steal II U5, 104
steigen to climb I
steinig rocky II U5, 93
Stelle place I

stellen *to put I
online stellen to post II U4, 74
Stelle/Stellt es in … Put it in … I
Stern star I
Steuer wheel I
Steuerrad wheel I
Stichwort key word I
Stiefmutter stepmum I
still quiet; still I
Stimme voice I
Stimmung mood II U1, 28
stolz (auf) proud (of) II U1, 13
stoppen to stop I
stören *to get in the way II U3, 64
Story story, stories (pl) I
stoßen to push II U4, 86
Strand beach II U4, 83
Straße road II U1, 22
Straße (in der Stadt) street I
auf der Straße in the street I
in der Straße in the street I
Strecke route II U1, 20
Streich trick I
einen Streich spielen to play a trick (on) I
Streit fight II U4, 76
(sich) streiten *to fight II U4, 86
Strom electricity II U5, 104
Stromausfall power cut II U4, 87
Stück piece I
pro Stück each I
Stück Papier piece of paper I
Student/-in student I
Studie survey I
Studium studies (pl) II AC1, 8
Stufe step I
Stuhl chair I
Stunde hour II U2, 49
Stundenplan timetable I
Sturm storm I
Such- search II U1, 25
Suche search II U1, 25
suchen nach to look for I
Süd- south II U2, 39
Südafrika South Africa II AC3, 73
Süden south II U2, 39
Südkoreaner/-in South Korean II AC3, 72
Südkoreanisch South Korean II AC3, 72
südkoreanisch South Korean II AC3, 72
super great; cool I
Es ist super zum/für … It's great for … I
Supermacht superpower II AC3, 73
Supermarkt supermarket I
Surfen surfing II U5, 93
süß cute; sweet I
Süßigkeiten sweets (pl) I
Szene scene I

T

Tabelle grid I
Tablet tablet II U4, 79
Tablette pill II U3, 59

die Tafelrunde the Round Table II AC4, 113
Tag day I
am nächsten Tag the next day II U1, 15
den ganzen Tag all day II U1, 18
ein Tag in … a day out in … II U2, 44
eines Tages one day II U2, 43
Tagebuch diary II U5, 106
Tagebucheintrag diary entry II U5, 106
Takelage rigging I
Talent talent I
Talentwettbewerb talent show I
Talisman lucky charm I
Tante aunt I
Tanz dance (no pl) II AC1, 8
tanzen to dance I
Ich singe und tanze gern. I like singing and dancing. I
Tanzveranstaltung dance (no pl) II AC1, 8
tapfer brave I
Tasche bag I
Taschengeld pocket money I
Taschenlampe torch II U1, 22
Tatsache fact II AC2, 34
Rollen tauschen to swap roles I
tausende (von) thousands of I
Taxi taxi II U1, 17
Team team II U1, 12
Technik Technology II AC1, 9
Technologie technology II AC3, 73
Tee tea I
Teenager teenager I
Teil part I
teilen to share II U4, 76
teilnehmen (an) *to take part (in) II U4, 74
Telefon phone; telephone I
Telefonanruf phone call I
Tennis tennis I
Test test I
teuer expensive I
Text text I
Theater theatre I; drama II AC1, 8
eine Theaterszene spielen acting a scene I
Thema theme I; topic II U1, 26
Ticket ticket I
tief deep II U5, 93
Tier animal I
Tierarzt/Tierärztin vet I
Tierpark zoo II U2, 39
Tierwelt (in freier Wildbahn) wildlife II AC1, 11
Tipp tip I
Tisch table I
Titel heading I
tja well I
Toast toast I
Toilette toilet I
toll great I; amazing II U1, 22
… ist ein toller Sport. … is a great sport. I
Tomate tomato, tomatoes (pl) I
Tombola raffle I
Ton sound I
Tonmodell model I

Tonpfeife clay pipe II U2, 49
Tonstudio recording studio I
Tor goal I
Torte cake I
Tortenguss jelly I
tot dead II U2, 48
Tour tour II U2, 42
Tourist/-in tourist I
Touristeninformation tourist information centre I; tourist board II U5, 97
Tradition tradition I
tragen to carry II U4, 80
tragen (Kleidung) *to wear I
Trainer/-in coach I
trainieren to practise I; to train II U3, 58
Training training II U3, 64
Training für den Mund mouth jogging I
Transport transport II U5, 94
Ich traute meinen Augen nicht. I couldn't believe my eyes. II U3, 61
Traum dream II U1, 19
Traum- fantasy I
traurig sad I
treffen *to meet; *to hit I
sich treffen *to meet I
treten to kick II U3, 54
Trick trick I
Trifle (englischer Nachtisch) trifle I
trinken *to drink I
Trip trip II U1, 13
trotzdem anyway II U2, 48
Tschüss! Bye! II U3, 58
T-Shirt T-shirt I
tun *to do; *to make I
tun als ob to act like II U4, 76
Tunnel tunnel I
Tür door I
Turnier competition II AC1, 9
Turteltauben lovebirds (pl) II U1, 13
Tüte bag I
Typ guy II U1, 13
typisch typical I

U

U-Bahn underground II AC2, 34
die Londoner U-Bahn the Tube II AC2, 34
Übelkeit verspüren *to feel sick II U3, 59
Üben practising I
üben to practise I
über about; over; across I
überall everywhere I
überall (in) all over I
überall (egal, wo) anywhere II U2, 40
überhaupt at all I
übernachten to stay II U5, 94
Übernachtung sleepover I
überprüfen to check I
überqueren to cross II AC3, 73
überraschen to surprise II U3, 65
überraschend surprising II U1, 28
überrascht sein *to be surprised II U2, 49

Überraschung surprise I
überreagieren to overreact II U4, 76
überreden to persuade II U2, 38
Überschrift heading I
übersetzen to translate I
   Übersetze/Übersetzt nicht … Don't translate … I
Übersetzung translation I
übrig left I
Übung exercise I
Übungsheft exercise book I
Ufer bank; shore II U2, 48
UFO UFO II U3, 62
Uhr clock I
   Um wie viel **Uhr**? What time? I
   Wie viel **Uhr** ist es? What's the time? I
Uhr *(Zeitangabe bei vollen Stunden)* o'clock I
um *(bei Uhrzeitangaben)* at I
   um halb acht at 7:30 I
   um … herum around I; round II U4, 87
   Um wie viel Uhr? What time? I
umarmen to hug I
(sich) **umdrehen** to turn round II U5, 104
Umfrage survey I
Umgebung set II AC4, 113
Lege/Legt … **umgedreht** hin. Put … face down. I
umgehen mit *to deal (with) II U2, 40
umher around I
umkippen *to fall over I
sich **umschauen** to explore I
umsteigen (in) to change (onto) II U2, 39
umziehen to move (house) II U5, 94
und and I
unfair unfair II U3, 58
Unfall accident II U3, 55
unfreundlich unfriendly II U1, 28
ungefähr about I
ungefährlich safe II U2, 42
Ungeheuer monster I
unglaublich amazing II U1, 22
Unglück disaster II U4, 86
unheimlich scary II U1, 28
unhöflich rude I
Uniform uniform I
Unordnung mess II U4, 80
unrecht haben *to be wrong I
unregelmäßig irregular I
uns us I
unser/-e our I
unten downstairs II U4, 86
   nach **unten** down II U2, 48
   nach **unten** gehen *to go down I
unten below I
unter under I
im **Untergeschoss** downstairs II U4, 86
unterhalb below I
Unterhaltung conversation I
unternehmen wegen *to do about II U4, 84
hier: **Unterricht** class II AC1, 8
Unterricht lesson I

unterrichten *to teach II U3, 60
Unterrichtsstunde lesson I
Unterschied difference I
unterschiedlich different I
unterwegs out and about II U2, 44
unverschämt rude I
unwohl sick II U3, 59
Urlaub holiday I
   Seid ihr im **Urlaub**? Are you on holiday? I
   Sind Sie im **Urlaub**? Are you on holiday? I
ursprünglich originally II AC2, 34

V

Vanillepudding custard I
Vanillesoße custard I
Vater father I
etw. **verändern** make a difference II AC1, 11
Veränderung change II U5, 105
Veranstaltung event I
verärgert angry I
Verb verb I
verbessern to improve I
   sich **verbessern** to improve I
verbinden *to put through I; to join II AC1, 11; to link II U4, 88
Verbindung link II U2, 45; connection II U5, 96
Verbrechen crime II AC4, 112
Verbrecher/-in criminal II AC4, 112
verbringen *(Zeit)* *to spend II U4, 76
verdienen to earn I; to deserve II U3, 60
   Geld **verdienen** *to make money I
Verein club I; society II U5, 105
verfolgen to trace I
Vergangenheit past II U1, 13
vergeben *to forgive II U3, 65
vergessen *to forget I
vergleichen (mit) to compare (with/to) I
verhaften to arrest II U1, 17
sich **verirren** *to get lost II U5, 101
Verkauf sale II U1, 16
verkaufen *to sell I
Verkäufer/-in assistant II U3, 62
Verkäufer/-in *(auf einem Flohmarkt)* seller I
Verkehrsmittel transport II U5, 94
   öffentliche **Verkehrsmittel** public transport *(no pl)* II U2, 37
Verkleidung fancy dress II U3, 64
verlassen *to leave II U3, 58
verlegen embarrassed II U1, 13
verletzen *to hurt II U3, 58
verletzt hurt II U1, 28
Verletzung injury II U3, 60
verlieren *to lose II U3, 54
verloren gehen *to get lost II U5, 101
vermissen to miss II U5, 94
vermitteln to mediate II U4, 78
vermuten to guess I
verneint negative II U5, 92
   verneinte Form negative form I
Vernissage gallery walk I

Verpackung wrapping I
verpassen to miss II U4, 83
sich den Knöchel **verrenken** to twist your ankle II U3, 58
verrückt crazy I; mad II U4, 81
   verrückt werden *to go crazy II U4, 79
Versammlung assembly II AC1, 8
versäumen to miss II U4, 83
verschieden different I; separate II U1, 20
Verschmutzung pollution II AC1, 11
verschwenden to waste II U4, 79
verschwunden missing II U1, 17
   verschwunden sein *to be gone II U3, 65
sich **versichern** *to make sure I
versorgen to supply II U5, 100
versprechen to promise II U5, 95
sich **verständigen** to communicate II AC3, 73
Verständnis understanding II U4, 77
(sich) **verstecken** *to hide II AC4, 112
verstehen *to understand I
versuchen to try I
   Versuch es mal mit … Try … I
verursachen to cause II U3, 66
Vervollständige/Vervollständigt … Complete … I
verwenden to use I
verzeihen *to forgive II U3, 65
verzieren to decorate I
Video video II U4, 75
Videochat video chat II U2, 36
viel much I; a lot I; lots (of); a lot of I
   viel zu lernen a lot to learn I
   Viele Grüße Best wishes II U5, 97
viele many I
vielleicht maybe I
Vielvölker- multi-ethnic II AC2, 34
vier four I
   Vier plus sechs ist zehn. Four and six is ten. I
Viertel nach/vor quarter past/to I
violett purple I
Vogel bird II AC1, 8
Vogelbeobachtung birdwatching II AC1, 8
Vokabular vocabulary I
voll (von) full (of) I
Volleyball volleyball I
völlig completely II AC4, 112
vollkommen perfect I
von from; about; of I
   von … bis from … to I
vor in front of I
vor *(bei Uhrzeitangaben)* to I
vor *(zeitlich)* before I; ago II U1, 14
   vor dem Lesen pre-reading I
vorbei over II U3, 63
vorbei (an) past I
vorbereiten to prepare I
sich **vordrängeln** to jump the queue I
vorgeschichtlich prehistoric II U5, 98
vorher before II U3, 57
Vormittag morning I
vormittags in the mornings I

vormittags (Uhrzeit) a.m. I
Vorschlag suggestion I
Vorsicht! Be careful! I
vorsichtig careful II U2, 42
vorstellen to present I
  sich (etwas) vorstellen to imagine I
  Stelle/Stellt … vor. Introduce … I
Vorstellung introduction II U3, 59
vortäuschen to fake II U3, 60
Vortrag presentation I
vorüber over II U3, 63
vorüber (an) past I

W

Wache guard II AC2, 35
Wachs wax II U2, 37
wachsen *to grow II U5, 93
Wachsfigur wax figure II U2, 37
Wächter/-in guard II AC2, 35
wackelig wobbly II U2, 48
Wackelpudding jelly I
Wahl choice II U2, 44
wählen to vote I
während (+ Nomen) during (+ noun) II U1, 13
während while; as I
wahrnehmen to notice II U2, 49
wahrscheinlich probably II U2, 38
Wald forest II U1, 20
Waliser/-in Welsh II U1, 20
Walisisch Welsh II U1, 20
walisisch Welsh II U1, 20
Wand wall I
Wandern walking II U1, 20; hiking II U5, 93
wann when I
  wann immer whenever II U4, 76
warten (auf) to wait (for) I
  Warte/Wartet und denk/denkt nach. Stop and think I
  Warte ab! Wait and see! I
Warteschlange queue I
warum why I
was what I
  was für ein what I
  Was fehlt? What is missing? I
  Was hast du? What's the matter? II U5, 104
  Was ist das? What's that? I
  Was ist dein/-e Lieblings…? What's your favourite …? I
  Was ist die Regel für …? What's the rule for …? I
  Was ist los? What's the matter? II U5, 104
  Was ist mit …? What about …? I
  was man … what to … I
  was noch what else I
  was sonst what else I
  Was um alles in der Welt …? What on earth …? II U4, 79
  … was ich tun soll. … what to do. II U4, 76
waschen to wash I

sich waschen to wash I
Waschmaschine washing machine II U4, 79
Wasser water I
Wasserrutsche water slide I
Wau! Woof! I
Webseite site II U4, 76
Website website I
Wechsel change II U5, 105
wechseln to change II U4, 74
  Wechselt euch ab. Take turns. I
Weg way I
  im Weg sein/stehen *to be in the way I
  im Weg stehen *to get in the way II U3, 64
weg away I
  weg sein *to be gone II U3, 65
  Es ist weg. It's gone. II U2, 48
wegen because of II U3, 65; for II U4, 75
wegnehmen *to take I
wegrennen *to run away I
wegwerfen *to throw away I
weh tun *to hurt II U3, 58
Weide field II U1, 22
Weihnachten Christmas I
weil because I
eine Weile a while II U2, 40
Wein wine I
auf andere Weise in other ways II U4, 81
weiß white I
weit far II U2, 41; wide II U5, 93
weitere more; other I
weiterführen *to go on I
weitergeben to pass (on) I
weitergehen *to go on I
weitermachen *to go on I
welche/-r/-s what; which I
  Welche Farbe hat …? What colour is …? I
  Welche … sind es? What are …? I
Welle wave I
Welt world I
  Was um alles in der Welt …? What on earth …? II U4, 79
wem who I
wen who I
  Für wen …? Who … for? I
wenden to turn round II U5, 104
  sich wenden an to turn to II U5, 105
Wendung expression II AC3, 73
ein wenig a little I; a bit II U1, 22
wenige a few I; few II U1, 22
wenn when; if I
wer who I
  Wer ist dabei? Who's in? II U3, 56
  Wer ist es? Who is it? I
  Wer macht mit? Who's in? II U3, 56
Werbespruch slogan II AC1, 11
werden *to become II U2, 42; *to get II U5, 104
werfen (nach) *to throw (at) I
Werkzeug tool II U5, 105
wert sein *to be worth I
West- west I
Westen west I

westeuropäische Zeit Greenwich Mean Time (= GMT) I
Wettbewerb contest I; competition II AC1, 9
ich wette I bet II U2, 40
Wetter weather I
Wettervorhersage weather forecast II U5, 96
Wettkampf contest I
Wettlauf race II U3, 54
wichtig important I
  wichtig nehmen to care (about) II U4, 77
wie like I
wie as II AC1, 11
wie how I
  Wie viele …? How many …? I
  Wie alt bist du? How old are you? I
  Wie alt sind Sie? How old are you? I
  wie der Mann aussah what the man looked like II U1, 17
  Wie geht es dir/euch/Ihnen? How are you? I
  Wie heißen Sie? What's your name? I
  Wie heißt du? What's your name? I
  Wie man … How to … I
  Wie spät ist es? What's the time? I
  Wie viel (kostet/kosten) …? How much is/are …? I
  Wie viel Uhr ist es? What's the time? I
  Wie wär's mit …? What about …? I
wieder again I
Wiederaufnehmen pick-up I
auf Wiedersehen goodbye I
wiederverwerten to recycle II AC1, 11
Wiese field II U1, 22
wild wild II U5, 98
Willkommen! Welcome! II U1, 22
willkommen heißen to welcome II AC1, 11
Wind wind II U5, 104
Windsurfen windsurfing II U5, 93
wir we I
  Wir sind aus … We're from … I
wirklich real II U1, 14
wirklich really I
wissen *to know I
  Du weißt, wie man … You know how to … I
  Ich weiß (es) nicht! I don't know! I
  Ihr wisst, wie man … You know how to … I
Witz joke I
witzig funny; fun I
wo where I
Woche week I
Wochenende weekend I
  am Wochenende at the weekend I
Wochentag weekday II U4, 84
Woher …? Where … from? I
wohin where I
  … wohin ich gehen kann. … where to go. II U2, 40
Wohlfahrt charity I
wohltätige Zwecke charity I

Wohltätigkeitsverein charity **I**
wohnen to live **I**
   wohnen bei to stay with **II U2**, 38
Wohnung flat **I**
Wohnzimmer living room **I**
Wolke cloud **II U5**, 104
wollen to want (to) **I**
Workshop workshop **I**
Wort word **I**
   die Kraft der **Wörter** *(Wortschatzübung)* Word power **I**
Wörterbuch dictionary **I**
Wörternetz *(eine Art Schaubild)* mind map **I**
Wortschatz vocabulary **I**
Wortschlange word snake **I**
Wortstellung word order **I**
Worum geht es in/im …? What is … about? **I**
Wow! Wow! **I**
wunderbar beautiful; wonderful **II U5**, 94
Wunsch wish **I**
sich etwas wünschen *to make a wish **I**
würde/-st/-n/-t gern would like **I**
   würde/-st/-n/-t sehr gern would love **I**
   Ich **würde** gern … I'd like to … *(= I would like to)* **I**
Würfle/Würfelt mit zwei Würfeln. Roll two dice. **I**
Wurm worm **I**
wusch whoosh **I**
wütend angry **I**

Z

z.B. *(= zum Beispiel)* e.g. *(= for example)* **I**
Zahl number **I**
zählen (auf) to count (on) **I**
Zauber- magical **II AC4**, 112
Zauberer wizard **II AC4**, 112

auf Zehenspitzen gehen to tiptoe **II U1**, 23
zehn ten **I**
   Vier plus sechs ist **zehn**. Four and six is ten. **I**
zehnmal ten times **I**
Zeichen sign **II U1**, 22
zeichnen *to draw **I**
Zeichnung drawing **I**
zeigen to show **I**
   Zeige/Zeigt auf … Point to … **I**
   Zeige/Zeigt darauf. Point. **I**
Zeile line **I**
Zeit time **I**
   (**Zeit**) brauchen *to take **II U4**, 79
   zur selben **Zeit** at the same time **I**
   die ganze **Zeit** all the time **II U2**, 48
   Es ist **Zeit** aufzustehen! Time to get up! **I**
Zeitschrift magazine **I**
Zeitstrahl time line **I**
Zelten camping **II U4**, 83
zelten to camp **II U5**, 106
zentral central **II U2**, 48
Zentral- central **II U2**, 48
hier: Zentrum heart **II U2**, 48
Zentrum centre **I**
zerbrechen *to break **I**
zerstören to ruin **II U3**, 65
Zeug stuff **I**
Zeuge/Zeugin witness **II U3**, 61
ziehen to pull **I**
Ziel goal **I**
Ziellinie finish line **II U3**, 65
Zimmer room **I**
Zimmergenosse/Zimmergenossin roommate **I**
Zinn tin **II U5**, 98
Zitrone lemon **II U1**, 28
Zoo zoo **II U2**, 39
zornig angry **I**

zu too **I**
   Zu dumm! Too bad! **I**
zu to **I**
   zu Hause at home **I**
zubereiten to prepare **I**
zuerst first **I**; at first **II U2**, 49
Zug train **I**
Zuhause home **I**
zuhören to listen (to) **I**
   Hör/Hört noch einmal **zu**. Listen again. **I**
Zuhörer/-in listener **II U3**, 61
zujubeln to cheer **II U3**, 58
Zukunft future **II U5**, 93
zum Beispiel for example **II AC3**, 73
zumachen to close **I**
zunächst at first **II U2**, 49
zuordnen to match **I**
zupassen to pass **II U3**, 54
zurück back **I**
zurückfahren to return **II U5**, 96
zurückgehen auf *to go right back to **II U5**, 104
zurückkehren to return **II U5**, 96
hier: zurückschrecken to jump back **II U2**, 43
zurückspringen to jump back **II U2**, 43
zusammen together **I**
zusätzlich extra **I**; additional **II AC1**, 8
zuschauen to watch **I**
zuspielen to pass **II U3**, 54
Zutat ingredient **II AC4**, 112
zuvor before **II U3**, 57
sich zuwenden to turn to **II U5**, 105
zwei two **I**
zweite/-r/-s second **I**
Zwilling twin **II U5**, 105
Zwillings- twin **II U5**, 105
zwischen between **I**
zwölf twelve **I**;

In the classroom

Die Wörter und Ausdrücke auf diesen Seiten musst du nicht auswendig lernen. Aber in vielen Situationen im Klassenzimmer wirst du sie nützlich finden!

Asking for help and information

Can you help me, please?	Kannst du / Können Sie mir bitte helfen?
How do you do this exercise?	Wie macht man diese Übung?
How do you spell … , please?	Wie schreibt man … , bitte?
Is this right? I'm not sure.	Ist das richtig? Ich bin mir nicht sicher.
Is it OK to …?	Ist es in Ordnung, wenn ich / wir …?
Is it true or false?	Ist das richtig oder falsch?
Sorry, I don't know. Ask …	Tut mir leid, das weiß ich nicht. Frag …
Sorry. Can you say that again, please?	Wie bitte? Können Sie das bitte wiederholen?
What does that mean?	Was bedeutet das?
What's for homework?	Was haben wir als Hausaufgabe auf?
What's that in English / German?	Was heißt das auf Englisch / Deutsch?

Vocabulary for instructions and activities

Act (out) one of the scenes. / Act (out) the dialogues.	Spiele eine der Szenen. / Spiele die Dialoge.
Add more words / ideas.	Füge weitere Wörter / Ideen hinzu.
Ask your partner questions.	Stelle deinem Partner / deiner Partnerin Fragen.
Answer your partner's questions.	Beantworte die Fragen deines Partners / deiner Partnerin.
Check your partner's text.	Überprüfe den Text deines Partners / deiner Partnerin.
Collect ideas.	Sammle Ideen.
Compare English and German.	Vergleiche das Englische und Deutsche.
Complete the answers.	Vervollständige die Antworten.
Copy the grid / the mind map.	Schreibe die Tabelle / das Wörternetz ab.
Correct the wrong sentences.	Korrigiere die falschen Sätze.
Describe your room.	Beschreibe dein Zimmer.

Decide who writes which part.	Entscheidet, wer welchen Teil schreibt.
Discuss different ideas.	Diskutiert verschiedene Ideen.
Draw a picture.	Zeichne ein Bild.
Exchange your flyers / questions.	Tauscht eure Flyer / Fragen untereinander aus.
Explain your answer. / Explain why.	Erkläre deine Antwort. / Erkläre warum.
Fill in your grid / the form.	Fülle deine Tabelle / das Formular aus.
Find somebody who …	Finde jemanden, der …
Find the rule / the right word order.	Finde die Regel / die richtige Wortstellung.
Finish your brochure.	Stelle deine Broschüre fertig.
Form expert groups.	Bildet Expertengruppen.
Get organised.	Organisiert euch.
Go back to your home group.	Gehe zurück zu deiner ersten Gruppe.
Guess the new words.	Errate die neuen Wörter.
Imagine you're one of the people in the story.	Stelle dir vor, du bist eine der Personen in der Geschichte.
Improve your text / part of the report.	Verbessere deinen Text / Teil des Berichts.
Learn your text by heart.	Lerne deinen Text auswendig.
Listen to the sentences / the dialogue.	Höre dir die Sätze / den Dialog an.
Look at the picture / the examples.	Schau dir das Bild / die Beispiele an.
Look up the words.	Schlage die Wörter nach.
Make a poster / a grid / a mind map.	Fertige ein Poster / eine Tabelle / ein Wörternetz an.
Match the sentence parts.	Ordne die Satzteile einander zu.
Name more sports.	Nenne mehr Sportarten.
Note down what is missing.	Notiere, was fehlt.
Peer-edit each other's work.	Kontrolliert eure Arbeiten gegenseitig.
Plan the scenes.	Plane die Szenen.
Record your final report / dialogue.	Nehmt euren fertigen Bericht / Dialog auf.
Scan the text for details.	Suche den Text nach Details ab.
Share the information with your partner.	Teile die Informationen mit deinem Partner / deiner Partnerin.
Skim the text for the gist.	Überfliege den Text und finde die wichtigsten Aussagen.
Sum up what happens in the story.	Fasse zusammen, was in der Geschichte passiert.
Practise your scenes / the dialogues.	Übe deine Szenen / die Dialoge.
Present the information from your text.	Präsentiere die Informationen aus deinem Text.
Put in the correct forms.	Setze die richtigen Formen ein.
Read your text aloud.	Lies deinen Text laut vor.
Repeat the sentences / the dialogues.	Wiederhole die Sätze / die Dialoge.
Say the words / the sounds.	Sage die Wörter / die Laute.
Show your brochure.	Zeige deine Broschüre.
Swap roles.	Tauscht die Rollen.
Take a card.	Nimm eine Karte.

Take notes.	Mache dir Notizen.
Take turns.	Wechselt euch ab.
Talk with your partner.	Sprich mit deinem Partner / deiner Partnerin.
Tell your partner about your hobby.	Erzähle deinem Partner / deiner Partnerin von deinem Hobby.
Think of ideas for …	Überlege dir Ideen für …
Trade your part with somebody else.	Tausche deinen Teil mit jemandem.
Translate the words / sentences.	Übersetze die Wörter / Sätze.
Use the ideas / the vocabulary.	Verwende die Ideen / die Vokabeln.
Work with a partner or in a group.	Arbeite mit einem Partner / einer Partnerin oder in einer Gruppe.
Write dialogues / a short text / a reply.	Schreibe Dialoge / einen kurzen Text / eine Antwort.
Write about your friends.	Schreibe über deine Freunde.
Write down school words.	Schreibe Wörter zum Thema „Schule" auf.

Useful words

activity – Aktivität	presentation – Präsentation; Vortrag
answer – Antwort	prompt card – Rollenkarte
class display – Ausstellung in der Klasse	puzzle – Rätsel; Puzzle
collocation – Wortverbindung	pros and cons – Vor- und Nachteile
description – Beschreibung	question – Frage
dialogue – Dialog	quiz – Quiz; Rätsel
dice – Würfel	quote – Zitat
draft – Entwurf; Konzept	report – Bericht
drawing – Zeichnung	revision – Wiederholung
example – Beispiel	rhyme – Reim
fact – Tatsache; Fakt	role play – Rollenspiel
folder – Ordner; Mappe	rule – Regel
game – Spiel	scene – Szene
grid – Gitter; Tabelle; Raster	signal word – Signalwort
heading – Überschrift	slogan – Slogan; Werbespruch
information – Information(en)	speech bubble – Sprechblase
key word – Schlüsselwort	story – Geschichte; Erzählung
list – Liste	task – Aufgabe
mind map – Wörternetz	theme – Thema
order – Reihenfolge	title – Titel; Überschrift
perspective – Perspektive	unit – Lektion; Kapitel
phrase – Redewendung; Ausdruck	useful phrases – nützliche Ausdrücke
picture story – Bildergeschichte	vocabulary – Vokabular; Wortschatz
point of view – Standpunkt; Ansicht	word cloud – Wörterwolke

Find more online:
mr5h4g

Irregular verbs

- ■ ■ ■ Grundform, *simple past* und *past participle* sind identisch
- ■ ● ● Grundform unterscheidet sich vom *simple past* und *past participle*
- ■ ● ■ Grundform und *past participle* sind identisch, nur das *simple past* hat eine andere Form
- ■ ● ▲ Grundform, *simple past* und *past participle* haben alle eine andere Form

■ Grundform	■ simple past	■ past participle	Deutsch
cost [kɒst]	cost [kɒst]	cost [kɒst]	kosten
cut [kʌt]	cut [kʌt]	cut [kʌt]	schneiden
hit [hɪt]	hit [hɪt]	hit [hɪt]	schlagen, treffen
hurt [hɜ:t]	hurt [hɜ:t]	hurt [hɜ:t]	verletzen, sich weh tun
let [let]	let [let]	let [let]	lassen
put [pʊt]	put [pʊt]	put [pʊt]	legen, setzen, stellen
set up ['set ˌʌp]	set up ['set ˌʌp]	set up ['set ˌʌp]	erbauen, errichten

■ Grundform	● simple past	● past participle	Deutsch
bring [brɪŋ]	brought [brɔ:t]	brought [brɔ:t]	(mit)bringen
build [bɪld]	built [bɪlt]	built [bɪlt]	bauen
buy [baɪ]	bought [bɔ:t]	bought [bɔ:t]	kaufen
feel [fi:l]	felt [felt]	felt [felt]	fühlen
find [faɪnd]	found [faʊnd]	found [faʊnd]	finden
get [get]	got [gɒt]	got [gɒt]	bekommen, erhalten
have [hæv]	had [hæd]	had [hæd]	haben
hear [hɪə]	heard [hɜ:d]	heard [hɜ:d]	hören
hold [həʊld]	held [held]	held [held]	halten
keep [ki:p]	kept [kept]	kept [kept]	(auf)bewahren, behalten
learn [lɜ:n]	learned [lɜ:nd] / learnt [lɜ:nt]	learned [lɜ:nd] / learnt [lɜ:nt]	lernen
leave [li:v]	left [left]	left [left]	(ver)lassen
make [meɪk]	made [meɪd]	made [meɪd]	machen, tun
meet [mi:t]	met [met]	met [met]	treffen
pay [peɪ]	paid [peɪd]	paid [peɪd]	(be)zahlen
read [ri:d]	read [red]	read [red]	lesen
retell [ˌri:'tel]	retold [ˌri:'təʊld]	retold [ˌri:'təʊld]	nacherzählen
say [seɪ]	said [sed]	said [sed]	sagen
sell [sel]	sold [səʊld]	sold [səʊld]	verkaufen
send [send]	sent [sent]	sent [sent]	senden, verschicken
sit [sɪt]	sat [sæt]	sat [sæt]	sitzen
sleep [sli:p]	slept [slept]	slept [slept]	schlafen
spell [spel]	spelt [spelt]	spelt [spelt]	buchstabieren

spend [spend]	spent [spent]	spent [spent]	ausgeben, verbringen
stand (up) [stænd]	stood (up) [stʊd]	stood (up) [stʊd]	(auf)stehen
tell [tel]	told [təʊld]	told [təʊld]	erzählen
think [θɪŋk]	thought [θɔːt]	thought [θɔːt]	(nach)denken, glauben
understand [ˌʌndəˈstænd]	understood [ˌʌndəˈstʊd]	understood [ˌʌndəˈstʊd]	verstehen
win [wɪn]	won [wʌn]	won [wʌn]	gewinnen, siegen

■ Grundform	● simple past	■ past participle	Deutsch
become [bɪˈkʌm]	became [bɪˈkeɪm]	become [bɪˈkʌm]	werden
come [kʌm]	came [keɪm]	come [kʌm]	kommen
run [rʌn]	ran [ræn]	run [rʌn]	laufen, rennen

■ Grundform	● simple past	▲ past participle	Deutsch
be [biː]	was / were [wɒz / wɜː]	been [biːn]	sein
blow (out) [bləʊ]	blew [bluː]	blown [bləʊn]	(aus)blasen, (aus)pusten
break [breɪk]	broke [brəʊk]	broken [ˈbrəʊkn]	(zer)brechen, kaputt machen
choose [tʃuːz]	chose [tʃəʊz]	chosen [tʃəʊzn]	(aus)wählen
do [duː]	did [dɪd]	done [dʌn]	machen, tun
draw [drɔː]	drew [druː]	drawn [drɔːn]	zeichnen
drink [drɪŋk]	drank [dræŋk]	drunk [drʌŋk]	trinken
eat [iːt]	ate [et]	eaten [iːtn]	essen
fall [fɔːl]	fell [fel]	fallen [ˈfɔːlən]	fallen
fly [flaɪ]	flew [fluː]	flown [fləʊn]	fliegen
forget [fəˈget]	forgot [fəˈgɒt]	forgotten [fəˈgɒtn]	vergessen
give [gɪv]	gave [geɪv]	given [ˈgɪvn]	geben
go [gəʊ]	went [went]	gone [gɒn]	gehen, fahren
know [nəʊ]	knew [njuː]	known [nəʊn]	kennen, wissen
see [siː]	saw [sɔː]	seen [siːn]	sehen
show [ʃəʊ]	showed [ʃəʊd]	shown [ʃəʊn]	zeigen
sing [sɪŋ]	sang [sæŋ]	sung [sʌŋ]	singen
speak [spiːk]	spoke [spəʊk]	spoken [ˈspəʊkn]	sprechen
swim [swɪm]	swam [swæm]	swum [swʌm]	schwimmen
take [teɪk]	took [tʊk]	taken [ˈteɪkn]	nehmen
throw [θrəʊ]	threw [θruː]	thrown [θrəʊn]	werfen
wear [weə]	wore [wɔː]	worn [wɔːn]	anhaben, tragen
write [raɪt]	wrote [rəʊt]	written [ˈrɪtn]	schreiben

Check-out solutions

Unit 1 Page 29

Exercise 1

They talked about the 'dreams' page. / They put the sports pages together. / They looked at Jay's ideas for the music pages. / They collected ideas for the puzzles page. / They took a photo of the yearbook team. / They made a list of jobs for next week.

Exercise 2

1. went
2. was
3. wasn't
4. invited
5. did you go
6. did
7. were
8. was
9. was
10. didn't stay

Exercise 3

1. When did you get up this morning?
2. Where did you go?
3. What did you see?
4. Why did your classmates laugh at you?

Exercise 4

1. Luke's dog Sherlock is **the craziest** animal in England. There's nothing **funnier** than when he chases his tail. It's always **faster** than he is!
2. The **cutest** pets for Holly are her two guinea pigs. Mr Fluff likes to explore. He thinks a trip in a bag is **more interesting** than a game on the floor! Honey isn't **as brave as** Mr Fluff.
3. Cats are **the most popular** pets in the class. Dave's cat Sid brings presents for the family. Some presents are **better** than others. The **worst** thing for Dave is a mouse in his bed!

Unit 2 Page 51

Exercise 1

1. The Frasers are going to have a picnic. / The Frasers are going to go on a picnic.
2. Luke and Sherlock are going to play ball in the park. / Luke and Sherlock are going to play in the park.
3. Mr and Mrs Azad are going to visit / see / go to the Tower of London.
4. Holly is going to go (inline) skating. / Holly is going to have fun on her skates.
5. Amir is going to take (lots of) photos / pictures.
6. Shahid is going to meet someone / his girlfriend / a friend (somewhere).

Exercise 2

1. anybody
2. someone
3. everybody
4. something
5. somewhere
6. everything
7. anywhere
8. nothing

Exercise 3

Lösungsvorschlag:
You take the S1 to Filderstadt. You change at Hauptbahnhof and take the U7 to Ostfildern. It's seven stops to Ruhbank. You get off at Ruhbank. / You get off there. From Ruhbank you walk to the Fernsehturm for about 11 minutes.

Unit 3 Page 67

Exercise 1

1 c)
2 e)
3 b)
4 a)
5 f)
6 d)

Exercise 2

1. Luke: Have you found any information on the internet yet?
   Dave: Yes, I have. I've already used some (information) in the report.
2. Luke: Has Jay drawn any mangas for his report (yet)?
   Dave: Yes, he has. He has created great new characters.
3. Dave: Have you seen the two new manga comics yet?
   Luke: Yes, I have. I've already finished one of them.
4. Luke: Have you seen Olivia today?
   Dave: No, I haven't. But I've just sent her a text.
5. Dave: Has Holly written about guinea pigs?
   Luke: I hope not! She's written about guinea pigs many times before.
6. Dave: Have you gone to the park with Sherlock yet?
   Luke: No, I haven't. But Irina has just gone for a walk with him.

Exercise 3

I love football. I think it's the best **game** in the world! I **watch** every **match** of my favourite team, the Wellsey. Do you want to **see** my new poster of the best player ever, Adriano Donaldo? He scores lots of goals with his head because he's very **tall**. He even **got** the **highest** score of three head goals in one match. My dream is to **become** a football star like him.

Unit 4 Page 89

Exercise 1

1 e) When my dad wants to relax, he watches football on TV.
2 d) When I want to know the words of a song I've heard, I look it up on the internet.
3 b) When my mum works away from home, she sends me text messages.
4 a) When I want to tell all my friends how great my holiday is, I post it on my social network profile.
5 c) When my sister wants to know about the coolest new clothes, she reads girls' magazines.

Exercise 2

1. Lösungsvorschlag:
   A: I really hurt my foot. I hope it isn't broken. / I think it could be broken.
   B: Does it really hurt?
   A: Yes, it does.
   B: Well, you should go to the doctor's. / Why don't you go to the doctor's?
   A: Yes, maybe you're right.

2. Lösungsvorschlag:
   A: I can't believe I missed my favourite show last night!
   B: Well, you could watch it on the internet. / Why don't you watch it on the internet?
   A: The internet doesn't always have everything.
   B: Have you tried looking yet?
   A: Well, no.

3. Lösungsvorschlag:
   A: Oh no, something is wrong with my bike!
   B: What's the problem?
   A: I don't know.
   B: Have you tried looking on the internet yet? / Have you asked Mum and Dad / Ben / … for help?

4. Lösungsvorschlag:
   A: I can't believe she posted those photos – they're really embarrassing.
   B: Have you talked to her yet?
   A: Yes, I have. She doesn't think they're embarrassing. And she thinks she looks really good in them.
   B: Well, why don't you tell her to cut you off the photos?
   A: OK, that's a good idea.

5. Lösungsvorschlag:
   A: I can't use my phone for a week because my parents are really angry with me.
   B: Well, maybe you should tell them that you're sorry.
   A: I've already told them, but they still took my phone.
   B: Just use my phone when you need it.

Exercise 3

1. Das Handy meines Bruders ist sehr alt, ich glaube, er muss (sich) ein neues kaufen.
2. Er hat Glück, weil er nicht selbst dafür bezahlen muss – er hat in zwei Monaten Geburtstag.
3. Ich habe noch mehr Glück, weil ich nicht so lange zu warten brauche / nicht so lange warten muss. Ich kann das neue Smartphone meines Vaters haben!
4. Aber ich darf meinem Bruder nichts (davon) erzählen – er kann sehr eifersüchtig sein.

Unit 5   Page 107

Exercise 1

1. will be	7. won't rain
2. will be	8. will be
3. won't be	9. will change
4. will be	10. will move in
5. will get	11. will start
6. will be	

Exercise 2

2. I have to work late today. – No problem. We'll cook dinner for you.
3. I didn't do my homework. – Too bad! Mum will say you can't play on your computer.
4. Hurry up! The train leaves in one hour. – Don't worry, it's not far to the station. We won't be late.
5. Let's book the train tickets now. Tomorrow they'll be more expensive.

Exercise 3

1. Jamie says **he knows** about the Celts from the Asterix stories. They're **his** favourite comics.
2. Irina tells me **I must take** some Celtic souvenirs! **She loves** everything Celtic.
3. My dad says Sherlock is really missing **me**! He must **come** with **me** next time.
4. Mum says / promises the whole family will go to Cornwall next year. **She's** going to make a list of places to visit when **I'm** back home.

Grammar solutions

Unit 1

G1 Two years ago we raised lots of money.

Dear Olivia,
Thank you for your e-mail and the photos. I like them a lot.
You **wanted** to know about our charity event. Well, last month we **organised** an event in the park and we **planned** lots of activities. First there **were** games for students, parents and teachers. After that we **sold** cakes. In the afternoon the students in Year 7 **did** some really cool tricks. And then it **was** the turn of the students in Year 8. They **created** a comedy show. The girls **wanted** to look funny so they **painted** their faces and **wore** some funny costumes too. In the evening the school band **sang** in the park – lots of people **came** to listen. Michael **was** the real star of their show. He **did** some cool moves!
We **raised** 400 euros in just one day!
Write soon.
Pia

G2 How did they know?

Lösungsvorschlag:
How old was he? – He was about twenty years old.
When did you see him? – I saw him at 10 o'clock.
Where did you see him? – I saw him in front of the sports shop in Trafalgar Road.
Did you see what he took from the shop? – Well, he had two bags full of T-shirts and shoes.
Was he alone? – Yes, he was.

G3 The police didn't know what the man looked like.

Man arrested
Greenwich. On 4th September a young man **broke into** a sports shop in Trafalgar Road. Yesterday the police **arrested** him. They **didn't know** what he **looked** like at first. But then they **got** an anonymous phone call. The caller **didn't give** them much information, but she **gave** them an address in Greenwich. When the police **got to** the house, two women **were** there but the man **wasn't**. So they **waited** till he **came** home and then they **arrested** him – he **didn't try** to run away. The police **found** the sports shoes and the T-shirts in the loft, but they **didn't find** the bike.

G4 An adventure course helps students to be more confident.

a) big – bigger – the biggest
bad – worse – the worst
happy – happier – the happiest
important – more important – the most important

b) 1. Luke is tall. Holly is taller. But Olivia is the tallest of the three.
2. The red car is expensive. The blue car is more expensive. But the black car is the most expensive of the three.
3. Hook Lane is a busy road. King's Street is busier. But London Road is the busiest of the three.
4. Luke has got a good idea. Holly's idea is better. But Dave has got the best idea of the three.

G5 Outdoor activities are as important as lessons in the classroom.

Lösungsvorschlag:
The Rhine is longer than the Spree/Oder.
The Spree is shorter than the Oder/Rhine.
Düsseldorf is as big as Stuttgart.
Cologne is bigger than Düsseldorf/Stuttgart.
The Feldberg is the highest mountain. It is higher than the Brocken/the Großer Arber.
The Großer Arber is about as high as the Feldberg.
The Saarland is the smallest state/region. It is smaller than Hesse/Saxony.
Hesse is bigger than Saxony.

Unit 2

G6 It's going to be fun.

Jay is going to go to Covent Garden. He's going to listen to the buskers there.
Amir is going to send/write a postcard home.
Olivia and Holly aren't going to see/visit Brick Lane with its street art/graffiti.
Shahid is going to go to a café with his girlfriend.
Mrs Azad isn't going to go shopping/to the supermarket.
Mr Azad is going to wash his car.

G7 It's something important.

Amir: Listen, **everybody**. I want to buy a little present for my aunt to say 'thank you'. Is there a good shop **anywhere**?
Olivia: What are you thinking of?
Amir: Well, it must be **something** special, but it mustn't be **anything** expensive.
Jay: **Everything** is expensive in London!
Holly: That's not true! I know a good shop where **nothing** costs more than £10.
Amir: OK. Let's go there and see if we can find **something** for her.

Unit 3

G8 Have you ever run in a marathon?

Lösungsvorschlag:
a) 1. Have you prepared for Sports Day yet?
2. Have you bought new sports shoes yet?
3. Have you already started eating healthy food?
4. Have you ever hurt your foot?
5. Have you found a name for your team yet?

b) 2. Have you bought new sports shoes yet?
- – No, I haven't. I don't need any new shoes. My old ones/ shoes are OK.
- – Yes, I have. I've just bought some new shoes. Look, they are in this bag.

3. Have you already started eating healthy food?
- – Yes, I have. I've already eaten two apples today.

4. Have you ever hurt your foot?
- – Yes, I have. I've hurt my leg twice/two times.
- – No, I haven't.

5. Have you found a name for your team yet?
- – Yes, I have. But I'm not going to tell you.
- – No, I haven't found a nice name yet.

Unit 4

G9   I'm writing to you because I need your advice.

Joe: I like your magazine **because** it's always got the interesting news on my favourite stars in it.

Ginny: I buy *TeenLife* **as soon as/when** I get my pocket money from my parents. I love it!

Michael: The concert photos are fantastic. When I look at them, it's **like** I'm there.

Lisa: **Whenever/When** I read Ruby's advice, I think she really understands our problems.

Sheila: **After** I tried the make-up in last week's magazine, I'm not going to buy *TeenLife* again! It looked awful on my face.

G10   I must fix it before your mum comes home.

You have to arrive early.
You needn't bring your own computer.
You must pay before the course starts.
You needn't / don't have to wear a uniform.
They can do fun things with computers.
Students can't / mustn't eat in computer room.
Students must / have to keep the computer room clean.

G11   You could look at a forum for help.

Lösungsvorschlag:
1. You should say sorry (to her). / You could ask if she needs help. / You should be more careful when you play netball.
2. You should tell Dave. / You could buy him a new book. / You could ask how much the book was and give him the money.
3. You shouldn't pull him out from under the bed. / You could put some food in front of the bed. / You could leave a gap between the bed and the wall. Then it's easier to pick him up.
4. You should say sorry (to her). / You could buy her new flowers for her garden. / Next time if you are not sure, you should ask her first.

Unit 5

G12   I'll miss you so much!

1. Olivia: I hope Dave **will love** his new school.
2. Holly: I'm sure the Prestons **will visit** Granny Rose and Aunt Frances in London soon.
3. Luke: I don't think the new home **will be** a problem for Sid. He **will make** new cat friends quickly. He **won't get bored**!
4. Gwen: I hope Dave **won't forget** us.

G13   He says the landscape in Cornwall is very wild.

Lou says (that) she loves climbing.
Tony tells me (that) his homework is difficult.
They say (that) they're winning that race.
Tony says (that) it's his iPod.

Text- und Liedquellen:
S.30 From *Middle School: How I Got Lost in London* by James Patterson. Published by Random House Children's Publishers. Reprinted by permission of the Random House Group Ltd.; **S.52** Excerpt from *The Copper Treasure* by Melvin Burgess, A & C Black Publishers Ltd, London, 1999/2002 © Melvin Burgess (adapted); **S.59** Excerpt from the brochure *Erkennen – Bewerten – Handeln: Zur Gesundheit von Kindern und Jugendlichen in Deutschland*, Robert Koch-Institut, Bundeszentrale für gesundheitliche Aufklärung, p. 33, Berlin und Köln, 2008 © Robert Koch-Institut; **S.68** „The Summer Table" from WONDER by R. J. Palacio, copyright © 2012 by R.J. Palacio. Reprinted by permission of R.J. Palacio and Alfred A. Knopf, an imprint of Random House Childrens's Books, a division of Random House LLC. All rights reserved; **S.78** „Friends" Text: Armato, Antonina/Dione, Aura marie/ James, Tim/Jost, David © Akashic Field Music/Antonina Songs/Good Songs Publishing A/S/ Universal/MCA Music Publishing GmbH, Berlin/Universal Music Publishing GmbH, Berlin/Rolf Budde Musikverlag GmbH, Berlin/Jost Music Publisching David Jost, Berlin; **S.90** Excerpt from *Ratburger* by David Walliams, HarperCollins Children's Books, a division of HarperCollins Publishers Ltd, London, 2012 © David Walliams 2012 (adapted); **S.100** From www.poetryarchive. org/poem/romans-britain, © Judith Nicholls; **S.108** Excerpt from „A Harp on the Water" from *Welsh Legends and Folktales* by Gwyn Jones (ed.), Oxford University Press, 1955 (adapted); **S.133** Excerpt from *Ratburger* by David Walliams, HarperCollins Children's Books, a division of HarperCollins Publishers Ltd, London, 2012 © David Walliams 2012 (adapted)

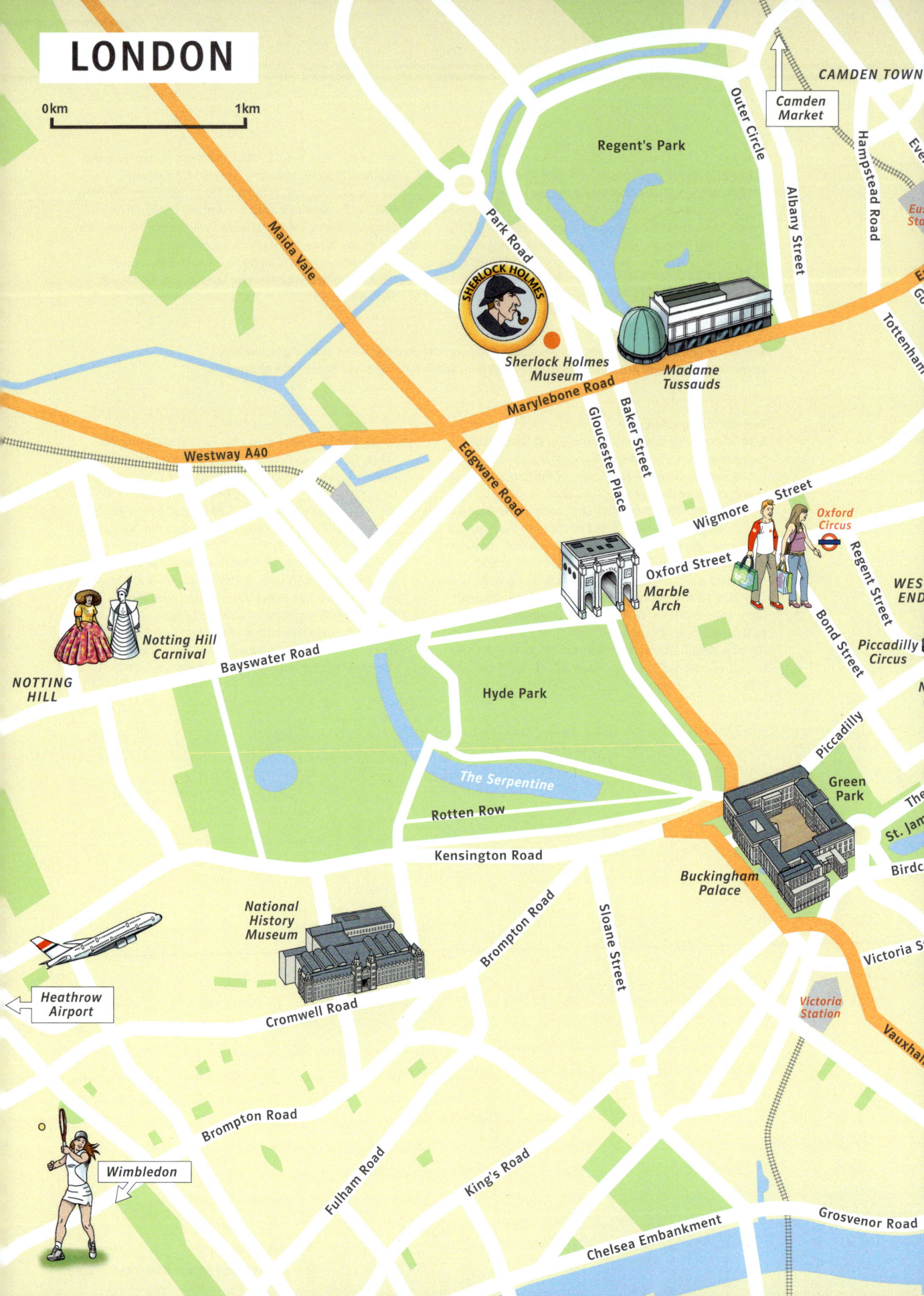

LONDON

0km 1km

CAMDEN TOWN

Camden Market

Regent's Park

Outer Circle

Hampstead Road

Albany Street

Maida Vale

Park Road

Eus
Sta

El
Go

Tottenham

Westway A40

Edgware Road

Marylebone Road

SHERLOCK HOLMES

Sherlock Holmes
Museum

Madame
Tussauds

Baker Street

Gloucester Place

Wigmore Street

Oxford Circus

Regent Street

WEST
END

Oxford Street

Marble
Arch

Bond Street

Piccadilly
Circus

Notting Hill
Carnival

NOTTING
HILL

Bayswater Road

Hyde Park

The Serpentine

Rotten Row

Kensington Road

Piccadilly

Green
Park

The

St. Jam

Birdca

National
History
Museum

Brompton Road

Sloane Street

Buckingham
Palace

Victoria St

Heathrow
Airport

Cromwell Road

Victoria
Station

Vauxhall

Brompton Road

Fulham Road

King's Road

Wimbledon

Chelsea Embankment

Grosvenor Road

Highbury

King's Cross Station

St. Pancras Station

City Road

Old Street

Great Eastern St.

Woburn Place

Gray's Inn Road

Farringdon Road

Clerkenwell Road

Bloomsbury St.

British Museum

City of London

Brick Lane

High Holborn

London Wall

Charing Cross Road

Avenue

Covent Garden

Covent Garden

Fleet Street

St. Paul's Cathedral

Tower of London

Shaftesbury Road

Strand

Embankment

Millennium Bridge

Blackfriars Bridge

Southwark Bridge

Trafalgar Square

Victoria

London Eye

Tate Modern

Southwark Street

Globe Theatre

The Shard

Tower Bridge

Horse Guards

London Dungeon

the London Dungeon

Waterloo Station

Blackfriars Road

SOUTHWARK

Docklands

Thames Barrier

Houses of Parliament

Westminster Bridge

Waterloo Road

Borough High Street

Westminster Abbey

River Thames

TMINSTER

Lambeth Bridge

Millbank

Albert Embankment

Vauxhall Bridge

GREENWICH

Mudchute Farm

Trinity Hospital

Thames

Swimming Pool (Arches Leisure Centre)

London

Greenwich

Cutty Sark

Playground

GREENWICH MARKET

Boating Lake

Greenwich Station

Fan Museum

Planetarium

Royal Observatory

Vanbrugh Castle

Tennis Court

Deer Park

Rose Garden

Thomas Tallis School

THE BRITISH ISLES

ORKNEY ISLANDS

ER RIDES

Highlands

Inverness

Loch Ness

▲ Ben Nevis

SCOTLAND

Aberdeen

0   100   200   300 km
0   100   200 miles

Firth of Forth

Glasgow

Edinburgh

Edinburgh Castle

Hadrian's Wall

Newcastle

Tyne

Giant's Causeway

HERN IRELAND

Belfast

ISLE OF MAN

Lake District

Pennines

UNITED KINGDOM OF GREAT BRITAIN AND NORTHERN IRELAND

York

Hull

Humber

Irish Sea

Dublin

Liverpool

Manchester

Nottingham

The Wash

▲ Snowdon

Trent

ENGLAND

St. George's Channel

Cambrian Mountains

Severn

Birmingham

Cambridge

North Sea

WALES

Oxford

London

Big Ben

Swansea

Cardiff

Heathrow

Thames

Stonehenge

Dover

EURO TUNNEL

Devon

ISLE OF WIGHT

Brighton

St. Agnes

Plymouth

Cornwall

Penzance

English Channel

ISLES OF SCILLY

CHANNEL ISLANDS

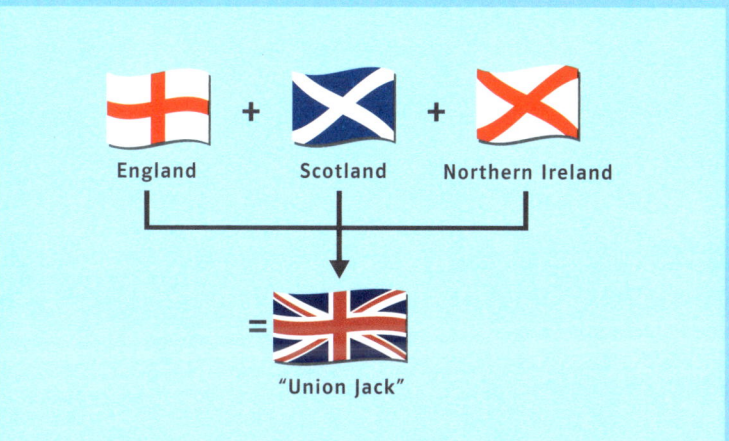

England + Scotland + Northern Ireland

= "Union Jack"

Atlantic Ocean

Galway

REPUBLIC OF IRELAND

Cork

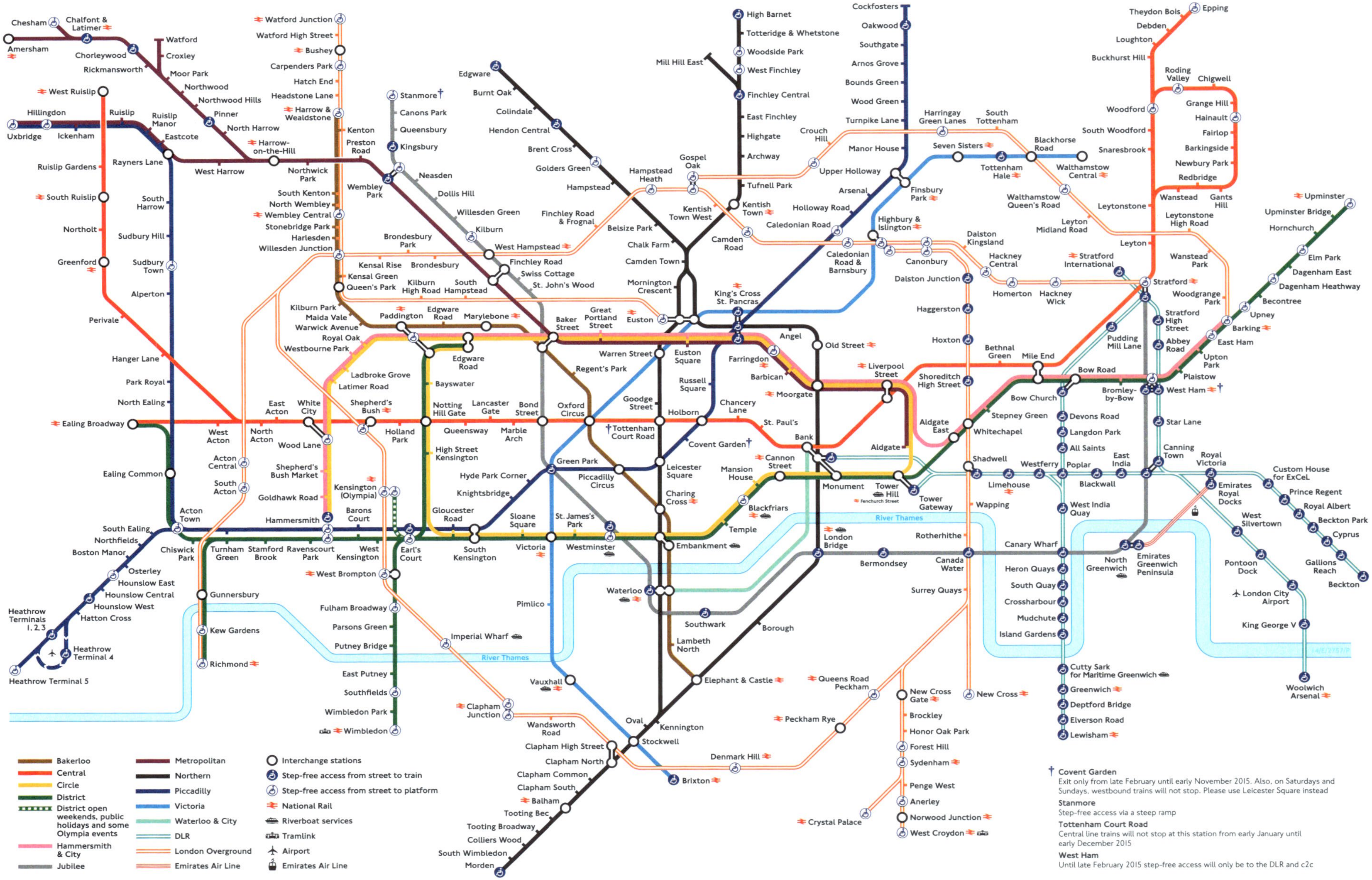

† **Covent Garden**
Exit only from late February until early November 2015. Also, on Saturdays and Sundays, westbound trains will not stop. Please use Leicester Square instead

Stanmore
Step-free access via a steep ramp

Tottenham Court Road
Central line trains will not stop at this station from early January until early December 2015

West Ham
Until late February 2015 step-free access will only be to the DLR and c2c

MAYOR OF LONDON

tfl.gov.uk

24 hour travel information
0343 222 1234*

Sign up for email updates
tfl.gov.uk/emailupdates

@TfLTravelAlerts

*Service and network charges may apply. See tfl.gov.uk/terms for details.

UNDERGROUND

TRANSPORT FOR LONDON
EVERY JOURNEY MATTERS

Reg. user No. 14/E/2757/P

Improvement works may affect your journey, please check before you travel

Version A TfL 12. 2014

Correct at time of going to print

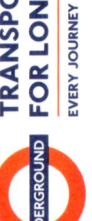

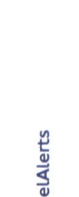